1974

# The
# Von Hassell
# Diaries

# The Von Hassell Diaries

## 1938–1944

### THE STORY OF THE FORCES
### AGAINST HITLER INSIDE GERMANY,
### AS RECORDED BY

## Ambassador Ulrich von Hassell

### A LEADER
### OF THE MOVEMENT

▼

### WITH AN INTRODUCTION BY
## Allen Welsh Dulles

▼

## GREENWOOD PRESS, PUBLISHERS
### WESTPORT, CONNECTICUT

# Contents

# CONTENTS

# Introduction

BY

ALLEN WELSH DULLES

Conspirators do not often keep diaries. Fortunately, Ulrich von Hassell, German Ambassador to Italy from 1932 to 1937, was an exception. His diary gives us a vivid contemporary account of the various plots against Hitler. It was written not after the events but in the midst of them, and the last entries were made a few days before his arrest and execution in 1944.

The Hassell family came from Hanover. Ulrich von Hassell, born in 1881, devoted his youth to preparation for a diplomatic career. After improving his knowledge of languages and of foreign affairs by studying in Switzerland and in England, he served in Tsingtau, China. In 1911 he entered the diplomatic service and served as Vice-Consul in Genoa in the years immediately preceding the outbreak of World I War. Then he joined the German Army. He was seriously wounded at the Battle of the Marne.

In 1919 he returned to the foreign service and served in Rome, Barcelona, and then as Minister to Denmark and to Yugoslavia. In Belgrade his British colleague was Nevile Henderson, and the friendship which started there brought the two men often together in Berlin in the dark days of August 1939 which led to war. Finally, Hassell returned to Rome as Ambassador to the Quirinal. Here the Hassell family considered the American Ambassador, William Phillips, and Mrs. Phillips, their most congenial colleagues.

Hassell's diplomatic career in Rome was largely devoted to trying to build a bridge between Germany and the states of western Europe. He felt that there was a common bond in the civilization of these states, and that a way must be found to bring Germany into this European culture for her own salvation and the security of her western neighbors. He took an important part in the negotiations leading to the conclusion, on June 7, 1933, of the Four-Power Pact between England, France, Italy, and Germany. The pact was never ratified, and as the Hitler-Ribbentrop policy unfolded Hassell found himself more and more in antagonism to the instructions which came to him from the Wilhelmstrasse in Berlin.

During the early days of the Nazi regime, while Hitler was consolidating his power within Germany, the Führer desired to present a peaceful face to the outside world. Hence he was quite content to allow the Ambassadors inherited from the Weimar Republic days to hold their posts. It was only when Hitler prepared to take off the mask that he began to clear the deck of the diplomats who refused to be tools for his policy of aggression.

In November 1937 Ribbentrop, then Ambassador in London, came to Rome and concluded the Anti-Comintern Pact between Germany, Italy, and Japan. He tried to win Hassell over to his views, assuring him that he, Ribbentrop, was soon to become Foreign Minister, and that Hassell had better play along with him. But the Ambassador to Rome, in his reports to the weak and vacillating Foreign Minister, Neurath, left no doubt of his opposition to the formation of the Axis and the inevitable reorientation of German foreign policy against England and France and toward world conflict. A few weeks later Hassell's mission in Rome was ended. He was replaced as Ambassador and retired from the foreign service. From that time on he became the diplomatic adviser of the secret opposition to Hitler.

As a convenient cover for his activities he joined an organization called the Central European Economic Conference which, as its name implies, was devoted to the study of European economic conditions. This gave him an excuse for spending much of his time in Berlin and permitted him to travel relatively freely, even after the outbreak of war. He journeyed to the Balkans, to Switzerland, and, as the Nazis swept over Europe, to the various occupied countries. Finally, when his enemies in the Foreign Office and in the Gestapo forced him to abandon these activities, he used the Institute for Economic Research as a cloak for his real work as a conspirator.

To get the proper focus, as one reads the diary, it is important to try to recall how world affairs stood at the time the entry was made, not how they look today. Hassell was not always right in his judgment as to what course was feasible to end the war, as his negotiations in Switzerland disclose, but by and large he was right in his assessment of the Nazi madness, and right when many in England, France, and America were wrong. Also, he was sound in his conclusion that one could not depend upon the military—"hopeless corporals," he called them—to stand up against Hitler. "These generals," he wrote, "would have the same government they wish to overthrow give them the orders to do so." Hassell was not one of those whose views were warped by contemporary German military successes. Some of his bitterest lines were written during the days when the Nazis were the masters of Europe. For him, the occupation of France was the death knell for his hopes of finding a way to end the war on a basis of understanding between Germany and western Europe.

Hassell's closest associates during these days of plotting were the two men who were at the center of the conspiracy, General Ludwig Beck, Hitler's dismissed Chief of Staff, and Carl Friedrich Goerdeler, the ex-Mayor of Leipzig. They were slated to become respectively Chief of State and Head of the Government, if the plot succeeded. And then through the pages of the diary pass in review the other important conspirators, Witzleben, Falkenhausen, Canaris, Oster, Thomas, and Stauffenberg among the military; Dohnanyi, Moltke, Peter Jessen, Leuschner, Popitz, Gisevius, and Schlabrendorff among the civilians—to mention only a few out of many.

The diary was largely written at Hassell's home at Ebenhausen, in Bavaria, especially in the latter days. Reasons of security made this necessary. It was not safe to travel around Germany with incriminating papers, and far too risky to keep them in Berlin. Under the ceaseless bombing, houses and even safes were torn to pieces. In his garden at Ebenhausen his diary was relatively safe. For a time the hiding place was a Ridgeway's Pure China Tea box, buried in the ground. But when it was unearthed after a wet summer in 1942, as Frau von Hassell tells us, the tea box had proved to be a very ineffective protection against the dampness. Then the diary was hidden in a grotto in the garden. When the Gestapo, after Hassell's arrest, searched Ebenhausen, the last pages of the diary, secreted in a photograph album, barely escaped detection. In the early days of the war, when Hassell could travel with a certain amount of diplomatic protection, he had succeeded in smuggling into Switzerland his notes for the years 1936 to 1941.

Hassell did not try to make daily entries. He was a great traveler, back and forth between Ebenhausen and Berlin, and then on trips to France and Belgium, the Balkans, and in the earlier days to Switzerland. He would often wait until his return to Ebenhausen, and then put down the events of a week or two. The last entry in the diary is dated July 13, 1944, just a week before the bomb was placed at Hitler's feet under the map table as he was reviewing with his generals the military events of the day.

Hassell knew what was afoot, and he went to Berlin, ready to play his part if the attempt were successful. He probably had little doubt as to the fate in store for him in the event of failure. He knew that he was the probable choice for Foreign Minister in the government the conspirators hoped to install after Hitler's assassination. He knew that many—too many— other people also knew this.

There had been some discussion among the plotters as to whether the post of Foreign Minister should be given to Hassell, whose diplomatic ties were with the west, or to Count Werner von der Schulenberg, the last German Ambassador to Moscow, who also was a member of the conspiracy. This uncertainty in turn reflected a division within the ranks of the conspiracy. Should Germany turn east or west? Should the new German Republic look to Soviet Russia, and have a

Foreign Minister who was a friend of Stalin's, or turn west and lean on the Anglo-Saxon countries?

With true but rather incautious German thoroughness the new cabinet lists had been prepared. The men who were to take the lead had burned their bridges, and when the Gestapo terror set in after July 20, Hassell quietly awaited in his office in Berlin the inevitable visit of the Gestapo. It was futile to hide, useless, even dangerous to flee, as Hassell's wife and children were within the power of the Nazis. On July 28 the Gestapo came. On September 7 he was haled before the so-called People's Court and its sinister Presiding Judge, Roland Freisler, and on September 8 executed. The calmness with which he faced the ordeal of those last days was doubtless reinforced by the knowledge that he was leaving a record on which he was willing that his own conduct as a consistent opponent of Nazism should be judged.

The vengeance of the Nazis was not satisfied by taking Hassell's life. Members of his family, including his daughter, were sent to concentration camps, and the two young children of the daughter, two and three years old, were taken from her and placed in an institution under false names. After the armistice, in July 1945, Frau von Hassell, after weeks of searching, by the greatest good chance finally discovered the children near Innsbruck. It was the Nazi plan, of course, that these children, too young to know who they were, should never learn that their grandfather was one of those who had fought the Nazis.

The evidence on the anti-Nazi conspiracy is not yet all before us. Some of it is irretrievably lost. We have ample information, however, against which to test the importance of the testimony given by Hassell. We have the accounts of Hans Bernd Gisevius and Fabian von Schlabrendorff, two of the survivors; a summary of the evidence by Rudolf Pechel; the letters of Helmuth von Moltke; and the testimony of the widows and orphans of the men of July 20, 1944. Judged by all this evidence, and a mass of other documentation which I have studied, the diary of Ulrich von Hassell ranks high as a document of historical importance. It also has the element of gripping human interest.

No one man, with the exception of General Beck and Goerdeler, and possibly General Oster from his vantage point in the German Counterintelligence Service, was kept informed of all that went on within the ranks of the conspiracy. It was not a closely knit affair. The military men did not always tell the civilians of their plans, and Hassell was absent from Berlin for protracted periods. But with the exception of the three men I have mentioned, and none of them has survived or left behind any extensive written record, Hassell was one of the closest to the center of the plot. Furthermore, he enjoyed the confidence of the leaders. Thus, not only for students of this dramatic attempt to overthrow a totalitarian regime, but for those who are interested in knowing what went on behind the scenes of Hitler's wartime Reich, this diary is an invaluable record.

# 1938

*Berlin, September 17, 1938, on the train between Berlin and Weimar:* Stormy international atmosphere. At home there is growing despondency under the weight of Party rule and fear of war. Heydrich again in Nuremberg in full regalia. Hitler's speeches are all demagogic and spiced with sharp attacks on the entire upper class. The closing speech at the Party conference was of the same sort, delivered in wild, boisterous tones. The mounting hatred against the upper class has been inflamed by the warnings of the generals, with the exception of Keitel, against war. At the same time there is growing aversion to all independent people. Whoever does not crawl in the dust is regarded as stuck up. Here also lies the explanation of my situation. Heydrich told Plessen in Rome that the Party considered me haughty. Ribbentrop cannot abide me either.

During the past weeks I have asked myself repeatedly whether it is right to serve such an immoral system. However, "on the outside," the slight chance of successful opposition would be even smaller.

*Wednesday, September 4:* At twelve forty-five I went to see Raeder, who was still very much impressed by Hitler's foreign policy. Hitler, he said, has had luck, and luck one must have. However, Raeder had received inaccurate information, which he somewhat prematurely passed on to the naval commands, that the Czechs had mobilized. Thereby, they would, of course, have placed themselves in the wrong. In the afternoon he hastened to let me know that he had been misinformed.

The political situation Wednesday morning was this: in spite of all the bombast, Hitler's speech on Monday left the door open for diplomacy and referred only to the right of self-determination. The deliberate brutality of Hitler's policies has once more repelled all the Great Powers, reluctant to go to war. As a result, Englishmen and Frenchmen today discuss quite calmly the holding of a plebiscite—unthinkable only a few months ago. That Hitler in reality wants more is something else. In spite of this step-by-step retreat on the part of the Western Powers, the odds on war at the time of my arrival seemed to be 10 to 1. This was owing to the irresponsible assumption of Ribbentrop and others that England would not fight.

Then came the great *coup de scène* of Chamberlain's visit. It was another tremendous success for Hitlerian bluff; on the other hand, it constituted the strongest possible moral pressure by England on Germany.

Knowing nothing about all this, I lunched alone with Henderson. He was very frank and friendly, but at the same time visibly agitated. He explained the English position to me convincingly as follows: (1) to work with all their might to preserve the peace, even if this involves sacrifices; (2) but if Germany resorts to force, and France finds it necessary to act, the English will march with France.

He complained bitterly about Ribbentrop, who was chiefly responsible for the fact that England and Germany were not getting along better. Furthermore, he was of the opinion that all might yet go well if the Nazi regime did not make itself so terribly hated throughout the whole world, and especially in England.

Finally he said that he had made a final attempt and induced the British cabinet to propose Chamberlain's visit to Hitler. It was decided yesterday evening. This morning at eight o'clock he had informed Weizsäcker and Woermann, and he was now waiting for an answer. Unfortunately Ribbentrop was off somewhere with the Führer. In my presence he then telephoned to Göring at Karinhall and explained the developments. He said something like this: "You will admit that it is of the greatest importance that the seventy-year-old British Prime Minister is ready to fly to meet the Führer this very day." Göring answered: "Of course!" and promised to telephone to the Obersalzberg.

Henderson had sworn me to secrecy, but when he heard that I was to see Keitel in the evening he asked me to tell Keitel what he had revealed to me. I did so and was surprised to observe that Keitel was manifestly astonished at England's readiness to march with France in case of conflict. During the conversation he showed himself quite uninformed politically; he figured with all the free-and-easy mathematics of a milkmaid on the chances for war and on the possibility that England might be on the other side. I told W—— of this conversation today and he was of the opinion that Keitel was simply too stupid to understand such things. The Keitel family, however, showed themselves substantially more sober. For instance, his daughter said many young officers thought the "Brown Shirts" should be the first to be sent to the front, for they were wagging their jaws too freely.

Thursday forenoon I went to see Schacht, who was extremely pessimistic about economic and financial matters. He is completely opposed to the regime. At the very beginning he called Hitler a swindler, with whom England would find it impossible to make binding agreements. He said Chamberlain's visit was a mistake, for it would not prevent war.

Today I met Schacht at the Foreign Office, where he went so far as to make what I considered the senseless remark that if Hitler now gets only the German border districts he will have suffered a serious defeat in foreign policy! Economically we had pumped ourselves more and more dry; the secret funds, foreign-exchange reserves (from Austria, et cetera), had already been used up in an irresponsible way. He thought we were even now in the red. So far as the finances of the Reich were concerned, it was often impossible to meet claims on the government. I cautiously referred to his share of responsibility in the matter, but he denied that he had any. To be a Cabinet Minister no longer meant anything—one was not even kept informed. He didn't know, he said, how they expected to get out of the mess except by printing money, and if that were required of him he would simply resign.

He seemed to think that a state which operated on such immoral principles could not survive much longer. I parried with the remark that many immoral regimes had lasted long. This he denied. The corruption, et cetera, practiced under these systems were condemned in principle. The state as such recognized ethical standards. But we now have a regime which in the administration of justice, for instance, *officially* proclaims immoral principles. There is some truth in this distinction.

He also told me that Goebbels was pretty much in disfavor because of his affairs with actresses and other women who are dependent upon the Propaganda Ministry for jobs. This was getting to be too much of a scandal. Hitler was in a rage, also, because Goebbels wanted to divorce his wife. Goebbels, knowing the mood of the people, was opposed to the rash war policy.

In the afternoon with Widenmann, Naval Attaché in London before the World War. He said openly what countless people think—that as a German one is today in a tragic conflict. If Hitler's drum-beating policies should succeed, it would be difficult to believe in the blessings of such a success.

*Friday, September the sixteenth:* At noon I went to see Woermann, who reported to me briefly on the Chamberlain visit. Ribbentrop was furious because he had not been asked to attend. In the discussion Hitler had demanded the "cession" of the German region as the only remaining possibility. The word "plebiscite" does not appear to have been uttered. Personally, Chamberlain had shown understanding but had, of course, made no commitments either for his own people or for the French. Weizsäcker told me today that apparently Chamberlain did not make it sufficiently clear that England would go to war if Germany used force. He was evidently under the impression that matters would continue peaceably. I asked Weizsäcker whether there was danger that conditions in Czechoslovakia would lead to an invasion. He thought not; the press reports were artfully exaggerated and in large part faked. At the moment the barometer indicated recourse to peaceful means. But we well know what differences may yet arise in high places. Woermann, as well as Weizsäcker, confirmed my opinion that Ribbentrop absolutely would not be-lieve England would go to war.

I hasten to add here that I talked to Eisenlohr, our Minister at Prague, today, shortly before my departure. He had been recalled so that the German representation in Prague might appear "thinner." This he rightly condemned. Just now he belongs in Prague. He was troubled and depressed about the methods used. He thought the whole business could not pos-sibly lead to any lasting good, even if another success was scored.

*Saturday, September 17, 1938:* In Weimar for a meeting of the Dante Society. From a world of stress and strain into a dream world.

*Wittenmoor, September 29, 1938, at Udo Alvensleben's:* In Berlin on the twenty-seventh there was a heavy atmosphere. The Sudeten business doesn't go so smoothly as many people thought it would. Although the Czechs promised the English and the French that in principle they would surrender the German areas to us, we are on the verge of war—world war—because Hitler's demands (immediate evacuation and occupa-tion of the predominantly German districts by German troops) are unacceptable to the Western Powers, if only for reasons of prestige. In this situation, that is in view of the expiration of the German ultimatum to the Czechs on the afternoon of Wednesday the twenty-eighth, and in view of the threatened German mobilization in the event of an unsatisfactory answer, the chances of war stand at 10 to 1.

On the morning after my arrival at the Adlon I met Kanitz, former Minister of Agriculture. He reports that people are in a chaotic state of mind as they suddenly begin to realize how serious the situation is. Dohna-Finckenstein, the SS man, had just told him that "the others (i.e., France and England) had betrayed us," and "we must now take the German districts by force!"

I had lunch with Heinrici, Popitz, Tischbein, and Sybel (Agrarian League) at the Continental. All very depressed. Popitz was extremely bitter; he was of the opinion that the

Nazis would proceed with increasing fury against the "upper stratum," as Hitler calls it. Every decent person is seized with a physical nausea, as the Acting Minister of Finance Popitz expressed it, when he hears speeches like Hitler's recent vulgar tirade in the Sports Palace. Before lunch I saw Stauss, who was one of the first business leaders to go over to Hitler. He is now filled with the greatest anxiety and disgust.

Afterward I saw Ullo Osten, who spent a long time in Spain as an officer. He praised the Italians and complained about the condition of our whole military organization, every branch of which, he said, was in poor shape. All sensible officers agree that it is foolhardy to toy with the idea of war under such circumstances. We really haven't even had a chief of the General Staff since Beck resigned, indignant and unbending. There is growing recognition that Keitel is weak and completely without judgment. Stauss thinks he is simply incapable of understanding things. Brauchitsch hitches his collar a notch higher and says: "I am a soldier; it is my duty to obey."

Yesterday [the twenty-eighth] was a most critical day. In the morning I felt the situation was almost hopeless. In Wittenmoor, at Udo Alvensleben's, we and the Kamekes sat constantly by the radio. The German version of the situation was untruthful in the highest degree. It was brashly denied that there had been an ultimatum and a threat of mobilization so they wouldn't have to admit that a postponement had been granted. Not a word was said about Mussolini having intervened at the request of England. The German radio represented today's meeting of the Four Powers as the result of Hitler's own initiative.

How will Mussolini conduct himself today? [The twenty-ninth.] I do not believe he will support Hitler unconditionally. On the contrary he may be pleased by the strong coalition against us which is now clear to everyone, and do all he can to avert war and arrive at a compromise that will save Hitler's face. Then he himself can return to Rome as peacemaker and *arbiter mundi*.

If it comes off ("It is all right this time," Chamberlain called out to the people), Hitler will bring the German areas into the fold and thereby achieve another great success. But the question is whether, in view of the methods used, this success may not prove quite different from all others. Hitler must now realize that he has brought us to the brink of war against half the world, and that those who thought England was in earnest were right. The world (but among the Germans, of course, only those who had a chance to hear something besides the German official reports) will be left with a very bad taste in the mouth. Hatred against Hitler and his methods must have grown in bitterness.

Will Hitler, for the first time, begin to tremble in his God-like position? This time he could not freely follow that inspiration he so blindly trusts. Pressure from the outside has become effective. The question is whether recent events produced any sort of inner shock and how this will affect him psychologically. It may be that he will relieve his feelings by more frenzied rages—perhaps on the domestic scene, against the hated upper stratum, which keeps warning him of dangers. In any case, we may be facing fundamental changes.

*Ebenhausen, October 1, 1938:* One of the few certainties today is the overwhelming and tremendous relief of the whole nation, or rather of all nations, that war has been averted. However, the Germans, or rather the great majority of them, have no idea how close they were to war. In Berlin, London, Paris, and Rome the four returning matadors were all received as "peacemakers" by their people with the same stormy enthusiasm. Hitler's brutal policies have brought him great material successes.

The day before yesterday we went in the afternoon with Udo Alvensleben from Wittenmoor to see the old Princess Herbert Bismark. Schoenhausen [her residence] makes an almost tragic impression. She thought her father-in-law no longer counted; that in fact his stature was systematically played down. This is true, and, in view of the spirit of our rulers and the successful Anschluss policy, very logical. In the beginning she was impressed by Hitler, but today thinks of him and his methods just about as Popitz does. R. Kassner, the philosopher, was also present—a gifted man, filled with the deepest bitterness by the cultural devastation wrought by the Third Reich.

I share Princess Bismarck's belief that a system employing such treacherous and brutal methods cannot achieve good ends. But I cannot follow her when she draws the conclusion (as do General Beck and a thousand others) that therefore the regime will soon collapse. There is not yet sufficient reason to think so.

Yesterday afternoon [September 30], on my way home, I stopped with Alvensleben in Neugattersleben. Werner Alvensleben was there too. He is the famous "Herr von A." of June 30, who has meanwhile been released from prison and banished to a hunting lodge in Pomerania. He is somewhat mysterious, more conspirator than politician. It is interesting that he was with Hammerstein (the general), who told him that Minister of Finance Schwerin-Krosigk had looked him up (or happened to meet him?), piping hot from an audience with Hitler on Wednesday, September 28, and reported the following incident. Krosigk, with Neurath and Göring, had gone to Hitler to persuade him of the utter impossibility of the war on which he seemed bent. Krosigk emphasized that financially we were already done for, and that we could in no case hold out during a war. Hitler apparently stood out against these arguments until the historic telephone call of Mussolini broke in upon the scene and compelled him to give in.

*October 10, 1938:* Traveled to Berlin on *October 4* for the funeral of poor, charming Princess Friedrich Sigismund, who at the age of forty-one, after a brief attack of influenza, suffered a weakening of the heart and died. It was really very sad, and a great loss to us personally. In Berlin the *principessa della luna* was always a good companion, full of charm and vitality. Indeed her death leaves a great gap, for she was such a good influence—a bridge between the Court and the world. Besides, her house was one of the few which could receive in good style. Her hearty ways of the old days had become more mellow. Huge crowds escorted the cortege from the church in Nicolskoi to the burial place at Glienicker Park. It was really very beautiful—the radiance and color of this autumn day, at the Havel Lakes, and along the road through the old park. But the impression of unreality was distressing: the hearse, drawn by four horses decorated with violet velvet and the royal coat of arms in silk, followed by a complete array of Prussian, Danish, and other princes, many wearing the orange ribbon of the Order of the Black Eagle, was like a fantasy. I rode back with General von Kleist, Commander of Hanover, earlier Dieter's commanding officer. He was very bitter about the irresponsible way in which political matters had been handled during recent months; he was also worried about developments in the Army. If we really had been pushed into war on the twenty-eighth, he said, there would have been no way to avoid catastrophe for Germany but for the military to arrest the leading politicians.

As Weizsäcker told me, Hitler had again expressed himself to the effect that the Czech problem must be liquidated within a few months. Weizsäcker was deeply distressed over Hitler's methods and about Ribbentrop, his own irresponsible, superficial, unrealistic chief. He said he simply could not imagine how this business could go on much longer.

Werner Alvensleben, it seems, did not report the events of September 27–28 quite accurately, although in essence correctly. Krosigk does not appear to have gone to Hitler; he expressed his opinion in writing. Neurath and Göring, it seems, were not actually present when Mussolini talked to Hitler on the telephone. Weizsäcker was in a rage because Neurath showed no sense of responsibility. The president of the secret Cabinet Council did not bestir himself at the critical moment; he preferred to go stag hunting. Only on Tuesday did Weizsäcker succeed in telephoning Neurath to come; Neurath now claims that he came of his own accord.

I wager Mussolini felt the greatest relief of his life when Chamberlain made his proposal. Incidentally, it was suggested by Daladier. Although Mussolini had refused to commit himself to Germany in private, he did venture very far in public, and on Wednesday at two o'clock he would have faced the dilemma of going to war or repeating 1915.

The Hungarians appear to have been somewhat fooled (only relatively speaking, of course)—they maneuvered too timidly!

A great question for the future is opening up in the East: Ruthenia. For Poland this is a fateful question of the first order.

On *October 6* I dined with Stauss. It was his birthday. Schacht was also there, and after dinner, unfortunately in the midst of a rather large circle, he dominated a superficial and witty conversation by making biting attacks on the regime under which, after all, he still holds a responsible position. In his private discussion with me his political remarks were obscure and full of contradictions. His beautiful and intelligent niece (daughter of the doctor), who brought me as far as Nuremberg in her car, told me that her uncle's habit of spouting satire kept her on tenterhooks.

The scandalous behavior of Goebbels is rapidly giving rise to a whispering campaign. It appears that his wife, not he, is seeking the divorce that Hitler forbids. Recently the actress Lida Barowa, slightly inebriated, made a painful scene in which she warned Goebbels: "You cannot treat me like the others." Title of the play: Restoration of family life!

Friday evening at the Deutscher Club. I sat between the guest of honor of the evening, Glaise-Horstenau, and the politician, Colonel von Xylander. Glaise talked quite interestingly and soberly. When I praised the old Austrian administration he commented that it was now being hopelessly wrecked and that nothing decent was being put in its place. Afterward he made an address which was much less unorthodox than our conversation. He is a true Austrian in his lovable adroitness, his humorous sarcasm, and his subtle self-criticism, as well as in his exaggerated modesty, not to say servility ("the Führer was very gracious when he received me!"). On the other hand, he told me that his frankness in stating his views during the critical days had cost him the post of governor (*Reichsstatthalter*).

*October 15, 1938:* Great to-do in Vienna. Before thousands of people in St. Stephen's Cathedral, Cardinal Initzer preached a sermon with some rather conventional exhortations, especially to young people, to fulfill their religious duties. But he made use of several injudicious turns of speech. His remarks

were received with great enthusiasm and there were demonstrations in front of the Cardinal's residence, as Glaise-
Horstenau told me today at the Bruckmanns'. Slogans in the
Nazi style were used, but with twisted meanings. The *Neue
Züricher Zeitung* reported that the crowds shouted: "We want
to see *our* Führer," and the Dollfuss song was sung. As a result
there were counterdemonstrations, especially by the Hitler
Youth, and serious acts of violence against the Cardinal's residence and also against his staff. One cleric was thrown out of
the window and had both legs broken.

The most stupefying part of the story, however, concerns the
conduct of the police. For hours they gave the mob a free hand,
Glaise thought because of fear of the Party, for it was assumed
that the Nazis had organized the affair. The Party, he said, is
superimposed upon the state. Glaise naturally deplored the fact
that the fight against the church has flamed up again after a
terribly violent speech by Bürckel. Glaise was in a very gloomy
frame of mind in general because of the developments in
Austria. It was today nothing but a robber state. There was no
single factor strong enough to counteract the disintegration—
certainly not Seyss-Inquart. Bürckel made dynastic politics like
a medieval duke; he wanted to be Gauleiter of a Greater
Palatinate and to "compensate" Bavaria by giving her the
Vorarlberg province.

Yesterday [*October 14*] Hitler was at the Bruckmanns' for
an hour and a half for Hugo Bruckmann's seventy-fifth birthday, bringing an abominable floral offering. He was said to
have been "human" and pleasant. But everything he said
clearly indicated that he had not yet recovered from the intervention of the Powers and would rather have had his war. He
was especially annoyed with England—that accounts for the
incomprehensibly rude speech at Saarbrücken. The dependable
friend is supposed to be Mussolini, who unquestionably would
have "marched" just as he—Hitler—would do for Mussolini
in a similar situation. In answer to Frau Bruckmann's question
as to whether he was not glad that it was unnecessary to shed
blood, Hitler growled only a half-hearted yes. When Frau
Bruckmann expressed certain doubts about the war sentiments
of the German people Hitler replied: "Only the ten thousand

in the upper stratum have any doubts; the people stand solidly behind me!" Does he really believe that?

*October 23, 1938:* Nostitz came from Berlin, from the Foreign Office, and confirmed the reports about Hitler's state of mind, at least he said that Ribbentrop was running about in obviously bad temper because circumstances had not permitted the use of force. Schmitt-Tiefenbrunn (formerly Minister of Economic Affairs), whom we visited last Sunday, also believes that Hitler will remain quiet only a short time. It simply isn't in him to do otherwise than plan for a new move on the chessboard.

At the moment the Hungarian question,[1] which almost led to military action about ten days ago, is much to the fore. However, for the future we have the Ukrainian problem which is already bubbling away in the pot.

Misgivings are increased by the recent report that Göring is avoiding all public appearances because of excessive demands on his time, and asks that no petitions be addressed to him outside his immediate jurisdiction. Why do that just now? Did he make himself that unpopular because of his warnings against war?

The Bruckmanns were here for lunch yesterday. He is an intelligent, cultured man, who tells interesting stories from his experiences. Frau Bruckmann was very depressed (she always feels somewhat responsible) about tales coming out of the Civil Servants' Indoctrination Camp at Tölz. Fritz Bismarck-Plathe had already reported some of them recently. To one participant, who mentioned that he was descended from seven generations of officers, the leader said, "Ah, somewhat decadent, stupid, and arrogant." On another occasion the leader had asked how many of those present still belonged to any church. When twenty-four out of twenty-five reported in the affirmative he said this fact was a disgrace to his course, and declared that he was surprised to know there were still so many fools around.

[1] Demand on Czechoslovakia from Budapest concerning a "reorganization" of the border districts.

*October 24, 1938:* Saw Rintelen [Military Attaché in Rome] on his way back to Rome following his operation. He said Hitler was really very angry with the generals who had, all too imprudently, expressed their views about our inability to wage a war. He is demanding their dismissal, and Brauchitsch must now contend with all his might against this move. Indeed, this has kept Brauchitsch so occupied that he says he cannot find time to cope with less important matters, such as the General Staff discussions which General Pariani keeps suggesting to discuss plans in the event of joint operations. Keitel, the stooge, was also frustrated because the Führer was of the opinion that no plans for any kind of mobilization could be made now because there was no way of knowing what the situation would be at the time!

Rintelen reported further that Brauchitsch was trying to get Hitler at least to agree that in the event of war Beck would be called to command an army. He opined that his successor, Halder, was a very good soldier but hardly a man of great caliber.

*November 4, 1938:* The dismissal of Beck and Rundstedt is now publicly announced. Rundstedt, I presume, because of "cowardice"? Keitel appointed colonel general.

Princess Bona of Bavaria (daughter of the Duke of Genoa) told us yesterday Mussolini had bluntly told Hitler that Italy could not go to war and thereby forced him to come around. If that is true, it throws a curious light on Hitler's repeated assertions that Mussolini had proved himself his one true friend.

The Vienna arbitration award[1] of Ribbentrop and Ciano has for the first time since the war, perhaps for the first time in history, given rise to anti-German demonstrations by Hungarians before the German Legation in Budapest. At the same time there were ovations for the Duce. One may well wonder whether, as a result of the peace of Munich, new groupings may develop, and when the first occasion for a German-Italian clash will appear.

In the eastern part of the new Czechoslovakia conditions

[1]The decision at Vienna, November 2, 1938, required Czechoslovakia to cede 12,400 square kilometers to Hungary.

exist which may lead to great conflicts. Is Hitler counting on the Ukraine?

*November 25, 1938, Ebenhausen:* I am writing under crushing emotions evoked by the vile persecution of the Jews after the murder of vom Rath. Not since the World War have we lost so much credit in the world. But my chief concern is not with the effects abroad, not with what kind of foreign political reaction we may expect—at least not for the moment. I am most deeply troubled about the effect on our national life, which is dominated ever more inexorably by a system capable of such things.

Goebbels has seldom won so little credence for any assertion (although there are people among us who swallowed it) as when he said that a spontaneous outburst of anger among the people had caused the outrages and that they were stopped after a few hours. At the same time he laid himself open to the convincing reply that—if such things can happen unhindered —the authority of the state must be in a bad way. As a matter of fact there is no doubt that we are dealing with an officially organized anti-Jewish riot which broke out at the same hour of the night all over Germany! Truly a disgrace! Naïve Party functionaries have freely admitted that.

To Hans Dieter one of them gave as an excuse for his lack of preparation for military billeting his "strenuous activities during the pogrom." A neighboring burgomaster, as early as Wednesday, the ninth, expressed his sorrow to Pastor Weber that he had orders to take action against a respectable Jew. He then added that on the tenth all the synagogues in Germany would be burning. They were shameless enough to mobilize school classes (in Feldafing, on the Starbergersee they even armed the pupils with bricks). In a Swabian village, Leyen says, the Catholic teacher gave in, but the Evangelical teacher refused to let the boys go.

There is probably nothing more distasteful in life than to have to acknowledge the justice of attacks made by foreigners on one's own people. As a matter of fact, in other countries they are making a proper distinction between the people and the group responsible for acts such as these. But it is futile to deny that the lowest instincts have been aroused; and the effect, especially among the young, must have been bad. One comforting thought is that this time indignation has gripped not only the great majority of the educated class but also broad sections of the people as a whole. It seems to me that the Nazi leaders sense this darkly. Subtle retreats are to be observed here and there. Only the *Schwarzes Korps* [newspaper of the SS] lashes out with blind rage against the grumblers.

Respectable people were shocked to read names like Gürtner and Schwerin-Krosigk among the authors of the decree prescribing penalties for the Jews. These men apparently cannot see how they are degrading themselves and how they are being used.

The day before yesterday, [*November 23*] at the Leyens' in Underdiessen (she is nee Ruffo—from Rome), they spoke of the unfavorable development of public opinion in Italy, inspired primarily by Mussolini's tendency to copy Hitler. Frequently heard witticism: Mussolini was the Gauleiter of the Gau [District] Italy. Mackensen is said to be stiff and clumsy.

A Belgian was there too on his wedding journey. He was in Germany at the time of the Jewish persecutions and was naturally shocked. He was arrested for no other reason than that he stood for a moment before a demolished shop. According to his stories the mobilized Belgian Army must have been in very high spirits. In his father-in-law's château soldiers and officers got terribly drunk and smashed everything, so that the nearest area commander had to be called on for help. On the Belgian-French frontier Belgian soldiers are said to have set up placards with "Vive Hitler!" on them.

*November 27, 1938, Ebenhausen:* The Bruckmanns were here for tea. Their horror at the shameless Jewish persecutions is as great as that of all respectable people. According to Bruckmann even thorough-going National Socialists, after witnessing the devilish barbarity with which the SS treated the unfortunate Jews, are now completely converted. Günther Schmitt of the SS Special Troops says that Himmler heard of the impending action against the Jews only on the evening of November 9—new proof, incidentally, that it was organized—

disapproved of it, and for that reason ordered a two-day confinement to barracks for the Special Troops.

Discussions are said to have taken place between Gauleiter Adolph Wagner and the Police President of Munich, Von Eberstein, as to "who was really behind it." Guilty consciences. Had conversations with B—— and Professor A. V. M—— as to what one could do to give public expression to the general abhorrence of these methods. Unfortunately without success; without office we have no effective weapon. Any action on our part would lead to our being silenced—or worse. The university professors, who occupied a good strategic position at the outset, have long since lost it through their own fault.

The Army, which alone still has "power," has suffered enormous losses politically. In addition to Beck and Rundstedt, Adam has also been relieved of his command because he too candidly pointed out the defects of the Army.

*November 28, 1938:* Russians and Poles are attempting to come to an understanding because of the pressure of the Ukrainian question, which is dangerous to both. New crisis in Europe.

A very interesting article in the *Observer* by Lord Lothian. He has hitherto been friendly to the Germans, but is now considerably cooler. He grasped the fact that Hitler wanted to use force in the Czechoslovakian question and was prevented from doing so. Lord Lothian sees and sets forth clearly the whole issue as between "totalitarians" and "democrats." He hopes that morality and freedom will finally win out over brute force, even in the totalitarian states.

I was asked today, as I have often been asked before, how one could explain the sudden swing of Mussolini into the use of Hitler's ideological bilge water. It is the old story: one who says A must also say B. The German National Socialist bloc became so tremendously strong overnight that Mussolini no longer saw any possibility of arming against it with the backing of the Western Powers. In that event it seemed better to go whole hog with Hitler!

On the racial question, for instance, there was a time when Mussolini could not make enough fun of the ideas of the "superior Nordic race." There is that famous article of his, according to which the Laplanders must logically be the bearers of the highest culture; and his angry declaration: "I do not feel that I belong to an inferior race." Now he has decisively executed an about-face, and the Italians (including, therefore, the good Arab-Sicilians) are speedily pronounced Nordics.

*November 29, 1938:* Professor von Bissing and Professor Karo here. A year ago Bissing had sent back his gold Party badge because of the persecution of the churches. Noteworthy courage, but unfortunately rare. Both were very distressed over our disgrace, but felt that the latest events would have at least one good result: create complete clarity on the situation.

*December 1, 1938:* Visit with Professor Cossman [partly Jewish] who lives here at Ebenhausen "back in the woods." He reads no papers, listens to no radio, and buries himself in his studies. He said that now, for the first time, he saw how much he had missed and had yet to study! He denied the rumor that he had again been arrested. On the contrary, the local government suggested to him through one of its officials, and apparently with friendly intent, that he take a trip during the critical days (pogrom). This he did.

It is humiliating to see this courageous fighter for German honor in the role of an outcast. He was imprisoned because a man whom he had once saved from starvation had denounced him. For months there were, of course, no court proceedings. He said the prison guards, men of the old school, had treated him well. But what they had told him about other cases, and what he had since been told by acquaintances and relatives, beggared description. The saddest thought for him, especially since these recent happenings, is that the foundation on which he had based his whole battle against the German atrocities stories during the World War had now been shattered, for he had always claimed that Germans were incapable of such bestialities.

We talked about Minister of Justice Gürtner, whom he had known for a long time. It was his opinion that the man was most unhappy but unable to do anything. If he were to resign he would have the worst to fear because he knows too much. Interesting address by Ciano. He pictures Mussolini's role in September as that of the real peacemaker, who at the critical moment persuaded Hitler to wait twenty-four hours. It is doubtful whether Hitler will enjoy having the fact of his yielding to Mussolini's pressure thus established before the eyes of the world.

At the same time Ciano asserts that Mussolini would most certainly have gone along with Hitler. That, too, we may doubt; but it costs nothing to say it now, it obligates Hitler to reciprocate, and it serves as a threat against the Western Powers. England is treated with friendly coolness. France is "cut" completely, and Poland and Hungary are admonished to keep quiet.

Daladier has won out against the general strike. Will this result in a strengthening of democracy? In Hungary the crisis continues between Liberal-Conservatives and Progressives, between Progressives and Nazis. In Rumania Codreanu has been done away with "while trying to escape." Throughout Europe the constitutional way of life is locked in a pitched battle with the totalitarian.

*December 3, 1938:* Ciano's warning to Hungary and Poland must be considered with the one reservation "if it only lasts." (namely, this attitude to the rising Ukrainian problem).

This question is now very much to the fore—following the organized Italian demonstration about Tunis and Corsica, which in turn were precipitated by a casual remark of Ciano's. Although this new demand for something that is an Italian objective serves for the time being only as a means of extortion, the situation may become very serious. Mussolini is fed up with playing second fiddle and can bring us into a very dangerous subordinate role overnight.

*December 11, 1938:* The correspondent Heymann, who came here yesterday fresh from Rome, is of the opinion that the Axis will hold. I asked him how the 120 per cent Nazi attitude of the *Münchener Neueste Nachrichten* (for which Heymann writes) can be reconciled with the mentality of a thoughtful man like Wirsing. He replied that the paper was submitted to Hitler every day and had to be appropriately dolled up.

Heymann has been traveling around Germany for three months and got the impression that the mood of the people was very gloomy. H. Nathusius told him he had heard young officers on active duty discussing quite openly their desire to make an attempt on Hitler's life. Leyen gave a similar report from a resort for officers of the Luftwaffe in Pommersfelden. In the presence of foreign air attachés these officers had spoken about the Third Reich in violent terms.

Lunched yesterday with Plessen. He gave a fantastic description of conditions in the Foreign Office, where, under the insane leadership of Ribbentrop, everybody's nerves ᴜᴇ beginning to snap. The new, young diplomats, for instance, are to be schooled in special Party training camps, which means that they will be without any real knowledge.

Maritschi Plessen confirmed the story that teachers had armed school children with clubs so that they could destroy Jewish shops on November 9.

*Berlin, December 20, 1938:* In Berlin—during a severe cold spell. These day⁻ are marked by a deep sense of shame which has weighed heavily on all decent and thoughtful people since the hideous events of November (pogrom). There is talk of little else. Apparently our rulers are fully aware of the disastrous effect of this stupid and vulgar undertaking. Even within the inner sanctum the majority of those responsible secretly condemn the pogrom, and everyone tries, shamefacedly, to make minor amends. But this does not change the essence of the matter one whit; on the contrary, one gets the impression that the paroxysm is spreading into all fields of public life, domestic and foreign.

Perhaps the worst of it is that Göring, who condemned the pogrom most sharply and openly before all the Cabinet ministers and Gauleiters, could not bring himself to quit his post and join with Brauchitsch to call a complete halt. This would have been a very opportune and psychological moment for a stroke which at one fell swoop would have made him the open defender of all good forces in Germany. Apparently he did say something about this being the last filthy business to which he would lend his name. This is reminiscent of the lieutenant in the café who, upon receiving a box on the ear, cried: "Sir, if you slap me once more I shall challenge you to a duel." Or, for that matter, it is like the Anglo-French policy toward Hitler's "offensives."

Arrived in Berlin in the *evening of the fourteenth* one hour late. Dinner for the board members of the Deutscher Club. Neurath and Krosigk, it seemed to me, were both somewhat uncomfortable in their sorry roles. Bodo Alvensleben is still relatively optimistic because he hopes the Army will do something to change the regime. He said Hoepner, the Commanding General of the Third Corps Area, who was present, was an especially useful man.

On *Thursday, the fifteenth,* Herbert Göring told me that Thyssen had made a great show of resigning as *Staatsrat* and *Reichsrat,* especially because of the organized attempt to murder Acting Governor Schmid (the so-called *Schweineschmid*) in his home at Dusseldorf. Schmid, who has a partly Jewish wife, barely escaped with his life because the wife of the janitor managed to hide him.

Lunch at the Weizsäckers', with the Magistratis, the Dieckhoffs, Ritter, and an intelligent Swiss banker, Rickenbach. On the whole a cautious Foreign Office atmosphere. Dieckhoff and Ritter told interesting stories about conditions and currents of thought in America. Weizsäcker told me Ribbentrop had said there was no point in his receiving me. As a matter of fact he has still not received Ambassador Trautmann, who returned almost half a year ago from China. He is no more inclined to listen to divergent views than his lord and master. The pace in the Foreign Office, it seems, borders on the unbearable; it is a frantic merry-go-round in which everybody's nerves are getting frayed. Even the highest officials—with the possible exception of Weizsäcker, and he to a limited extent—know nothing about the political objectives and general lines of policy.

Visited Kurt Hammerstein [former Chief of Staff of the Reichswehr]. His attitude toward this regime of criminals and fools is just about as antagonistic as one could imagine. He doesn't place much hope in the decapitated and dishonored Army. Brauchitsch, he said, is a good soldier but has no political sense and no power, owing to the new and deliberate reorganization of the High Command.

Wilmowsky [Baron von Wilmowsky, a partner in Krupp's] called on me in the evening and talked very intelligently and sympathetically about some vague financial prospects for me. He also spoke of the really mad pace of rearmament, which one can view only with the gravest concern. Dinner with the Brauchitsch family. Next time they want to invite me informally with their cousin, the general, so that I can work on him.

*Friday, December the sixteenth:* Called on Weizsäcker in the morning. He gave me rather an alarming description of the foreign policy of Ribbentrop and Hitler. He thought it was obviously aimed at war. It had not yet been decided whether to strike out right away against England, while keeping Poland neutral, or to move first against the East, in order to liquidate the German-Polish and the Ukrainian questions, as well as the Memel problem. The latter, in Hitler's opinion, would not require a resort to arms, but merely a registered letter addressed to Kaunas! For the time being immediate action has apparently been once more postponed.

In the anteroom I met tall Mr. Sahm, who is supposedly about to be dismissed, and Carl Burckhardt of Danzig. The latter, understandably enough, was not in a happy frame of mind; he said he was playing a role like that of the Bey of Tunis and would prefer to resign. The Nazi leaders in Danzig, especially Forster, he says, were disagreeable people who had lied to him continuously. It is characteristic of Ribbentrop that he first kept Burckhardt waiting and then had him told to be brief, since he had little time. Burckhardt replied to the attaché with polite irony that he would take only five minutes of the Minister's time. When he emerged afterward he told me Ribbentrop had asked him to stay on.

I saw Hentig at the Foreign Office. He rightly pointed out that all this complaining about conditions is useless. The situation is so threatening that one must begin to prepare for action. But how? That is the big question. There is no chance of creating an organization. The one positive approach in this direction, which has already been made, is the surveillance of the entire Party through the Intelligence Section (Canaris) of the Army.

Saturday, December 17, at ten o'clock I called on Neurath, who is reduced to a room at 74 Wilhelmstrasse—an undignified setting. He is slated eventually to move over into the Reich Chancery, but this does not improve his position. He seems to be in a resigned mood, but covers it up with a lot of hollow phrases. It's interesting that the Turks (he had attended Ataturk's funeral) had told him that Soviet Russia was almost on the point of falling to pieces.

In Potsdam to lunch with Kameke. He told me about Kerrl's [Reich Minister of Church Affairs] tactics in convening a synod to put the affairs of the Evangelical Church in order. The basis of his plan was that external matters should be entirely separated from spiritual matters, and the former (finances!) should be put in the hands of the state. Kerrl had Winnig in mind as chairman, but he had refused because the whole thing was phony. If the state controlled church finances it would control everything. Meiser, Wurm, and Marahrens had rejected the idea, so the matter was limited to the Old Prussian Union. Wilmowsky had finally consented to serve in place of Winnig.

Popitz, with whom I lunched today, was of a different opinion: Kerll, to be sure, was not orthodox; nevertheless he was a Christian who was known to have told Hitler (and for a Party member this was quite something): "If you steer a course against Christianity I shall not follow you." Moreover, Kerll was an honest chap. Popitz does not believe that the meeting of the synod will be a success, but he feels that tactically it would be an error to refuse to participate, especially since the "German Christians" are very angry with Kerrl and dislike the idea of a synod.

Incidentally, Popitz tendered his resignation to Göring after the pogrom, and Göring promised to transmit it to Hitler. Popitz said he felt it necessary to take this action at least since those responsible—Gürtner, Schwerin-Krosigk, and Neurath— though Cabinet Ministers, had once again failed ignominiously. Neurath, he said, was simply lazy and negligent. For

instance, when Popitz wanted to talk matters over with him
Neurath simply sent word through a secretary or the like that
he couldn't do it now. This story is indeed typical of Neurath.
Popitz said that he himself discussed this subject candidly with
Göring and clearly pointed out its significance to Göring's
future position and the impossibility of going along with this
sort of thing. Göring was deeply moved and apparently entirely
convinced. But in the end this proved not to be enough, for
Göring is completely dependent upon Hitler and is afraid of
Himmler and Heydrich. Nevertheless Göring is reported to
have talked to them very bluntly, and to have said that he
would burn up the honorary uniforms the SS had given him.
He thundered away at the Gauleiters so that the whole house
shook. Olga Riegele-Göring is in complete despair; she is being besieged with petitions from all sides to influence her
brother.

I asked Popitz about Himmler's attitude toward the pogrom,
which I can't quite figure out. Popitz confirmed the story that
Himmler had created a subtle alibi for himself by writing or
wiring Hitler to the effect that he could not carry out the
orders. Then when he received no reply he carried out the
orders anyway. Now he can say that he did what he could.
Very strict orders seem to have been issued by Hitler himself,
and detailed mimeographed instructions as to methods of destruction were sent to the provincial governors. Popitz had told
Göring that those responsible must be punished. Göring answered: "My dear Popitz, do you wish to punish the Führer?"

*Sunday, the eighteenth:* Spent the afternoon in Achterberg
near Soltau to visit Fritsch. The Army had put this charming
manor house on the training grounds at his disposal. Long
political conversation. The substance of his views is: "This
man—Hitler—is Germany's destiny for good and for evil. If
he now goes into the abyss—which Fritsch believes he will—
he will drag us all down with him. There is nothing we can do."

I objected to this spirit of resignation, but have to admit
that I see little ground for hope of halting this journey into
disaster. Fritsch considers Göring a particularly bad specimen,
always engaged in double-dealing. Göring began to conspire
against him, Fritsch, as early as 1934, that is after June 30,

because he regarded him as a potential leader of a *putsch*, or at least as the coming commander in chief—a position which Göring had persistently sought for himself.

In considering Göring's personal history, it is interesting to note that in the spring of 1934 he had sought to get Fritsch as a confederate against the ever-growing threat of the SA. In this connection he emphasized the importance to the Army of the fight against the SA, especially now that an officer (Heydrich), who had been expelled from the Army and who hated the officer corps, had become head of the Gestapo. To Fritsch's question "How is it possible that such a man should be appointed to this post?" Göring replied: "The Führer has so decided."

*Monday, the nineteenth:* Went early to see Schwerin-Krosigk: well-bred and as agreeable as always, but he has lost all his punch. He feels uncomfortable in his awkward situation. In an attempt to justify his conduct in his own eyes he holds that it had been necessary above all else to get things into a "legal channel." There he is wrong. A while ago I chanced to meet Mrs. H—— at the railway station. She is the first educated person I know of who goes so far as to defend the pogrom.

At twelve o'clock with Woermann at the Foreign Office. He imparted to me the interesting fact that Magistrati handed in a strange document to the effect that the Tunis demonstrations were a spontaneous movement of the people and were not engineered by the government! The Italian Government indeed did not wish to take the offensive now in the question of Tunis. Furthermore, the document continued, "in order to change the subject," Italy would be very glad to be of service in bringing about an understanding between Germany and England. It appears to me that Italy has got wind of our plans for war and wishes to establish an alibi, so that afterward it cannot be said that Italian demands in the Mediterranean were the cause of the conflict.

Lunch with Schacht. Unfortunately he is getting a reputation (so say Beck, Popitz, and Fritsch) for talking one way and acting another—i.e., he won't stand his ground on a position he has agreed to take. In his conversation with me there was also apparent some kind of inner conflict. He was just back from England, where he had been discussing business matters only —not politics—such as a plan to finance Jewish emigration (the Warburg plan). The English were eager to work with us, but first wanted a very clear understanding about our policies. They ought to see things clearly by now! Naturally Schacht regards our present development, even the economic part of it, as very grim in spite of all "prosperity." He himself takes the position that he must hold out at his present post until the impossible is demanded of him (inflation, for instance). He had bought Rauschning's book[1] in Basel and found it brilliant.

With Beck in the afternoon. A refined and intelligent man, and a decent soldier. This whole trend disgusts him, and the irresponsible attitude of our leaders toward war angers and horrifies him. He dwelt on the outrageous way these people have of toying with the dangerous idea that this is "certain to be only a very short war." Apparently he has written another memorandum on the real conditions under which a war would be fought. I forgot, incidentally, to mention that Schacht absolutely rejects Ribbentrop's idea of a "decadent England"; our nerves, he said, would make a poorer showing if exposed to a great test. Beck thinks so too.

I went with Ilse Göring to the Deutsches Theater in the evening to see *Minna von Barnhelm.* Good performance; Loos as Riccaut, especially brilliant. This unfortunate bearer of the name Göring is very distressed at recent happenings and worries about the domestic and political affairs of her brother-in-law and Uncle Hermann. Emmy [Göring's wife] had conducted herself splendidly the whole time, and had spoken her mind stoutly and openly.

*December 25, 1938, Ebenhausen:* I forgot to mention the piquant detail that, after the murder of Codreanu, which followed closely upon the heels of King Carol's visit to Germany, Hitler ordered that the Rumanian decorations just bestowed should be returned; the German decoration intended for the Crown Prince was not given to him. The battle of King Carol against "Hitlerism" in his country and for his own dictatorship

[1]*Revolution of Nihilism.*

assumes a fundamental significance, within the limits of the somewhat oriental conditions prevailing in Rumania. The situation is similar in Hungary.

After returning from Berlin I went at once in the evening to Schoen's [former Minister in Budapest] to meet Welczeck. The latter described Ribbentrop's visit to Paris very vividly. He was apparently driven by a peculiar, almost pathological desire for recognition and a childish vanity. He made it plain that anything arranged in his honor would have to be staged in as extravagant a style as possible "Whenever feasible to surpass the splendor of the reception for the King of England." Welczeck had the impression that Ribbentrop was simply mad.

Day before yesterday at the Bruckmanns'. Frau Bruckmann is in growing despair because of the man on whom she had staked everything (Hitler). She clings to the last shreds of her sentimental attachment and her hopes, but in her mind she has completely rejected him. In addition to the outrages against the Jews, she is shocked by the contemptible campaign against poor Spann [Professor Spann, Austria] conducted in the paper *Schwarzes Korps*.

*December 29, 1938, Ebenhausen:* Yesterday afternoon with Schmitt [formerly Minister of Economic Affairs] at Tiefenbrunn. His son Günther did not get the Cecil Rhodes scholarship. Both father and son believe—and are indignant—that he was rejected because he belonged to the SS and because he left the church. If that were true it would be easy to understand, for it is the duty of the committee to send people to England who do not give offense.

The domestic and economic situation discourages Schmitt as it does all of us. He considers Goebbels and Heydrich the most dangerous of the Party leaders. On the other hand, he is not ready to give up Himmler entirely; although, of course, Himmler had some wild notions (i.e., the Church) which cannot even be discussed with him. In many other fields, said Schmitt, his views were not so bad.

Among the Gauleiters there were some obvious rascals and utter gangsters; others were better. Among the worst he numbers Streicher, Mutschmann, Wagner (Munich), and

Schwede; among the better, first of all Köhler (Baden), Wagner (Silesia), and Terboven; Murr was harmless; Koch (East Prussia) doubtful; Görlitzer (Berlin) was evil and corrupt.

In the evening to the Bruckmanns' for further information. The usual subject. Pietzsch, that faithful follower of Hitler, was horrified at the dangerous economic situation: the immoderate, stormy tempo of a production drive that is seriously overstraining all energies and resources. The present breakdown of the railroads at Christmastime was indicative of the general situation. It was characteristic of the present state of things in Germany that the whole country, so to speak, was covered with ruins, that is with all kinds of unfinished buildings that cannot be completed. The deterioration in the quality of everything was tangible evidence not only of the scarcity of materials but also of a rise in prices. Today's tax burden was already so great that an honest business profit and a healthy accumulation of capital were simply not possible.

Hitler had no understanding of all these things; he refused even to discuss economic affairs. For a year and a half he had not spoken to Pietzsch. In addition we had corruption. A man like Undersecretary Reinhardt paid taxes on a 350,000-mark income and earned even more because he got a handsome sum for each copy of a publication that every finance official was compelled to buy.

Equally scandalous were the earnings that Amann derives from Party publications (sale of *Mein Kampf*, for instance). Hitler held fast to his corrupt associates. The obscenities practiced by Schaub and Brückner, who are in Hitler's company every day, were followed by a season of disgrace; then they were reinstated and flourished again. The photographer Hoffmann, according to Frau Bruckmann, is almost the worst of all—a kind of evil spirit, a Caliban. On what foundation his relationship to Hitler rests is a dark secret.

On December 23 Hess spent two hours with the Bruckmanns. They said he had never before been so depressed. He left no doubt that he thoroughly disapproved of the action against the Jews; he had presented his views to the Führer in very clear terms and had implored him to stop the pogrom. Unfortunately his efforts had been in vain. Hess pointed to Goebbels as the real instigator.

On December 24 Hitler called at the Bruckmanns' but spent only half an hour. Apparently no real conversation got under way. He had acted "very satisfied" with everything and wrote in the guest book, beneath my (!) name and that of Hess: "My happiest Christmas." There is increasing evidence that these words may come to have another meaning than was intended.

Frau Bruckmann said that from her knowledge of his character she believed Hitler persecuted decent people so recklessly because he expected them to offer no defense, whereas he always spared and protected the rogues because he was afraid of them.

In Buchan's *Augustus*[1] there are some remarkable passages:

"A revolution, if it is to endure, must be in large part a reaction, a return to inbred modes of thought which have been neglected."

With reference to an upper class that limps along behind the times: "Much pride of ancestry but without hope of posterity."

And: "being too much governed, men had forgotten how to govern themselves."

[1] John Buchan [Lord Tweedsmuir, Governor General of Canada], *Augustus*.

# 1939

*January 17, 1939:* Visit from Hans Grimm. He gave a vivid description of the snooping and trailing to which he is subjected. Some time ago he was urgently summoned to Berlin by Goebbels. Since he was not feeling well, he at first said he could not come. Finally he had to travel to Berlin after all, where he was received by Goebbels in the presence of an unknown man in SS uniform. Goebbels immediately burst into an uncontrolled tirade and upbraided him for being opposed to National Socialism.

The documentary evidence offered was comical: first of all, a two-and-a-half-year-old (!) letter written by Grimm to Frick, a National Socialist Minister. It was a frank letter criticizing the unbelievable beating of somebody in Grimm's home town at the instigation of an SS leader. In addition Grimm did not end his letters with "Heil Hitler." Furthermore, he had not attended the Writers' Convention at Weimar. And, finally, he had sent word through a secretary to a government official "acting on behalf of Undersecretary" Hanke and, instead of traveling to Berlin, took the liberty of inviting Hanke to tea (he was traveling about in the neighborhood anyway)!

Then Goebbels dressed him down. If he did not adopt a different attitude he would break him just as he had broken Furtwängler, no matter how much of a row this might create in foreign countries. He was in the habit of sending recalcitrant writers to a concentration camp for four months, and at the second offense they would never get out. This interview was a "friendly warning" to which he had better give heed!

Grimm said he received an impression of unbelievable baseness; here was a level to which one simply could not descend. This sudden offensive, Grimm thought, could be laid at the door of the Party's fear that, since the pogrom had backfired, centers of opposition might be forming throughout the country. He may be right about this, but not in the sense that Goebbels, as Grimm assumed, wanted to sound him out. My opinion is that it was an attempt to intimidate him.

Grimm said that in his reply he had merely questioned the consistency of the reproaches, and explained that he didn't consider "Heil Hitler" a pleasant way to close a letter. He had emphasized that he could perceive no friendliness in Goebbels's "friendly warning"; he saw only force and pressure.

Grimm then inquired of some high-ranking person close to Hess whether he could do anything about such treatment, but was advised to keep still, otherwise he would be squashed like a fly on the wall. He intended to appeal to Göring, in his capacity as "Protector of the Prussian Academy," to institute any proceedings. But this will hardly succeed. The whole incident shows what methods we must now expect.

In the afternoon at Professor Goetz's (Dante scholar) with Gessler [former Minister of War], Hamm, and Sperr, last Bavarian Minister to Berlin. The political atmosphere is one of great anxiety. Hamm and Gessler are old Democrats; Goetz, an early follower of Naumann. Between their views and those of the old German Nationalist Party there is today no material difference. Politics makes strange bedfellows.

*Trip to Berlin, January 22–28, 1939:* Lehnich, an early Nazi and the highest functionary in motion-picture affairs, was on the train. Very vigorous and frank. Deeply depressed over Schacht's leaving. Now all restraints are gone. The one possibility of escaping economic collapse he saw, strangely enough, in economic domination of the Ukraine.

Then Lehnich described the shameless conduct of Goebbels in film affairs. Movies in which Lida Barowa (Goebbels's mistress) appeared were hissed off the screen. The actor Fröhlich is said to have boxed Lida Barowa's ears because he claimed prior rights to her. Goebbels himself is said to have been given a drubbing by Fröhlich.

These incidents gave rise to two jokes: "Emergency prayer: Dear God, let me be 'Fröhlich' [happy] just for twenty minutes!" Other Goebbels joke: "Why has Victoria (the statue of Victory) been raised several meters? So that Goebbels cannot reach her!"

Goebbels's period of disgrace with Hitler seems now to be over. Likewise, Esser, Bavarian Secretary of State, who was in disgrace because of his shameful carryings-on (he was beaten up in a beer hall over an affair with a woman), was not even dismissed. He was simply transferred to a subordinate post and now has been promoted again to a position as undersecretary in the Ministry of Propaganda. Which is just where he belongs!

It is noteworthy how our lords and masters are beginning to talk about one another. When the generals, some time ago, challenged Streicher for having insulted the nobility, Buch, the Party judge, quashed the matter on the grounds that Streicher was not considered normal by the Party. Göring once told me in Florence that Ley (one of the highest bigshots) is allowed the freedom of a court jester. And recently Göring said of Goebbels that he hoped he had now finally broken his neck.

*Tuesday, January 24, 1939:* Lunch with Popitz and others at the Continental Hotel. All were laboring under the effects of Schacht's dismissal.[1] Everybody is wondering how Funk will manage to carry on. The general impression is that some form of inflation is unavoidable. What the effects, or at least the immediate effects, will be is considered uncertain in view of the rigidity of currency controls and the official regulation of prices and wages. Popitz, of course, has received from Göring no answer to his request for retirement.

In the afternoon to see Frau von Weizsäcker. She was not very well informed politically. I had the impression that her position, as well as that of her husband, whom I saw on Thurs-

---

[1]January 20, 1939, Funk succeeded Schacht as President of the Reichsbank and Minister of Economic Affairs.

day, was being undermined. The same is true of Schwerin-Krosigk and other officials.

Wednesday, January 25, to call on Schacht: I found him noticeably and deeply upset. His first words were: "You have no idea how exuberantly happy I am to be out of all this!" But this did not ring true. My impression was that the blow fell unexpectedly and has left him speechless.

It is a great pity that a man who could have served our cause immensely by resigning at the proper time is now thrown out of his job like an incompetent employee. When I said that he himself had very likely taken the initiative, Schacht thundered back at me: "On the contrary, he threw me out!" According to his story he had had a somewhat frosty conversation with Hitler as early as last December, in which Hitler told him that he wished to go over the whole question of finance with him in January; moreover, Hitler knew what to do to procure money; after all, the resources were there. Schacht had replied that, since he was about to submit a memorandum on financial reforms, this subject might well be included in the discussion. This memorandum, supporting the thesis that government spending must be balanced by taxes and loans, was sent to Hitler on January 7. A few days later it was followed by a similar memorandum prepared by Schwerin-Korsigk after discussions with Schacht. Then silence.

Finally, on January 20, at nine-fifteen, he was summoned to Hitler and was received with these words: "Mr. President of the Reichsbank, I have asked you to come here in order to hand you your letter of dismissal!" Whereupon he produced the document. Schacht remained silent. Then Hitler, who thus far in the four or five minutes of conversation had said nothing about the memorandum, accused him of not having made an effort to fit himself into the National Socialist system. He cited as proof that at a party for the employees of the Reichsbank he had said that the events of November (Jewish pogrom) were a disgrace. Schacht says he replied: "My Führer, if I had known that you approved of these proceedings I would have kept silent!" Unquestionably a good answer. Then Schacht, as he says, made a reference to his not-inconsiderable services for the last six years; whereupon Hitler de-

clared that certainly he acknowledged those services, and for
that very reason wished to retain him as a Minister, providing
(and this is a strange utterance from the mouth of Hitler,
who obviously wished to get rid of Schacht) that he, Schacht,
did not himself desire to leave altogether.

In answer to my eager question as to what answer he. had
made, Schacht said: "I was silent!" and continued: "You
look at me as if to say I should have accepted the proposal (to
leave)!" I: "As a matter of fact, that course would have been
worthy of serious consideration, and it would interest me very
much to learn your motives for not doing so." Schacht walked
about for a few moments with his hands on his hips and then
said: "I did not want to blow up the bridge; he should do
that!"—which was not at all convincing to me. Schacht added
that Hitler apparently wanted to create disunity among the
directors of the Reichsbank for of the sixteen out of seventeen
members who had signed the memorandum he had dismissed
only two. Schacht was furious with Brinkmann, but also with
the business leaders who had behaved in a very cowardly way.
With the exception of the board of directors of the Deutsche
Bank, not one of them wrote or telegraphed or called on
him. Schwerin-Krosigk congratulated Funk, but to Schacht,
at their next meeting, he had not one word to say.

We then discussed the general financial situation. He thought
that even an authoritarian government could not prevent the
effects of an inflation—not even of a veiled one—upon wages
and prices. This was especially true under this particular
authoritarian government which permitted the all-too-limited
financial cover to be pulled at from all sides "by order of the
Führer": one must build airplanes, another highways, the
third guns, et cetera, and everything else was of no concern
to Hitler.

I hear also that Wiedemann was most brusquely "kicked up-
stairs" by Hitler personally; curiously enough with the remark:
". . . in case you wish to accept the post.'" From a well-informed source it was learned that Hitler also said to Wiedemann he wished to spare him conflicts between his own concepts and "those of the Führer."

---

[1]Wiedemann, adjutant of Hitler, was appointed Consul General in
San Francisco.

At midday Wilmowsky visited me to talk over his ideas about my becoming active in southeastern European economic affairs. He said industrial leaders were considering whether they should try to talk to Hitler in view of Schacht's dismissal. But probably nothing would come of it.

Wilmowsky came directly from a meeting of the laymen's church council, over which he presided—at Kerrl's request—in the place of Winnig. He was very proud of having reached a unanimous resolution: first of all he appointed a provisional synod; next he arranged for parish elections, and finally he decided that from among the local church elders a constituent synod is to be elected. He gave his project a 20 per cent chance of success. I raised the question whether we should help these people at all; he replied that the way we had been brought up we would always do it. Dibelius, he admitted, had told him the matter was simply this: Wilmowsky had confidence in Kerrl, whereas, in Dibelius's opinion, Kerrl was not playing fair.

*Thursday, January 26, 1939:* At twelve o'clock to see Weizsäcker. He thought the barometer indicated peace even in the east, where at the most one might expect action against Poland. On the other hand, Hitler's program still demanded a complete settlement of the Czech issue.

Afternoon tea with Olga Riegele [Göring's sister]. She tells fabulous tales about the Goebbels affair. Frau Goebbels had gone to Emmy to complain about "that devil in human form"; Goebbels, however, had gone to Hermann to complain tearfully how cold she was and how he had to seek his pleasures elsewhere. Hermann was actually impressed and told Emmy that she must look at it from his side too. Any feeling of responsibility and decorum seems to be absolutely foreign to this man, not to mention the infamy of exploiting actresses who depend on him for their jobs. Olga did not know whether or not there was any truth in the reports that Hermann was slated to be Chancellor.

Spent the evening at the house of my friend Brauchitsch. At last I met the Commander in Chief Brauchitsch and his new, common, but energetic wife. He impresses me as soldierly, intelligent, and rather reserved; when he speaks at greater length he cannot quite free himself from a kind of embarrassment. I can hardly imagine that he carries much weight with Hitler. He was rather impressed by Hitler's speech to the generals! Apparently Hitler had very cleverly keyed his speech to the psychology of the generals. He had spoken of the "old aristocracy" which had deteriorated by reason of bad and plebeian influences and which must now be regenerated through a process of fusion with the products of National Socialist education. Brauchitsch's leitmotiv was: the good will win out in the end.

He himself apparently helped to draft the new regulations concerning the pre- and post-military functions of the SA. His intention was to bring the SA under the influence of the military. He said we should have to wait and see who would gain the upper hand. In any case the measure was aimed by Brauchitsch against the SS, whose leader (Himmler) was in a rage about it.

*February 18, 1939, Ebenhausen:* Launching of the *Bismarck,* with a superficial speech by Hitler. The name was chosen chiefly in order to throw dust in the eyes of gullible Germans, many of whom will regard this homage paid the Iron Chancellor as a sign of Hitler's patriotism.

Whither we are traveling is indicated by shameless rabble-rousing on the subjects of "bureaucracy" and the "upper crust" on the part of that filthy dog, Goebbels, who is again in the good graces of Hitler. Decent people are defenseless against that sort of thing.

Sybel, member of the Reichstag and former leader of the Agrarian League, has been nabbed by the Gestapo. He belongs to the luncheon group of the Acting Minister of Finance, Popitz, and was arrested after a personal enemy had denounced him because of "remarks inimical to the regime."

Unpleasant discussions between us and the Navy about the launching of the *Tirpitz.* Mother Tirpitz vehemently refuses to christen the ship. The old naval officers object to Trotha as the speaker because they accuse him of abjectness toward the Party.

The German press, apparently on instructions, has commented decently on the death of the Pope [Pius XI, on February 10, 1939]. But at the same time the Catholic Theological Faculty in Munich is to be closed because of a dispute about an appointment. The intolerable part of such incidents is that the public is permitted to hear only one side.

According to the official Italian press, Ciano wants a mild, non-political Pope, presumably in order to facilitate an understanding with the Third Reich.

There is considerable agitation, caused on the one hand by the capture of Barcelona and the approaching end of the civil war, and, on the other hand, by the apparent stalling of the Japanese advance into China, despite the simultaneous occupation of Hainan. In Spain an obvious conspiracy has developed between Franco and the English by which the latter sought to prevent—and have succeeded in preventing—the occupation of Minorca by the Italians. The result is that the Italians made air attacks on Mahon from Majorca without Franco's permission. Things are getting complicated down there.

In China there is some evidence that the Japanese would tolerate a southern rump China under Chiang Kai-shek if they themselves could take a firm grip on the remainder. In the eyes of Wolf (who has just been there) this arrangement would be a kind of *partie remise,* with the better chances in the long run resting with the Chinese.

*February 25, 1939:* It is becoming more and more evident that England and France are following a tactical procedure, involving a highly accelerated rearmament program combined with simultaneous pronouncements of solidarity [February 6, 1939] by means of which they seek to exert "peace pressure" on the "totalitarians." They seem to believe it will work. At the same time England is attempting to reach an economic agreement with Germany. With respect to this latter project, the *Temps* comments, not entirely without justice from the Entente viewpoint, that England should be careful lest she increase the economic war potential of Germany.

Roosevelt pursues a somewhat different course, shaped to a considerable extent by the exigencies of domestic election issues.

He conjures up the picture of "the inevitable war with the aggressive totalitarians."

A few expressions from the man in the street: According to my somewhat garrulous barber, people's spirits are sinking rapidly. High Party officials are being cursed in a tone and with a recklessness without precedent. I asked: What are the principal complaints? Answer: Just about everything. "Joseph" [Goebbels] is the principal object of public scorn. But people complain particularly about the way the Government and Party work at cross-purposes.

Stories told me by Rommell, lawyer for the Allianz Insurance Company, are to be taken more seriously. He manages the insurance of local government officials and travels about continually among the local administrations. He said it was unbelievable what these people, often old Party members, tell him in the first five minutes of conversation about conditions in general, and specifically about financial matters. Out in the country things look most discouraging, particularly because of the labor shortage. A peasant had told him that Darré was seriously beaten up by the peasants at a session of the Bavarian Peasant Council, after he had answered their practical complaints with stupid slogans.

Herr von Praun, representative of BMW [Bayrische Motoren Werke], told me that at an "educational" conference of the Party, arranged for the engineers of his company, the chairman had sounded off: "Russia is made up of twenty-nine states, each one of which is now being undermined by our Party members; in this way bolshevism will collapse and with it the unity of Russia. All twenty-nine states will thereupon plead: 'Führer, send us leaders!' "

Following this erudite instruction, the eighty people had to listen to the recital of a song; afterward they had to repeat it; then they had to sing it, at first sitting, then standing, and finally marching in the hall. In the afternoon they had to stomp through the streets, in columns of four, braying the song in chorus. Praun said that in his business there were hardly any Nazis, no SA men, and no SS men. A murderous hatred against Ley prevailed among the workers.

*March 22, 1939, Ebenhausen:* The move against Czechoslovakia which I had heard about as early as January has now been made [March 15, 1939, occupation of Prague]. This is the first instance of manifest depravity, exceeding all limits, including those of decency; brilliantly executed in its technical aspects, to the utter astonishment of the world, which is looking on aghast. The violation of all decent standards now proven, among other things by the theft of the gold reserves. A violation of every acknowledged pledge and every healthy national policy. The whole business was conducted in defiance of the dictates of good faith. Duff Cooper: "Thrice perfidious traitor!" Even if all goes well at first, I cannot believe that this can end in anything but disaster.

England shows the strongest reaction and apparently wants to build up a strong defensive front against us. But since there is no real determination to resist anywhere—and on this fact Hitler is counting—nothing will happen for the moment. But the point at which Talleyrand left Napoleon has certainly been passed.

Hitler very likely needed the Czech gold, but it can help him only temporarily. It is almost tragically comical that Brinkmann (Director General of the Reichsbank) suffered a nervous breakdown after Schacht's dismissal. The Reichsbank, therefore, is at this moment without a real head. Schacht will surely talk of Nemesis. Brinkmann is supposed to have been found in a bar directing the orchestra, and also appears to have promised all his clerks wages of a thousand marks a month, and to have written out some orders in verse.

*April 3, 1939, Ebenhausen:* In Berlin since *March 25.* First, the ordination of Alfred Tirpitz. Ordination services were conducted rather impressively by Pastor Gollwitzer instead of Niemöller. At various places in the sermon references were made to poor Niemöller and to other victims. Frau Niemöller afterward came to the Tirpitz house for a short time, where old Professor Sering held forth in all his glory against our political methods. Frau von Keudell, on the other hand, talks more like a Nazi than is even faintly consistent with her nature. Her husband is a reed swaying in the breeze. Erika Rheinbaben was of the opinion that people in general were shocked by the sinister gangster tactics employed.

After the ordination I spent the evening with the Kamekes. He was desperate about the willful destruction of all ethical values and institutions in order to enhance the glory of the Nazi regime. Example: the senseless abolition of the truly irreplaceable Travelers' Aid Mission in favor of the NSV (National Socialist Peoples' Welfare). Kameke clings to astrological prophecies that the Nazi splendors will soon come to an end in a way I cannot understand.

The treaty with Rumania [March 23, 1939]—concluded in spite of all opposition—and the Memel business[1] have, understandably enough, made a considerable impression in Germany and have had the effect of stilling the fears of some of those people who were openly upset by the Czech affair. But regardless of the fact that the treaty with Rumania is, for the time being, only a frame—to be sure a beautiful one—it is becoming increasingly clear that these two events (Rumania and Memel) have had more alarming repercussions throughout the East than the Czech affair. The Soviet Union and Poland have pulled over markedly toward the west in spite of the fact that Stalin had until lately posed as the enemy of the Western capitalists, who would not succeed in provoking him into antagonism against Germany—least of all by the empty specter of alleged German plans for the Ukraine.

Poland's fear of us is rapidly mounting, and England, contrary to all her traditions, has given Poland a kind of guarantee [March 31, 1939] which would oblige her to join the anti-German front. It is, however, typically English that the *Times* immediately ran a commentary that qualified this obligation. According to letters from Italy, anti-German sentiment there is almost as strong as in 1934.

*Monday, March 27,* in Berlin I met Schwendemann, with whom I discussed my trip to Spain and at whose house I met Kiep, just returned from England. He was deeply impressed by the almost universal and rabid anti-German feeling there. In his view the English are anything but decadent and flabby;

[1]By a treaty with Lithuania on March 22, 1939, Memel was returned to Germany.

they are absolutely determined to make an end of appeasement. The one question remains whether they are militarily well enough prepared to strike if Hitler should again become aggressive.

I saw Ilse Göring at the theater (very charming performance of *Madame Sans-Gêne*). In spite of all doubts she has been impressed by the successes in the foreign field and has become somewhat more favorable to the regime. She thought Hermann had been kept informed by Hitler during the Czech affair and that he was fully in accord with the proceedings.

Heydrich is the Görings' principal *bête noir* at the moment. Everything else they put up with. Even Himmler was entirely unimportant and basically harmless!

*Tuesday, March 28, 1939:* After my Spanish lesson I visited Canaris, who was about to leave for Spain by air.

Lunch at the Continental with Popitz, Heinrici, Sybel (who is just out of the concentration camp and, like one who has returned from a vacation, now dines merrily with the Prussian Minister of Finance!), Tischbein, Kempner, and Planck. Everyone is shocked about the miserable role Schwerin-Krosigk is playing in the new finance scheme. Planck very intelligent—a man with whom one can work. He told me that he had visited Brinkmann in the sanatorium. The latter had met him at the station and in the car had said "he should excuse him for a short time because it was his custom to shoot one more sparrow and a hawk." In other words, completely cracked!

*April 5, 1939:* It goes without saying that none of us undertook the journey to Wilhelmshaven with joy. With his latest move Hitler has maneuvered Germany irrevocably into the role of public enemy. Each new step may bring catastrophe upon us, and it is psychologically improbable that he will remain quiet for long. The launching of the *Tirpitz* is exactly the sort of gesture of opposition to England which makes it possible for Tirpitz's policies to be unjustly exploited and falsely interpreted.

Many old friends among the guests; Seebohm full of humor but at the same time bitterly ironical about the Party. It was worth while to see the Austrian general, Bardolff, and the Minister, Glaise-Horstenau, both in the uniform of German generals, eying each other's garb in genial astonishment. The Austrian lightheartedness, which they both possess, is a quality which the *Altreich* [Germany proper] could use to advantage. Himmler spoke to me about our chauffeur, Schuhknecht, who has just been kicked out by him. We know Schuhknecht's side of the story. He had been with us for six years and took a job with Himmler after we left Rome. Once, at a crossroads, he had a minor accident in which neither the empty car which Schuhknecht drove nor the motorcyclist involved was more than superficially damaged. As a result, Schuhknecht, without being given a hearing, was locked up for six weeks in the deepest cellar of the Gestapo; he couldn't even let his wife know his whereabouts. Still without a hearing he was released and came to us, completely down at the heel, looking for help, although he had been forced to pledge silence. This good, reliable man still trembles all over. In this matter Himmler did not demonstrate any of the vaunted "comradely" spirit [*Volksgemeinschaft*]; on the contrary, he assumed pretty much the manner attributed to the despised "upper class." Interesting that he, the highest officer of the Gestapo, ventured to tell me that Schuhknecht wanted to talk out of school about us. But with this kind of thing, of course, he would have nothing at all to do. "The man shall work for me, but not talk about his former employer," he said.

In *May 1939* I traveled to Spain for the Munich Reinsurance Company.

*May 30, 1939, Ebenhausen:* Trip to Berlin and Hanover, *May 1939.* Arrived in Berlin on *Monday evening, the twenty-second.* To my horror it occurred to me on the way that Ciano was still in Berlin,[1] and at the Adlon, of all places. So the former Ambassador to Rome stole into the Adlon like a thief in the night to avoid meeting Ciano and his outfit. They had all just marched off to Dahlem to see Ribbentrop.

[1]His visit of May 21–23, made after the meeting in Milan on May 5–6, 1939, at which the military alliance was signed.

On Tuesday one of the guests told me about the tremendous banquet that was given by Ribbentrop at his villa there. The affair took place in the garden under gigantic tents decorated with a fantastic display of flowers. We also learned of the astonishingly undignified behavior of Ciano—but that was no surprise to us. As spring had not arrived according to schedule, hundreds of electric stoves were pressed into service to provide warmth.

Detalmo Pirzio Biroli, who visited us here for a few days paying court to my daughter Fey, told amazing things about the low state of morale in Italy; feeling runs strong against domestic political trends as well as against us. It seems that the presence of numerous Germans, above all Gestapo agents, aviation technicians, et cetera, arouses great ire. The principal cause for anger is, of course, the fact that Mussolini has completely swung about to sail in our wake. The current joke: "*Si stava meglio sotto Mussolini* [Things were better under Mussolini]."

Everyone fears war. There is a little hope that the alliance just concluded may work for peace because Mussolini may act as a kind of brake; he must know that Italy cannot fight a world war, either militarily, materially, or morally. Detalmo, on the basis of his own experiences as a reserve officer, tells amazing things about the poor state of the Army. He said that in fascism two tendencies are in conflict: a "good" one—stifled at the moment—Grandi, Balbo, De Vecchi, De Bono; and a "bad" one—now in the saddle—Ciano, Starace, Farinacci. Mussolini was coming more and more under Ciano's influence and was being hamstrung by Signora Petacci.

*On Monday, May 22,* I paid a visit to Elisabeth and Ernst Albers-Schönberg at Frohnau. They were both very much depressed about domestic developments, especially moral ones. For instance, the Hitler Youth organization, with its idiotic, extravagant demands, was leading their son to shiftlessness and lying. In spite of this the son was opposed in every way to the Hitler Youth.

Grotesque description by Ernst of the officially inspired "popular" demonstrations in honor of Ciano. The people are weary of these things to the point of nausea, and when the

Party was unable to scrape together enough of a crowd for the first day's celebration, the Labor Front was called into action. At a time when man-power mobilization had reached its peak, the industrial leaders were literally begged to send their workers out on the streets—of course with full pay. Then the employers were compensated on a percentage basis; in the case of Ernst Albers-Schönberg, for example, it was 25 per cent.

Wilmowsky has interested himself further in the church question, although his first mediation proposal had simply disappeared into the pigeonholes of Kerrl's desk. He thought the prospects for success were somewhat rosier now. The Godesberg declaration of the "German Christians" was generally regarded as an error. I cannot share his optimism, however; I feel that the outlook for the Evangelical Church is very black. They want to strangle it.

Incidentally, I saw the wenches—so they must really be called—who belong to the National Socialist Travelers' Aid Service. They are now supposed to replace the old and worthy Station Mission, but their efforts only arouse much antagonism and little confidence.

*Wednesday, May 24,* I visited Henderson. The poor chap told me he had cancer of the mouth, but hoped to be saved by radium treatment. He is naturally very much depressed over the political situation. In England they accuse him of letting Hitler lead him about by the nose. It is understandable that he speaks most bitterly about Hitler's breach of faith. Hitler had broken every promise made at Berchtesgaden, Godesberg, and Munich. All faith in him is destroyed. He believes that the seizure of Czechoslovakia was a great mistake from the German point of view. He had, of course, received the news that is everywhere filtering through concerning the increasing tension in Czechoslovakia: Frank's brutal policies of oppression and the helplessness of Neurath. Seyss-Inquart has also been completely bypassed in Austria.

*June 1, evening in Hanover.*

*On Friday, June 2,* I rode first of all to Nienburg; met there by Friedrich Bodelschwingh in his little car and taken to his parsonage at Schlüsselburg. He gave a description of the hopeless conditions in the Evangelical Church which, itself disunited, is gradually being strangled by the National Socialist state. Real leadership is lacking in the struggle. I inquired about his uncle Bodelschwingh, but it seems that, despite his great abilities, he too sees no way to get a hold on the situation. Bodelschwingh and those like him now see only one way left—that of indefatigable, faithful congregational work and contact with like-minded colleagues. But how long will that be permitted? And what will happen to the community as a whole? Will the Church go back into the catacombs? Of course there are already denunciations in the congregation. Friedrich was arrested once, and when the Bethel Academy was closed, his house was searched.

About political feeling among the people, he said that an increasing indifference prevailed among those not personally interested in the regime. The chief Nazis everywhere were the old communists; their views, naturally, were unchanged.

*June 20, 1939:* Striking example of the quivering fear of German editors is provided by the blue penciling of my article on Spain. Herr Wirth really thinks exactly like every other human being who is not completely befuddled, and yet he makes up the *Deutsche Zukunft* as if Goebbels were its editor. The few raisins which I was able to leave in my article were meticulously dug out; any spot where a penetrating imagination might discover something like an independent thought; also anything that might reflect a gentle criticism of Franco or a comparison with National Socialism.

Ever-increasing tension in Czechoslovakia. A vivid description of the bad conditions there was given to Schmoller by Dr. Walther, a German provincial administrator in that country. There are two sets of authorities of which one, the Czech, can be thankful if it is not jailed by the other. There and in Austria the old South German conception of the Prussian, the *Preiss,* is coming to the fore again, regardless of the fact that the old, genuine Prussianism is a very different thing indeed. Two stories illustrate this point: Two Austrians sit in a café in Vienna. The first says, "Hm," and the second, after

a long silence, answers: "Hm." The first repeats: "Hm," and
the second: "Well, we finally got rid of the Turks too."

Also in Vienna: an old woman, looking at a banner stretched
across the street: "I can't read what's on there!" An SS man
explains: "It says: 'We have been freed!'" The woman:
"*Ach,* have the Prussians left again?"

A wild speech by Goebbels in Danzig. Is this the signal for
a solution by force or just bluff?

There is increasing tension in the international field. English
policies appear to be completely stymied. The Soviets, recognizing this situation, blackmail England. In a desperate effort
to get an agreement, she yields one position after another. The
Japanese, presumably in co-operation with Germany and Italy,
treat the great British Empire just as the Great Powers were
once accustomed to deal with Haiti.

According to all reports, Ribbentrop is the man who has the
most influence with Hitler.

In Germany the strain is increasing every day.

Yesterday a lecture by Fabritius, German minority leader
in Rumania, before an invited audience (Party people and the
Organization for Germans Abroad [*Verein des Deutschtums
im Ausland*]. What he said about the practical work of the
minority group was sensible and quite interesting. For example, he warned against the unsuitable education given the
young Germans who were brought into the Reich for schooling.
If one continued to accustom them to standards and notions far
too grandiose for them, instead of training them for the simple,
Spartan peasant life, one would do more harm than good.

He also strongly emphasized the necessity of avoiding a
conflict with the churches; the work of the national minority
group rested directly upon church foundations. He said the
Church, furthermore, was heart and soul behind the (National
Socialist) leadership of the minority group. Bishop Glondys
was a Party member.

In the middle of all this Fabritius slipped grotesquely, saying: "We are now so strongly entrenched in the Evangelical
Church that we could have Evangelical, Catholic, or Jewish
services read in the church whenever we wish!" Nevertheless
he made this rather amusing closing remark: "Gentlemen,

we do not intend to do everything in Rumania by ourselves. You settle this church question in the Reich first, and we shall follow right along!"

The important part of his speech, however, was the political section, and that was the most abominable kind of imperialistic demagogy, fit only for dairymaids. I certainly should like to know how this outburst affected the audience, for the most part composed of people without discrimination. Upon a partly factual foundation he built up a cardboard political structure compared to which the ideas of the Pan-Germans were an example of *Realpolitik*.

Afterward I sat for a while with Berthold, Fabritius, and the teacher, Florian Kramer from Veprowac, in Yugoslavia. In meeting my objections Fabritius was the calmest and most reasonable of the lot. After he had gone I asked Berthold how to account for the inflammatory parts of his speech, whereupon Berthold said: "Very simple! Fabritius has spent a week in Berlin and was continually exposed to the effusions of Himmler, Lorenz, *et al.*

*June 21, 1939, Ebenhausen:* Last evening I was visited by two South Tyrolean leaders, Dr. Tinzl from Schlanders, and Franceschini, now a German citizen, who lives in Vienna. I had already informed them that I was now a private person and without influence, but they insisted on coming anyway to present their views and to seek advice. It is a grotesque situation. For years, even before going to Rome, I did nothing but work for reasonable co-operation with Italy; then I was recalled because I was not sufficiently pro-Axis (having opposed the military alliance with Italy and also the Anti-Comintern Pact); and now the South Tyroleans take me into their confidence!

Tinzl and Franceschini were completely crushed by their observations in Germany. According to instructions from "above," no one dared to discuss public affairs with them. Lorenz, a chief group leader and director of the office for German Minority Groups, expressly told them that he was no longer permitted to deal with South Tyrolean affairs. The only person Franceschini managed to see was Göring. Nothing-could now be done for the South Tyroleans because Chief Group Leader Kaufmann, a German citizen, upon orders of Ettel [the Nazi Party leader for Italy] had rather tactlessly organized a camping trip to Meran for German citizens living in the South Tyrol, and got himself arrested.

This incident was said to have enraged Hitler. He went so far as to forbid the use of the expression South Tyrol, and to order that all German citizens, mostly Austrians of course, and some with large property holdings south of the Brenner, were to be brought out of South Tyrol immediately. Orders were also given to prepare the resettlement of the South Tyroleans proper. An office had already been opened at Innsbruck, of all places, staffed by people who knew nothing at all about local conditions. The direction of this resettlement scheme had been assigned to Himmler, who was to carry it out in direct negotiation with Attolico. As for the South Tyroleans, they could not even find out what was going to happen to them. Everything was handled with incredible carelessness, and at the same time with the Byzantine methods of the imperial era. Franceschini added that Ribbentrop was the worst offender in this respect. For example, in a recent discussion with Germans from Slovenia, who wanted to save southern Styria, he explained that their project was hopeless because he had just concluded a twenty-five-year pact with "Slovenia"—thus confusing Slovenes and Slovaks.[1]

Franceschini and Tinzl already knew about the wild imperialistic plans that Fabritius had dished out day before yesterday. They were afraid that the South Tyroleans were to be carted off into the eastern provinces. After first proclaiming the principle of nationality as the basis of his policy, Hitler had completely reversed himself, first by seizing Czechoslovakia and now by sacrificing the Germans in South Tyrol. As for the South Tyroleans themselves, the only course open to them was to denounce this policy, and to claim for themselves the right of self-determination. In this they would, for obvious reasons, find the approval of the Western Powers.

*June 23, 1939:* Throughout the last few months there has been a stream of unpleasant reports from Fey about her labor

[1]Treaty with Slovakia, March 25, 1939.

camp at Münnerstadt. An obstinate, foolish, and very inferior woman is camp leader. Her senseless orders endanger the health of the girls. Everybody breathed easier when she went on vacation and a sensible assistant took her place. Now the latter has been transferred to another camp. This has resulted in complete pandemonium. In addition there are always men about the rooms.

However, this is really nothing as compared with the cases Major Blattmann and the painter Erbslöh described today. A girl they knew wrote to her parents from the camp: "Please don't thrash me when I come home with a baby, otherwise I'll report you." Another young girl, known to them, wrote from her work camp or school that the director, a woman, had informed one mother that to her joy her daughter and five other girls from the camp would before long "present the Führer with a child."

There is increasing evidence that things are beginning to "creak" in high places. The building and festival mania is now so rampant and, on the other hand, the financial stringency has become so evident that—one would not think it possible—an "Association for the Promotion of Large-scale Projects" has been founded "so that our Führer, who has so far generously paid for these things, may be relieved of this care." Nothing but a new form of extortion in the place of unpopular taxes.

Former Undersecretary von Kühlmann received a visit from a uniformed representative of this association, traveling in a huge Mercedes. Bruckmann was solicited by letter, but both men bravely refused to contribute. Annual membership fees run from 300 to 500 marks. Initiation fee, 250 marks. Instead of annual contributions one single payment of several thousand marks is permitted. The representatives told Kühlmann he had already recruited one hundred members in Bavaria. Apprehension is enormous. By this kind of financing fantastic things are made possible.

A second art museum is to be built opposite the first. Here are to be housed gigantic facsimiles in Nymphenburg porcelain of floats from various processions which Hitler had commended and which thus qualified as artistically meritorious. The porcelain manufacturers are wringing their hands over this order. Similarly, a statue of Minerva three yards high is to be wrought of silver as enduring evidence of German artistry in handicrafts.

*July 4, 1939:* The students' harvest service, which has become necessary as a result of the man-power shortage, has met with surprisingly open resistance in Munich, and, according to what one hears, also among the Heidelberg students, who are fed up with not being able to settle down to their studies. The interesting thing about these demonstrations is that this kind of resistance is possible at all, above all without organization, which is, of course, out of the question. A Party speaker was hissed out of one student gathering; in another he was bombarded with eggs, and the affair resulted in about ten students being sent to Dachau. The halls of the university were plastered during the night with inscriptions "Down with Hitler" and with slogans comparing Hitler with Napoleon, whose rule also had a quick end.

General intensification of the nervous tension and fear of war is being accepted almost as a decree of Fate. The tone adopted against England, particularly in an article by Goebbels, beggars description. As a German one is ashamed.

To the chapter on illegitimate children Dieter adds the following: in a village in the Palatinate he himself read an announcement by the burgomaster to the effect that he had at his disposal a fund which was to be used for the support of girls who wished to present a child to the Führer. The girl and her father, however, must first report to the authorities. "Re-establishment of the family as the moral foundation of the nation!"

*July 11, 1939:* Yesterday I had a conversation with Prince Constantine of Bavaria. His stories about the Labor Service indicate that he had hardly discovered a single 100 per cent National Socialist. Everybody was either angered or bored by the methods of the Party rulers; there was general complaint about the economic stringencies caused by current policies; everybody longed for a change. Naturally motives vary greatly.

Most people center their hopes on the Army as the one factor still intact. In public the camp functionaries spoke an entirely different language than in private, especially with him as a prince. Furthermore, all grades of labor-service officials below the rank of superintendent were very inferior. For money, food, automobile trips, and similar inducements, one can get anything. A worker told him if war came the Army would certainly take things in hand. Every officer who had been kicked out by the Nazis, like Fritsch, would immediately get a position because one could assume that he had shown independence.

*July 13, 1939:* Visited Professor W. Goetz with former Cabinet Ministers Hamm and Gessler. Detailed discussion on the necessity of preparations in the event of a Nazi collapse. Gessler is convinced that in this case one must aim at a monarchy. But how? Gessler does not expect much from the Army in its present shape, since all independent brains have been systematically removed. Hammerstein, Fritsch, and Beck were not slated to receive commands in the event of mobilization. Gessler was in England for several weeks and conferred with many prominent people. He had the impression that Hitler had effectively aroused the English with occupation of Prague on March 15. But the English still entertained a slight hope that Hitler, impressed by their awakening, might relent and become reasonable. If not, they were resolved not to make peace with Hitler and his friends. He heard especially vehement expressions about Göring. Goebbels was worth his weight in gold to the English.

Gessler said propaganda guns were being brought up in England. The letters of King-Hall—earlier regarded as anti-German and now considered rather pro-German—were being translated into foreign languages and distributed in Germany, among other countries. Goetz, Hamm, and Gessler had received some of them (quotes from Rauschning were included). King-Hall told Gessler that the correct system was to report actual facts briefly; then one could occasionally sandwich in a thick lie. Goebbels's practice of producing lies as a steady diet and now and then including a piece of truth was the wrong way to do things.

British strategy apparently called for offensive action in full strength against Italy, in the Alps, on the sea, and in Africa, and remaining on the defensive against Germany. Italy was considered a weak adversary to be crushed; after the fall of Mussolini the monarchy was to be supported and Italy forced to make a separate peace.

*July 18, 1939:* Through a remarkable coincidence, Goebbels's article on the King-Hall letters appeared the very morning after my conversation with Gessler. It constitutes the most vulgar concoction of words ever to flow from the pen of a German Cabinet Minister. Meanwhile, in a roundabout way, I received a King-Hall letter. It strikes me as poor propaganda. And this fact makes the tremendous to-do of Goebbels's counterattack the more incomprehensible. The sole explanation lies in Goebbels's determination to undertake something every single day to undermine English prestige. Some blind patriots will, of course, think: "Goebbels really handed him one this time!"

In London a large Moseley gathering has been given new treatment by the English press; not hushed up, as they have been lately, but simply belittled. I wonder whether there is really something behind this? Is the man paid by us?

In Paris the French press has revealed cases of bribery by the Germans; this would explain the weak stand frequently taken by French newspapers—even the *Temps*.

Captain Scheibe was here and told how shamelessly the Nazis, after having seized power, broke the most solemn promises they had made to the German National Party. For this the latter have only themselves to blame.

*July 22, 1939:* A few days ago the Bruckmanns visited us. They are disgusted by Goebbels's article. Everybody is weary, they say, of the many celebrations and flags. "All these red flags in the Ludwig Strasse!" exclaimed Hitler's most faithful woman friend. Her husband declared that he was simply delighted when it rained on the Day of German Art. Eyewitnesses give a comical description of the condition of Hitler's rostrum during the festival. Because of the downpour the canvas roof

—the blue "heaven"—had to be propped up with poles, whereupon veritable streams of water poured down upon the rostrum. Hitler was in a very bad temper, having sent his raincoat over to his "friend," Fräulein Braun.

Glaise-Horstenau told the Bruckmanns that if an election were to be held in Austria now less than 10 per cent would vote for Hitler.

*August 1, 1939:* Guttenberg was here. Told about the rough handling Revertera had received from the Gestapo, and reported further that the editor of the *Fränkischer Kurier* was informed of the seriousness of the international situation by high personages in the Propaganda Ministry. Is this bluff? Doesn't seem likely to me. According to them, about August 20 the Poles will be attacked by us and by the Lithuanians, to whom we have apparently promised Vilna. Shortly before that the usual propaganda is to be turned loose.

The decision was reached after Mussolini "finally" agreed to go along. Hitler is supposed to have thanked Mussolini, adding that he appreciated it the more since Italy would have to bear the brunt of the first thrust. To be sure Mussolini is said to have declared that to the extent Russia had obligated herself to the Western Powers he would refuse to be drawn into a war. Therefore, if Russia should make a pact with the Western Powers, Hitler would announce his demands to the whole world, but postpone their fulfillment for two years.

If these reports are correct, Molotov has the fate of the world in his hands.

The *Neue Züricher Zeitung* reprinted an astonishingly frank article from the *Deutsche Volkswirt,* describing the mistakes and dangers inherent in our economic policy, especially with respect to public spending. Enthusiasm cannot replace experience.

I have received many reports about the wretched conditions in Czechoslovakia, particularly about the brutal methods of Hermann Frank.

*August 3, 1939:* Widespread war psychosis.
One might well believe that the Soviets are deliberately

planning to bring about a European war by their vacillating conduct.

*August 7, 1939:* News from Nostitz (Foreign Office): the third and last wave of partial mobilization against Poland is now in progress. On August 26 or 27 everything will be ready. The decision whether or not to march (in conjunction with sudden naval action against Gdynia) has not yet been made.

At the top, very bad tempers and wavering for the first time: orders and counterorders, for instance with reference to an earlier plan to stage a naval demonstration off Danzig. Ribbentrop behaved like a lunatic, was unbearable in the office, and has no friends at all. Involved in a great fight with Goebbels, he is in bad with Göring, and of late has not been on a good footing with Hess. Göring still appears to be the most sensible but—as I heard today from another source—"does not wish to be discredited again as a 'coward.' "

Nothing is to be hoped from the generals. Let's not even talk about Keitel; even Brauchitsch is in the hands of the Party. Only a few have kept clear heads: Halder, Canaris, Thomas. Ribbentrop is said to have been in disgrace with Hitler for weeks, (1) because he had misinformed him about England, (2) because he had advised him to take Czechoslovakia first and then Danzig.

Nothing serious seems to be in the air with the Soviets, although Hitler, according to many indications, wants an understanding. Molotov is said to have been most reticent during a conference with Schulenburg, who had clearly pointed out the desirability of "normalizing" Russo-German relations.

The Prime Minister of Hungary recently addressed a remarkable document to Hitler and Mussolini. In the event of a general conflict, Hungary would synchronize its policies with those of the Axis Powers. While the meaning of this message was being mulled over a supplementary note arrived. In order to avoid any misunderstanding, it said, it should be made clear that in the event of a German-Polish conflict Hungary could not go to war.

Horthy is said to have told an old Austrian comrade recently that he thought the days of the Axis were numbered; if it broke up, Hungary would stick to Italy. Whether or not this story is true it certainly represents the mood of Hungary. But whether this decision will stand in the face of realities is another question. Nostitz thought Yugoslavia was of late turning more and more toward the Western Powers.

Most important recent event: ten or twelve days ago Attolico called on Ribbentrop (after having seen Weizsäcker) and finally Hitler, with a message from the Duce to the following effect: the meeting of the Duce and the Führer at the Brenner, set for August 4, would be useful only if something tangible should come out of it. And, in view of the entire situation, this something could only be a decision to call a Six Power conference (Italy, Germany, France, England, Spain, Poland) in order to solve the Italian-French as well as the German-Polish conflicts. If this were not done now it would have to be done in four to six weeks' time. This message had the effect of a thunderbolt.

The first (and entirely groundless) "consolation" offered thereafter by the Italians took the form of a tapped telephone conversation between Ciano and Attolico, during which the former most forcefully emphasized his loyalty to the Axis pact. The second hope was that Attolico had, as usual, said more than he had been authorized to say. (In September 1938 he had also worked for peace on his own responsibility.) But Weizsäcker's report on the clarity and precision of Attolico's remarks left no room for this interpretation. A few days ago a preliminary and evasive answer was given. Consideration is now being given to taking care of the Polish matter without Italy.

This looks to me very much like one of Mussolini's frequent personal impulses. He must suddenly have realized the gravity of the whole situation for Italy. If he meets resistance to his proposal in Berlin he will simply drop it.

*August 10, 1939:* Many things conspire to create a high degree of bad humor and defeatism: scarcity of gasoline and raw materials, as well as of many foodstuffs even before the start of war. In addition there is constant and sometimes contradictory interference in business affairs. Complaints and grumblings are louder and less cautious than ever before. Ilse went to the Bavarian Co-operative in Wolfratshausen today to get some oats, and was fairly overwhelmed by the vehemence of the director's criticism of the regime in the presence of the workmen. We had a similar experience yesterday at our garage in Starnberg.

The press is turning the heat on Poland. The line, however, is not "atrocities," which would offer an excuse for intervention, but rather "Polish impertinence," which creates dangerous conditions leading to war. It doesn't sound as if causes for war were being manufactured yet.

Sunday [*August 6, 1939*] at the Müfflings' (publisher of *Deutschlands Erneuerung*). Müffling, prototype of the German idealist, had at one time gone over to the Party with flags flying. Now he is bitterly disappointed and disgusted, and speaks of the "sub-humans" who rule over us.

Day before yesterday I had tea with Miss Tomara, who had interviewed me in Rome. An attractive, intelligent Russian, a correspondent for the New York *Herald Tribune*. After all they have experienced the Russians no longer take things tragically. They no longer have a fatherland and observe everything in an historico-philosophical light. The expulsion of individuals and whole races from their homeland does not astonish them. Even so she was deeply impressed by what she had seen in unhappy South Tyrol. Politically and militarily critical of the Italians. They are tired, she says, of continually "living like lions."

Yesterday an Italian officer who is here on language duty told our Italian groom, Filippo, that Mussolini was no longer a very well man; he also had had bad luck with his associates. "We are waiting for Umberto. He will put everything in order." Ilse then asked Filippo whom he would choose, Mussolini or the House of Savoy. Without a moment's hesitation he answered: "Naturally *Casa Savoia*."

Miss Tomara had no good impressions from her visit in Germany. Public morale had sunk very considerably during the past year. In the Foreign Office someone had told her that the chances of war or peace stood at about 30 to 70.

In contrast to last year she had been favorably impressed in

France: *"Recueillement!"* The French are calm, even in contemplating the possibility of war; she had the feeling that everything—for instance air-raid shelters for women and children —was well organized.

In America there was a strong pro-war feeling. If Roosevelt chooses to run again he will be elected. He, and particularly his wife, is very popular. The sentiments of the well-to-do Americans traveling in Europe, who are concerned about their money, are of no consequence.

*August 11, 1939:* Today Ciano and Ribbentrop meet in Salzburg. Perhaps the die will be cast there for war or peace.

Conversation with R. A. Bosch (spark-plug manufacturer), a man old in years but lively, intelligent, and energetic. A good representative of the captains of industry of his generation. It is difficult to imagine that it would be possible to develop personalities of this type today. He considers the economic policies of the Third Reich and the entire system of government as ruinous, the leaders as fundamentally incompetent and entirely without ethics. He had had a conference with Hitler in 1933 and was most unfavorably impressed. He admits he made an error in judging how long such a system could last.

In answer to my question as to whether we who have eyes to see must hurl ourselves into the abyss, he made pointed remarks about progress in creating an organization designed to meet a difficult crisis. But it did not seem to me as if he knew anything concrete. He had a low opinion of the political abilities of the Army and of industry, particularly of the Rhenish-Westphalian industrialists, who seemed satisfied with making profits; that was why they had been completely fooled by Hitler.

Bosch has large land holdings; he said agriculture was going down rapidly. If war began now we would go into it in the same shape we were in when forced to surrender in 1918. Furthermore, he believes that the people would rebel after a fortnight. He was not clear, however, as to just how all this was to be effected.

In Tübingen the atmosphere is pessimistic. The city, without the colorful students' caps, makes an unhappy impression. But withal it looked as beautiful as ever. In the morning I was wakened by the trumpeting of the hymn *"Wache auf, so rufet uns die Stimme* (Wake up! a voice is calling us)." Before me in brilliant sunshine lay the market square, with the old Rathaus and the spring around which we always gathered to raise our glasses in celebration of May Day. I climbed up to the castle and looked out over the countryside along the Neckar, spread out at my feet in its full splendor. Down in the city people were streaming toward the college chapel, whose bells pealed forth comfort and peace. This picture represents the real German character.

*Westerland, August 17–18, 1939:* Political situation: the strategic design of the "others" is apparently to effect a "peace front" (with Soviet Russia) and then to present us and the Italians with the alternative: either to accept certain conditions and give guarantees, so that the unbearable tension bedeviling the whole world at present may be brought to an end, or to reckon with a reaction backed by force of arms. Under these conditions Mussolini concluded that Germany and Italy had better seize the initiative in calling a conference. Ciano brought this proposal to Salzburg and to the Obersalzberg and met with a flat refusal. The deadlock was so complete that they couldn't even agree on the wording of a communiqué. I hear that Mussolini formulated his position thus: that, in the event his proposal was rejected, responsibility for the consequences would be ours.

Hitler proceeds in an entirely different way. The very threat of a conference makes him more aggressive. He wants to take the lead even at the last minute. The most dangerous game one can imagine has already begun. It is highly probable that war with Poland is imminent and I cannot believe (as Hitler pretends to do) that the Western Powers will remain neutral.

Some people believe we must go through the catastrophe of a world war, in which the chances of defeat are 80 per cent, in order to achieve healthy conditions here at home. I cannot share this view, and consider the whole business an irresponsible adventure, both from the National Socialist point of view and from that of an enemy of the Nazi regime. All clear-headed people should do everything in their power to prevent war. The only question is what one can do. The ideal moment for a coup would come directly before or at the moment of the outbreak of war. But, practically speaking, simply to wait for that moment means taking a terrible risk, the more so since apparently not much is to be expected from the present leaders of the Army. The last speeches of Brauchitsch and Raeder vie with each other in Byzantine expansiveness.

Hitler has made one more effort to win Danzig peacefully by receiving the League of Nations Commissioner, Burckhardt and inducing him to report his ideas to the English. But he may have done so chiefly to create an alibi and to make it more difficult for England to intervene. I know nothing about the result.

The wild tone used by the press against Poland and against the "fantastic idea of calling a conference" seems to indicate an unfavorable outcome.

*Back in Berlin.* The first person I met was Magistrati. He was obviously troubled. In answer to my question he said that he, too, had been in Salzburg and Berchtesgaden. He said with emphasis that it had been very interesting. I ventured: there were doubtless difficult subjects to be discussed? Yes, very difficult! But, I asked, did everything go off well? "Yes," he answered, after considerable hesitation. "Yes, I think so."

*Monday, August 14, 1939:* At ten o'clock I saw Goerdeler in his lodgings on Askanischer Platz. Fresh, clear-headed, active. Perhaps a bit sanguine. One hears generally that he is imprudent and is being closely watched. It is a relief, though, to speak with a man who wants to act rather than grumble. Of course his hands are tied, just like ours, and he is desperate about the losses we have suffered in the Army since February 4, 1938.

Nevertheless, he believes there are elements of resistance already growing again throughout the country, even though scattered and without organization. We were agreed that a world war offers no solution, that it would be a terrible catastrophe. Whatever influence we have must be used to prevent it.

Goerdeler appeared again at the Hotel Adlon with his comrade in arms, Dr. Gisevius, whom I had already met once at

Herbert Göring's. Gisevius was formerly with the Gestapo, then became active in industry, and has now reentered the civil service. Goerdeler and others praise him to the skies. He is no doubt intelligent, informed, and active. But I don't quite make him out.

As I had an engagement with Wolf Tirpitz, the four of us lunched at the Esplanade. There we found a veritable stock exchange: Dirksen, Stauss, Richard H. Wolff, Mann, H. Pönsgen. Pönsgen stated that we had, at the outside, only six weeks' supply of raw materials for war. I asked Dirksen whether he was on a holiday or if he had been summoned. He replied scornfully: "Of course I was summoned to the Obersalzberg!" (Dirksen had tried for weeks to get an appointment with Hitler.)

*August 14, 1939:* Afternoon tea with the Weizsäckers in their new and beautiful residence next to the verdant garden of the Krupp building. He was rather done in. His chief, Ribbentrop, causes him great worries. He had given him but scant information about events in Salzburg[1] over the telephone. Weizsäcker quite properly raised the question what the Italians would do now that they had been turned down. As a matter of fact they are no longer free to choose.

*August 14, 1939:* This evening I dined alone with Beck. A most cultured, attractive, and intelligent man. Unfortunately, he has a very low opinion of the leading people in the Army. For that reason he could see no place there where we could gain a foothold. He is firmly convinced of the vicious character of the policies of the Third Reich. I discussed with him as well as with Goerdeler the idea of a meeting disguised as a board meeting of the *Weisse Blätter.*[2]

I have changed my mind about arranging this in Neustadt. Berlin is better. Furthermore, things have developed so rapidly since my discussion with Guttenberg that there is hardly time for such detours.

*Tuesday, August 15, 1939:* In the morning I visited Schacht in his new bachelor quarters. He was very lively and bucked

---

[1]Meeting of Ribbentrop and Ciano, August 11-12, 1939, at which no agreement about Mussolini's conference proposal could be reached.

[2]Periodical published by Guttenberg in Neustadt on the Saale.

up by his travels, and seemed to be sure that his judgment would soon be vindicated. A few days ago he spent four hours with Funk, who now realized that the economic and financial policies of the Reich were up a blind alley.

Someone had said of Undersecretary Reinhardt that he seemed like a clown in the circus, always running along behind the juggler and trying to imitate him. Whoever told the story expressed the fear that Reinhardt would soon break his neck, whereupon Schacht had answered: "The clown never breaks his neck; but the juggler well may."

Schacht's view is that we can do nothing but keep our eyes open and wait, that things will follow their inevitable courses. I am only worried that while we wait great values will be irretrievably destroyed and one day a complete catastrophe will suddenly confront us. Schacht spoke favorably of Goerdeler. I forgot to mention—Goerdeler maintained that Göring no longer has much to say; Himmler, Ribbentrop, and Goebbels are now managing Hitler.

*August 15, 1939:* At twelve-thirty I went to see Henderson. He received me with the words: "Madhouse or hospital?" I answered: "A madhouse." He apparently knew nothing yet about Salzburg. He thought the result would probably tend more toward war than peace. Notes have been exchanged recently between Poland and Germany which justify the worst expectations. As I was leaving, Attolico was announced. I am curious whether he has already indicated that Italy wants peace, but unfortunately . . .

I told Henderson that one of the most dangerous notions circulating here in Germany was that England would no longer deal with Hitler at all. If this thought took root I was afraid that it might possibly result in lining up the whole of Germany behind Hitler. Henderson replied that the English certainly would prefer to deal with someone else, but they were even now ready to talk with Hitler if he gave certain guarantees. In the course of our talk he pointed out that the occupation of Prague was the straw that broke the camel's back. Now it was impossible for Chamberlain to fly here again with his umbrella.

In the afternoon Gisevius came to me in great excitement. The army commanders were informed yesterday at the Obersalzberg that Hitler had decided to strike at Poland. For this reason he would call off the Nuremberg Party rally. Suitable provocations of the Poles would now be got under way, particularly in Upper Silesia. Hitler did not believe the Western Powers would interfere. Nevertheless, if this did happen, he would change his plan; he would soon put an end to all doubt about it.

I told Gisevius I could not imagine what Hitler meant by the latter remark. Gisevius couldn't either, but he thought it was not seriously intended—simply a lie that he put out to the soldiers to calm their fears. Gisevius thought we should not yet use up all our ammunition by putting extreme pressure on the military, for action now would be futile, and then, later, when the decisive moment arrived, we could not do it all over again. Goerdeler, sustained by our recent discussions, was, however, in favor of going immediately to Brauchitsch. I replied that after what Gisevius had reported I, too, was in favor of postponing direct action for the moment. Gisevius thought the days before August 27 would be the decisive ones, perhaps from August 22 on.

The most sensational news brought by Gisevius was that a thoroughly dependable person, who had himself read the telegram, reported Hitler had instructed Schulenburg once more to attempt to reach an agreement with Molotov; he was to inform him that Hitler was ready to go to Russia to see Stalin! This left me agape. Gisevius thought Stalin would certainly invite him!

Afternoon tea with Frau von Brauchitsch. I sharpened up her anti-war sentiments and begged her to tell her cousin that I was absolutely convinced that if an attack were made on Poland the Western Powers would intervene. She telephoned me the next morning to say she had had an opportunity to pass the word on. Brauchitsch had looked at her intently, offered no comment, and sent his regards to me. I went to see him myself, but was informed by a woman member of the secretariat that he was extremely busy. In the evening, at Frohnau, Elizabeth gave me the interesting news that her friend, Fräulein von Oven, who worked in another department of the Ministry of War, had to inquire by telephone as to my visit and its purpose, and said that the Foreign Office had also been asked if I was still on active service. The answer was that I had inactive status. If all this originated with Brauchitsch it proves that nothing can be done with him. Either he is afraid or he doesn't understand what it is all about, and that I have "nothing to sell him."

Today's newspaper reports indicate an aggravation of the crisis. It is significant that Upper Silesia is played up as the scene of Polish terror, just as Gisevius had predicted.

*Berlin, August 27, 1939:* This day, on which the celebration of the anniversary of the battle of Tannenberg was supposed to have taken place, may go down in history as the day of a very great decision. Whether there will be a world war or not will ultimately depend on what Henderson brings back today from London.

The most acute stage of the crisis was reached when we signed the pact with the Soviets [August 23, 1939]. Gisevius had the facts straight, although he perhaps mistook Hitler for Ribbentrop. The conclusion of this pact is regarded by the whole world as a tactical master stroke and at the same time as proof of absolute unscrupulousness and lack of principle.

Hitler's expectation that the Western Powers, as well as Poland, would now yield has not been realized. Strategically the result has been to make it clear to England that it is all or nothing, and that further loss of prestige would be an unmitigated catastrophe for the Western Powers. Hence the immediate conclusion of an almost unconditional alliance with Poland. Furthermore, all elements in Europe which saw in us a protective wall or weapon of offense against bolshevism have turned away from us. Yet it is still an open question how far the pact is merely a dishonest expedient for both authoritarian regimes or how far it goes toward drawing the two countries close together on the basis of further nationalization of the Soviets and the bolshevization of the Nazis. A considerable cooling off in our relations with Japan is also to be noted.

This apparently extraordinary tactical success will naturally be welcomed at first among the German people as a resumption of the historic policy of friendship with Russia, but above

all as increasing the chances for peace. So far as the Italians
are concerned, the pact will have the immediate effect of giving them courage to live up to the Axis pact; but that will not
last. The feeling of inner weakness and anxiety over the unpredictable nature of our adventurous policies will soon gain
the upper hand again.

For all those who believed in effective help from Italy the
real sensation of these last days was a letter from Mussolini to
Hitler the night before last. It said that Italy would join in the
world war only if the Germans made certain promises of raw
materials and military equipment—this coming at exactly the
moment when, as Mussolini must have known, mobilization
was getting into full swing and when the invasion of Poland
had been scheduled for the first morning hours of that very
night. This communication appears to have come as a bomb-
shell—especially to Ribbentrop, that anti-Comintern, pro-
bolshevik, former Anglomaniac and now Italomaniac. Incomprehensibly to me, Hitler apparently still counted on immediate
military assistance from the Italians, and seems to have timed
his own aggressive action accordingly. The result was that
the whole business was called off.

If, as we must assume, the English know about the marching orders as well as their cancellation, and perhaps also about
the Italian position, they will consider this move as an indication of German weakness and will stiffen their own resistance.
The question now is whether the longing for peace among the
Western Powers is still deep enough to impel them to grant
concessions to Hitler, which he could hold up before his people
as successes and thus justify his withdrawal. In any event the
revocation of orders already given is psychologically very
hazardous for him. The element of surprise will thus have been
lost.

Henderson, who flew to London with a memorandum from
us, asked whether there would still be time if he came back
today, and was told that our people hoped so, but that the
utmost speed would be necessary.

I spent the evening in the White Room of the Imperial
Castle. Reception for the archaeologists.[1] In view of the situ-

[1]International Congress of Archaeologists in Berlin, August 21–26, 1939.

ation it was grotesque. Englishmen, Frenchmen, and Poles had already been recalled. Boring concert, during which my thoughts wandered elsewhere. Afterward a banquet. I was at Rust's table. He played host loudly and often tactlessly. A silent exchange of glances with Popitz at one moment almost cost us our self-control. The very agreeable Bulgarian Minister of Education and Paribene were near me, the latter gaily eating with his knife. The whole affair in these rooms (Schlüter Room), with Sutter and Wegener as caterers, was a burlesque.

*Saturday, August 26:* I visited the Foreign Office in the morning. Saw Wiehl with Ritter and Clodius. Everything is up in the air; orders terribly confused. The Reichstag is to meet within a few hours, nay, minutes; thrice called into session and dismissed. Situation obscured. I went afterward to the chancery with Weizsäcker. He thought the chances for peace seemed somewhat better. We might, after all, tone down our demands. In the corridor of the Foreign Office I spoke briefly with Attolico, who was obviously deeply worried. Then a short visit to the new chief of personnel, Kriebel (an old officer and an old Party member, with two souls). Goerdeler has left for Sweden.

It is clear to me that the Rusians made the pact with us in the same spirit in which they dragged out the negotiations with the Western Powers. That is to encourage us and to set all nations of Europe against one another.

*August 27, 1939:* There is news everywhere but it is not easy to verify. In any case the higher-ups are in a "state of mind," and the people in the throes of great unrest and anxiety. Every chauffeur is asking if there will be war. Mobilization goes on apace. War weddings for weeping couples. Ration cards, scarcity of foodstuffs—all that even before the war begins.

Of the substance of our proposal to England I could get no authentic information. The most plausible conjecture is: "Let us have our quarrel with Poland to ourselves, then we will make some generous arrangement with you."

As far as Mussolini is concerned, the situation is this: we have accepted the fact that he will not come along but that he should act "as if he would!" He also seems to be in a bad humor. Nostitz said they were looking for someone they could send down there to straighten things out. Would I know of somebody? A grotesque inquiry to make of me. Anyway, I know of no one.

Someone told me today that I was in danger. They are talking about my being here for the purpose of making preparations to help take over the rescue work in case the regime falls.

*August 29:* "Between battles." The world keeps on mobilizing. The normal lives of all peoples and international intercourse are being throttled more and more. The fear of war rises higher and higher in the nation. As the governments of England and France want to do everything in their power to avoid war, it may still be possible for Hitler to achieve a partial success which he could represent to the nation as the fruit of a well-calculated policy pursued, as he says, "with fixed determination up to the very verge of war."

Yesterday morning Weizsäcker announced that the crisis was no less acute. Everything is held in abeyance pending the arrival of the English. Henderson got back late yesterday evening.

Last night I saw in the movies a disgusting example of how human misery is exploited for purposes of propaganda. Weeping women and children are shown and in voices choked with tears they describe their sufferings in Poland. The audience remained completely passive; there was only very weak applause at the showing of military pictures, not taken up by the bulk of the audience.

Seven o'clock. The general tension seems to have relaxed; the odds on war have somewhat decreased. Just because the measures for mobilization have been in effect for some time, the probability of war diminishes every day. Of course there are still enough elements of danger. The question is whether Hitler will be able to obtain enough by negotiation to manufacture a "success."

My first bulletin of the day was from Magistrati, whom I met in the Adlon; evidently in excellent spirits—presumably because he felt sure of Italian neutrality. He pointed to the anti-aircraft batteries across from the Adlon and said this was the third time he had seen this picture in Berlin. He set the odds on war at 4 to 1 and said that the chief concern was whether the Poles would be "reasonable" under English and French pressure.

I went on to the Foreign Office to see Wiehl who reported that after the morning conference there was only slight hope of maintaining "peace."

The English seem to have replied that they would be happy to consider Hitler's wish for a general agreement, but that the German-Polish conflict must first be solved by free negotiation between the two parties on the basis of equal rights, accompanied by adequate guarantees. To this end the English offered their services. According to Popitz certain definite suggestions as to the nature of the solution were also submitted. Perhaps it was these that provoked the pessimism at the Foreign Office. Hitler has indicated to Henderson that his answer would be ready today.

I called on Henderson toward noon. He was somewhat fatigued—which is understandable—but not entirely pessimistic. Whereas last time, at the Obersalzberg, Hitler had fabricated wild stories about English plans to strangle Germany (to which he, Henderson, would have liked to say: "Nonsense!"), this time he was much more approachable. Henderson sketched the English answer as similar to what I have already written. Hitler must now demonstrate, he said, whether he wishes to be a Genghis Khan or a real statesman. England wishes peace, but is absolutely determined to go to war if we use force.

The chief danger lies in the disastrous counsels of Ribbentrop, who has already done enough mischief. If it were not for the act of aggression against Prague everything could now be arranged easily. The last time, or time before last, when Henderson was at the Obersalzberg, Hitler told him reproachfully, "And I sent you the best man!" To which Henderson could offer no reply. Today Göring participated in the deliberations, and this, he thought, was a good sign.

Lunch with Popitz, Tischbein, Heinrici, Kempner, Sybel. The last named, a member of the Reichstag, told about Hitler's speech on Sunday [August 27, 1939]. He thought Hitler had made a miserable impression. He had declared that certain minimum demands must be met unconditionally if he was to forgo war, namely: "Danzig to return to the Reich" and the "solution" of the Corridor question. The latter could even be carried out by stages. In other words, rather modest! Why, then, does he publish his letter to Daladier, in which he categorically demands the Corridor?

About the Russian pact Hitler said that he was in no wise altering his fundamental anti-bolshevist policies; one had to use Beelzebub to drive away the devil; all means were justified in dealing with the Soviets, even such a pact as this. This is a typical example of his conception of "Realpolitik."

He said we must not misunderstand the Italian position, that it really works to our advantage. This sounds very much like sour grapes. Popitz expressed his conviction that the whole thing was an enormous failure, and this held true even if a face-saving success could still be produced. After the first moments of joy over the preservation of peace the inner rottenness of the situation would again become apparent. That would be the time to be constantly on the alert to stem the tide.

This morning Frau von Brauchitsch called on me to say that it would be better for the time being not to make any attempt to influence the general; he had become heavily involved with the Nazis, largely through the influence of his rabid wife.

*August 30:* Yesterday I forgot to record that Henderson said with considerable emphasis: "The Italians? They want peace —nothing more!" With respect to the British reply, I heard yesterday evening from an authentic source that no territorial problems are under discussion.

In the note we sent yesterday (according to A. Kessel) we agreed in an arrogant way to negotiate with Poland, provided that a Polish plenipotentiary came immediately (within twenty-four hours) to Germany. Kessel thought Ribbentrop was already lusting for war. Kessel, too, was afraid that our inevitable political defeat would not be thorough enough to serve as a remedy.

The Foreign Office received word today from the Ministry of Economic Affairs that there would be no war, and that further preparations were unnecessary. This light-hearted conclusion was justly received with indignation. Weizsäcker told Wiehl over the telephone in my presence that these people must be drunk. He said the tension remained undiminished. Everybody is now waiting to see if a Polish negotiator will come. Should Ribbentrop feel firmly in the saddle again the Poles, if they come, will be presented with unacceptable demands.

I had the impression that this present crisis introduced for the first time some touch of a twilight of the gods, or rather a twilight of the false gods of the Party.

*August 31, 1939:* This morning at seven twenty-five Weizsäcker called me and asked me to meet him at eight-forty. He explained that he had to deal with the following situation: since nothing had been heard so far from the Poles, Ribbentrop had called for Henderson last night and had railed at him, exclaiming that these delaying tactics of the English and Poles were contemptible. The German Government had been prepared to make a very acceptable proposal, which he read to Henderson. Essentially it contained the following points: Danzig to be ceded to the Reich, but demilitarized; referendum in the main part of the Corridor, and, depending upon the result, either a German east-west traffic route or a Polish south-north route to Gdynia, which would remain Polish. But these definitely modest terms were of course no longer open as no Polish negotiator had come. Therefore there was nothing left for Germany but to take action to secure its rights.

After this unfriendly interview, which did not constitute a complete break, Hitler had made it known that the other side had now put itself clearly in the wrong, and that therefore an attack might begin this afternoon. Weizsäcker considers the situation extremely serious; matters stand exactly where they were on Friday. Must we really be hurled into the abyss because of two madmen?

Of course one can never be sure with Hitler; it is not entirely out of the question that he will recoil at the last moment. But we agreed that we could hardly expect this to happen since, after all, Hitler had really decided on war Friday and had given orders to that effect. Under the circumstances Weizsäcker could see only one hope—that Henderson should immediately persuade the Polish Ambassador and his own

government to urge Warsaw this very morning to send a plenipotentiary at once, or at least to have Lipski announce this
intention to Ribbentrop before noon. Could I "privately" influence Henderson to this end, and could I perhaps also warn
Göring about the rash decisions of Hitler? Göring should be
made to understand that Ribbentrop was digging the graves of
the Reich and of National Socialism. Karinhall would go up in
flames! I said I was prepared to try my luck.

My impression was that Ribbentrop and Hitler are in a spirit
of criminal recklessness. They are running the most fearful
risks, involving the whole German people, merely to save their
own prestige by some minor success—all this, of course, being
only a temporary stopgap. So far as I am concerned the one
vital thing is to avoid a world war.

I found Henderson at breakfast; he had got to bed at four
o'clock. He was, above all, shocked at Ribbentrop's bad man-
ners. Ribbentrop was evidently determined to play in this war
the baneful role Berchtold had played in the last one. Henderson said Ribbentrop had read him the German proposals very
hurriedly ("had gabbled them"), had not given him a copy
because they were now "water over the dam." The peremptory
character of our latest move was destroying all efforts to keep
the peace. I explained the situation to him and emphasized
that I came entirely as a private person and without orders,
and had only the desire to help in reaching a peaceful solution
by making clear to him the stupendous significance of the next
few hours.

He said that during the night he had been in touch with
London, as well as with Lipski, and that he would continue
his efforts. The chief difficulty lay in our methods, particularly
the way in which we expected the English to order the Poles
around like stupid little boys. I told him that the persistent
silence of the Poles was also objectionable. This Slavic behavior, with which he doubtlessly had become familiar in
Petersburg, was dangerous. He said, nostalgically, he wished
those times would only come back—times, I countered, with a
poor attempt at jesting, in which he had almost strangled his
ambassador.[1] Now, it seemed to me, he was in a mood to

---

[1] An episode in Petersburg under the Czarist regime, when, instead of
a supposed burglar, Henderson had seized his ambassador.

strangle others. In conclusion, Henderson said it would be easy to reach an understanding between England and Germany if it were not for the calamitous Ribbentrop. With him it would never be possible.

About nine-thirty I went to Olga Riegele, told her that the situation was terribly serious, and asked her to arrange a meeting between me and her brother Hermann. Tearfully the good woman did so at once. She was successful in reaching him at his "battle station," as he later put it, and I had a long conversation with him. He asked at once whether I wanted to talk with him about the Italians. I said, "No," but stated that I was a friend of Henderson who was doing all he could to keep the peace. Göring asked why, in that case, he had been so "snooty" during the latest discussions. I answered I did not believe that was his intention, but possibly it was difficult for some people to get along.

Göring said he liked Henderson but that he was too slow. I answered that naturally he was an Englishman and not a Latin, but he was doing his very best. Göring said he thought our proposal was really modest, to which I replied that it had been described as no longer valid. Göring thereupon became very animated and asked how Henderson could have reached this conclusion since the proposal would become invalid only if no Polish negotiator arrived. I answered that this point was most important, that I would tell Henderson at once and urge him to exert himself further in that direction.

Göring: "Yes, but he must come at once."

I: "That is technically impossible; it must suffice if the Poles declare that they will send one."

Göring: "Yes, but he must come very quickly. Go tell the Foreign Minister immediately what you have heard from Henderson."

I: "I do not know whether I can do that, but, in any case, I will tell Weizsäcker."

My impression was that Göring really wants peace. Olga had previously told me, weeping, that recently he had put his arms about her and said: "Now, you see, everybody is for war, only I, the soldier and field marshal, am not."

But why, then, does this man, at this moment, sit in Oranienburg? And Brauchitsch and Halder are flying about over the West Wall!

I went back to Henderson at once and told him what Göring had said. He was greatly interested and wrote down the most important parts. Then to Weizsäcker, to whom I reported the steps I had taken.

After an hour Weizsäcker called for me again. Henderson had requested the text of our proposals in order to have something to show to the Poles. Officially Weizsäcker was not permitted to give it to him. Did I think it possible to give Henderson a more detailed knowledge of the contents, which meant perhaps to put the paper itself into his hands? The document lay before me on the table.

At that moment a telephone call came from Ribbentrop, and immediately thereafter a second. The gist of both was that Henderson should not be given the proposals. He himself would call and tell him that the Poles had been plainly told they would get the proposals if they sent a plenipotentiary. We agreed that under these conditions it was now impossible to give Henderson the document or any further details.

Ribbentrop had forbidden Weizsäcker to have any further dealings with Henderson and had added that Hitler had ordered all advances be rebuffed. That was proof for Weizsäcker that Hitler and Ribbentrop wanted war; they imagined their proposals had furnished them an alibi. This seems nonsensical to me if the proposals are not given to the Poles.

Ribbentrop further stated that during the next half hour it would be decided whether the proposals should be made public. If this is really under discussion it is altogether incomprehensible why the proposals should not be given to Henderson, unless they want war.

Weizsäcker said Rome was making efforts to mediate in London. Mussolini is said to have declared that a *fait nouveau* had to be created and the best move would be for Poland to cede Danzig to Germany at once. Weizsäcker was very doubtful whether the Poles would do that. London, for its part, informed the Italians that the only question now was one of honor: whether we asked Lipski to call or whether he was to come of his own accord. With this in mind I discussed with

Weizsäcker whether I should go to Henderson once more to induce him to get Lipski out of his hole. But we agreed that Henderson knew the situation and would do all he could anyway. Perhaps I shall still go to see him.

Afternoon. I did go to call on Henderson and met him in front of the embassy. I told him everything depended on Lipski's putting in an appearance—not to ask questions but to declare his readiness to negotiate—but at once. He wanted to support this suggestion immediately. I also told Henderson that Göring had arrived. Young Kessel had just seen him drive in.

At the Foreign Office I had met Moltke [Ambassador in Warsaw] and arranged to have lunch with him at the Adlon. As I arrived at the hotel Kessel appeared in great alarm to tell me that Lipski had presented himself, but that there was reluctance to receive him. Since Moltke had told me the same thing a few minutes before, I tried first by telephoning Olga Riegele to influence Hermann Göring, with the request that he give me a hearing if possible. I did not succeed, however. Kessel declared the danger was extremely grave. Weizsäcker had told him the best thing would be to persuade Mussolini to telephone Hitler at once.

Could I go to see Attolico? I was not very anxious to perform this mission, but in view of the situation I said I would. Attolico received me at once. He swore that once upon a time he had done everything possible for me! And promised absolute silence concerning our conversation. He understood instantly what was at issue, and promised to telephone Rome at once.

*September 1, 1939:* Yesterday I had lunch with Moltke. He was furious at having been forbidden to return to Warsaw. Dined at the house of our Brauchitsch. I complained about the Commander in Chief being absent on a day of such decisions. In the course of the night the "proposals" were made public.

At ten o'clock today I heard Hitler's weak speech from my hotel room. Few people on the streets, only official enthusiasm over the closing of the border.

My final conclusions about the week's events up to September 1 are as follows:

Hitler and Ribbentrop wanted war with Poland and know-

ingly took the risk of war with the Western Powers, deluding
themselves to varying degrees up to the very last with the belief
that the West would remain neutral after all. The Poles, for
their part, with Polish conceit and Slavic aimlessness, confident
of English and French support, had missed every remaining
chance of avoiding war. The government in London, whose
ambassador did everything to keep the peace, gave up the race
in the very last days and adopted a kind of devil-may-care
attitude. France went through the same stages, only with much
more hesitation. Mussolini did all in his power to avoid war.
His mediation proposal of September 2 offered no more hope
of success because England no longer could or would back
down. The attitude of France on this day is not quite clear.

In spite of all war preparations the feeling that war is really
here has not yet penetrated the public mind. They are for the
most part apathetic and still look upon it as a sort of Party
project.

*October 11, 1939:* Last night Goerdeler came to see me in
Munich. We dined together at the Continental, where, because
of poor train connections, I remained for the night. Whom
should I meet there but Rümelin, who explained he was just
traveling about without any fixed destination. He declared it
was certainly better for the moment for people "like him and
myself!" to look on from the "balcony." He told a long, not
altogether plausible story, of how he had spoken up against
Ribbentrop and had won out over the Party.

With Goerdeler I talked about the political situation. He
agreed in every detail with my basic conceptions. He also
thinks that the war policy was criminally irresponsible and that
our Russian policy in its present form is an enormous danger.
In this hopeless situation into which Hitler and Ribbentrop
have maneuvered us, co-operation with the Soviets is looked
upon as the only way out. To meet their immediate needs the
Nazis have burned what they had worshiped and worshiped
what they had burned. And thus they have wrecked their own
philosophical foundations, hollow though they were from the
beginning.

The resultant intellectual confusion is already very noticeable in the Party. We sacrificed the most important positions, the Baltic Sea and the security of our eastern boundary—in order to rescue ourselves momentarily from a dire emergency that we brought upon ourselves. Not to speak of the politically unethical abandonment of the Baltic countries which now seriously endangers our *dominium maris Baltici*. In case of a conflict with Russia even the transportation of ore from Sweden is imperiled. But all this pales in comparison with the nonchalant handing over of a large and important part of the Occident—in part of German-Lutheran culture, in part old Austrian—to that same bolshevism against which we ostensibly fought to the death in distant Spain. The bolshevization of the hitherto Polish sections has already started on a broad front.

It is quite possible—according to Hitler's speech before the Reichstag [August 27, 1939], and even probable—that Hitler secretly plans to attack Soviet Russia later. If this be the case the criminal character of his policies is only corroborated.

The advance of bolshevism on the whole front along our borders, together with the necessary socialist consequences of a war economy, will also have political results of the most dangerous nature inside Germany. An additional problem is the exchange of populations started by Hitler, which condemns many hundreds of thousands, or even millions, of people to an uprooted existence, and destroys ancient German traditions. Moreover, Hitler's remarks can only strengthen the will of the other side not to rest until the southeast is also revolutionized.

This fraternization with the Soviets has two good aspects. First, it may help to open the eyes of the Germans, especially the better elements within the Party; second, it ought to encourage the Western Powers to preserve a healthy, vigorous Germany, but certainly not under a leadership that is half or three quarters bolshevist.

The whole situation leads me to the conclusion that it is high time to apply the brakes to the runaway cart. Goerdeler is of the same opinion. He sees things even blacker than I do. He believes that if it is not possible to put a stop to these political adventures soon, a catastrophe, domestic and foreign, is inevitable. According to his information our economic situation is very much worse than appears on the surface. He is convinced that the first serious difficulties will develop very soon, even in the matter of war matériel, munitions, and vital industrial supplies.

Russia can help only on a very modest scale. Within six months we must expect severe shortages in numerous fields, and we can't hold out for more than eighteen months. I am somewhat skeptical about such predictions. Therefore, (1) the watchword of the enemy is a long war. In no case will they compromise now. Therefore, (2) a very low dietary level for us, peace offensives, and morbid reflections on how to achieve victory quickly.

The nerves of the generals are said to have suffered already —Halder's, for instance. A few (he mentioned Canaris) had come back from Poland entirely broken, after they had seen the results of our brutal conduct of the war, especially in devastated Warsaw. I told him of young fellows in the Labor Service who witnessed the way villages were surrounded and set on fire, because of civilian snipers, while the population inside shrieked frantically. The Polish atrocities in Bromberg and elsewhere were also true.

Goerdeler said that he and General Beck had listened to an English broadcast; an English general told how before the World War he had been attached to a crack regiment of the German Army and had been enthusiastic over the spirit of the men and the decency and chivalry of the officers. During the World War this spirit had still prevailed. Where were these German officers and soldiers, now that this cruel method of waging war had been initiated in Poland? Then the English general had spoken of Fritsch, had commended him highly and asserted, quite correctly, that he had sought death. Now, the officer continued, he wanted to honor Fritsch in the German manner, whereupon three verses of *"Ich hat einen Kameraden"* were played. . . . Beck was overcome at that point.

We were agreed that Fritsch's conduct was not easy to understand. He should have sought an opportunity to make use of his life or to sacrifice it in some other way. Nevertheless, his death seems not to have been altogether in vain, for it has apparently made a deep impression in the Army as well as among the people. Unfortunately it is generally assumed he was murdered by the SS.

Goerdeler reported further that Hitler is testing out three alternative policies: (1) an air and naval attack in full force against England. For the time being this plan has been rejected because of huge airplane losses in Poland and lack of heavy bombers. Moreover, weather conditions are becoming unfavorable for air attacks. (2) a break-through on the Maginot Line. The Army was against this plan, as a decisive success was improbable, the losses would be very heavy, and the French heavy artillery was in a very advantageous position. (3) A drive through Belgium and Holland. In spite of the warnings of Brauchitsch and Halder, Hitler had now ordered that preparations be made for this operation.

We were agreed that before this could take place everything possible should be done to bring about a change. I counseled urgently that no great hopes be placed on Brauchitsch, and asked about other generals. Goerdeler thought that of the army leaders in the west Witzleben and Hammerstein were good men. So were most of the deputy commanding generals at home and their staffs. According to Goerdeler, so far as foreign policy was concerned, the goal must be an expressed readiness for peace based on: (1) moderate demands (German parts of Poland to us, the remainder to be independent, a new arrangement in Czechoslovakia); (2) the restitution of the rule of law in Germany; (3) general disarmament, with specific guarantees in the case of Germany (control of airplane and submarine production); and (4) the restoration of world commerce.

I warned against foreigners making demands of a domestic political nature. The controls Goerdeler proposed for Germany also seemed questionable to me. He thought that domestic conditions must be created that would permit the making of peace on such a basis. The people would welcome a peace of that kind with tremendous relief.

He asked me whether in my opinion Göring was a possibility. For, in spite of serious doubts, he had come to the conclusion that Göring was the only solution—temporarily, of course. Beck also had finally come to that conclusion. I agreed with this view.

It is interesting that, according to the report of my visit, high functionaries from Göring's entourage had sounded him out as to whether we might be inclined to use Göring to put things in order. The latter had apparently grasped the seriousness of the situation and was deeply disturbed. Goerdeler had answered: Yes, but only with certain guarantees, including the restitution of a state of law, with modifications for the transition period, permitting immediate arrest without warrant, but with the right of appeal to a special court. Also supervision of public policies by some representative body of a corporative nature.

The Göring people had agreed to that. If this report is correct, my essay, "Stein's Conception of the Organic State," which has just appeared in the *Weisse Blätter* will be very timely!

Discussing the question as to how we could ascertain at the proper time the readiness of the other powers to come to terms on this basis, my visitor reported that someone from the American Embassy had approached Schacht. He was asked whether he could bring about a peace and, if necessary, come to America. We were not sure what was behind all this, nor were we sure that Schacht could be entrusted with such a mission.

In this whole matter Goerdeler was of the opinion that such a peace offer should be made to Hitler. If he accepted it he would be swallowed up by subsequent developments; if he refused, we would have good reason to proceed without him.

This whole idea has not yet crystallized properly. We decided to hold further discussions in Berlin.

On *October 19, 1939,* I spent the evening with Guttenberg in Würzburg. My essay, "Baron vom Stein's Conception of the Organic State" has appeared in his *Weisse Blätter.* I have sent it to many people, especially to some of the more moderate Party chiefs. My purpose is to express for once the thought that the present form of government cannot last forever; that it must gradually be converted into an organic state based on the rule of law and operating under popular controls. Prime

Minister Siebert seems to have understood that point, for he writes that he has read the essay *and its conclusions* with great interest.

At the baptism in Schlüsselburg Uncle Friedrich von Bodelschwingh preached in an extraordinarily popular and effective manner. Afterward I had a long conversation with him and young Friedrich about the desperate situation of the Church. Uncle Friedrich, the former bishop, thought the war might create just the conditions for an improvement of the situation through the church directorate that Kerrl had established: Marahrens, the German-Christian Schulz (Mecklenburg), and the neutral Professor Hymmen. Could not Göring receive Marahrens? It is significant that in desperation everyone looks to Göring as the only hope—significant because it makes clear how little hope there really is, for basically Göring is not a man in whom one can have confidence. He lacks both character and real determination to see things through.

On the trains everywhere lots of soldiers on leave. Good material on the whole, but for the most part little discipline. In Berlin I heard that the infantry showed considerably less offensive spirit than in 1914. Therefore the officers had to expose themselves unduly and suffered heavy losses.

In Bamberg, Ilse was shown a few pages of the *Adelsblatt* by the porter; both he and one of the waiters were deeply shocked by the interminable list of death notices. There is every evidence that the hatred of the Party for the nobility and the so-called intelligentsia is growing ever stronger. While the youth of the nobility is killed in droves, their class is jeered at unrebuked in such magazines as the *Koralle*. No wonder that more and more people are firmly convinced, like Goerdeler, that Hitler wants to exterminate the nobility and the educated classes.

Among well-informed people in Berlin I noticed a good deal of despair. In wide circles there is still rejoicing over the "inspired chess move of the pact with Russia," over the victories in Poland, over the performance of the submarines and the Air Corps against England. But among informed people there is growing awareness of our impending disaster.

The principal sentiments are: the conviction that the war

cannot be won militarily; a realization of the highly dangerous
economic situation; the feeling of being led by criminal ad-
venturers; and the disgrace that has sullied the German name
through the conduct of the war in Poland; namely, the brutal
use of air power and the shocking bestialities of the SS, especially toward the Jews. The cruelties of the Poles against the
German minority are a fact, too, but somehow excusable psychologically. When people use their revolvers to shoot down a
group of Jews herded into a synagogue one is filled with shame.
A light court-martial sentence pronounced against some of
these criminals was set aside by Brauchitsch; a second sentence,
likewise light, was voided by the disgraceful general amnesty
for such deeds. And all this time a man like Niemöller has been
sitting for years in a concentration camp!

I hear that Blaskowitz, as commander of an army, wanted
to prosecute two SS leaders—including that rowdy Sepp
Dietrich—for looting and murder. But in vain. Those who saw
Warsaw, with its devastation and the many thousands of dead
bodies lying around, came away with horrible impressions. Of
course the commander of the city should not have permitted
this to happen, but the Nazi determination to bring the war
to a quick end was primarily responsible.

My political impressions from Berlin can be summarized
thus: depressing through and through, but for the first time:

> *Doch sah ich manches Auge flammen,*
> *Und klopfen hört ich manches Herz.*
>
> *Yet saw I many eyes aflame,*
> *Heard many a heart beat true.*

The situation of the majority of politically clearheaded and
reasonably well-informed people today, while Germany is in
the midst of a great war, is truly tragic. They love their country. They think patriotically as well as socially. They cannot
wish for victory, even less for a severe defeat. They fear a long
war, and they see no feasible way out; the latter because there
is no confidence that the military leadership possesses enough
insight and will power to assert itself at the decisive moment.

Brauchitsch is said to have some understanding but no determination; he also appears to suffer from a stomach ailment. Halder is more reasonable, but has less power; physically he is not at his best—a matter of nerves. No one expects anything of Raeder, and I have spoken often enough about Göring in these pages. Among the army leaders there are excellent people: Rundstedt, Blaskowitz, Bock, Leeb, Witzleben, List. But in their local commands they are not near enough to the helm. Hammerstein, who had commanded an army group in Cologne, was first ordered to a less important command and has now been put on the shelf altogether.

On *Monday, the sixteenth,* in the afternoon, I went to see Beck. He saw no great chance of success either in a break-through on the Maginot Line or in Belgium and Holland. His opinion of the leading people is of the very worst; that goes for Göring too. I asked him about his connections with the present group of generals. It appears they are not paying much atten-tion to him (out of fear, of course). He thinks highly of Goerdeler, even though he considers him too sanguine and imprudent. We were agreed that the worst thing that could happen would be an invasion of the neutral countries.

Interesting conversation with Welczeck [Ambassador in Paris], who is very active. His sphere of activity includes mem-bers of the SS High Command—Stuckart and Höhn. He maintained that these two men thought fundamentally as we do, and were already considering whether Ribbentrop should be thrown to the wolves. The formation of a new cabinet was under consideration there. He had been asked whether he would accept the post of Foreign Minister, but thought him-self not qualified and suggested Wohltat or myself. I am afraid these people are to some extent playing a double game. Popitz later warned me against Höhn, whom Welczeck wanted me to meet; Stuckart was all right, but cautious and without much punch.

At noon I met Goerdeler. He has revised his somewhat wild plans. He realizes that demands concerning our domestic affairs must not be made openly from abroad. This is not the moment for us to advance our cause through peace offers. Ac-cording to all reports, the various feelers emanating from Hitler's side, especially from Göring (American Senator Dawis [*sic!*], and others), have come and will come to naught. Hitler had ordered all such moves stopped; proposals will be examined only if the initiative is taken by the enemy. He is in a bad nervous condition and would certainly be glad to wriggle out of this situation, but after Chamberlain's speech he has returned to the tactics of intransigence. At the moment he favors a drive through Belgium and Holland.

*Afternoon of October 17* I went to see Weizsäcker. Rather cut up, understandably enough, over Heinrich's death and everything else. He has gradually come to see things very clearly, considers Hitler possessed, and Ribbentrop at least partly so. Our only hope of salvation, he thinks, lies in a military *coup d'état*. But how?

*Wednesday afternoon* [*October 18*] went to see Raeder. I gave him my book and then questioned him thoroughly. He spoke of Ribbentrop apparently without much sympathy. He declared categorically that the Navy was not in favor of a drive through Belgium and Holland. The Belgian harbors were exposed to the fire of British long-range artillery. The Army was not for it, either, but the Luftwaffe was—whether Göring himself he did not know. In answer to my question he said he had stated his views in writing.

In the evening, in pouring rain, I went to Dahlem to the Hammersteins'. He, too, held the view that from a military standpoint an attempt to break through had little chance of success. He considers Brauchitsch a man of little political discernment and reluctant to act. Like myself, he believes a drive through Belgium and Holland would be a great disaster.

*Thursday morning* [*October 19*], another discussion with Goerdeler at the Bristol. The man is alert and extremely active, but very optimistic. He is now planning a visit to Göring, which will be arranged for him, and if possible to Hitler also. His aim is to be sent to some enemy country (preferably England) in order to arrange conditions of peace which Hitler cannot swallow, and which will bring about his overthrow. I do not see how this plan could be carried out.

At eleven o'clock to see Popitz. Detailed conversation, very much to the point. He sees very clearly. Although the principal factor is still lacking, namely, a general readiness to act, he is of the opinion that we should plan even now, in a limited group, what needs to be done at the decisive moment. Goerdeler and Planck were suitable collaborators. The former, however, was always unduly imaginative in his estimates and in his plans. Popitz's objectivity and deep concern commanded my respect.

Finally we talked about the question of the monarchy which, unlike Goerdeler, he would like to keep on ice for the present. So far as the choice is concerned Prince Oskar appeals most strongly to him as regent because of his impeccable character.

At the Kamekes', Winnig told of his lectures in industrial cities and at large factories. According to his observations the overwhelming majority of workers are quite opposed to National Socialism. Again and again he had observed that active Party members among the workers were avoided by the others; managers told him they had to arrange for these people to work separately. Kameke is full of hope, in part because of his trust in God, in part because of a prophecy that after 1940 the black-white-and-red flag would wave over Germany!

On the day of my return Ilse lunched with Schacht in Munich. The fickle old democrat claimed to be a thoroughgoing monarchist. His candidate is Prince Wilhelm, who had expressly told his father he had never given up his claim to the throne. Schacht does not believe a situation favorable for action will be created without a "small defeat." He is pessimistic about the outcome of the war.

*Berlin from October 29, evening, until November 2, evening:* Goerdeler asked me to come. He is to go on a business trip to Sweden for Robert Bosch and made my Scandinavian connections an excuse for his visit.

*October 30:* In the morning I took a walk with Goerdeler. According to his information this is the situation:

(1) MILITARILY: We must absolutely have a short war and Hitler saw only one way to achieve it—invasion of Holland

and Belgium. The Army was opposed to this, including Brauchitsch, and Halder even more so. Hitler is said to have summoned the generals recently for a morning conference and announced he wanted the invasion, but the plan submitted did not suit him. He had taken time to revise it the previous night and asked Brauchitsch to present it. Brauchitsch did so, whereupon the only general to speak against it was Reichenau, of all people, because an impossible assignment had been given to his army group. Hitler gave the impression of being nervous and thoroughly tired; it is said he wore pajamas. Result: further preparations were to be made, and the attack, which was first to have taken place on the twelfth, then on the sixth, then again on the twelfth, was now postponed for a few more days, the exact date to be fixed by the High Command when it considered the Army ready.

(2) ECONOMICALLY: Goerdeler declares all reliable reports indicate a very bad situation for munitions' production as well as for raw materials and food. We could hold out eighteen months at the very most; long before that, however, the wear and tear on nerves and resources would become dangerously evident.

(3) POLITICALLY: The situation being what it is, every effort for peace must be made. Under the present leadership, however, peace negotiations could neither be initiated nor entertained. Our goal must be to go into action the minute the order for invasion is given. If Hitler should decide against this solution, we would have some more time. If it should prove impossible to organize resistance against the order, the show would simply have to go on and the first setback would have to be exploited. Of course the chances to get a decent peace would then be considerably smaller, although the domestic situation would be riper.

(4) PROSPECTS: Goerdeler does not believe that Brauchitsch can be persuaded to act. At best there was a possibility that, with the help of Halder, he could be persuaded to "tolerate" action. Everything else was easy to arrange; the necessary number of determined generals is ready to proceed quickly and energetically if the order comes from the top. Herein lay the whole problem. Goerdeler said he maintained constant con-

tact with key people of the High Command of the Armed Forces. A memorandum presenting the case against the invasion and for seeking an early peace had already been prepared by groups within the Army and the Foreign Office (Etzdorf), and presented to Brauchitsch.

I asked Goerdeler whether anything ever came of the mission planned for Krupp-Bohlen. Goerdeler said Krupp had declined to take action (I never expected anything else), making an irrelevant reference to the flight of Thyssen which had compromised the industrialists.

My final impression: Goerdeler bases everything on Morgenstern's phrase "that which may not be, cannot be." He views matters with great optimism, gives credence to everything unfavorable to the Nazis, especially in economic matters, and rejects everything that is favorable. He also has many illusions about the generals. I expressed my doubts on this score, and warned him further against the assumption that after the invasion of Belgium it would still be possible to get a decent peace. I agreed with him fully that every effort must be made to induce the Army to refuse to carry out the invasion.

In spite of the weaknesses indicated Goerdeler is, without question, one of the few really active and fearless men. I promised him to use all my connections to work along the lines agreed upon.

When last in Berlin I noticed symptomatic creakings in the timbers. Now they are louder. The conduct of a man like Reichenau is significant. He always hears the grass grow. For some time now he is said to have been critical; he even risked a word of protest against the SS bestialities in Poland. The principal factor, however, is still lacking: a soldier in a position of decisive authority willing to take the initiative. Halder is not equal to the situation either in caliber or in authority.

I went to see Popitz before dinner [*October 30*]. He still hopes we can work this out with Göring, to whose outfit he belongs. He tells amazing things about his conversations in Hermann's immediate entourage. Gritzbach, one of Göring's intimates and constant companions, told Popitz that Hitler was mentally ill and ought to be removed; he indicated that in the last analysis Göring thought so too. According to Popitz the real trouble was Göring's paralyzing fear of the Gestapo, which has documentary evidence against him. If it could be guaranteed that these documents would be turned over to him unread he would act at once. I rather doubt this; he is too attached to Hitler.

In the afternoon I called on Olga Riegele. Her own mood and her impressions of her brother may well be gauged by the fact that she is constantly in tears. She senses the danger. She intimated that Göring has since reproached himself for not having taken decisive action after his interview with me on *August 31.*

*Tuesday, October 31, again in the Tiergarten with Goerdeler:* He has seen Funk and maintains that in his innermost being Funk is as pessimistic about the economic situation as he himself. Goerdeler thinks that among the generals there exists a strong aversion to the "Hammerstein group," and for that reason it would be difficult to use Planck. Tomorrow Goerdeler goes to Sweden for a few days.

Late in the afternoon I went to see Schacht. He sees things more soberly than Goerdeler, especially the question of an economic breakdown. He cannot yet bring himself to believe that the invasion will take place. Could Hitler be bluffing? But, if so, who would be fooled by his bluff?

At about 8 P.M. I met Goerdeler again in the Nürnbergerhof.

In the evening invited to Horcher's [restaurant] by Stauss, his wife and son. Excessive eating and drinking. The whole place full of big businessmen, film stars, and Party bigwigs. The latter very likely make it possible for Horcher to have everything on his menu. In one corner this interesting clover leaf: Helldorf, Gisevius, Colonel Oster (Canaris's representative in the Foreign Office).

*Wednesday, November 1:* In the morning Governor Diels (formerly Gestapo boss, first at Cologne, now Hanover)—an obscure but certainly intelligent man paid me a visit. His visit to me also evidences how low the barometer stands. He described the awful conditions of chaos prevailing throughout the administrative machinery, which the Third Reich had brought about through the competition between Party and

State and through the multiplicity of "bureaux." Such an apparatus could not survive the great test of war. In Hanover alone there were now twenty-eight more or less independent offices dealing with matters which formerly were under the jurisdiction of the provincial government.

For hours he had held forth on all this to Göring, but he had little hope of change. These people do not really know what a state is. Moreover, Göring will not listen to unpleasant things if he can help it. Popitz, the Acting Minister of Finance, cannot even get to see him. To a subordinate who conveyed Popitz's desire to be received, Göring said: "I know all he wants to tell me, but I cannot bear to hear it now!"

Later with Hueber, Göring's brother-in-law and Undersecretary in the Ministry of Justice, a pleasant, sensible man. As an old National Socialist and believer in a Greater Germany, he had long fought for union with Austria. Now he views the whole development with concern, without realizing the full magnitude of the danger. I tried to make him see how necessary it was to restore the rule of law in Germany; I also tried to indicate the tremendous responsibility that now rests on his brother-in-law, since Göring seems to listen somewhat to Hueber's wife. Hueber himself does not have much influence and, like all the better elements of the old Austrian National Socialism, he is really on the shelf.

Welczeck recently told me that he had talked with Horthy, who most openly expressed his absolute rejection of Hitler and his methods. A report from another quarter confirmed the story that Hitler had tried to treat Horthy à la Schuschnigg and Hacha, but that his attempt had misfired. Doubtless we have now maneuvered Hungary into the most impossible domestic and foreign situation.

Toward evening I went to see Beck. He sees the situation exactly as I do and told me he had taken Goerdeler severely to task for his overoptimistic attitude, and had urged him to look at things more soberly. He considers a military success out of the question, and read me a memorandum about the situation, clearly substantiating his pessimistic judgment. He called Brauchitsch and company "sixth graders" when it comes to looking beyond the narrowest military limits. He does not consider Halder much of a personality either. Like most officers he wants to have nothing to do with Göring because he considers him one of the worst of the lot; for this reason he cannot support Popitz's plans.

I went to see the Brauchitschs in the evening. At the moment there is little contact with their cousin, who is not in Berlin. But I did my best to show them the tremendous responsibility the general now bears. A commander in chief is not just a divisional commander who does nothing but obey. He must also consider the political ramifications of strategy, to say nothing of the military question whether or not a certain move promises sufficient success to warrant the risk and sacrifice involved.

*Thursday, November 2:* A visit from Gisevius. He is considerably more pessimistic than Goerdeler about the prospects of action by the generals. He thinks the invasion of Belgium is sure to come and that we cannot hope to act before that. Afterward there might be a better chance. All of us who are without government posts lack power of leverage and are without influence. For that reason he argued that a journey to America should be arranged for Schacht as a semi-official representative of German industry. With such a mission he could work for peace. I then made a remark about his elaborate dinner at Horcher's with the police president of Berlin, to which he replied he had known Helldorf since the days of his own police service, and was certain that he was of the same mind as we are.

Afterward, at his suggestion, I called on Otto Bismarck at the Foreign Office. He did not wear his Party emblem, and talked in a highly critical and subversive manner.

Lunch at the Deutscher Club, at the so-called Mitropa table. Afterward I talked with Brandenstein alone; he seemed to be rather well informed. He thought Witzleben was the general from whom one might expect action. But he was stationed at Kreutznach. He was planning to visit him there.

*Saturday, November 11, 1939:* Stag dinner, arranged by Schoen, for Crown Prince Rupprecht in Munich. Schoen had invited me to meet a "friend of the Greeks" and "grandson of the founder of the Glyptothek," which I didn't quite understand. Since I had seen the Crown Prince only once I did not recognize him immediately. Very interesting conversation, especially between the two of us. He is very attractive and cosmopolitan. Knows all countries and is remarkably well educated, especially in the history of art. In Italy he knows his way about better than I. What he had to say about military and political matters was also well thought through and bespoke rich experience and considerable judgment. I stayed the night with Schoen, since there was no way to get back.

At the Café Luitpold we met Princess Pilar. She is a nurse in a hospital. On the way from the café to the restaurant Pilar was stopped because her flashlight was not properly dimmed. The policeman rudely declared he had to confiscate it. We interceded for Pilar on the ground that, as a nurse, she absolutely needed it. He then became more reasonable. When, in answer to his question, she gave her name as "Princess Pilar of Bavaria," he pulled himself together, as if by habit. "Pardon me," he said, "I did not know that." He regretted that he had to act as he did, and murmured: "Yes, times are hard, times are hard." The flashlight, of course, he left with her.

The English White Paper (Henderson's final report) states quite accurately that Hitler had argued: (1) that England would not dare go to war; (2) that England had wanted war for a long time and was responsible for it! "Explain to me, Count Oerindur, this paradox of nature."

*November 16, 1939, Ebenhausen:* All Germany is discussing the attempt on Hitler's life at the Bürgerbräu [November 8]. The press is quite unable to cover up the fact that there is absolutely none of that "fanatical indignation" which prevails, described by official propaganda. Rather, there is an astounding indifference and many people quite openly express regret that the explosion came so late.

With cold-blooded insolence, immediately after the explosion of the bomb, the report was put out that the lines of suspicion led to England. Naturally, it is being whispered about that this was "another Reichstag fire," instigated by the Party in order to arouse hatred against England. I do not believe this, although the stories put out by the Gestapo would naturally arouse this suspicion. Most probably it was the act of dissatisfied elements within the Party. What will be the effect of this attempt on Hitler's life? I sense that confusion and helplessness are increasing.

I am beginning to believe that the invasion of Belgium and Holland has been given up. For weeks the foreign press has been full of reports on the fear of the Belgians and Dutch and their extensive preparations. The step taken by King Leopold and Queen Wilhelmina was the result of this anxiety and has made matters more difficult for Hitler. The opposition of our military men is also a factor.

A notable event in foreign affairs is the proclamation by the Comintern on the anniversary of the October Revolution. With remarkable *sang-froid* we are thrown into the same pot with England and France as capitalistic slave traders. The incident demonstrates what they dare say about us, apparently for the purpose of quieting their own party members. Since this proclamation also berates the Italians as future hyenas of the battlefield, who will enter the fray when the victory of one party is assured, the Italian press, on official instructions, has taken the field against Moscow and notes that apparently the *accordo* between us and the Soviets was not quite perfect.

Pietzsch came to see us. Very depressed. He completely understands that the fantastic policies of Hitler are leading Germany into ruin. Then, in the midst of it all, he falls back almost automatically into a state of admiration. He tells awful things about the economic disorganization which makes any rational management impossible. Without any knowledge of the matter in hand, Hitler interfered for political or military reasons, made altogether impossible demands—for instance, on behalf of Italy—and thereby turned the whole apparatus upside down. It appears to me that we ourselves are contributing to the English "destruction of German economy."

Characteristic of the deceptive methods of the leaders of the press, I was told by an editor: The papers were permitted recently to mention the anniversary of the death of Johanna von Bismarck[1] but were strictly forbidden to mention her piety. Moreover, all magazines and periodicals must publish something against England in each issue. The Comintern proclamation was of course suppressed and so are railroad accidents. The French and English replies to King Leopold and Queen Wilhelmina were reviled but not published.

I met Guttenberg in Munich. It appears that Gessler has the confidence of the Wittelsbachs. Interesting conversation with General Geyr, who had commanded an armored division in Poland. He must have experienced terrible things and was so strongly affected by them that he is in a sanatorium here with a heart condition.

Among other things he told that he had received orders at the Bug River not to permit the thousands of fleeing Poles, who were streaming back to us in terrible fear of the bolshevists, to recross the river. Of course, wherever possible, he had permitted it anyhow.

During his time as Military Attaché in London the Party had attacked him violently because he maintained that England was not bluffing, but that once a certain point had been reached she would fight. As late as June Reichenau had sneeringly asked him whether he still believed that the English would go to war. Reichenau, of course, thinks differently now. The only ones who had believed him were Beck and Fritsch. I remember in Rome, after the occupation of the Rhineland, how Göring assailed the service attachés in London who had "lost their nerve." Geyr[2] said the three of them together had sent a very matter-of-fact telegram to the effect that the chances of "war" stood fifty-fifty. He said that ever since the occupation of the Rhineland [March 7, 1936], the English had been suspicious and had begun to prepare themselves for war. The top military officers who were friendly to Germany were replaced by Francophiles throughout.

*November 23, 1939:* Yesterday it was announced that the would-be assassin had been caught. An astonishingly frank

---

[1] Wife of Chancellor Prince Bismarck, died November 27, 1894.
[2] At the time Military Attaché in London.

man whose attitude is puzzling. Otto Strasser and the British "Secret Service" are mentioned, without evidence, as the wire-pullers. There is a story of the Gestapo men who, camouflaged as "revolutionary German officers," had decoyed two members of the Secret Service into Germany and arrested the chief of the Western European Secret Service operating from Holland. The incident was reported in the foreign press a few days ago; it was stated there that the two Englishmen had been carried off by the SS after some shooting on Dutch territory. Of course the English radio denies everything. It is possible they will now try to hold Holland responsible. Today the old propaganda theme, "Otto Strasser," is being played in the German press.

A. Kessel writes that the western offensive is still under discussion. I hear nothing of any opposition. Rumors are flying thick that Brauchitsch has gone or is under arrest.

Santa Hercolani and Detalmo Pirzio Biroli are agreed that, according to information from Rome, something very close to hatred of Nazi Germany now prevails in Italy. At the same time fascism is losing ground while the monarchy is gaining. Mussolini himself is still impressed by Germany's military might and has not yet given up the idea of entering the struggle at Germany's side.

*December 5, 1939:* Wilmowsky asked me to see him. Ostensible reason, his Viennese project, which—alas!—has failed, at least so far as I am concerned. The main point really was that Popitz had asked him to summon me in the interest of concentrating all forces against the immediate threat of the Belgian-Dutch plan.

On this occasion Karl Heinrici produced a masterpiece of political ineptitude. Popitz had told him too that it would be good if I came, whereupon Heinrici made a telephone call to Wolf Tirpitz, compromising all four of us simultaneously. He said Popitz wanted me to come, but since my correspondence was probably watched, Wolf should try "harmlessly" to weave into a letter the desirability of my coming! Wolf went to him at once and gave him the devil. Popitz almost fell off his chair when I told him about this. In this chapter there also belongs another item, as Udo Alvensleben reported it to Kameke in great anxiety: an officer of the staff on which Alvensleben serves stated that a certain resistance was crystallizing and that it was centering around me.

I had informed Goerdeler that I was coming to Berlin and would be glad to help him with additional information for his Scandinavian trip for Bosch. I had hardly arrived at the Adlon when he entered my room. This man, usually so enterprising, was in black despair. By the way, he often reminds me of Kapp. I hope the cognomen is not an omen (*nomina non sunt omina*).

According to his account, all opposition of the military leaders to the drive-through-Belgium plan has collapsed. This in spite of the fact that Brauchitsch and Halder, as well as all the others, are convinced the result will be disastrous. But they feel they must obey. Göring also was still against it, but could not make up his mind to resist; instead, he confined himself to a certain sabotage of the plan on the pretext of bad weather, which has caused large-scale flooding in north and central Germany, as I saw on my trip, and also in Holland.

The worst thing is that there is absolutely no co-operation between Göring and Brauchitsch. The former does not like Brauchitsch and the latter, like almost all generals, mistrusts Göring's character in the highest degree. On the other hand, Brauchitsch, like many others, seems subject to Hitler's witchcraft.

Goerdeler told me that Halder had given the following reason for obeying the order: (1) Ludendorff had also made a last desperate effort in 1918, and had not thereby damaged his historical reputation. One can hardly believe one's ears. Of what importance to us is the historical reputation of a general! Besides, it is damaged, and, above all, the effort did fail! (2) There is no great man available. Such a man can only reveal himself in the course of action, and if he doesn't show up it simply can't be helped. One cannot, for that reason, let a crime be committed that would plunge Germany into catastrophe. For even if we are victorious it would necessarily be a Pyrrhic victory, quite apart from the necessity of putting a stop to the inner destruction, the demoralization, and the unspeakable bestialities in Poland, which are a disgrace to the name of Germany and for which the Army must share responsibility.

Keitel is said to believe that our marching into Belgium and Holland would induce Italy to go along with us; Pariani, who has been dismissed, had written him something like that. I do not share this opinion. Particularly now since the Russians, with our consent, have fallen upon Finland [November 29, 1939], which we had once helped to liberate from them. In such company we now appear in the eyes of the world as one big band of robbers.

(3) We ought to give Hitler this last (*sic!*) chance to deliver the German people from the slavery of English capitalism. How propaganda has affected the guileless Germans! Now they want to pursue a *Realpolitik* because their former policy was too "sentimental." Just like a certain type of officer who left the service in 1918, completely ignorant of business methods, and, upon becoming a merchant, thought he had to cheat, although previously he had never so much as stolen a pin. In just this way we have now come to think that a "realistic" policy means we must ignore all decencies and principles, and we do not even see that in doing this we are destroying our own foundations.

(4) One does not rebel when face to face with the enemy. But it is not the Army which is facing the enemy in this age of total warfare, but the entire people, and the issue is whether or not the nation shall be ruined.

(5) Opposition had not yet matured enough. It is interesting, by the way, that the leaders of armies always use this argument. There is some truth in that. But can one wait for this when everything is at stake? Of course, theoretically, it would be better to wait a while, but practically speaking we cannot.

(6) One could not be sure of the younger officers. That may be partially true. But if the generals are united and give out the right orders the people and Army will obey.

The question I discussed with Goerdeler, and again in the evening with Wilmowsky, is: (1) Can we still do something to influence the generals? (2) How, without changing Germany's tactical situation for the worse, could the generals get a guarantee that a decent peace is still obtainable, but could no longer be had after marching through Belgium and Holland?

Goerdeler was, as I have said, rather pessimistic. It seems that Hitler spoke to the generals for three hours (Thursday, November 25) with the wild persuasiveness of a shyster lawyer. He impressed the harmless soldiers, whereas his more intelligent listeners got the impression of a raving Genghis Khan. Hitler said, more or less: humanitarianism was an invention of the nineteenth century. Neutrality was no obstacle. If he were destroyed in this undertaking, Germany would plunge with him into the abyss.

It is interesting that it is Reichenau, of all people, who continues to oppose the break-through most sharply; he also says so openly and has submitted a memorandum.

Goerdeler, whom I saw once more early Wednesday before he left for Sweden, thought that despite everything the "massaging" of the generals should not be given up. He suggested bringing on Reusch, who knows Halder well. In order to test out the possibilities of peace one could, for instance, ask Gessler to go to Rome and visit the Vatican; he could bring back a statement from the Pope to the effect that he would continue to support a decent peace.

Dined with Wilmowsky. He is just as well informed as Goerdeler and just as pessimistic. His brother-in-law, Krupp, was also dining in the Esplanade with his wife and several of their children. Wilmowsky said it was hopeless to attempt to urge him to action. He also reported a conversation with a friend of his, a highly respected landowner, Conrad, from the province of Posen. He had told him that what was being said about the brutalities in Poland was unfortunately true. The last thing he had seen there was a drunken Kreisleiter [district Party leader] who, with his henchmen, had ordered the prison opened; he had shot five whores and attempted to rape two others. Only after considerable efforts did they succeed in having him arrested.

Wilmowsky reported sorry things from Vienna: it had sunk to the level of a dead provincial city. Engineer Neubacher, the Mayor of Vienna, though an old Nazi, had confessed to him in a fit of profound depression that he feared the worst if there were the least setback.

Early *Thursday* [*November 30*] I went to see Canaris, with whom I spoke quite openly. He has given up all hope of resistance from the generals and thinks it would be useless to try anything more along this line.

In the afternoon I visited Maria Pecori [wife of the Italian Military Attaché in Berlin]. The Finnish affair has caused an outburst of sympathy among all decent Italians.

Toward evening I went to see Beck. In his own sphere he has done everything imaginable; he even went so far as to tell Brauchitsch that he was prepared to carry out the matter [the *coup d'état*] if Brauchitsch would give him a free hand. Naturally without success. He has repeatedly presented his view to the Quartermaster General, orally and in writing.

*Friday, December 1:* In the evening I went to see Kameke in Potsdam. He firmly believes that God will finally intervene. Furthermore, he thinks he is in a position to know that the stars, which Hitler trusts, are very unfavorable.

*Saturday, December 2:* return trip. Spoke to Gessler in Munich and encouraged him to go to Halder in Berlin.

*December 15, 1939, Ebenhausen:* The Finnish affair continues to inspire ever-stronger reactions against the Soviet Union and against us; up to now, however, only in a moral sense. England and the Scandinavian countries appear confused and powerless. It is interesting and understandable that in France there is now a strong movement advocating a break with Russia, whereas England holds back in fear of unforeseeable consequences. I have already mentioned that, according to reliable information, Hitler has said he will occupy Sweden if ore exports are blocked.

In the Belgium-Holland affair there is increasing evidence that the weather has stymied the plan for the moment. But who knows?

In the meantime the destruction of German economy continues, even though apparent only in isolated instances. The professional and middle classes face extinction.

Had tea day before yesterday at Hamm's with Gessler, Goetz, and Sperr. They unanimously judge the economic situation as extraordinarily serious. The English blockade strikes at one of our most sensitive spots. On the other hand, the losses and difficulties of shipping to and from England are undoubtedly great. I am convinced that with a change of regime in Germany we could even today get a decent peace, but for how much longer? The Nazi regime and Germany are coming to be looked on as one and the same.

Goetz told me that recently a conference of financial experts was convened in Berlin and reached a very pessimistic conclusion about financing the war; but it finally adopted a memorandum that tended to be more optimistic.

Sperr said that not long ago several people had gathered at the home of an acquaintance and had indulged in some critical utterances. Suddenly there was a call from the Gestapo: "You are warned not to continue this conversation." The call was prompted by his own daughter (a member of the Hitler Youth). She had eavesdropped at the door and informed the Gestapo by telephone.

*December 21, 1939:* On the *eighteenth* I met Gessler and Reusch by appointment at the Hotel Regina. The purpose of our meeting was gone, as the offensive had been postponed indefinitely. However, since the idea is not being abandoned, I thought it important to encourage Reusch to continue working against it through Halder.

I found Reusch rather pompous, a typical captain of industry, before whom everyone kowtows. Gessler also showed a rather obsequious attitude toward him. But he is no longer young and not in first-class physical condition. He emphasized very strongly that he was well informed, that he was in constant touch with the most important persons, et cetera, so that it was not very easy to establish a give-and-take atmosphere in our conversation or to make personal contact. He was of the opinion that at the present time it would be better to do nothing about the matter that interests us. The generals were tired of being continually exposed to influence from all sides, and were deliberately shutting themselves away. Although Halder had written that he wanted to visit him in Oberhausen, he was not sure whether the general would come. The main argument of the generals against action was that there was not yet enough public sentiment in favor of it, and that they were not sure of the officers from the rank of major down. This argument could not be lightly dismissed. I pointed out the danger that if we waited for complete readiness the right moment might very easily be missed—for a decent peace and for keeping the Army intact. I admitted that we would probably have to be quiet at least until the middle of January.

When I left Reusch I was rather depressed about conditions in general and our own helplessness. I had twice made up my mind to give up the trip to Stuttgart to see Robert Bosch, to whom I had already announced my arrival. Troubled with thoughts like Carlyle's in the Rue de l'Enfer, I wandered back and forth between the streetcar, the Isar Valley Railway Station, and the ticket windows of the Central Railway Station. Stuttgart finally won out, and I am happy about it now.

I made a melancholy three-and-a-half-hour trip in the dark to Stuttgart. The passengers vigorously questioned the conductor as to why he did not properly black out the train with curtains so that one could at least read, and a Swabian remarked: "This train isn't fit for a pig to ride in." Whereupon the conductor retorted: "That's the way it goes; some put up with it and some just won't."

Went to see Bosch early Tuesday. Grand old dynamo, unfortunately severely hampered by a bladder ailment. He called in his highest-ranking director, Walz, and both of them explained to me the desperate condition of our economy, and, above all, of our finances. They saw things very black indeed: the criminal irresponsibility of the war was sucking Germany dry and destroying the foundations which had been built up with so much effort. There is no better preparation for bolshevism. Bosch said that he himself was more of a technician than a businessman, and spoke with pride of the contribution of his firm to the victorious Messerschmitt planes and the recent and apparently extraordinary successes of the air force. But he sees clearly what we are heading for. Director Walz impressed me as a splendid, intelligent man.

Typical of the phony conditions we are living under: Walz was called out to attend a brief conference with SS people. When he came back he wore the SS button in his lapel, having put it on in a hurry for that purpose; he then went on to speak vigorously about the disastrous policy of the Hitler government.

Elsa Bruckmann enthusiastically telephoned to Ilse that Hitler had been there for his annual Christmas visit. He had been very healthy and confident and had stayed an hour and three quarters. All her doubts are dispelled by such a visit! They are just like enthusiastic monarchists, whose severest criticism is immediately silenced when His Majesty condescends to notice them.

*December 22, 1939:* As the Bruckmanns have just told me in detail, Hitler made his annual Christmas visit to them day before yesterday. Both were very much affected by this gracious act. Bruckmann was considerably impressed by Hitler's views, but she told Ilse she had not changed her critical attitude. Hitler had been in fine health, not at all cramped in his style, but in good spirits and optimistic. It must be added that he is a very good actor. However, it may be that he is sure of the success of our arms. He does not realize that the final result of a destructive victory over England, such as he wants, would mean the ruin of Western civilization; nor does he understand the domestic difficulties.

This man, who has just congratulated Stalin tenderly on his sixtieth birthday, is unscrupulous and utterly uncivilized. He had declared that with his magnetic mines and other fabulous means (20,000 bombers) he would force England to her knees in eight months. Thereafter would begin the glorious construction of a Reich that would extend far beyond the present borders of Germany. England had unfortunately obstructed him for an unnecessarily long time in establishing this empire. In the Bruckmanns' guest book he wrote: "In the year of the struggle for the building of the great German-Germanic Reich!" What does "German-Germanic" mean?

Hitler was very suspicious about Holland, Sweden, et cetera. He also spoke at some length about Warsaw, of which only a small fraction was worth rebuilding: most of it was a hopeless pile of ruins. He betrayed no feeling whatever in saying this and only mentioned that he had tried in vain to urge the commander to capitulate earlier; he had not been able to employ the tactics of Franco at Madrid. Actually, a few weeks of siege would have sufficed to prevent the tragedy. When Elsa remarked that it was regrettable we had taken Lemberg, et cetera, at the cost of bloodshed, only to relinquish it to the Russians, he answered that this was unavoidable because the Russians deployed three days too late and a vacuum had to be avoided.

*December 23, 1939:* General Vogl, who is on leave at his house in Irschenhausen, visited me. He is very depressed because of a possible offensive through Belgium and Holland, the political consequences of such action, the great losses to be expected, and the doubtful military results. Militarily and technically he considers us superior, but he sees little prospect of a really decisive victory because of the over-all situation. The four months' rest, that is to say, training period, had been very necessary for the troops. The vast majority of the higher officers thought as he did; they are full of concern and of the most serious political doubts. The younger ones were different; for them Hitler was still taboo, but not the other Party chieftains. The effect of any open resistance of the generals to an order of Hitler's was therefore very problematical. After the easy Polish campaign these people needed really severe battle experience to make them see the light.

This morning a remarkable article in the *Münchener Neueste Nachrichten* (and, I assume, in the rest of the press) containing threatening hints about possible Anglo-French attempts to extend the theater of war either in the southeast, via Turkey, or in the north, via Norway and Sweden, in connection with the Finnish-Russian war. The latter, by the way, would not be a bad idea from the Entente point of view. The moral arguments are to encircle us there and to cut off our ore imports. Does Hitler want to beat them to it? (Cf. his "German-Germanic" dreams.)

*December 25, 1939:* This afternoon Nostitz was with us. Very deeply worried. There is to be another meeting on the *twenty-seventh* to discuss what we should do. The Holland-Belgium undertaking is still in the limelight. Perhaps that explains why today, during Christmas week, Goerdeler asked me to come to Berlin (on *December 28*).

Gogo Nostitz, very depressed, told about absolutely shameless actions in Poland, particularly by the SS. Conditions there as regards sanitation defied description, especially in the Jewish district and in the resettlement areas. The shooting of hundreds of innocent Jews was the order of the day. Furthermore, an increasingly insolent attitude was adopted by the SS toward the Army, which they did not salute but jeered at and undermined.

Blaskowitz had written a memorandum describing all this quite frankly. It also contained a sentence to the effect that, judging from the conduct of the SS in Poland, it was to be feared they might later turn upon their own people in the same way. Blaskowitz, as a matter of fact, had executive powers only in case of a "revolt." Otherwise he had nothing to say outside the military sphere. Frank was carrying on like a megalomaniacal pasha. Neurath could learn a lesson from him in that respect, since he (Frank) let nobody interfere, but ruled like a sovereign, whereas Neurath gave magnificent hunting parties but in reality served only as an "extra." Perhaps we may hope that the behavior of the SS will be the quickest way to enlighten the Army.

Gogo [Nostitz] reports from Italy that Mussolini bluntly expressed to Mackensen his misgivings about the Finnish affair. He described the bolshevists as swindlers. Large parts of Ciano's speech have been suppressed here, for very good reasons. Among other things he emphasized that on concluding the alliance it had been agreed that in the next few years a conflict would have to be avoided. He also underlined the differences that developed at the Salzburg conference and reaffirmed his anti-bolshevist attitude. This last point brought thunderous applause from the Chamber, which had remained impassive during all the passages relating to Germany.

*December 30, 1939:* I arrived in Berlin on the *twenty-seventh,* an hour and a half late. Looked up Popitz first. His estimate of the situation was considerably more optimistic than last time, because the reign of terror of the SS in the east and the arrogance of these people toward the Army were gradually opening the eyes of the soldiers to this German shame and this robber state within a state. In the west the SS has already assembled behind the Army, to the annoyance of the latter, in order to take Belgium and Holland in hand at the proper moment. It seems that Hitler has ordered that in these countries—unlike Poland—the executive power is to remain in the hands of the military. But nobody relies on these declarations any more, above all not on their durability.

Popitz describes the situation about as follows: Brauchitsch has been written off among the higher generals. The plan now was to have a number of divisions stop in Berlin "in transit from west to east." Then Witzleben was to appear in Berlin and dissolve the SS. On the basis of this action Beck would go to Zossen and take the supreme command from Brauchitsch's hands. A doctor would declare Hitler incapable of continuing in office, whereupon he would be taken into custody. Then an appeal would be made to the people along these lines: prevention of further SS atrocities, restoration of decency and Christian morality, continuation of the war, but readiness for peace on a reasonable basis. The problem is—with or without Göring?

Popitz said all were agreed on one point: that only after completed action, if at all, could Göring be asked whether he wanted to co-operate. The advantages and disadvantages of taking Göring in are obvious. Of great significance in this respect is the question as to whether the truth of the information Popitz was given by Goerdeler is authentic: that Göring had recently sent out peace feelers behind Hitler's back. These feelers supposedly went through Prince Paul of Yugoslavia (perhaps with Prince Philip of Hesse as intermediary), and were based on the following points: Göring instead of Hitler, monarchy, frontiers of 1914, German territories such as Austria and the Sudetenland to remain German.

I can't quite believe that Göring would behave in this way toward Hitler. In my opinion this step would be a tactical error in dealing with the Allies. Yet it is possible that Göring is entertaining the mad idea of proposing the candidacy of his slave Philip.

Popitz stated that in furtherance of the plan just discussed Colonel Oster had gone to Witzleben. Goerdeler was to meet him or Witzleben himself in Frankfurt; afterward Witzleben was supposed to discuss the matter with Beck. Time, of course, is short, especially since on the day of my visit to Popitz the Belgian-Dutch show was scheduled for March 1.

Popitz told me that Goerdeler has a plan for dispelling the doubts of the generals about the chances of a decent peace. He plans to go with a general to the King of the Belgians, who is a friend of his, to inform the King of our views and the possibility of a change in regime, and to arrange for a confidential but authoritative response from Paris and London. Popitz has expressed doubts about the plan and asked that I be heard. I stated that I shared his doubts. At best Goerdeler could talk with the King in his own name, but only for the purpose of ascertaining the King's attitude.

Popitz also reported that Schacht had declared himself ready to co-operate and to "stick his neck out"; I expressed some doubts. Furthermore, Goerdeler had visited the "Great Grand Admiral," and Raeder had volunteered his conviction that conditions were unbearable; he would co-operate if the Army would act; but in any event the action would have to be taken by the Army.

Popitz also said that the not-overintelligent Ambassador Mackensen had arranged for Hitler's visit to his father, old Field Marshal von Mackensen. In the flurry of the visit the old gentleman had suddenly regained his enthusiasm and had saluted the Führer with a *"Sieg Heil!"* Now they wanted Popitz to go to Mackensen and bring the old man back to his senses—a task Popitz does not relish. I said that all this would not be of much use; the suggestion that Mackensen, as the oldest officer, should go to Brauchitsch and appeal to his honor as a German officer to take a stand against the SS bestialities does not hold out much hope of success. But he can make the attempt, at least if he wants to.

In the afternoon I visited Olga Göring, who has spent Christmas at Karinhall. On Christmas Eve sixty people (including the servants) sat at one table. Nice speech by brother-in-law Hueber plainly underlining the desire for peace, for which Göring had thanked him warmly. The Wieds were there also and fed Göring a great deal of crude flattery. Olga Göring told of dismal news from Austria. Göring's brother spoke with daring frankness of the necessity for doing away with Hitler.

During the forenoon of the *twenty-eighth* I spoke briefly with Goerdeler, who arrived three hours late from Frankfurt. Had lunch afterward with him and Dr. Reuter (of the *Deutscher Volkswirt*) at Borchardt's and then stayed on with him alone. It did not seem to surprise him that I had opposed his plan for approaching the King of the Belgians. He did not even insist on it, but claimed he had been 100 per cent successful with Witzleben. Witzleben would soon come to have a final talk with Beck. Goerdeler stated that Hitler is said to have told Greiser and Forster he expected them to make Posen and West Prussia German land again within a few years. "And you, my dear Frank, will meanwhile have to continue your satanic duties in Poland."

Goerdeler intends in the next few days to speak with Reichenau, who has begun to wobble. It seems he has been tempted by the prospect of an easy success against France and England.

Spent another hour with Popitz before lunch, and discussed at length the practical procedure of forming a new government. The personnel problem is very difficult because the old machinery has been destroyed. Popitz emphasized the need for an immediate change in the structure of the Reich (division into states) and for the proclamation of genuine national and social principles, with Christian morality, after the best German tradition. I pointed to the necessity of building the state on the basis of local and corporative self-government.

In the early evening I went to see Beck. He continues to be pessimistic about the prospects for an offensive in Belgium and Holland, or any decisive success against England. He spoke even more openly than usual about the action planned. Afterward Goerdeler came and joined us.

# 1940

*January 11, 1940, Ebenhausen:* According to news from Berlin the plans for an offensive have been temporarily abandoned. The press systematically draws attention to the north, that is, to the supposed Anglo-French plans to send decisive help via Norway and Sweden to Finland, now putting up quite a successful defense. A rather obvious threat is being made to the effect that we may try to take preventive action. Such a step would completely ruin our moral position.

Wolf told me about a telegram from Schulenburg covering his conversation with Potemkin. The latter had said thousands of Poles and Jews who were not wanted in Russia were constantly attempting to cross the border. The Russians would not let them cross and they were shot down in droves by the German SS. How long, he asked, can this kind of thing go on?

Schulenburg: "What shall I answer?"

This beastliness has become absolutely intolerable. Dieter said that on his leave train the soldiers had behaved in a way he could not even imagine possible in 1918.

Detalmo is all agog to establish connections via Italy between the decent Germany and the English "appeasement" group.

Ilse Göring is always an interesting barometer, inasmuch as she mirrors Hermann's attitude toward Hitler. Around Christmastime, at any rate, their relations must have been strained; according to her, one of Hermann's peace feelers, through a

Swede, came to Hitler's knowledge and put him in a violent rage. One observes that in Göring's entourage the idea is slowly gaining ground that, if need be, one ought to write off Hitler and strive for peace under Göring's banner.

*Ebenhausen, January 28, 1940. Trip to Berlin:* Goerdeler asked me to come to Berlin on very short notice. Traveling conditions more and more uncomfortable; trains run less frequently, are getting more and more crowded, and are tremendously late. Just before leaving I met Schmidt in the Wolff Hotel. He drew a picture of Berlin which was quite in accord with his impressionable nature, fundamentally very unfavorable, but with occasional flashes of optimism. When Funk tells him that the persistent orders and counterorders for the offensive against Belgium and Holland are really a well-calculated war of nerves, he believes it. Göring, he said, had spoken "calmly and with judgment." But he was horrified at Himmler, who with wobbling pince-nez and a cruel expression on his vulgar face said the Führer had given him the task of seeing to it that Poland should never rise again. In other words, a policy of extermination.

In Berlin, after the barbarous cold spell of recent weeks, there was milder weather, and the streets began to improve. The jokes told are indicative of the trend of public opinion. For instance, Göring and Goebbels talk about what they want to do after the war. The former says: "I've always dreamed of making a bicycle tour around Germany someday!"

Goebbels answers: "Fine; and what are you going to do in the afternoon?"

Another: The two Gs and Hitler are talking on the same subject. Göring says he will probably find a job as a forester; Goebbels says that with his able pen he could return to newspaper work.

Hitler: *"Ach,* it will be much simpler for me. I'm an Austrian!"

Or: "What is an opportunist?"

"A man who resigns from the Party now!"

Or a new category of blessedness: "Blessed are the half-educated, for the Third Kingdom [*das Dritte Reich*] will be theirs."

The public is worrying about the coal shortage and the lack of many things—potatoes, for instance. The railways appear to be gradually disintegrating. Of the 8,000 locomotives and 140,000 cars, which Dorpmüller urgently requested a long time ago, only a fraction are in course of delivery. The personnel is overworked and disgruntled—according to Goerdeler—because of the role played by Party affiliation in promotions. Despite all inconveniences the people, in my opinion, continue to be touchingly patient, and the petty bourgeois are still enthusiastic pillars of the Party.

Those who are in the know (that is to say very few) have been chiefly impressed by two events: the Mussolini letter and the air fiasco at Malines. I heard of both from Goerdeler first, but later received confirmation.

Mussolini, it seems (apparently aware of the offensive planned for January 17, 1940, against Belgium and Holland), sent a letter to Hitler through Attolico on January 9. It was a historical document of the first order. The main points seem to be:

(1) A modification of the Ciano speech as a final statement of the Italian position. German propaganda had tried to present it as an expression of Ciano's personal wrath toward Ribbentrop.

(2) Sharp condemnation of Hitler's policy toward Russia. Every revolution had its principles; there were, of course, occasions when one or another of these must be temporarily played down. But abandonment of a fundamental attitude, preached to the people as gospel, did not meet with his approval, and neither Italy nor Spain could follow that course. Both would adhere most firmly to their anti-bolshevist line. If Hitler—which Heaven forbid!—should continue in this course, he would get no support in Italy and this would have serious consequences for Germany. Out of consideration for Germany, he had instructed Ciano not to mention Finland in his speech; otherwise a storm of applause would have resulted.

(3) At present Italy could still help Germany; her mobilization tied up several hundred thousand of the enemy. But Hitler must clearly recognize that he could not win the war. (In this connection he took a potshot at Ribbentrop: "Since England

and France, contrary to Ribbentrop's prediction, have entered the war . . .") Therefore he ought to aim at the restoration of peace. To this end it would be necessary in the first place to moderate his war aims—a reconstituted Polish state (Mussolini clearly disassociates himself from present conditions in Poland), and, above all, an abandonment of the offensive. This offensive could not bring final victory, even if it went as far as Paris; it would only destroy all possibilities of peace. Mussolini then offered his diplomatic support in any peace effort.

This document seems to have resulted in an outburst of rage on the part of Hitler: "my cowardly friend" and "just for that, I will!"

Whether he was affected differently in his innermost being is another question. Actually, the first result was to continue plans for the offensive. Dieter writes that the soldiers took a tearful and alcoholic leave of their quarters, and, accompanied by the sobbing population, began their advance along foul roads and in bitter cold for sixty-five kilometers (that is to say almost up to the Belgian-Dutch border). Spirits were rather tepid and there were signs of exhaustion. Then came the order: back to the old quarters—at which all signs of exhaustion immediately disappeared. The abandoning of the offensive is apparently due to the weather and event No. 2.

The plan for the offensive, with all details, fell into the hands of the Belgians on the eleventh or twelfth, when a German plane landed in Malines instead of at Cologne. At first I thought this a fairy tale, then I thought of treason. But it was officially hinted, with a wink, that it was intentional. Both the latter possibilities have been ruled out by those who know the facts. It is simply a case of unbelievable irresponsibility. An officer of the Air General Staff was charged with taking the plans to the Air Commander in Cologne and had express orders to use the railway. After having missed the train, allegedly because of a drinking party, he flew on from Muenster, encouraged by air force officers, and landed in Malines instead of Cologne. Kameke naturally believes that both this improbable story and the abnormal weather evidence divine intervention.

From Ilse Göring I heard that Hermann was beside himself

for a number of days. The air general in Cologne and his chief of staff have been relieved of their duties.

At three-fifteen I went to see Goerdeler at the hotel. The hopes he had entertained at our last meeting have turned to water. The "legitimate" concentration of troops near Berlin, as demanded by Witzleben, could not be arranged. The result was that the order to attack was carried out with blind obedience. Prussian discipline is no longer really dependable where it is absolutely indispensable, namely, among the troops and in the officers' corps. But at the upper levels, where obedience should be supplemented by judgment and political responsibility, it is applied all the more slavishly and against better knowledge. These generals who want to overthrow governments demand orders from these very governments before they will act!

Goerdeler was depressed by complete failure with Reichenau. The latter told him that the offensive had good prospects of success and must be carried through. Upon being confronted with his earlier opinions to the contrary, he made a significant reply: "Yes, at that time I still thought we could get peace with Hitler; now I know that that is not the case; now we must go through with it." What the fox really thinks remains doubtful.

This argument shows how tactically wrong it is to demand a change of regime from outside. This frightens the generals who remember 1918. It must remain a strictly internal affair. Nevertheless, Goerdeler is not quitting the race. The domestic situation is becoming more and more obvious, even to the blindest. The temporary abandonment of the offensive gave us a breathing spell which must be used. Goerdeler no longer believes that the plan can be managed with Göring; the generals absolutely reject the idea.

Early in the evening I went to see Beck. Very intelligent and calm, but he sees no way out at present. Goerdeler chanced to come by too. We dined at the "Krug" in Dahlem and then went to Popitz's. Talked until one o'clock about the first measures to be taken in case of an overthrow of the regime. We were all quite aware of the unfortunate theoretical nature of this discussion; yet it is necessary. Popitz and I were in almost complete agreement. Goerdeler, oddly enough, wants to have a plebiscite immediately; he is much too optimistic about the results. Popitz has had some maps made showing the new division of the Reich into states; his plan is too strongly influenced by the requirements of administrative efficiency and too little by political sensitivities.

On the *morning of the twenty-fifth* I called on Schacht. He is busily occupied with the question of preparing a peace feeler, and is obviously thinking of his mission to America. The trouble with him is that he is self-centered and hence is liable to act precipitately—and in the process his principles fall by the wayside.

Toward noon I went to see Kirk. He showed me a nice letter from Henderson. As Kirk sees it, America is not at all enjoying the war boom, which seems to be colossal, but hopes for peace. In this respect there is a certain resemblance to Italy, with which, according to Kirk, relations are good.

Ribbentrop is in bed. He ordered the Mussolini letter and the air fiasco to be kept strictly secret. Nevertheless, both leaked out.

On the *morning of the twenty-sixth* Planck called on me. Clever, pleasant man; the generals, unfortunately, seem to look on him as a disciple of Schleicher, and therefore mistrust him.

Then Wilmowsky came, sad at the crash of his nephew Krupp, the second son, and the most promising one. He views the situation with great pessimism.

Afterward a lieutenant colonel from Blaskowitz's staff visited me. He poured out his heart about the whole miserable situation, especially about the shameful conditions in Poland. Blaskowitz was weak, he said; he had drawn up a memorandum, to be sure, but afterward he had failed to send it on to Hitler.

Tea with Attolico. Eleanora was very excited and urgently implored me to encourage her husband, who was downhearted, to continue working for peace. I did the best I could. After a cautious approach I mentioned his visit to Hitler. When he realized that I was informed he began to talk. He said he was absolutely discouraged especially as he had heard nothing from Hitler for the last eighteen days.

Afterward I called on Nostitz. My former impressions were confirmed. He was surprised when I told him that I had seen Colonel Oster only once, and then for but a second. Apparently, he had assumed that we were always together. Bismarck inquired in a roundabout way about Goerdeler. I was vague.

Early on the *twenty-seventh* went walking with Etzdorf. He sees things quite clearly but has no confidence in the generals. Of the three top commanders he considers Bock vain, thinking only of his future pension, Rundstedt as soft in the head, and Leeb as the only one with whom something might be done. He told about the brutal exactions of the Russians, who have actually extorted the heavy cruiser *Lützow* from us.

In the afternoon I saw Welczeck. He had nothing new to say; his zealous political activity seems to be hibernating.

*February 1, 1940:* Extremely malicious speech by Hitler on the lowest possible level.

From the west one hears of increasing lack of discipline among the troops and workmen.

Typical joke: Why doesn't the Führer visit the front any more? Because on his departure the soldiers would cry: "Führer, we will follow you!" Or: "We want to go home to the Reich!"

On the *afternoon of the thirteenth* I went to see Schmitt (Tiefenbrunn). He has been in Berlin for some time. His impressions were rather depressing; confusion of economic requirements, breakdown of transport facilities, obvious perplexity in "high quarters" as to what to do next in military, financial, and economic matters.

Gürtner and Schwerin-Krosigk had impressed him as pathetically played out. Lammers, to whom he had poured out all his anxieties and explained the necessity for a peace drive, had not been at all opposed to the idea of telling this to Hitler. However, sickness had prevented Schmitt from getting around to it. Funk had finally given way and complained to him about conditions in general. He had observed: "In order to put up with all this confusion one has to be either crazy or drunk—I prefer the latter!"

Most remarkable of all was that Schmitt did get through to Göring. I heard later from another source that Göring had also called in other people, Planck for instance (as the new head of the Otto Wolf Corporation).

Olga Riegele told me her brother had telephoned her, which had never happened before, and asked why she didn't come out to Karinhall any more, and if she didn't care to, et cetera.

Symptoms of inner unrest and insecurity. In his conversation with Schmitt, Göring had reacted to Schmitt's insistence on a peace drive by launching into long-winded statements which vacillated between the assurance that he and the Führer both wanted a decent peace and fulminating declarations to the effect that "if the others don't want to come to an agreement, then they will be decisively licked."

Göring had added that new tactics were being employed in London. At first they had hinted they would not play ball with Hitler, but only with Göring; now they were not even ready to do that. He may be right.

In general the process of identifying the Nazi regime with all of Germany is persistently gaining ground. Goerdeler told me Vansittart had sent him his regards with the comment that now it would not be so easy to put through the old Reich frontiers in the east.

As to the prospects of victory, Göring told Schmitt he based his confidence first on the fantastic technical innovations which were in process of development (Professor Petersen, AEG), and then upon the strategic genius of the Führer. He would go down in history as the greatest military commander of all time, and in an offensive he would maneuver the enemy into exactly the positions where he wanted them. The generals were not worth much; they had no guts, but were merely excellent general staff officers à la Beck, who sat with wrinkled brows bent over their maps and would really prefer to sit down at a table with Gamelin and Gort and settle things with a pair of dice.

Upon Schmitt's objection that in Poland the generals had done a splendid job, Göring replied no, the Führer had done it all alone; the generals would have maneuvered slowly and cautiously. Yes, the troops and the lieutenants, above all his fliers, were excellent, but the leading generals, no.

Concerning peace, he added that one could still discuss the future of Poland, but the Führer refused any discussion about the Czechs.

In these comments Göring's tactics, playing on two pianos, as Popitz remarked, are just as obvious as his inner uncertainty.

*From February 14 to 17 in Berlin:* Arrived in Berlin four hours overdue, the last hour owing to the derailing of a sleeper on an open stretch. Traffic conditions in Berlin are very bad. Minor càtastrophe: the doors of the elevated no longer open readily, so that passengers often cannot get out and have to be shoved through the windows. Topics of conversation: the cold spell, lack of coal, food shortages. All in all, the public is touchingly patient, almost slave-like; nothing is done with enthusiasm. When a man on the elevated remarked: "Well, about the middle of July it will be getting a little warmer!" there was a ripple of merriment.

I saw Goerdeler immediately after my arrival. He was desperate about the indecision of the generals; Brauchitsch has to be written off entirely; his position was in danger, and Reichenau had been seen in Berlin!

Halder was thinking more clearly, and had to be worked on more. But now the visit of Sumner Welles was in the offing and this gave the generals the impression—wrongly, since it was not so intended—that the other side was ready to negotiate with Hitler and therefore one dared not deprive him of his chance. Goerdeler thought we ought to try to manage that Welles should not go from Rome directly to Berlin, but first to Paris and London. There he would be so enlightened that he would give up the trip to Berlin. I did not consider this plan very promising. The only thing one could do was to see to it that Sumner Welles was properly indoctrinated in Rome, and that he should afterward get correct impressions of the situation here.

After dinner I went to see Weizsäcker. He didn't take the visit of Sumner Welles so seriously, especially since it was purely informative and influenced by domestic political considerations—the elections.

Ribbentrop and Hitler were quite snooty and wanted to treat Welles brusquely. I doubt whether they will actually dare do so. On the other hand, Hitler and the Americans speak such entirely different languages that an understanding is almost unthinkable.

Weizsäcker thinks it should be suggested to Sumner Welles that he get down to certain principles and proclaim them to be decisive factors. He mentioned nationality, with historic modifications, as the basic formula for peace. Welles should not discuss personalities. If the objection were then raised that the Americans did not really want to make peace with this regime, Welles should reply that he could say nothing about that, but he personally was convinced that a name like Ribbentrop's should not be placed on any peace document.

Weizsäcker thought that if one keystone were removed the whole structure would begin to totter. I differed. Ribbentrop was not enough. Hitler, whom Göring was trying to influence against Ribbentrop anyhow, would readily drop the latter and toss him to the wolves without batting an eye. This might even lead to a strengthening of the regime.

Weizsäcker then told me the Gestapo had objected to my getting newspapers from Rome (because of their objectionable contents). We decided not to give in on this point, and an excellent man in the Personnel Department straightened the matter out.

I passed the evening with the Koenigs. He was unhappy about the breakdown of transportation. Years ago he had insisted on a large building program, but super-highways and Party buildings had been given priority.

Early on the *fifteenth* I called on Popitz. He was somewhat more optimistic about the generals because of the increasing number of those whose eyes are being opened. The Deputy Commander in Dresden, Falkenhausen, was very active. Because of his stay in China he had a more adventurous spirit. Nevertheless, there was little hope of coming to a decision before the American visit.

Goerdeler was right in thinking that the "summer" weather could easily revive spirits in general. Popitz reported the ninety-year-old Mackensen had visited him, youthfully vigorous, and had declared himself willing to write to Brauchitsch about the atrocities in Poland, appealing to the honor of the German Army and to Christian morality.

Hitler has been having wild tantrums. It is reliably reported that not long ago he took off his shoes and hurled them about the room.

I invited Kirk to breakfast and summoned up all my diplomacy to put him on the right track. I urged him to have Sumner Welles meet other than strictly official personages. I mentioned the names of Planck and Popitz.

Lunch at the Weizsäckers'. Popitz told me that Signora Attolico had quoted very optimistic utterances to the effect that, with Mussolini's help, we would soon have peace. Weizsäcker said this was pure fantasy, as indeed I had assumed. Mussolini had received no answer to his letter.

I asked Weizsäcker about the new trade treaty with Russia, concerning which Roediger at the Foreign Office had made a very optimistic speech at the Deutscher Club about advance deliveries. The treaty actually appears to be advantageous. At first Stalin had rejected the German interpretation that for a long time Russia would have to deliver in advance; but as it was finally worked out we should, in fact, always be a few months ahead. Of course whether this is carried out remains to be seen.

In the afternoon I went to call on Olga Riegele. Nothing new. She confirms the belief that Göring is strongly opposed to Ribbentrop. Then I saw Goerdeler again for a few minutes. Late in the afternoon I called on Beck. The pernicious character of the regime, above all in an ethical sense, becomes more and more apparent.

Beck told me that a prominent personage was about to undertake a mission abroad, but that he had declared he must first inform himself about the happenings in Poland. This individual had gone there and had found his worst expectations surpassed. He had drawn up a sort of memorandum which

Beck had read. Among other things it was reported that the SS had taken 1,500 Jews, including many women and children, and shuttled them back and forth in open freight cars until they were all dead. Then about two hundred peasants were forced to dig immense graves, and afterward all those who had taken part in this work were shot.

I forgot to mention that Olga Riegele told me that Hermann Treskow-Radojewo had been carried off by the Poles as a hostage. When he could no longer talk and fell by the roadside, they had simply shot him. His wife had now got through to Göring and had begged him to uphold the honor of the German name and to stop the terrible atrocities against the Poles and Jews! This incident had given him a real shock.

Tea at Frau von Schnitzler's. Elegant prewar "five o'clock." Frau von Schnitzler and Erna H. talked about the wonderful atmosphere of tension in Berlin, in which all elements were really working hard toward final victory. Restrained assent on the part of Frank-Fahle. Afterward, when he was with me, Frank-Fahle expressed his unmitigated horror at the whole situation.

*Trip to Arosa:* [Through the mediation of Hassell's son-in-law, Detalmo Pirzio Biroli, an English associate of Lord Halifax was to contact Hassell in Arosa. The arrangements for this meeting were camouflaged so as to make the English contact appear as a specialist attending the eldest son of Hassell, who was ill in Arosa. Detalmo wrote to Hassell on February 20, 1940:

I gather that in order to arrange your affairs it would be most useful to you to have an "assurance" of the Madre Manassei (Halifax) about what steps you must take in the future. I understand that for such an "assurance" to be of value, it would have to be made with the necessary authority and precision. I understand that the written form would be the most desirable and the most useful. . . . I have had about forty conversations with Mr. . . . He always took the initiative. His plan would be to see you, to speak with Signora Manassei [Halifax], then to see you again immediately. He would like to be the bearer of two messages: the first from you to the Signora (Halifax); the second from the Signora to you.

In this way he hopes to be able to bring you the "assurance" you need.]

*Arosa, February 22, 1940:* As the result of a telegraphic misunderstanding, Mr. X has already spent four days waiting for me in Arosa. I arrived on the evening of *February 21, 1940.* About noon of the twenty-second X came to the hotel, where I opened the door for him myself, as I had been on the lookout for him.

Two days earlier (Sunday) he had breakfasted in the hotel in order to get the lay of the land; when he saw my wife eating alone he rightly concluded that I had not yet arrived. He deliberately spoke loudly of Rome and a village called Detalmo with a man who happened to sit at his table, so that my wife suspected he was the party we were waiting for. The way he conducted these matters and the personal impression he makes give me assurance that he has a certain experience in such things.

On the *twenty-second,* before lunch, in the afternoon, and in the evening, as well as on the morning of the *twenty-third,* I spoke at length with X, and finally gave him the attached (but unsigned) statement on a durable peace. X's aim is to get a statement from Halifax to the effect that he would use all his influence to achieve a situation—more or less on the basis of my statement—in which an eventual change of regime in Germany would in no way be exploited by the other side, but, on the contrary, would be used constructively as a means of arriving at a lasting peace. Above all, the English would in this event attempt to arrange an armistice immediately.

Mr. X considers a negotiated peace with the present German regime an absolute impossibility, even though—and he emphasized this—Ribbentrop should be sacrificed to achieve it.

Main points which I stressed to Mr. X:

(1) My statement is valid only if a peace along these lines could be achieved soon, that is, above all before major military operations are undertaken. Mr. X himself seemed to be for speedy action in view of the possible German offensive.

(2) In answer to a question from Mr. X: "I am not in a

position to name the men who are backing me; I can only assure you that a statement from Halifax would get to the right people." Nevile Henderson, by the way, was well informed on conditions and persons in Germany.

(3) Sumner Welles must ask questions and not make statements; he should ask questions about principles and not about personalities or individual problems. It is important that he should also see unofficial personages in Berlin.

(4) Non-German sources should never demand a change of regime in Germany or the resignation of certain persons, et cetera. This must be an exclusively German affair.

(5) The principal obstacle to any change in regime is the story of 1918, that is, German anxiety (above all on the part of the generals) lest things develop as they did then, after the Kaiser was sacrificed.

(6) Therefore, unless there is some authoritative English statement on this point in the sense discussed, there will be no prospect of a change in the German regime auspicious for a negotiated peace.

(7) In answer to remarks by Mr. X indicating that conservative Englishmen hoped for a monarchy: "A monarchy is very much to be desired, but that would be a problem of the second stage."

[EDITOR'S NOTE: The following is Hassell's own English version, in which no changes have been made.]

### CONFIDENTIAL

*I. All serious minded people in Germany consider it as of utmost importance to stop this mad war as soon as possible.*

*II. We consider this because the danger of a complete destruction and particularly a bolshevization of Europe is rapidly growing.*

*III. Europe does not mean for us a chess-board of political or military action or a base of power but it has "la valeur d'une patrie" in the frame of which a healthy Germany in sound conditions of life is an indispensable factor.*

*IV. The purpose of a peace treaty ought to be a permanent pacification and restablishment of Europe on a solid base and a security against a renewal of warlike tendencies.*

*V. Condition, necessary for this result, is to leave the union of Austria and the Sudeten with the Reich out of any discussion. In the same way there would be excluded a renewed discussion of occidental frontier-questions of the Reich. On the other hand, the German-Polish frontier will have to be more or less identical with the German frontier of 1914.*

*VI. The treaty of peace and the reconstruction of Europe ought to be based on certain principles which will have to be universally accepted.*

*VII. Such principles are the following:*

*1. The principle of nationality with certain modifications deriving from history. Therefore*

*2. Restablishment of an independent Poland and of a Czech Republic.*

*3. General reductions of armament.*

*4. Restablishment of free international economical cooperation.*

*5. Recognition of certain leading ideas by all European states, such as:*

*a. The principles of Christian ethics.*

*b. Justice and law as fundamental elements of public life.*

*c. Social welfare as* leitmotiv.

*d. Effective control of the executive power of state by the people, adapted to the special character of every nation.*

*e. Liberty of thought, conscience, and intellectual activity.*

At the request of Goerdeler I undertook a trip to Berlin, *March 6–10, 1940.*

*Ebenhausen, March 11, 1940:* The strategic situation at the time of my departure was marked by the following new developments:

(1) Successes of the Russians in Finland. Passive and irresolute attitude of the Western Powers. In contrast, attempts of the Germans to mediate between Finland and Russia with the help of Sweden. A peace thus effected would mean a considerable success for Hitler.

(2) New tactics adopted by the English toward neutrals and against German trade and shipping; a deliberate underscoring of their determination to use every means to make English supremacy prevail on the seas and to enforce the principles of the blockade. All this partly in order to raise the morale of their own people, to intimidate the neutrals, and to demonstrate to Germany that the English are not doddering but are the heirs of Drake and Raleigh. For the same reason, the astounding, aggressive move against the *Altmark,* made within Norwegian territorial waters [February 16, 1940], motivated above all by the thought that British prestige could not allow four hundred English seamen to be transported from the La Plata to Europe.

(3) Growing recognition by our leaders that time is working against us; therefore, ever-stronger inclination to push the offensive.

Recently there have been added to Point 2 the operations of the English against Italian coal ships.[1] This action sprang from the conviction that Mussolini would not fight over this point, but, if he did, there would, perhaps, be advantages for England.

On the train I met Pietzsch and Seldte. The latter gave a most colorful account of his battles for economic reasons, ineffective though his efforts are. Pietzsch theorized a great deal, as usual, in the most beautiful Saxon dialect, but his vision is clear. Both were of one mind about the shocking economic confusion, caused by lack of real leadership. Both, however, are politically naïve.

Upon my arrival I called on Popitz first of all. He views the future with gloom. He still saw an offensive through neutral territory as very imminent. This would destroy every possibility of a favorable outcome of the war for a long time to come. Discussions of these matters with the military leaders—Halder, for example—are simply grotesque. They grasp the point, but insist that something can be done only when the offensive has got under way, which means after everything has been settled.

---

[1]As a result of the blockade (March 1, 1940) of German coal shipments via Rotterdam to Italy, then still neutral, Germany was obliged on March 13 to meet the coal requirements of the Italians by using land routes.

Meanwhile, the SS gains in power and its atrocities continue. The SS is the real cancer in our body politic and at the same time the backbone of the tyranny.

Goerdeler thinks the offensive is in the offing. He does not believe all the talk about it being mere bluff; neither do I, nor does Popitz. On the other hand, it is of course possible that for one reason or another Hitler will get cold feet at the last minute.

Goerdeler has talked with the King of the Belgians, who again assured him that definite opportunities for peace existed and that he was ready to be of assistance. But not with our present regime. I told Goerdeler about the Arosa discussions, whereupon he said he had been asked by some American in Switzerland to meet an agent of Daladier's. He was holding off this meeting, however, for the time being. At the moment the only thing to do was to exert all efforts to open the eyes of the military to the terrible danger.

From the observations of Goerdeler, Popitz, Kirk, Attolico, and others, the results of Sumner Welles's visit [March 1, 1940] appeared as follows:

On the surface all went smoothly. There were no hitches and he was politely received, contrary to Weizsäcker's expectations. His talk with Ribbentrop was not a success. Ribbentrop had made a psychological slip when he pictured Germany as desiring a kind of Monroe Doctrine for herself and her sphere of influence to the east and the southeast, exactly as America had done.

Hitler appears to have managed things more cleverly. He had presented Germany as being the victim of an attack and without war aims. Only the others had war aims; we wish only to be master in our own house.

At the conclusion of the talk Sumner Welles had said something like this: "Then your war aim is peace?" to which Hitler had offered no reply.

According to all reports, Hitler assumes that the sole purpose of Sumner Welles's visit was to prevent an offensive. Sumner Welles talked with Göring for three hours and twenty minutes. Göring emphasized Germany's power and the possibilities that lay before her. It is interesting that Sumner Welles suggested remaining in direct contact with Göring. His conversation with Hess was, of course, without significance.

Sumner Welles's talk with Schacht was most remarkable, if only because Hitler was forced to summon Schacht beforehand, thus contributing to Schacht's triumph. It was Sumner Welles who had asked for the interview.

Hitler gave Schacht instructions in line with his own conversation with Sumner Welles and, in doing so, had intimated that Sumner Welles only wanted to prevent an offensive. But from now on time was working against us! This is the first time Hitler has admitted this. Who knows where Stalin and Mussolini will be in a year's time? Hitler recently called all the Gauleiters together secretly and told them we must act. Our offensive would be such "that it would completely crush the enemy."

Schacht was much encouraged by the whole affair, especially because Sumner Welles had expressed the desire to remain in direct touch with him—which would mean a departure from official channels. Schacht told me he had said to his visitor that if the other powers did not want to deal with the regime they would have to say so plainly.

I told Schacht as well as Goerdeler about Arosa. Schacht reported Sumner Welles had emphasized that dismemberment of German national territory was by no means the intention of the United States. Asked whether he thought Sumner Welles's visit would have any result, Schacht said yes, if he, Schacht, were sent to America. But Ribbentrop would not consent.

Another interesting point from Schacht's report: he does not believe in the offensive. The prevention of the offensive he thinks is in Hitler's interest, paradoxical as it may sound. In view of its inevitably unsuccessful outcome, Hitler could be saved only if the offensive were not to take place!

On *March 7* I dined with Frank-Fahle at the Deutscher Club. As a businessman he appraises the situation very much as I do. It is typical of us Germans and of our odd ways that the next day Frank-Fahle sent me a long letter dealing with a philological question on Dante which we had only touched the day before. I showed it to Kirk, who remarked: "Yes, that is why you people accomplish so much."

On *Friday morning, the eighth,* I went early to see Schacht. He lauded the reserve he himself had maintained so far. Now he had indeed been summoned. Those Nazi upstarts could not long manage without help. "They finally have to summon people like you and me when the going gets hard." I do not see things quite in this light.

In the afternoon, tea with Frau von Brauchitsch. She thinks that her cousin will carry out the offensive. He had said we should have to seek a military decision. Later she called me up to correct what she had said: at heart he was uncertain and very troubled; if he could be relieved of the responsibility for taking action he would "tolerate" it.

Late in the afternoon I went to see Attolico. He looked wretched, and in his ornate green dressing gown he resembled the portrait of a sick Pope in a canopied bed. Fundamentally pessimistic. He is naturally absorbed in the question of whether or not Mussolini will receive a proper answer. He said that in his letter Mussolini had urged Hitler to make the gesture of creating an independent rump Poland, and do it on his own initiative.

Beethoven brought me a brief moment of exaltation above all these worries.

*Saturday, the ninth,* had luncheon with Kirk. He laid great emphasis on the courtesy with which Sumner Welles had been received and how well the whole thing had gone off. However, he did not seem to have much hope of concrete results. He had taken Sumner Welles (who, incidentally, knows German well) to an excellent performance of *The Marriage of Figaro.* It is to be hoped that this was not Welles's only good impression. One has only to read Halifax's speech to the students at Oxford to see how wide a chasm separates his world from that of the Nazis.

In the afternoon another long visit with Popitz at his home. He will try again to get to Brauchitsch. He reported that one of his higher officials had asked for leave of absence in order to take over the civil administration of Belgium. From Nostitz I learned that an entire staff under the direction of Posse is all set to go there too.

The Governor of Stettin had been ordered by the Ministry

of the Interior to move all Jews into the Jewish reservation in Poland. In order to be sure he made inquiry at the Ministry of the Interior and found they had no inkling of such an order. Heydrich had distributed the order on stationery bearing the heading "Ministry of the Interior." The order was canceled after all preparations had been made.

*March 15, 1940:* The peace concluded between Finland and Russia [March 13, 1940] means a loss of prestige for the Western Powers that will have repercussions throughout the world. According to various communications, it seems doubtful that we participated in the arrangement.

The common man in Germany and elsewhere in the world mistakenly regards this peace treaty as a step toward a general peace. He similarly interprets the meetings of Ribbentrop and Mussolini and Ribbentrop and the Pope, and is confirmed in his error by their apparent connection with the Sumner Welles mission.

On the anniversary of the occupation of Czechoslovakia Hacha sent Hitler a very carefully worded telegram. Neurath more than made up for Hacha's caution, and, one must say, in a most dishonorable way. He sent a telegram—no doubt dictated to him word for word—which far exceeds anything Neurath had hitherto perpetrated along this line. It contained a solemn promise of unswerving loyalty in the name of the entire population of the Protectorate!

*Berlin, March 19, 1940:* Left for Berlin on the *fifteenth*, evening. Stayed until the morning of the *twentieth*.

On the train Frau von Mendelssohn (née Bonin) told me a really good joke. Hitler and Göring are in a boat on the ocean.

Hitler: "Can they see us from the shore?"

Göring: "Yes."

Hitler: "Then row on."

Hitler: "Can we still be seen?"

Göring: "I think so."

Hitler: "Then let's go further! . . . Still in sight?"

Göring: "No, impossible!"

Hitler: "Then stop! I'll try to walk on the water."

In Berlin I went first to see Popitz. He said tension had increased at home. The question was now acute whether the Army will tolerate further disintegration and loss of power, and whether it is prepared to wreck all chances for peace by undertaking an offensive through neutral countries—an offensive whose outcome is highly questionable.

With the help of the Army High Command (Keitel and Jodl—"Jodl-Army"), that is, Hitler's personal supreme command, an independent second army is to be created out of the SS. Brauchitsch is being treated more and more badly and pushed into the background. Nothing definite has been done about the SS atrocities. Todt is to be Minister of Munitions.

Ley made a speech before the district propaganda chiefs in which he declared that the Army was good for nothing, that in Poland the SS had done everything. The Army, he said, simply was not schooled enough in the ways of National Socialism, but still clung to the principles of Christianity.

Popitz has now actually seen Brauchitsch and frankly described the situation and the necessity of wresting power from the talons of the black pirates (SS), cleansing the authority of the state, and stabilizing it on the basis of the Army as the sole armed force. B. listened to everything and said very little. Like Schwerin-Krosigk and others, he gave Popitz the impression of an inwardly broken man. One of the few times he interrupted was to ask whether we still had a chance of securing a decent peace. Popitz answered that as far as he could judge the possibility still existed.

Lunch with the Weizsäckers. He is alarmed because, on the occasion of Ribbentrop's visit to Rome (eighty pages of protocol), on March 10–11, Mussolini refrained from uttering a single word of protest against the offensive, but spoke of our "brotherhood in destiny" and of his intention to enter the conflict. He had, however, made reservations regarding the date of his action.

My explanation is this: Mussolini received the distinct impression that Hitler is determined to attack. This being so, he thinks it would be a tactical error to issue further warnings and now prefers to show himself sympathetic. If, contrary to expectation, things go well and if everything else looks favorable, he will come in on our side. Should matters go badly, he still has an alibi and can work out a way to extricate himself.

Many expected, however, that Mussolini would sound a warning yesterday [March 18] in the course of a tête-à-tête at the Brenner Pass. But it seems no real tête-à-tête developed, and the tone was the same as it had been in Rome. Mussolini, nevertheless, will certainly not burn his bridges, particularly not those leading to America. Mussolini, when he returns to Rome, will certainly not tell the true gist of the conversations to Sumner Welles, who had postponed his departure when he heard of the meeting at the Brenner. He will, instead, perhaps, urge him to attempt a quick mediation.

About noon to see Nostitz. So far as he knows the offensive is being prepared with great energy and will be directed toward Belgium and Holland as well as toward Denmark and Norway.

At the request of Oster and Dohnanyi he asked me to see Beck in the afternoon, which I did. I found him alone and discussed the situation with him thoroughly. Oster and Dohnanyi came in later; they read me some extraordinarily interesting documents covering the conversations of a Catholic intermediary with the Pope.[1] Following these conversations the Pope established contact with Halifax through Osborne [British envoy to the Vatican].

The Pope was apparently prepared to go to surprising lengths in his understanding of German interests. Halifax, who spoke definitely for the British Government, was much more cagey in formulating his statements and touched on points like "decentralization of Germany" and "a referendum in Austria." On the whole, the desire to make a decent peace is quite evident, and the Pope emphasized very strongly to the intermediary that such things as "decentralization" and "plebiscite in Austria" would certainly be no barriers to the peace if there was agreement on other points. The prerequisite for the whole

---

[1]These talks, arranged through the Pope for the purpose of laying a foundation for the discussion of peace terms after a change in the German regime, are generally referred to as Operation X. The confidential agent (x) is an attorney, Dr. Josef Müller. Even in the final report his name is not mentioned; this so-called X-report was meant to induce the generals to take action. For that reason it had to be formulated with an eye to the danger that it might fall into the wrong hands.

thing, naturally, is a change in the regime and an avowal of Christian morality.

The purpose of this talk with me was: (1) to hear my views on the foreign aspects of the problem; (2) to ask me to present the matter to Halder, because no other intermediary had much chance of success.

*Sunday, the seventeenth, at Potsdam:* Kameke, in his Christian-astrological certainty, was convinced that this time, too, the offensive would be prevented "from on high."

In the evening at the Chvalkovskys'. We had no more than exchanged a few words of greeting when he began to describe the events leading up to the fifteenth of March 1939 and the events of the day itself. He obviously is very agitated and filled with a burning desire to explain his conduct during that period. He was accurate and, it seemed to me, quite objective in his recital.

The position in which Hitler placed Hacha and Chvalkovsky as a reward for having supported a policy of co-operation with Germany was, to use one of Hitler's beloved expressions, "historically unique." It was a brutal action, dictated neither by political necessity nor by any farsighted considerations.

I afterward asked Chvalkovsky how he envisaged the future. In this connection it should, of course, be remembered that his future is mortgaged and that in the event of a German defeat he will be hanged. However, it was of interest to me that he thought things could be arranged very easily—one would need only to yield a point of honor. Czechoslovakia should regain the name and character of a formally independent state and should have a free hand in managing its domestic affairs. After that, it would without question fit itself, militarily and economically, into the realm of the Reich.

Chvalkovsky told two remarkable stories: A German detachment marching into Prague on March 15 had come to a bridge where a crowd of excited people had gathered. They insisted that they had rather be shot than give way, and proceeded to sing the Czech national anthem. Thereupon the German commanding officer ordered: "Halt! Attention! Pre-

sent arms!" By means of this decent as well as clever conduct
he persuaded the crowd to disperse.

The other story: Foreign Minister Chvalkovsky went walking in Prague one evening with his wife. As usual they spoke
French, since she is not a Czech. Suddenly a student came up
and spat at them. So great was the hatred against the French
and English because of their betrayal of Czechoslovakia.

*Monday, March 18, 1940:* With Dohnanyi at Oster's home;
we again discussed the matter of informing Halder of the
Pope's action.

Lunched with Goerdeler. He said that at the last minute
Halder had refused to see him. But that did not matter, as he
had received from another source the assurance that under-
standing was growing in that quarter. Among other things
Halder now wanted to see me, but as a preliminary move
Thomas has asked me to call on him tomorrow morning.
Goerdeler was so insistent that I decided to postpone my de-
parture.

On *March 19, 1940,* in the morning, I had a very important
conversation with Thomas.

My points: an offensive through neutral territory can in no
event be beneficial to Germany. Victory, defeat, stalemate—all
will cause a terrible destruction of moral and material values
in Europe. Above all the destruction of all chances of a sensible
and durable peace. Such a peace, I urged, must be our only
aim.

Are there any prospects of a tolerable peace?

Yes, although of course no one can give absolute guarantees.
We could be certain of only one thing, that after an offensive
the chances for peace would be gone. Therefore we must fight
against the offensive and strive for peace.

There are two prerequisites: a Germany that is intact, and,
above all, an intact Army so that our enemies would run a considerable risk if they persisted in continuing the war. Unfortunately disintegration was already in process, militarily
(second SS army) as well as morally (SS atrocities in Poland).
It was high time to call a halt. How about the conscience of the

soldiers? All doubts must stop at the point where the Army itself is threatened with destruction.

Possibilities of negotiation?

After March 15, 1939 (occupation of Czechoslovakia), and other events (atrocities in Poland), the regime ceased to be a fit partner for international negotiations. But a change of regime was a domestic German affair. Any such demand from a foreign source must be rejected. It is possible to get peace only if there is a change of regime. Is peace possible? There is no guarantee; but there are definite indications.

Thomas agreed with me entirely and described the dreadful conditions in his sphere of activity. Halder wanted to talk with me; the date was fixed for after Easter. I gathered from this discussion that Goerdeler saw Halder after all, but that the latter wished to pretend he had not.

*Ebenhausen, March 22, 1940:* Detalmo, in Italy, sends news that his friend [Mr. X] cannot come to Arosa for the moment (or for ever?).

I saw Gessler yesterday. He has been to Switzerland on what appeared to be a similar mission. He mentioned so many of the same things that I assumed he knew about the same events. In the course of the discussion he urged very strongly a re-establishment of the monarchy (the old democrat!), but opined that the Hohenzollerns would be unacceptable for southern Germany. I had the impression that he was very keen on Crown Prince Rupprecht as Emperor.

*March 24, 1940. Easter:* I've been reading about a conversation that took place between Moltke, Bismarck, and Roon after 1870. Bismarck expressed the opinion that after such tremendous events life held little that was worth while. Whereupon Moltke remarked dryly: "We can still watch a tree grow."

*March 27, 1940:* After a short glimpse of spring it is snowing again as if it were the middle of winter. Spring planting as well as the offensive must wait.

After the Finnish peace, the partially successful aerial attack at Scapa Flow, and the insignificant results of the counterblow against Sylt, one gets the impression that the Western Powers are somewhat confused—the more so since information that has leaked out about the Brenner conference indicates that Mussolini did not play the pipes of peace—far from it! At present the psychological situation is so very unfavorable for the Allies that one might well expect Mussolini to show an increased readiness to step in on the German side at a propitious moment in order to be in at the kill. To bring this about, however, a conspicuous German success must be achieved. Can this be done? The military are doubtful.

Our neighbor [Geyr von Schweppenberg], commanding general of a tank corps, told us about the Polish campaign. He did not think much of the higher Polish leaders, but thought that their problem had been insoluble in view of the general situation. He praised the officers and soldiers. They had gone down honorably. One example: after a number of mines had exploded along the line of march, he had summoned a prisoner, an officer of Engineers, to tell him where the rest of the mines lay. Answer, delivered with a soldierly bearing: "Herr General, I am an officer."

He said the difference between the Poles and the Czechs was tremendous. Geyr thought that even if the Czech Government was unable to do anything it was incomprehensible that not one military leader had offered resistance at some point. I pointed to the sociological differences between the two peoples: the Poles, a nation made up of an aristocratic and a lower class with a weak middle class that had developed very late; hence proud and bellicose. The Czechs, a nation of middle-class people who are awkwardly surrounded and penetrated by Germanic influence. Now the Poles and the Czechs have been presented with the prize question: who will come out ahead in the long run? Those who fought bravely to defeat and now have a terribly devastated country, or the cowards who gave themselves up and whose economy and populations are largely intact?

Geyr said the personnel policy of the Army indicated a tendency to put independent and self-reliant souls in cold storage, or at least to place them in unimportant posts. This was true, for instance, of most of the commanders of tank divisions, who had been superseded by insignificant troopers. In like manner, Manstein was removed from his post as chief of staff of an army group and given command of a corps at a place which surely will not figure in the offensive. The same had happened to Geyr himself. Leeb and Witzleben likewise were intentionally placed at the southern wing of the front. He thought, incidentally, that Witzleben entertained extraordinarily radical views about the regime. Low opinion of the character of Guderian.

*Ebenhausen, April 6, 1940:* Trip to Berlin. Left on the *evening of the second,* returned *April 5.*

My uneasiness [over lack of news from Berlin] grew into certainty after a telephone call from Reuter to the effect that "something had gone wrong." I arranged a meeting with Goerdeler by letter.

Soon after my arrival in Berlin, Goerdeler came to see me and confirmed my suspicion that Halder had got cold feet. He showed me a letter in which Halder refused for the time being( ! ) to take action for very naïve reasons. (England and France had declared war on us, and one had to see it through. A peace of compromise was senseless. Only in the greatest emergency [come, now!] could one take the action desired by Goerdeler.) Halder, who had begun to weep during the discussion of his responsibility, gave the impression of a weak man with shattered nerves.

Furthermore, it seems too late now for anything, for, according to Goerdeler's information, action against Denmark and Norway is imminent. Goerdeler had the impression that Halder had talked to his chief, Brauchitsch, and that both had agreed to give an unfavorable reply, i.e., to yield to Hitler.

In the forenoon I also saw Wilmowsky, who was very much impressed by the rapid decline in our export trade; we could sell enormous quantities, especially in the southeast, but could not deliver, and with the decrease in exports the import of necessary raw materials, et cetera, must inevitably decline. He said that his brother-in-law, Krupp, had spent two and a half hours with Hitler. But Hitler had not said a word about the economic situation; he had spoken only about production of arms. He (Hitler) is becoming more and more of a universal genius—at least in his own opinion!

The general assault on the Army continues. The SS is organizing its own aviation (which will please Göring!). Todt has become Minister of Munitions [March 20].

In the afternoon at the Weizsäckers'. She looked pale and thin, and he seemed very much run down. His position is hideous in every respect. He really has nothing to say, but is held accountable nevertheless. The Swedish Minister has been to see him to inquire about an allegedly imminent action against Scandinavia. His answer was that he could tell him nothing, inasmuch as he received no information on military matters. The Swede must have done his share of thinking. The Swedish Military Attaché also indicated to our Military Attaché that the northern countries are expecting a German attack.

I cannot conceive that the English are neglecting to make their calculations accordingly. If, in spite of this, they permit the action to succeed, they deserve to be conquered. Weizsäcker was very unhappy about Mussolini, who "apparently has also gone insane."

I met Oster and Dohnanyi at Oster's house. They reported that the attack in the north had been ordered for the morning of April 9. Since, in addition to airplanes (paratroop divisions), troops are to be transported by boat and put into action, the enterprise must be under way already.

They then showed me further notes of Dr. Josef Müller, from which it would appear that the Pope and the English hold fast to their viewpoint. We discussed, without coming to a conclusion, whether Gessler's information had to do with this or with some unrelated action. It is still doubtful to me how my transactions with my conferee in Arosa fit into the picture. Did he fail to come again because Halifax "gives up," or because the man had no authority, or because Halifax does not want to proceed along several lines at the same time?

From Müller's notes it is further apparent that the discussions between the Pope and Ribbentrop were entirely fruitless because the latter had held forth in his Party jargon. We then considered whether anything further could be done. First of all, in view of Halder's refusal to see me, Thomas himself was to have taken the matter to Halder day before yesterday.

We further decided that Oster should at once send an intermediary to Falkenhausen[1] in Dresden to make a canvass of various army leaders, including Leeb, Witzleben, List, Kluge. He is to persuade them to join him in making a personal and energetic approach to Brauchitsch for the purpose of moving him either to do something himself or to permit others to take action.

I see hardly a chance now. There might be another opportunity, however, after the Scandinavian attack is over or is ebbing, and before the attack on Belgium and Holland has been launched. We may expect the second offensive to follow the first very quickly.

Popitz is disappointed that his visit with Brauchitsch was apparently fruitless. Everything we had tried to do was of no avail and at best could only relieve our own consciences. At nine o'clock I visited Beck, and found Goerdeler there too. We were not in a happy frame of mind and felt the menace of an inescapable fate. Goerdeler read a memorandum which he wants to use in connection with the Falkenhausen mission.

On the *fourth* I had Wolf von Tirpitz to breakfast. He could not imagine that the northern invasion would succeed, especially in its naval aspects. As one who knows Norway well, Weizsäcker had already told me that those who had initiated this campaign had no idea of the geographical conditions up there, especially the vast distances and barren nature of the far northern part of Norway, where hardly anything grows.

*Arosa, April 15, 1940:* Left for Arosa on *April 10.* The world is shocked by the occupation of Denmark and the Norwegian harbors (April 9, 1940). I cannot understand how the English managed to be taken by surprise again.

German leadership brilliant; but the whole project is politically—and in the eyes of all prudent people—an insane undertaking from the military point of view. Will it finally open the eyes of the generals?

[1]This messenger was Lieutenant Colonel Groscurth.

As a result of unexpectedly strong resistance by the Norwegians, our military strength, particularly our air power, has been so heavily engaged that there is a certain chance of a postponement or abandonment of the Holland-Belgium offensive. Our generals would thus have yet another opportunity to act in advance. To be sure, with a nature like Hitler's, the unsatisfactory progress in Norway might well lead to abrupt and quite insane decisions.

Hatred for the Germans has reached the peak in Switzerland. And that despite the fact the English played into the hands of our propaganda again, because the public really believed in the beginning that our action was in answer to the laying of English mines and the attendant publicity.

I received a telephone message from Detalmo that his English friend was to be here yesterday.

Mr. X reported that he had given my notes to Halifax who, allegedly without mentioning my name, had shown them to Chamberlain. According to X's account, Cadogan has also been informed, though without knowing about me or the details.

Halifax told Mr. X that he was most grateful for the communication, valued it highly, and was in complete agreement with the principles set forth. He could not give a written assurance, such as Mr. X had suggested, because he had already done so through another channel just a week before.

Mr. X intimated that his people were very skeptical about the chances of arranging anything like this. In addition, he freely admitted that they were slow and difficult to move. He (Mr. X) was therefore much worried as to whether this "other channel" was a good one. I replied that as far as the "other channel" was concerned, I could not be completely sure what it was all about, but that I assumed it concerned a serious action known to me, and one which on our side had reached the same group with which I was in contact. If my assumption was correct, I could only heartily welcome Mr. X's information as a kind of confirmation. Above all, however, it was important to know whether, after recent events, London would continue to maintain this position; that is to say whether it still wished to arrive at a decent peace with a respectable national Germany, which would employ other political methods than those used by the present regime.

Mr. X answered in the affirmative, although the battles now raging in the north naturally absorbed all attention and pushed the interest in political negotiations into the background.

Mr. X was obviously relieved that I seemed to know about the "other channel." He had said to himself: either I would know about it, in which case there was something to it, or I would not, which would indicate that it was a false lead.

We next discussed what there was still to do. I referred him to Rome which, then as now, was a focal point. The Western Powers, however, should be under no illusion that Mussolini is closer to joining forces with our side today than at the time of our last meeting. Mr. X declared he would attempt to make his way to Mussolini and to the Pope, that is to say Maglione, [the Papal Secretary of State]. I indicated that I saw little promise in the former, much more in the latter.

This morning I took another walk with Mr. X. I gained the impression that Halifax and his group had no real faith in the possibility of attaining peace in this way, that is, through a change of regime in Germany. But Mr. X affirmed again that Halifax's viewpoint had undergone no essential change.

We talked at length about Mussolini's attitude. I emphasized that Mussolini might very possibly consider participation in the war on our side as the only way out. Of course he might again waver in his attitude, should things go wrong for Hitler in Norway.

Mr. X again and again raised the question of what Hitler thought he could gain from the destruction of the British Empire. Such an outcome would have the same effect as the destruction of Germany. It would only bring injury to all Europe and to the white race. Mr. X evidenced great pessimism as to domestic affairs in England in the event of a long war; victory or defeat alike would bring great and revolutionary changes.

*Ebenhausen, April 29, 1940:* Trip to Berlin, from *Sunday evening, April 21,* to the *morning of April 27, 1940.*
In Berlin I first familiarized myself with the situation by

talking to Popitz and Nostitz. Principal indications: deep pessimism because of the attitude of the generals, who are becoming increasingly resigned to Hitler's plans. There was even a certain ambition among the army leaders to win fame for themselves, after the previous undertakings of the High Command had met with only partial success.

According to unanimous reports Hitler is very angry over the course of political events in Norway. He holds Habicht and Breuer (who has since been placed on the reserve list) accountable for the Norwegian resistance because they relied strongly on Quisling and insisted on him as against King Haakon. According to a reliable source, Hitler is reported to have said, absurdly enough, the north did not interest him and that the generals could finish that business.

As for the attack through Belgium and Holland, the bulletins are changing continually. The latest information is to the effect that it has now really been decided upon.

Principal cause of anxiety: "What will the Italians do?" Mackensen upholds the view that they will soon enter the war. The Naval Attaché takes the opposite position, as I learned from Oster. Mackensen denies that Ciano is working against participation. Other sources say Ciano is actively opposed to it; there are even rumors that he is about to be kicked out. It is certain that the Throne, some of the generals, the Church, and the people are in opposition. I personally believe that Mussolini has not yet made his decision. The great noise in the press is no sure indication.

It is still difficult to prophesy future developments in Norway. It is certain that the German fleet is in a bad way. At the moment not one large ship is really seaworthy, and only two or three of the cruisers. Moreover, Narvik is theoretically lost; the evacuation was ordered once before, I am told, but was postponed because the English are proceeding with remarkable timidity.

In general the campaign of the Allies is not impressive, although they have landed at many points, including some important ones. South of Trondheim they appear to have advanced carelessly and too hurriedly. On the other hand, it is difficult to understand how we can gain a really decisive success there.

As for ore, the situation looks bad. For that reason the political struggle is at the moment concentrated on Sweden.
Economically, the occupation of Denmark and Norway is a
burden for us, all things considered. To be sure it also has very
serious consequences for England (timber!). On the whole
we are one step farther along the road toward the destruction
of Europe.

In Norway it appears that the Nazis intend to rule with the
usual iron fist. Hence the despatching of Gauleiter Terboven
with two SS battalions and of SS Group Leader Weissmüller,
a tyrant who "won his spurs" in Prague.

On the domestic front a very ominous sign: the dismissal of
Josef Wagner, the rather sensible Gauleiter and Price Commissioner.

The quality of the Party bosses is clearly demonstrated by
the fate of Streicher, whose fall has finally been accomplished
after years of the most beastly activities.

In the afternoon I had a visit with Weizsäcker—very depressed and with no hope of a change. I told him I had received confirmation of the English attitude from my visitor in
Arosa. Weizsäcker thought the English should not always insist
that their goal was the destruction of Germany. On the other
hand, Weizsäker did not fully agree with my view that the
enemy powers should make no demands of a domestic nature,
but should leave this up to us! He saw no objection to Allied
insistence that there can be no peace with Ribbentrop.

Late in the afternoon I went to see Beck. For the past fortnight he has had no real connection with our group and had
therefore concluded that all opportunities were blocked. It is
true that the attempt to set Falkenhausen in motion came to
nothing, because Falkenhausen first spoke with Thomas, who
felt that it was useless to try anything in the present situation.
We must let events run their fateful course. I agreed with Beck
(as with Popitz and Goerdeler) that we should continue to
hammer away at the generals, despite the extremely poor
prospects of the moment. I called on Thomas and maintained
the same point of view, but he was without hope since the
documents he had presented Halder had had no effect.

On *Thursday afternoon* [April 25], my address. Afterward a

stag dinner. Long conversation with Fromm, General of Artillery, and chief of the "Home Army," who made a soldierly impression but is something of a stuffed shirt. He was always considered very reasonable and clear-sighted, but has now apparently been touched by war fever. "We will push through Holland and Belgium at one blow, and then finish off France in fourteen days; the French will run like the Poles. France will then make peace, England will fight on alone for a while but will finally give up too. Then the Führer will make a very moderate, statesmanlike peace."

I stated that I could say nothing on the score of military prospects, but that I had other views about Hitler's peace plans.

Before noon on Friday the good Courten visited me. Invited to lunch by Keudell at the Continental along with Kameke, Wolf, and "Schweineschmid." Keudell is a peculiarly confused man. He signs his letters to me with "Heil Hitler" and then invites himself to such a meeting of the opposition. Schmid is fed up to the gills with the Party, which he has closely observed at work. He no longer has hope in the generals, either. Kameke keeps trusting that God will not permit an offensive through Belgium and Holland to take place. He maintains that he has talked with someone who actually saw Himmler in a hospital with an injured lower jaw and a wounded leg. Just who gave him this information is doubtful.

*Trip to Arosa and Zürich, May 10–17, 1940:* The invasion of Holland and Belgium which, in spite of Kameke, took place on May 10, 1940, made my intended trip to Spain impossible for the moment, for the entrance of Italy into the war had to be taken into account, and all Swiss entry visas became invalid. But Dr. Ritter, the Swiss Consul General in Munich, at my request arranged with Berlin and Berne shortly before my projected departure on Saturday, the *eleventh,* that my diplomatic visa should remain valid. Thus, although my companion could not travel, I went alone to Switzerland on the first lap of my journey.

The president of the railroad administration in Munich informed me by telephone that the frontier was not yet closed, but that of course it might be at any minute; if he were in my place he would risk it. Very considerately he sent a man to the station to tell me the Swiss State Railroads had just telegraphed they had found it necessary for the present to discontinue international express service, but that freight would still be accepted. Nevertheless, I decided to go on.

At the border German officials were skeptical and said all German travelers were being sent back by the Swiss. But I was not to be deterred. The passport officials at St. Margrethen were at first inclined not to honor my visa, although a fellow passenger, Miss Tobler, secretary at the Swiss Consulate General in Munich intervened heroically for me. Finally they called the police department in St. Gallen and, happily, received a favorable decision.

I telephoned Ilse in Arosa so that in the absence of other means of transportation she could pick me up by car in Chur late in the evening. For this purpose I had to have the help of the military border patrol, whose leader, a corporal or sergeant, was exceedingly friendly and carried on a lengthy conversation about the war. He was amazingly moderate in his views. In general, however, a genuine panic has seized Switzerland. One gains the impression of a highly mobilized, yes, even belligerent country—much more so than in Germany itself!

Everywhere one fairly trips over troops. Aliens have had to turn over all weapons, and even old Frau H. had to surrender her tiny pistol. There is talk of interning the Germans, and the good burghers of Zürich, Basel, are taking their wives and children to the mountains. Their great fears are parachute troops and the Fifth Column. In Zürich one sees barbwire barriers, and road blocks, before public buildings and on bridges. They are also afraid of Mussolini. But above all, of course, they fear us, and with a burning hatred.

*Berlin, May 24–27, 1940:* An entirely new situation has been created through the unbelievably great successes of the Germans in the west. The vastly superior tank and air forces, together with other modern weapons, the morale of the troops (nothing succeeds like success), and excellent leadership, along with criminal negligence and bad leadership on the other side —all these things add up to something new. The skepticism of most of the generals, above all Beck's, is proved wrong; the swaggering Fromm has been proved right. The credit due Hitler and Göring for producing these weapons and Hitler's personal success in directing the campaign are undeniable facts.

Göring, who was fundamentally opposed to the offensive as he had been opposed to the war, saved his skin by a speech in which he praised the "strategical genius" of the Führer.

The Army fights anonymously as far as its leadership goes. One can clearly see what this will lead to: the destruction of everything that remains of the old tradition.

But that is only a partial picture. One must now reckon with a new structure for Europe, in Hitler's image, achieved through a peace supporting his wide aims. They are already preparing to wipe out the peace of Westphalia at Münster and Osnabrück; but it remains an open question whether, as now appears likely, the accent will lie on the complete emasculation of France, accompanied by a certain toleration of England overseas, or whether the main effort will, after all, be applied to the destruction of the British Empire.

Domestically, the new forms will become evident through the ascendancy of Hitler's brand of socialism, the destruction of the upper class, the transformation of the churches into meaningless sects, et cetera.

Since National Socialism, as it has now developed, is completely soulless, its intrinsic creed being power, we shall get a godless nature, a dehumanized, cultureless Germany, and perhaps a Europe, conscienceless and brutal.

Weizsäcker thought there was some consolation in the knowledge that very often in history great transformations have been wrought by criminals. I did not contest this, of course, but did reply that all this was bearable only if the "agents of Fate" are capable of carrying out forward-looking ideas. In our present case I simply cannot believe it possible. Whatever there is, or was, of progressive thoughts in National Socialism has now been blotted out by its destructive aspects.

At the dinner of the MWT [Central European Economic Association] I sat next to an economic adviser at the Reich Chancery [Willuhn], who, to my astonishment, expressed similar concern. He deplored the destruction of three things: faith, character, and discipline! Instead of "discipline" I would say "all scruples." The worst is, perhaps, the frightful devastation wrought on German character, which often enough has shown a tendency to servility.

*May 29, 1940:* The Allied position in Flanders has been lost with the capitulation of the Belgians [May 28, 1940], unless Weygand is able to manage a break-through in some most improbable way. The crux of the matter then will be whether the Allies are able, militarily and spiritually, to hold out until time itself weighs in the balance against us.

Will America recognize her own interest in this Anglo-French affair and join with them before it is too late? It is indeed doubtful; perhaps they already look upon the effort of the Western Powers as a lost cause and a bad investment.

Russia is an unknown quantity because a German hegemony must seem threatening to her. Yet she has neither the offensive power nor the courage to tackle us as long as we are intact. Rather, she might take action against Rumania—an unpleasant event for us in any case.

In Italy official and inspired voices shriek wildly for war, despite the opposing sentiments of the Throne, the Vatican, and popular opinion. Mussolini has two objectives: one, realistic and imperial; another, psychological, aimed at vindicating Italian military prestige. For the latter it is almost too late; his attitude is that of a hyena. But this makes the first objective even more pressing. The Spaniards, too, are shouting for Gibraltar. The capitulation of Leopold III may free the throne of some of its inhibitions, but the real problem even for Italy is whether Germany isn't getting too strong. How can this problem be met? By getting together as much as possible from the legacy of the English-French Empire? Or by a private war in the Balkans to protect that area from a German monopoly? Or by refraining from doing anything for the time being?

Alfieri, who, it seems, has replaced the lukewarm Attolico at the express wish of the Germans, says in Berlin that action will begin very soon. Donna Carlotta acts in a very warlike manner too.

Among the upper strata in Berlin I found some who were indulging in unrestrained triumph, accompanied by plans for dividing up the world in great style. Others were thrown into the deepest despair because now we would have to count on the unrestrained tyranny of the Party for a long time to come. Among the people in general there was, to be sure, joy over the victories which they thought would bring peace nearer, but at the same time there was an astonishing apathy. The demoralization of the Germans has never before shown up so clearly. No one, of course, puts out his flags spontaneously; all wait for orders.

I am of the opinion that, however discouraging the prospects are for the present, we must not throw in the sponge; we must prepare to fight on against Hitler under changed conditions. Just after victory great tensions will inevitably develop in this gigantic Reich which may provide the possibility and the necessity for taking action.

Weizsäcker said he had to stay in office; he had not contributed to the victory, and really had nothing to do with it. I wonder, however, whether he should not have resigned at the time of the invasion of Holland and Belgium.

Davignon[1] is said to have given Ribbentrop a piece of his mind: every word in the memorandum was a lie and he, Ribbentrop, did not even believe it himself.

*Berlin, Friday, May 24, 1940:* Talked with Goerdeler in the morning. He was naturally very shaken but doesn't give up the battle. He is still fooling himself a bit.

At midday I went to see Nostitz, who has had a quarrel with Ribbentrop and was to be kicked out. In the end he emerged from the episode completely justified, but anyway is to go to Geneva to take Kessel's place. Kessel will take Nostitz's place. Kessel, with whom I had dinner, is completely resigned and wants to study archaeology. I tried to cheer him up.

Afternoon tea at Popitz's with Beck and Goerdeler. Beck is puzzled by the negligence and bad leadership of the English

[1]Davignon, Belgian Ambassador in Berlin. Reference is to a memorandum handed to him by Ribbentrop on May 10 to justify Nazi invasion of Belgium.

and French. He believes, however, that they may still pull themselves together.

*Saturday, May the twenty-fifth.* Lunch with Oster, Dohn-anyi, and Guttenberg at Kroll's. I tried to buck up their badly shattered spirits. The very soldiers, who used to be skeptical, are now in an uncomfortable situation.

Toward evening I went to see Kirk. He is completely crushed and without hope. He thought America was drawing nearer and nearer to war.

*Sunday, the twenty-sixth,* attended service at the cathedral. Doehring preached well. Large congregation. Very many men, young ones, too, and many soldiers. The congregation was earnest and composed—a favorable sign.

Luncheon at the Schuberts' (the former Ambassador); coffee at the Pecoris'. Signora Pecori left in the evening for Rome. Pecori said the naval leaders had pointed out to Hitler the heavy losses to be expected in the Norwegian campaign, to which he replied: "It is worth it."

Among our adversaries, Pecori said, the Belgians fought best. Pecori drove me in his car to Wolf T., where I had tea and admired his marvelous poultry runs.

Later Sell came in [Freiherr von Sell, until recently in Doorn]. He told us of Prince Wilhelm's death in battle. From the standpoint of the Hohenzollern family the brave death of the eldest grandchild of the Kaiser is a helpful factor, if one may still think in those terms. And there will be one complication the less in the family. According to Sell, the Kaiser con-ducted himself in Doorn with dignity and courage. He refused all offers of the Dutch and English royal families. He would stay where he was; he had once before been accused of running away!

The German High Command had forbidden officers to pay calls on him. But a Lieutenant von Braunschweig, who with eighteen men had Sunday guard duty at Doorn, asked—in the name of his men—for permission to participate in divine wor-ship. He stayed on even after Dommes (aide-de-camp to the Kaiser) had pointed out to him that he might get himself into difficulties. After the service the Kaiser spoke to the soldiers and said something to the effect that it made him happy to see

German soldiers; they had accomplished tremendous things and borne many hardships and would continue to do so; they must, however, always remember that both came from God.

Sell reported further that letters from the Scandinavian states breathed bitter hatred.

*June 24, 1940, Ebenhausen:* I was in Arosa *from Monday the tenth* until *Sunday the sixteenth.* Traveled by car as far as St. Margrethen with Nostitz, who has been transferred to Geneva. During his first "neutral" night in Geneva English bombs fell on his hotel. Dead and wounded only fifty yards from him!

I found Wolf-Ulli really improved, thank God, although still weak. I cannot foresee further developments, but we can really begin to hope. Ilse is a magnificent nurse, better than words can say, and is admired by all. In spite of being incredibly occupied she found time to prepare, with passionate eagerness, a very effective little essay for ——— to combat his tendency to take a more favorable view of Hitler after his military successes.

Goethe, in *Poetry and Truth,* Book 20, gave us the best possible characterization of the devilish powers that disturb the moral order of the world.

Y, who had been so critical after the invasion of Belgium and Holland, I now found completely shaken by our tremendous military successes. He expressed no political opinions. Z, on the other hand, was inclined to believe, on religious grounds, that a man who achieves such success must be a man of God.

I am indeed convinced that Hitler, and Göring too in a somewhat different way, made a decisive contribution to these successes; yet the accomplishments of the military leadership, the inherited qualities of the old army, and the achievements of individuals, from Gessler and Seeckt to Beck and Fritsch, have been shamelessly suppressed. Nobody can contest the proportions of the success achieved by Hitler. But that does not alter the real nature of his deeds or the cruel dangers now threatening all our higher standards. A demoniac Spartacus will wreak nothing but destruction if the opposition does not act in time.

It is tragic not to be able to rejoice over such achievements. The masses of the people take everything with an astonishingly stolid indifference; deafened, I suppose, by seven years of listening to loud-speakers.

On the *evening of June 18* I traveled to Berlin. Politically I found the city in a "between-the-battles" state of mind: in foreign affairs, the repercussions of the French capitulation are not yet clear [June 17, 1940]; on the domestic front, we are all agreed that at the moment there is nothing we can do; but we are agreed that immediately after victory there will be new opportunities and obligations to fight on against the regime.

Schacht, as well as Goerdeler, is very pessimistic as to what will happen if England should continue the conflict (which is generally expected). They think great economic difficulties will inevitably arise after a few months. That is probably true, but I do not believe such difficulties will soon be great enough to endanger the German position (and that would be necessary), particularly since, for that very reason, England would be fiercely attacked.

The military, incidentally, apparently think it will be extremely difficult to make a landing.

America still represents an X in the equation, although military intervention appears unlikely for a long time. That England, America, and Russia might get together is now conceivable, but not yet a reality. However, the Russian advance in the Baltic area is an indication of how they look upon the tremendous increase of German power.

The Italians, with their declaration of war [June 11, 1940], not followed up by deeds, do not play a very brilliant role. Their sole accomplishment to date is a defeat by the English on the Libyan frontier. However, if Mussolini were able to reap the whole harvest without shedding Italian blood he would be the great man in the sense of the classical slogan: *Italia fara da se* (Italy does it alone).

*Ebenhausen, August 10, 1940:* As I am concerned with the question of the reconstruction of economic relations with the southeast, with special emphasis on the reconciliation of German-Italian interests, I have been having innumerable conversations on general and special subjects. Funk was reasonable. At a luncheon at Alfieri's he drank my health resoundingly: "To our old friendship."

After all I experienced in Rome it is really tragicomic that I should again be concerned with the psychologically correct treatment of the Italians and regard for their interests.

I am in frequent touch with the Balkan Ministers. Andric, the Yugoslav, a poet of some standing, is a pleasant, intelligent man. Draganoff, the Bulgarian (a former officer), and Romalo, the Rumanian (a businessman), are also remarkable people. My work continues to develop step by step because the situation in the southeast is still quite uncertain, in view of the disagreement between Rumania and Hungary, Russian pressure, and the domestic uncertainty in Yugoslavia (particularly the Croatian matter). The intentions of Italy in this territory are also highly conjectural.

Until recently peace feelers have been sent out by the National Socialists to England through various neutral countries. These talks, however, never seem to have progressed beyond vague declarations. Through Oster I learned about the latest attempt of this kind, with Carl Burckhardt and Paravicini (Swiss Minister to London) mediating between Kelly (British Minister in Bern) and Hohenlohe of Rotenhaus at the beginning of July. Kelly immediately raised the question as to whom Hohenlohe represented, which was tantamount to his hinting at the possibility of a change of regime in Germany. Hohenlohe naturally did not fall for this.

In London the Duke of Alba is working zealously to keep Spain out of the war with the implication that Spain may get Gibraltar by peaceful means.

Among other items of information furnished by Oster this one is interesting: Huntziger has offered to undertake an offensive against Mosul with the Syrian Army, working with the Axis. German reaction was sour, as there was no desire to give France a trump card for the peace treaty.

In North Africa, according to reliable information, a highly fluid situation seems to have developed in the French colonies; in other words, there is some doubt as to whether the people there will obey Pétain. Meanwhile, Italy, numerically superior, is preparing an attack toward Egypt, though she had recently declared again that she was not yet ready.

Our people, at Hitler's command, are making preparations for the landing in England—"in case it should become necessary." However, the Navy will not be ready before September 15, and then we will have unfavorable flying weather. The order is a superficial and in part a childishly amateurish document. After perusing it I was left speechless. This is definite evidence that, apart from the excellence of the Army, luck must play a great role in Hitler's successes.

It is characteristic of his whole mentality that he already has his eyes fixed on an attack on Russia for the spring of 1941, in case he should not be completely successful against England. No wonder, therefore, that a Russian-English-Turkish understanding is being worked out in feverish haste, especially with respect to the Straits. So far the plan has not met with success; but it is remarkable how little inclination Turkey is showing to play ball with us.

I had a talk recently with Matschoss, the well-known engineer, about conditions in Russia, where he had just been. The last time he had been in Moscow was in 1929 (about the time of our trip to Petersburg). At that time his impressions were very gloomy. Now he was overwhelmed by the difference: marvelous city planning; splendid, spacious public squares; clean streets; the great majority of the people clean and dressed decently; happy faces, laughter, and music. For the fun of it he had sat in a café and counted the people whom the doorkeeper at the Adlon Hotel would probably have turned away. They were not more than one fourth. Of course behind this Moscow façade there is still much misery, dirt, and unhappiness, but the progress, he says, is extraordinary.

This parable was told at the same luncheon as to the possibility of doing business with the Soviets. "An industrialist was dickering with a Negro chieftain about a railway concession. Everything was arranged satisfactorily, when suddenly the chieftain belched loudly and said, 'Pardon me, but yesterday I feasted on my grandmother!' In such a situation should one break off negotiations, or, rather, say, 'I hope she agrees with you, Chief!'"

Negotiations between the Rumanians and the Bulgarians are going along very well in the southeast.[1] The Bulgarians had inquired in Berlin where the line ran between Germany and Russia down there. The German answer: "Russian interests end at the Prut!" had delighted the good people of Sofia very much. *Pourvu que cela dure.* So far no bridge between Hungary and Rumania.

Hitler wrote a very urgent letter to Carol admonishing him to come to an agreement. Maniu works with all his might for concessions to Bulgaria and absolute resistance to Hungary. The situation is very uncomfortable for Berlin. Hitler shudders at the prospect of having to act as umpire but offers border guarantees in case of immediate agreement.

It is evident from Oster's reports how terrible conditions are in the Government General of Cracow; unparalleled destruction and distress.

Oster knew this much about Hitler's peace conditions: German terms at the moment, Alsace-Lorraine, Briey, Malmédy, et cetera; Norwegian ports on the Atlantic; our old colonies; the Belgian Congo; the Moroccan ports on the Atlantic (otherwise French Morocco to Spain). Italian terms: Nice, Corsica, Tunisia, Algeria, Djibouti, British Somaliland, a land connection between Ethiopia and Libya, neutralization of the Straits of Gibraltar, alliance with Egypt.

Three days ago I had a long conversation with Goerdeler's friend Gisevius. He said that Goerdeler, after all other hopes had vanished, was arguing purely on a moral basis: such an immoral system could not last. This argument Gisevius and I dismissed as historically untenable. Nevertheless, as Gisevius sees it, moral principles, as well as religious convictions, which are steadily gaining in strength, are of great importance in our preparations for a change of regime. Gisevius no longer expects anything from the highest generals; they are being fattened on titles, decorations, and gifts. But in somewhat lower ranks resistance was probably developing against the whole horror, particularly against the SS.

*September 22, 1940:* Intensive activity at the MWT. A good platform for me, very effective, and a good cloak. I am gradu-

[1] On July 23, 1940, Rumania ceded the southern Dobruja to Bulgaria.

ally getting my bearings in this work in spite of the fact that much remains difficult and obscure.

*September 1 to 3*. Trip to Vienna, Essen (*September 13*), Düsseldorf. Attended a meeting of the Dante Society in Weimar—an improbable, unreal interlude that made the Third Reich and the war suddenly seem far away. As always I enjoyed the atmosphere of the Hotel Erbprinz and the park in Weimar, which is always inspiring. It is significant that there was hardly a person in the whole Dante gathering who could be considered a follower of the ruling party.

At the Industrial Club at Düsseldorf I made an address— not entirely without apprehension—before an audience of economic experts, extremely conscious of their own importance. Not one of some ten captains of industry present wore the Party badge.

Great to-do in Vienna about the opening of the Fair. Schirach, as the new Gauleiter and host, Funk, Ley, Ricci, Italian Minister of Corporations, Andres, Sagaroff, Varga, the Ministers of Economic Affairs of Yugoslavia, Bulgaria, and Hungary, two other Yugoslav Ministers, Kosutitsch (son-in-law of Raditsch and Secretary General of the Matschek Party, treated with special deference by the Yugoslavs), Sidorowitschi, the Rumanian Youth Minister, and others. Shortly before the opening of the Fair Ciano and Ribbentrop made the Vienna arbitration award in the dispute between the Rumanians and the Hungarians.[1] It was advertised as the "final pacification of the Danube area." Actually it revealed how fluid the situation still is, especially between Italy and Yugoslavia.

During luncheon at the Hofburg my two neighbors, the Finnish Minister and the Rumanian Cabinet member, drank toasts to each other with the remark: "We shall recover what the Soviet Russians have taken away from us!"[2] Funk made a sensible and factual opening address.

Schirach's line was to demonstrate on every possible occasion the differences between his methods and Bürckel's. Schirach, whose countenance reflects treachery, played the role

---

[1] Second Vienna arbitration award, August 30, 1940. Rumania ceded two thirds of Transylvania to Hungary.

[2] On July 1, 1940, Rumania yielded to a Russian ultimatum of June 27, and ceded Bessarabia and the northern Bucovina to the Soviet Union.

of "generosity and sympathy personified," and in his speech praised the princely house that had made Vienna the capital of an empire and Maria Theresa and Joseph II its distinguished representatives.

At the reception for the guests he showed himself adroit and amiable. Every now and then, however, the bombastic Party ruffian would come to the surface. As, for instance, at lunch, when he sat between Ricci and the Turkish Ambassador, he carelessly glanced over all kinds of papers which were brought to him—a needless but intentional showing off.

We were served on imperial porcelain and silver by servants in the imperial livery—a demonstration of bad taste which caused good General Bardolff resignedly to shake his head. The food was brought over from a hotel, so that we sat at the table in torture for two hours and a quarter. In despair, Schirach finally declared the meal at an end, just before the cheese course.

At the reception in the Rathaus, following a performance of the lovely *Magic Flute,* Schirach behaved like a sovereign with the daughter of the "Reich-drunkard" Hoffman; he was accompanied by an adjutant, heavy with gold braid, who whispered the names of the guests. But later on he took his place, like a *petit bourgeois,* beside his august wife.

The blustering bravado and certainty of victory demonstrated by the Government, the Party, and the Air Force have recently, and with good reason, yielded to the feeling that victory before winter—which they had expected so confidently —has become highly doubtful. Indeed, the outcome of the entire struggle now seems decidedly uncertain. England, under Churchill, is proving herself a very tough adversary, in spite of the terrific efforts of our air raids, particularly on London. Supremacy in the air has not been won. Flak and the new American Curtiss pursuit planes have proved most effective.

The landing in England has had to be postponed. In the consequent embarrassment, extravagant plans are being hatched on all sides against Russia and in the Mediterranean. Two things emerge with increasing clarity: first, the criminal irresponsibility with which Hitler, Ribbentrop, Keitel, *et al.,* began this war; second, the terrifying destruction which is now under way in Europe. We call the English fliers "pirates" and "incendiaries," and protest that they attack on purpose things like Goethe's garden house, Heidelberg, and Bethel, while we ourselves attack everything in our path with unrestrained brutality.

A particularly disgusting piece of propaganda swindle has been perpetrated with respect to the Bodelschwingh institutions. First of all, they kicked out Reich Bishop Bodelschwingh and tried in every conceivable way to weaken his institutions. They set in motion an inhuman and completely incoherent mass of legislation aimed at killing off the alleged or actual incurables among the feeble-minded inmates of Bethel. Then they praise this "father of mercies, whose life-long labors are maliciously destroyed by English dogs." During all this Bodelschwingh's deputy is in prison or in a concentration camp because he dared raise his voice against the methods of the government.

At the same time economic and moral conditions in the occupied areas grow worse. The Party "bulls" are, of course, not up to their jobs; all moral restraints are relaxing more and more; they steal and misbehave in every way; and meanwhile hatred increases everywhere.

In France political developments are getting ever more hazardous. De Gaulle's followers are increasing in number.

All reports agree as to the general picture. Popitz, Planck, and others have gathered shocking impressions during their travels.

Meanwhile Hitler sent the following edict to Keitel: after the war we shall have many rebellious peoples to rule; in order to manage them he wishes to put in control not the Army but the combat units of the SS. He therefore wants the SS transformed into a special-service branch, equipped with all arms, including air weapons, and under his personal command.

In all conferences with Beck, Popitz, Goerdeler, Oster, *et al.*, we keep asking ourselves in vain whether the generals do not at last sense what is going on; do they realize what a terrifying responsibility they bear, both for domestic developments and for the outcome of the war? We are agreed that we must once more attempt to do everything possible to convince them that they must not allow things to go along in this way lest we find ourselves confronted with or overwhelmed by catastrophe: widespread destruction at home and defeat abroad, or both.

As to the latter, it is significant that a Party historian (Johann von Leers) recently told my fraternity brother Zur Nedden (director of dramatic art at the National Theater in Weimar) that there was now such hatred between the two contending branches of the Germanic peoples as could be compared only with that between the Vandals and the Visigoths. However, he forgot to mention that of these two tribes not a trace remains. In this sense, the present war between Germans and Englishmen is truly suicidal for Europe.

Meanwhile, the German people are getting more and more war weary, and at heart they are indifferent. Two jokes characterize this state of mind: fourteen fliers want to get into heaven. St. Peter admits only seven, and the others protest. St. Peter appears again and says: "I am sorry, but we stick by the official army communiqués."

Goebbels complains that he has not been promoted. Hitler: "Never mind; after the war Göring will be World Marshal, and you Half-world (demi-monde) Marshal!" "And Himmler?" queried Goebbels. "Underworld Marshal!"

*October 8, 1940, Ebenhausen:* From now on every Pole must wear a "P" on his clothing, and to justify the treatment of this nation it is being said openly that there are no decent Poles, just as there are no respectable Jews. It is small comfort that with increasing frequency young officers, officials, or even SS men, try to avoid service in the occupied areas because "they are ashamed of being Germans."

On the other hand, Berthold, a young lawyer who works with the Governor General in Cracow, told me he had observed how the young National Socialists of his generation were losing all sense of values. Surrounded by vulgarity, they abandon their critical faculty as pointless, follow the pattern of their environment, and think exclusively in terms of their own advantage, whether it be a matter of position or a matter of personal enrichment.

Berthold painted an awful picture of conditions in Poland.

The hungry workers are gradually getting weaker, the Jews are systematically being exterminated, and a devilish campaign is being launched against the Polish intelligentsia with the express purpose of annihilating it. For the death of one SS man, who allegedly had been murdered while looking for a cache of arms, five hundred intellectuals were taken at random from the lists of lawyers, doctors, et cetera, and murdered. Among them was a lawyer who had been working for months with the administration as an expert on social policy. General ——— told me, deeply shocked, that stealing was being done on a large scale in the west. From the Reich Marshal on down, figures were being juggled between "public" and "private" thefts. There is no doubt that if this system prevails Germany and Europe will face fearful times. But if it should bring defeat to Germany the results will be unthinkable.

As the scheduled defeat of England did not materialize in the fall, Hitler and Mussolini are like two tigers in a cage who hurl themselves against the bars. For the time being they express themselves in words rather than in deeds; first the one and then the other makes new war plans.

Action against Russia seems to have been pushed into the background for the time being in favor of plans for an offensive in the Mediterranean. But the reaction of Spain to these plans is still rather sour, and she asks a great deal even before joining in. The Italians are gradually getting used to the idea that the expected short war may turn into a long one. A very uncomfortable prospect for a people who view the war with reserve and indolence and whose one wish is that it may quickly come to an end.

In England considerable, but not as yet decisive, successes by German fliers; also effective work done by our submarines. A shift in the Cabinet, with a bearing on air defenses, shows that everything is not going well. But the will to resist seems unshaken. As a countermove—that is as a move to frighten the United States out of taking an active part, as well as to influence an often intractable Russia—Hitler has turned the Anti-Comintern Pact with Japan into an alliance [September 27, 1940]. The U.S.A. must therefore reckon with a two-front war. However, I do not believe the situation will change much, for that would demonstrate its gravity all the more clearly to the Americans.

The English failure at Dakar revealed shocking amateurishness.

*Ebenhausen, October 20, 1940:* The landing in England has apparently been definitely put off; a real success of the air attack on London is possible but improbable; new plans are being made, especially for the Mediterranean; German divisions have taken over Rumania under the guise of "training troops" [October 10, 1940]; the thought of an attack on Russia has been pushed far into the background, and in its place there is abject wooing of Russia. Hitler (or Ribbentrop) has written Stalin (or Molotov) a long and suppliant letter offering to come to Moscow.

A few days ago Westrick, who has just come back from the United States, said that hostility to Nazi Germany was 100 per cent fanatical. Social intercourse was almost out of the question. Nevertheless, the chances of Willkie against Roosevelt were 50-50. If Roosevelt were elected it would mean the gradual and formal entry of America into the war; Willkie's election, a gradual return to neutrality. The German alliance with Japan, according to Westrick, was at first a shock because of the thought of a two-front war, but in the long run it actually sharpened war feeling.

Pétain wants to be allowed to increase French military power, using British attacks as an argument, and would most of all like to conclude a peace. Under certain circumstances he would even like to join the fight against England, because the present situation is becoming utterly intolerable. We seem to be quite ready to meet the former request, but because of German-Italian difficulties Weizsäcker sees no prospect of concluding a peace.

*November 11, 1940, Ebenhausen:* Back from a second visit to Brazzà and a trip to Belgrade and Zagreb. A discouraging impression of the situation in Yugoslavia. The Heerens were very kind, and it was a pleasure for me to stay in my old legation again. The city has not yet changed a lot, although there has been much building. Still that remarkable mixture of village and metropolis, Orient and Europe.

From Prince Paul's charming palace, Beli Dvor, a magnificent view over the whole countryside, particularly the Koschutniack. Lunched with him and the always lovely Princess Olga. We talked as frankly as possible about our various worries. The young King was there too. He reminds one of his father and grandfather (Ferdinand), slight, somewhat stooped, pale, reserved, but not uncongenial.

The relations of the royal family with the Heerens are very cool; no real contact from the beginning, but now even more pronounced through the Prince's break with Stoyadinovitch, to whom the Heerens are still attached. Frau von Heeren is so unswerving that she enthuses constantly about her good relationship with him. She thereby provides gossiping tongues with unnecessary material; Prince Paul implied as much.

Prince Paul's position is very difficult because he has no real contact with anyone in Serbia—though some with Croatians —but the question is whether the latter would not coldbloodedly betray him.

According to my observations, Heeren has not a bad position in Yugoslavia, but certainly not a strong one. In addition he is too lazy and fundamentally timid. Even in a circle of trusted German friends he doesn't dare make the slightest reference to domestic politics. In his relations with the Prince he has lost even more ground because, like the Italian Ambassador, he was charged with making a protest to Prince Paul against any attempt on the life of Stoyadinovitch! The Prince answered something to this effect: "I am no murderer, such as one sees nowadays in other countries."

Meanwhile the Italians, to our surprise, have attacked Greece [October 28, 1940]—a highly precarious undertaking, particularly if things go as badly as they have hitherto. Results so far: the English are in Crete.

There are a few things to add here from the days preceding my departure. The more likely a long war becomes, the more danger in our domestic and foreign situation. The dictators and their crowd sense this too, although they hide their fears under strong words. Witness Hitler's speech in the Löwenbräu in which he appraised himself, in an almost pathological manner, as the strongest man in centuries. At the same time the opportunity begins to drift toward the opposition. The industrialists of Düsseldorf, who bet on victory over England by November 5, have lost.

On *October 28,* at the Industrial Club (that is in the same room of the Park Hotel in which Hitler, escorted by Thyssen, of all people, won over the leaders of heavy industry), I spoke on the subject Politics and Industry in the Mediterranean— Then and Now. Numerous attentive listeners. I heard considerably less big talk from the industrialists than two months ago. The highest ranking police authority in the west, an SS chief group leader, was there too. He took me to the station during an air-raid alarm; otherwise I should not have made the train.

The predecessor of this police officer had been killed by a bomb while driving one night. Therefore it was quite heroic for his successor to make this trip with me. Whoever wants to take a ten-o'clock or eleven-o'clock train must be at the station between eight and nine o'clock, and then, very likely, wait in an air-raid shelter for trains leaving promptly, regardless of bombardments. The public was apparently quite accustomed to this procedure and remained quiet and well disciplined in spite of heavy bombardments.

Conversations with Popitz, Goerdeler, and Oster before my trip proved that the authority of the government in domestic affairs is dwindling with great rapidity. This is the government which claims to rest upon the "leader principle." The governors, particularly in agricultural areas, act like disobedient satraps and barricade their provinces against food exports; just like the much-condemned Bavarian and Württemberg "particularists" in World War I! At the same time wages and prices are rising ever higher, either in roundabout ways or openly, with considerable local differences. The worst conditions, amounting often to real distress, exist in some of the occupied areas.

Popitz has conferred at length with General ——, who is of the opinion that for the moment nothing can be done, but that in two or three months the tension will be so great that the pear may perhaps be ripe for picking. Meanwhile, the brutalities in Poland and elsewhere continue. In Baden several weeks ago all Jews were suddenly chased head over heels across the border toward Alsace, including reserve officers with the Iron Cross, First Class.

The most important event in foreign affairs was the last conference at the Brenner Pass [Hitler and Mussolini met October 4, 1940], which was conducted in a minor key. This is evidenced by three reports I have read. Although differing in details they agree on the whole. Both participants, to be sure, boasted extravagantly to each other about their military achievements and potentialities, but actually their spirits seemed somewhat dampened. Mussolini announced that the attack on Egypt was imminent and added, amusingly, that his generals were not really behind the enterprise, but that he had summoned Graziani and dressed him down.

Meanwhile, there were also the meetings of Hitler and Laval [October 22, 1940], of Hitler with Pétain [October 26, 1940], and between Hitler and Franco [October 23, 1940]. At the first two they did not get beyond generalities. Franco, to be sure, pledged absolute loyalty to the Axis but reserved to himself the timing of his participation.

At the Brenner Pass, Mussolini formulated rather moderate demands on France. So did Hitler.

Afterward there was a stiffening of attitudes by both the French and the Italians. Mussolini wrote a long letter to Hitler [October 22, 1940] with respect to an agreement with Pétain and backed down considerably. At the same time he announced that the offensive against Egypt would have to be postponed until after Christmas, and maliciously alluded to the fact that the landing in England wasn't going so rapidly as planned either. Result: the meeting at Florence [October 28, 1940], where Mussolini "delighted" his guest and friend with his entry into Greece. What the result of the Florence meeting was I don't know as yet.

In Air Force circles there was bad blood because Göring was on a fourteen-day shooting trip at Rominten during the main attack on England.

A few significant stories. The first is said to be actually true.

Someone comes into a Black Forest village and on entering a farmhouse says "Heil Hitler!" An old peasant woman replies: "How do you happen to hit upon that name?"

In an air-raid shelter. Upon entering, those who have already been asleep say: "Good morning." Those who have not yet been to bed say: "Good evening." Those who are still asleep say: "Heil Hitler!"

Indoctrination in the air-raid shelter: "Whom are we to thank for the night fighters?" "Hermann Göring." "For the whole Air Force?" "Hermann Göring." "Upon whose orders did Hermann Göring do all this?" "On the orders of the Führer!" "Where would we all be if it were not for Hermann Göring and the Führer?" "In our beds!"

Neville Chamberlain died on November 9, [10] 1940. A tragic end for a man of good will.

The next few days will perhaps show whether Hitler, by promising Constantinople, can coax the Russians out of the stable—against Turkey and England. In the first place it would be a blow to his enemies, but also a long step toward the complete destruction of Europe by the "hardest German that has appeared for centuries," as Hitler styles himself in his paroxysm.

*Ebenhausen, November 23, 1940:* The war drags on. On the one hand heavy destruction of towns in England, truly a nightmare of warfare. Considerable losses in merchant shipping. On the other side defeat of the Italians in Greece.[1] One would hardly think it possible; and a highly successful attack by English torpedo planes on the Italian Navy at Taranto [November 12, 1940]. Fifty per cent of the large warships are temporarily out of commission.

I heard the close of Mussolini's speech on the anniversary of the voting of sanctions and found his voice nervous and over-excited. Our good Corso Pecori, with whom I recently lunched, traced the defeat in Greece, above all, to the reports of Jacomoni, "Viceroy" of Albania, who had definitely predicted an insurrection of the Albanians in Epirus. Weizsäcker told me the whole undertaking was an ill-considered proposal of Ciano's,

[1]On November 22, 1940, the Greeks took Koritza in Albania.

worked out in conjunction with Jacomoni. Now that the English have occupied Crete and all islands in the Aegean, and are also sitting tight in Salonika, whence they can easily bomb the oil fields in Rumania, Hitler is faced with the question whether or not to march with the Bulgarians to Salonika and drive out the English; this would mean an extension of the theater of war and therefore possibly the involvement of Turkey as well.

I hear from Weizsäcker, among other things, that an improved atmosphere has developed from Molotov's visit,[1] but there have been no other definite results. Molotov is said to have spoken with great reserve about Turkey, and indicated that this was strictly a Russian problem.

I talked with Weizsäcker about the attitude of the generals on domestic matters, and hinted there was a growing realization of the fearful domestic developments and the complete shattering of all ethical foundations. Weizsäcker doubted that, and referred to a conversation he had had with his fellow Swabian [Neurath], who, with complete naïveté, was reveling in dreams of victory. In the course of the talk he had demonstrated, for one in his position, a scandalous ignorance of elementary statistics—for instance, in the matter of submarine warfare. And when Weizsäcker took well-founded exceptions to the fantastic figures mentioned, Neurath had said resignedly that information about naval and air matters was systematically withheld from him.

As for myself, I have the impression that the Navy juggles with the truth very recklessly. For instance, they recently reported that a battleship (*Scheer*) had stopped a large convoy in the Atlantic and completely destroyed it. The truth is that as a result of the heroic self-sacrifice of an English auxiliary cruiser it was possible for the greater part of the merchant ships to escape. A naval officer, with whom I discussed the affair in the riding stables, was incensed over this kind of reporting, but was convinced that nothing could be done about it. Presumably instructions had come from high quarters to report the episode in this way.

My impression of the officer corps of the Navy, especially of

[1] Visit of Molotov in Berlin, November 16, 1940.

the higher and middle brackets, is not very good. A guiding spirit is lacking. The rudeness of the ignorant *miles gloriosus* is combined disastrously with a lack of civil courage and moral stamina.

The Navy, of course, is only symbolic of the whole development. Goerdeler and Popitz told horrible things about moral laxity in the occupied areas as well as here at home. For example, the systematic and uncontrolled killing of the so-called "incurably insane." It is typical that Hitler declined to draft a law, but authorized Bouhler in a backhanded way to go ahead with it.

Hitler has issued an order on the future conduct of the war that sounds quite scatterbrained. "In case we should have to fall back on a landing in spring, it must be better prepared." The possibility of war against Russia is still being considered. At the moment they are squabbling with the Spaniards about an undertaking against Gibraltar. Hitler did not get on well with Franco, who was very reticent; he said Franco was probably a pretty good soldier but had become the head of his state only by accident. Suñer he called the worst kind of "business politician."

Popitz and Goerdeler have looked into the food situation. In Germany we can get along until August 1 if we made use of all reserves; in some of the occupied areas there will be acute food shortages pretty soon.

A speech by Greiser (Governor of the Warthegau), delivered several weeks ago, is most enlightening as to the state of mind of our rulers. He had orders from the Führer to see to it that no Pole, no matter of what class, shall receive more than three or four years of schooling; the Poles were to learn reading, writing, and arithmetic only to the point where they could understand their own account books. German teachers were too good for this kind of work; after the war he would commandeer 7,000 non-commissioned officers to do the job. After three or four years of school the Poles would be marched into the turnip and potato fields!

To serve the same purpose, the Czech university at Prague has been closed. In this manner they wish to build up Europe! Little wonder that a Yugoslav German, the famous industrialist August Westen from Cilli, with whom I had dinner night before last in Berlin, is desperate. We dined at the Excelsior so that I could be sure to reach the Anhalter Station through the connecting tunnel in case of an air alarm.

*December 9, 1940, Ebenhausen:* I gave my Düsseldorf lecture on politics and economics in the Mediterranean at the National Club in Hamburg on *November 30,* and on *December 6* in Berlin before the World Economics Society (Governor Schnee). In Hamburg political optimism still holds sway, which is surprising in view of the fact that the war naturally hits those people very hard.

Otto Bismarck, who was just then spending a few days in Germany, had heard of my lecture and invited me by telephone to come to Friedrichsruh; indicative of a cooling off of his friendliness toward the Nazis. He was pleasant and also interesting, in that he told all kinds of stories from Rome. Since the defeats in Greece the morale there is very low. Ciano looms larger in the picture. Under his influence Mussolini has surrendered more and more of his independence and has adopted Hitler's policies. Italy has been plotting a dangerous course. This at least presupposes "heroic" qualities, not to speak of other factors. The striking phrase: "They are too weary to live like lions" is now becoming more justified than ever. If the English would pursue a strategy with definite aims and did not shy at sacrifices, they could exploit a very weak point in the Axis by striking hard at Italy.

I saw the vault at Friedrichsruh; impressive in its simplicity. How simple and unpretentious these people were! This is evident in the house, too, which was originally a village tavern. Herbert B. has done much remodeling; workrooms and bedrooms remain as they were. The present Princess has decorated the house tastefully.

No air raids, either in Hamburg or Berlin. In the high circles of Berlin, waves of optimism; one hopes soon to bring England to her knees by the destruction of her cities and the action of submarines. They are speculating on a Labor Cabinet (Bevin) which would make peace. Fundamentally, however, the plutocrats are already weaker than the workers. From America come voices that give food for thought. I foresee no peace with Hitler, for our adversaries recognize Italy's weakness and the difficulties that confront us.

Meanwhile, we are collecting great—almost comically great —additions to the Tripartite Pact: Hungary! Rumania! Slovakia! [November 20–24, 1940]. Shameful conditions obtain in Rumania under our protection: murder and robbery. Without German troops terrible chaos would be inevitable. Bulgaria is being wooed by us and, in unmistakable fashion, against us, by the Soviets. The latter worries Boris, and so he weaves back and forth in indecision. The plan of winning Yugoslavia over through the promise of Salonika is now being tried. Prince Paul and his people, however, still hesitate.

At home we are steering an increasingly obvious course. The most revolting aspect at the moment is the unrestrained mass slaughter of the so-called incurably insane. Bishop Wurm of Württemberg has had the admirable courage to take a firm stand against it.

The activities of Ley are especially threatening; he very purposefully seeks to build up his own power. With his almost unlimited funds he gained control of the People's Car factory, the home-building industry, and the construction of sixty Strength-Through-Joy ships, and a large tractor factory.

*December 23, 1940, Ebenhausen:* The political situation is increasingly menacing. Shamelessly demagogical speech by Hitler, on the lowest level that a leading statesman has ever sunk to—a sign of anxiety over the growing dissatisfaction of the workers and at the same time a sign of the "red" course upon which he has embarked and in which he has become hopelessly entangled.

Ley, an accomplished but not very effective agitator, promises every worker not only a car but also an airplane. The admonition of the Bible about riches (the camel and the needle's eye) was so much foolishness. It should read: "You shall all be rich."

A brilliant lecture recently by Popitz on The Idea of the Reich, before the Wednesday Society. Afterward I had a long conversation about the situation with Popitz, Sauerbruch, and a young economist, Jessen, a Nazi in the very early days, now a bitter enemy. In the few days following a series of conferences with Popitz, Goerdeler, et cetera, about the necessity of doing something very soon. Popitz represented the view that one should immediately set up the monarchy as a firm central pillar. But that raises the difficult question of candidates. Popitz thought only Louis Ferdinand could be considered.

There is to be a serious discussion with Falkenhausen from Brussels some time in January. General Rabenau has been feeling out Brauchitsch.

The food problem is getting to be a burning issue.

Foreign situation: England is pretty exhausted but not shaken; morally strengthened by her military successes, including the current ones in North Africa and Italy.[1]

In Italy the situation is deteriorating; there is aversion to the war and dissatisfaction is mounting; reproaches are flying back and forth between the civil and military authorities. Italians in Germany are held more and more in contempt, which adds difficulty to my task. In Italy itself the Party attempts, very unjustly, to make a scapegoat of good old Badoglio.

In France, Pétain has pulled himself together, encouraged by Weygand in Africa, in opposition to the corrupt Laval, has thrown Laval out, and placed him in protective custody [December 15, 1940]. This is a heavy defeat for Ribbentrop and his Abetz. Even if we now force them to take Laval back into the Cabinet the situation has shifted much to Germany's disadvantage. Hitler has ordered preparations for occupying all of France. He will take this opportunity to get to the Mediterranean since: (1) Spain has refused to co-operate and an independent expedition against Gibraltar appears to be too risky; (2) the advance toward Salonika has temporarily foundered on the indecisive attitude of the Bulgarians.

Yugoslavia appears to be as unwilling as Bulgaria and Spain to tie itself up with Germany so soon. Such a decision is a nightmare for the Bulgarians, who fear that they will thereby definitely lose Macedonia. Draganoff, at whose house I recently attended a luncheon in honor of Ministers Schwerin-Krosigk and Todt, who had just been decorated with the

[1]December 12, 1940, Sollum and Fort Cabuzzo in English hands.

Grand Cross, expressed this fear in a very biting speech containing insulting references to the countries (Hungary and Rumania) which had to prove their friendship to Germany by means of special pacts (unlike Bulgaria), and to those people (the Yugoslavs) who now hasten to join up.

# 1941

*January 19, 1941, Ebenhausen:* The great destruction continues; all restraints are cast off. There is growing awareness of the developing evil, too, but no rift in the clouds which conceal the way out. Goerdeler remains firmly optimistic. I reported to him my conversations with two commanding generals and another high military figure; although they grasp the situation clearly they cannot free themselves from the stubborn military mentality which thinks with its hands on its trouser seams. To this Goerdeler replied blithely and incredibly that he could offer just as many examples of a different attitude.

I said today to Brocke, Trotha's pleasant son-in-law (Landrat and reserve officer), that to think in terms of simple, military duty was all right for officials and officers up to, roughly speaking, the rank of divisional commander, but then political responsibility should begin to play a part. I cited these examples: Neurath, in his role of Protector, the commanding officer in Poland, not to mention the Commander in Chief.

Goerdeler reported that conflicts are growing within the Party: (1) the Hitler group; (2) the Party group (Bormann); (3) the SS; (4) Ley. Ley is lined up with the first. The Party organization and SS are sharply antagonistic. The SS is already toying with plans of going into action under the slogan: against corruption and bolshevism. A dangerous slogan, because it is alluring, but it hides only a brutal battle for power. Such developments as these should make the Army realize that as the only decent factor remaining it must save the country and that it must shoulder the responsibility for what happens now.

Nothing has come as yet from Falkenhausen. General von Rabenau is soon to talk with Brauchitsch, but is to be coached in advance by Goerdeler and myself.

The following is significant for the inner drive toward bolshevism brought about by this uncontrollable war. At the Rheinbaben luncheon Gramsch, who is fundamentally a conservative man in the good sense, said that our policies in the occupied areas (Belgium, Holland, Denmark, and Norway) were wrong. We are working, he said, with the old upper class, for example with the Stauning Government in Denmark, with the large bankers in Holland, who allowed their money outside to work against us, and with the Norwegian shipping interests, who let their ships carry goods for England —all elements that were actually against us. In their stead we should, he said, use the new classes.

I interjected that perhaps he was thinking of Mussert, Degrelle, and Quisling, who certainly hadn't much to recommend them.

He: "No, perhaps not these, but entirely new elements from below."

I: "A bolshevization process, then!"

He, with a helpless gesture: "Yes, what else is there to do?"

A drastic example of the criminal flightiness of those carrying out the murder of the insane: a couple we know brought their feeble-minded daughter home quickly when it was announced that she was to be taken to "another institution." Shortly thereafter they received an official notice: "To our great sorrow we must report that your daughter has passed away!" Actually she was safely at home.

Berthold visited me and brought his friend Frauendorfer (a wearer of the gold Party badge, an official working in Poland under Frank). His desperation over the events in Poland and, in general, over the whole development (Hitler's speech) was most impressive. From another source I heard that the disreputable crowd of district and local group leaders who had failed at home and had been kicked out of their jobs had been given posts in Poland.

Signs of the war situation: heavy air raids on England are hampered by the weather, but certainly successful. Effective attacks by the English, especially on Bremen. Fewer successes for the submarines.

Heavy defeat for the Italians in North Africa,[1] further reverses in Albania. The Laval crisis is unsolved. Pétain has not yet given in.

Roosevelt came out strongly in support of England and against the dictators (no direct reference to Germany).

German planes in the Mediterranean are having substantial successes.

The tiger hurls himself against the bars! A large undertaking through Bulgaria directed against Greece (and Turkey?) is, in the foreground. Small supporting actions are planned for Italy in Albania and North Africa. Further preparations are slowly being made for a campaign against Russia. The landing in England is in the background for the time being.

*February 3, 1941, Ebenhausen:* Back from Paris and Switzerland. A meeting between Hitler and Mussolini at the Obersalzberg [January 20, 1941] has not, so far as I could discover in Berlin, yielded much that is new; the two dictators indulged to a great extent in generalities. According to my information Mussolini rejected help in Albania. On the other hand, German tank troops are soon to go to North Africa as a precaution against Weygand. Mussolini is to try once more to work on Franco[2] (strangely enough, the Italian is chosen to do this, although Italy is even less popular in Spain than Germany).

It seems to me that the bad situation in Spain and the shaky authority of Franco hold out little promise for this attempt. The more so since Italy is suffering further defeats, not only in North Africa but also in Abyssinia, and the U.S.A. emerges more and more strongly and firmly as a real ally of England.

It is interesting that [January 26, 1941] Ciano, Bottai, Ric-

[1]January 5, 1941, Bardia in English hands.
[2]Meeting of Mussolini and Franco in Bordighera, February 12, 1941.

cardi, and other Ministers have suddenly gone to the front as soldiers—a peculiar activity especially for a Minister for Foreign Affairs.

On the evening of my departure [January 24] I had dinner with Sauerbruch. He is intelligent, lively, very interesting. . . . Beck, Popitz, Jessen were also present—a very high level of discussion.

Because of a derailed freight train I was five hours late in Duisburg; this gradually grew to eleven hours. Rerouted by way of Brussels (through Herbesthal—memories of my journey in 1914 as a wounded soldier), where we managed to have the sleeping car attached to the train for Paris. Arrived in the morning instead of evening.

In Paris there was not a ray of sunshine all three days. Even without this the impression was one of gloom. Little traffic. The stores are still elegant but getting emptier. The people on the streets seemed, on the whole, very normal; in the evenings some gaiety was noticeable, some laughter heard. Elegant women were not lacking in the picture. The subway was very full and functioning normally; a medley of Frenchmen and soldiers in field-gray uniforms. At the Place de la Concorde the guard is changed at noon with bands playing; the population appears uninterested. Between the Jeu de Paume and the Orangerie soldiers are drilling. Wolf and I went to several churches Sunday morning, among others St. Eustache, St. Germain-des-Près. Both were full. In one a bearded monk preached animatedly to a very attentive congregation. Soldiers are forbidden to attend.

I spent the evening with the military commander in France, Otto Stülpnagel. He is intelligent, but somewhat overworked, deaf in one ear, of no great caliber. Understandably enough he suffers under the mad confusion in France, the conflicts among authorities, et cetera. He has a pretty clear understanding of things, but seems to lack decision. At another table sat Karl Haniel and Field Marshal von Reichenau, with whom we conversed briefly. The latter is cut of different cloth than Stülpnagel but is really a highly colorful character.

Tuesday afternoon—characteristic of the whole grotesque situation—there was a centennial exhibition of Rodin and

Manet in the Orangerie. Not a very happy combination when one considers the difference in character and genius of the two artists. Still very much worth seeing. German soldiers—that is to say students thrust into uniform—wandered about the exhibition with pathetically eager faces.

Then at the Embassy. The beautiful palace seems dishonored by the present incumbents. Abetz was in Berlin. His deputy, Consul General Schleyer, received me. He was formerly a merchant and a Party group leader. He looked the part exactly. What he said was not too bad. He made bitter complaints about the fatal lack of any vestige of integration in the policies toward France. While Pétain is called to Montoire to confer with Hitler about a workable system, Bürckel expels the Lorrainers in the most brutal fashion, and destroys whatever there was of a willingness to co-operate with Germany.

He also admitted the complete miscarriage of the childish maneuver with the ashes of the Duke of Reichstadt.[1] Pétain has now waited many weeks for an answer from Hitler to two letters, the first of which was very pointed, and in Berlin was considered most impudent. Schleyer thought Hitler was now inclined to let the French stew in their own juice. This is, however, no less detrimental to us than to France. In general even the Embassy seems to have grasped the point that the present situation is intolerable.

I lunched at Raindres with Ambassador Chambrun, along with Marie (formerly Murat, née Rohan) and Wolf. I was greeted very warmly by my former opponent, who, since he is Detalmo's uncle (the African explorer Brazzà was married to Chambrun's sister), has become a relative of ours, so to speak! In this unusual situation Germans and Frenchmen consult about plans for rescue with one another like passengers on a ship in distress.

In the afternoon I passed the very impressive statue of Clemenceau on my way to see the Countess Dolly de Castellane (née Talleyrand). A charming salon, with pictures and busts of her great-uncle Talleyrand, of Dorothea of Courland, and

[1]Transfer to Paris of the body of the Duke of Reichstadt, King of Rome and son of Napoleon I, as a gesture to the French.

other contemporaries; concentrated history breathing an irre-coverable past.

A summary of my conversations with Frenchmen about the situation in France would be about as follows: the structure created by the armistice terms could have been useful if it had been devised for a period of two to three months, followed by a final peace (or a renewal of hostilities). As a permanent ar-rangement, and in the absence of a concrete political settle-ment, the demarcation line is intolerable for France and dangerous for Germany—politically as well as economically.

The economic distress of the French, especially those of low incomes, and the economic difficulties for the Germans are increasing every day. Whereas at one time the people were not hostile toward the foreign invaders, who at least had brought about a cessation of fighting and a certain order, this attitude is rapidly giving way to a veiled enmity, particularly since our failure to make a landing in England and the defeats of the Italians gave rise to the hope that there might be a change of fortune.

It is politically impossible to rule this divided country. There is no one authority able to prevail. Only the name "Pétain" means something; the French cast furtive glances toward De Gaulle, and above all they look more and more in the direction of North Africa, to Weygand. The threat to occupy all of France does not have much effect. An overseas France under Weygand (or Pétain), which can victoriously engage Italy, rises on the French horizon—and on ours.

The fall of Laval [December 15, 1940] has demolished all budding hopes for a final agreement. It is the unanimous opinion of the French that Laval would have been successful, that is, he could have got France behind him if he had not come with empty hands. If we had given him a few hundred thousand prisoners of war and promised gradually to withdraw the demarcation line (instead of evicting the Lorrainers), he would have been hailed as a savior. To the public at large Laval is washed up, a traitor in the pay of Germany. Political circles still stand by him firmly (perhaps only for lack of any-thing better), as the only person who might be capable of finding a way out.

Laval's friends deny that he is bribed. They believe that if we would really give him something to offer he could even now find a way out of the impasse. It seems questionable to me, however, whether he would still have the necessary authority. One comes to the conclusion that the situation is quite insoluble.

During my last hour in Paris I received a telegram from Detalmo telling me that the "doctor" [English intermediary] was in Lisbon and wished "information about Wolf-Ulli." I wired him that I would be in Arosa through Saturday, February 1. There I found a second and similar telegram which seemed to me not an answer to mine but to have been sent simultaneously with the first. I therefore confirmed my telegram and made arrangements with Wolf-Ulli in case the doctor should appear. It is interesting that the doctor announces himself again. But his superior is no longer at the helm![1]

It is also significant that Professor Carl Burckhardt, who is active in the Red Cross, looked me up in Geneva [January 30, 1941], and gave me for any use I might make of it (he thought primarily of Weizsäcker) the following information: very recently the Finnish art historian, Professor Borenius, who has lived in London for many years, came to him to explain, apparently on behalf of English officials, that a reasonable peace could still be concluded. He had very intimate connections with —— and was personally convinced that sentiment was favorable in the English Cabinet; of course Eden's succession to Halifax was a handicap.

In reply to Burckhart's questions Borenius had said: Holland and Belgium must be restored; Denmark to remain in the sphere of German influence; some kind of Poland (minus the former German provinces) to be resurrected for reasons of prestige, "because the Poles fought so bravely for England." Otherwise no special interest in the East (not even for Czechoslovakia). Former German colonies to Germany. The British Empire to remain otherwise unshorn. England had no special passion for France.

[1] December 23, 1940, Lord Halifax was appointed Ambassador in Washington and Anthony Eden appointed his successor as Foreign Secretary.

To a question concerning Italian claims, this counterques-
tion was asked: Did Germany still seriously support these
demands? France would naturally remain a factor. Contrary
to the contentions of German propaganda, the war-minded
people in England are to be found particularly among the
lower middle class and the workers. The air raids, which have
struck especially the poorer sections, have been largely responsible for engendering war fever; namely, a fury against
the specter of enemy invasion. There is also a certain feeling
against the rich, but much less than against the enemy.

The question with whom peace could be made in Germany
was broached very cautiously by Carl Burckhardt, both in his
talks with Borenius and with me. But the clear impression
nonetheless emerged: one was highly reluctant to make peace
with Hitler. The main reason, one simply can't believe a word
he says. The English Consul General also told Carl Burckhardt
recently that in no event would peace be made with Hitler.

*March 2, 1941, Ebenhausen:* Three and a half weeks with
Ilse—finally!—in Berlin. We go out or have guests almost
every day for dinner or luncheon. Especially rewarding were a
luncheon given by us for Beck and Sauerbruch and a dinner at
Popitz's with Sauerbruch and the intelligent, typically north-
German Jessens. We often saw Italians (Cosmelli, Casardi,
Pecori), with whom we still maintain the old and intimate
relationship. They are very depressed. At Casardi's I had a
long conversation with the Brazilian Ambassador, who sharply
criticized our war policies and evidently does not believe that
we shall succeed—a view which is spreading rapidly.

The joke of the month: a conversation between Speer and
Furtwängler. Furtwängler: "It must be wonderful to be able
to build in grand style according to your own ideas!" Speer:
"Imagine if someone should say to you, 'It is my unshakable
will that from now on the Ninth Symphony shall be performed
exclusively on the mouth organ!'"

Finally I got to know Falkenhausen from Brussels through
Oster and Dohnanyi. Intelligent and clear-headed, but apparently he got nowhere with Brauchitsch; didn't even get to
present the main points. There were, however, interesting con-

versations between Brauchitsch and General von Rabenau. Rabenau seems to have painted an unvarnished picture for his colleague; he urged him especially to listen to me, whereupon Brauchitsch is said to have answered that if he listened at all to civilians it would be to Hassell, but that it was probably too early. Rabenau then angrily suggested that Brauchitsch might as well call the Gestapo and have him arrested! Popitz, Goerdeler, and I conferred with Rabenau as to whether and when this matter should be pushed further.

Salient points in the situation: rapidly developing food crisis, which will be absolutely threatening if Hitler really attacks Russia in the spring. This latter insanity is being defended on two grounds: (1) the necessity for occupying the Ukraine, (2) the necessity for defeating the "potential allies" of our opponents as a "precaution!"

The real results will be: (1) the cutting off of imports from Russia, since the Ukraine will be useful only after a long time; (2) a new and unprecedented strain on war matériel and energies; (3) complete encirclement, deliberately arranged.

Ribbentrop, supposedly, is still fighting for the alternative plan of an attack on Turkey. Meanwhile, the rumor is being systematically broadcast that all this is bluff; that an invasion of England really will take place.

*March 16, 1941:* I forgot to mention that Oster recently showed me an account of a conversation between Canaris and Halder, which plainly disclosed the weak position and the lack of information of the latter. Halder and Brauchitsch are nothing more than caddies to Hitler.

Hitler's last speech in Munich on the anniversary of the founding of the Party is characteristic of the whole situation. It was on an unbelievably low level. Professor Sauerbruch's chauffeur said: "He can't think of anything new." Popitz's chauffeur commented: "Always the same."

But certain classes of people, especially the half-educated and also, in part, the educated bourgeois let themselves be influenced. For instance, Pinder thought "the speech considerably strengthened the confidence of the people." A woman remarked to Ilse: "We can rest easy now, because he said he was prepared for all eventualities."

On the other hand, Ilse had an astonishing experience in a shop where the owner, in reply to some remark of Ilse's to the effect that everything was getting quite difficult, said: "Difficult? It is nothing short of tragic!" And then, violently attacking the destruction of all morals through our present rulers, he went on: "If we don't return to Christianity we shall be ruined."

A poem called *"Ten Little Grumblers"* is currently creating a great furor. It is passed from hand to hand and was recited and copied for me by a schoolboy.

The English radio made a big hit with its listeners by imitating a speech by Hitler in an air-raid shelter. In an unmistakably Hitlerian voice he declared he would have to withdraw Göring's pledge that no bomb would fall on German territory during the war, but, instead, he would act as godfather to every baby born in an air-raid shelter.

Another joke: in Germany the temperature is still being measured according to the foreign standards of Celsius and Réaumur. Hitler orders that in the future measurements be made according to the "German" Fahrenheit. We thereby gain 65 degrees of heat and automatically solve the coal shortage!

Very good jokes. But for all decent people the dominating factor is their own inner tragedy. They can wish neither for defeat nor for victory; they cannot wish for the latter because the victory of these people opens up terrible perspectives for Germany and Europe. Distressing news comes from Poland, Norway, and Holland. An indescribable hatred is piling up against us.

At supper with Wohltat and Thomas. Wohltat told impressive stories about Holland, where he must defer to Seyss-Inquart and Fischböck. He is to go to East Asia, a strange but significant move for a man who is so extremely valuable here.

Little favorable news comes from Japan about the situation in China; there is great corruption in the Army. Matsuoka is coming to Berlin and Rome. We want Japan to attack England. But things look different in the Far East, especially since America supports the other side more and more.

Nevertheless, during the last week the barometer in Berlin

began to rise noticeably. First, because it is hoped that in summer the submarine and air attacks will be more successful. Second, because the invasion of Bulgaria [March 2, 1941] went off without a hitch, with the Bulgarian Army standing aside. Some conclude from this that eventually we can also come to an understanding with the Turks. To this end we will march into Russia as far as the Caspian Sea and take the Turks between the pincers from Cape Matapan to Baku. Third, it is believed that Yugoslavia will join the Tripartite Pact. Heavy pressure is being applied to that country but she is still resisting. Perhaps she will have to yield, but in any event will do so with great reluctance. Furthermore, as Minister Draganoff clearly indicated to me day before yesterday, the Bulgarians look upon this business with great suspicion. Fourth, because things in Libya have come to a complete stalemate. There is even some thought of launching an offensive.

Two interesting conferences at Popitz's, one on *March 10*, with E.'s friend, Albrecht Haushofer, who is still being used by Hess for occasional missions. He says there is an urgent desire for peace in high quarters. He himself now thinks as we do (after going through a few spiritual detours in the direction of Ribbentrop), and recognizes that the "qualities" of the regime constitute a barrier for any kind of useful peace in view of the distrust and abomination in which the whole world holds Hitler. We discussed how we could capitalize my connections via Switzerland, so that Haushofer could come home with an authentic confirmation of this idea (the possibility of peace negotiations after a change of regime).

On the *eleventh* I had a conference with Goerdeler and General von Rabenau as to whether or not to arrange a new approach to Brauchitsch. Popitz and I were against it at the moment because of the general increase in optimism, which makes such a step seem fruitless. Goerdeler disagrees and maintains that the present optimism is not only unjustified by the facts (which may be correct) but also not very widespread (which I nevertheless believe). Rabenau is confused; he is himself a living example of the new mood of optimism. Popitz and I, however, agreed heartily that action should be taken on Goerdeler's plan of presenting to Brauchitsch the misgivings of members of the Reich Supreme Court "with respect to the complete decay of justice."

It is illustrative of the collapse of law that after Gürtner's death [January 22, 1941] Himmler suggested to Hitler that the administration of civil law should be placed under the Ministry of the Interior, with the Ministry of Justice liquidated, and that all matters of penal law be placed under the police department (Heydrich). Unfortunately, Lammers and others prevented that, for the whole world would thus have learned of the true state of affairs!

During the last few days the Italians wanted to attack in Albania, in the presence of Mussolini, in order to achieve a Vittorio Veneto before German pressure on Greece becomes effective. But they were stopped again.

*Trip to the southeast, March–April, 1941. Belgrade, March 20, 1941:* First political impressions in Zagreb revealed the great tension in which this land is gripped, both in its domestic and foreign relationships. Freundt [German Consul in Agram] and all Croats with whom I spoke emphasized the great differences between Croatia and Serbia. In Croatia there is no opposition whatever to Germany (with a few exceptions); on the contrary, a desire to co-operate. In Serbia, really bellicose sentiments against Germany and Italy, fanned by the military party. Franges maintains that English propaganda has become so effective recently that the English national anthem has often been called for in night clubs and that those present have stood to sing it. At the same time the tenor of Russian propaganda is such that if a pact with Germany should ever come about one would likewise be concluded with Russia.

This morning Heeren told me that Stoyadinovitch has been shoved off to Greece, probably with Egypt as his ultimate destination.

Shortly after my arrival I was invited to luncheon by Prince Paul, although I had not announced my presence. This was particularly piquant as Weizsäcker—because of the tense situation—had asked me not to request the authorization now required by Ribbentrop. Diplomatic representatives are no longer permitted to arrange for audiences of visitors with

Chiefs of State, Prime Ministers, Presidents, or Foreign Ministers, without Ribbentrop's permission. But I can't help it if someone invites me!

This was Heeren's opinion too. Before dinner he gave me a detailed picture of the course of the negotions with Yugoslavia, from the visit of Cinzar-Markovitch and from the latter's joint visit with Zvetkovitch to the Obersalzberg [February 14, 1941], the secret visit of Prince Paul to Hitler, and so on. According to him Germany retreated step by step before the Yugoslav conditions under which they would join the Three-Power Pact: territorial guarantees (first of all, naturally, against Italy); no military assistance and no march through Yugoslav territory; recognition of the right of access to the Aegean Sea (Salonika). In the midst of all this there was a hitch when Ribbentrop, on the evening after the most important concession was made, telephoned that the refusal of military co-operation was valid only in so far as Greece was concerned, but that it could not hold otherwise, else the Three-Power Pact would be undermined.

After that, there was a stiffening on the part of the Yugoslavs with consequent gains by the Serbian military, who saw in the occupation of Salonika as a preventive move the sole security for Yugoslavia. The Germans finally yielded this point also, and later discussions concerned only details (communiqués, the secrecy of the agreements, et cetera). But, according to Heeren's observations, there was no great joy on the part of the Yugoslavs over German acquiescence.

Today the Yugoslav Crown Council met. As I drove to Beli Dvor I observed the members of that assembly. The Prince told me right away that the meeting had just taken place, and he thought that now, perhaps, Yugoslavia would work more closely with Germany; only we made it so difficult, psychologically, for our friends.

My impression that the Crown Council meeting had led to a positive decision, even though the Yugoslavs would continue to play coy for a while, was confirmed in the course of the conversation. Princess Olga participated, too, mostly as a listener, but at times actively. In all two hours, with an interruption for a family lunch, that is with the two sons, in a small sitting room for guests on the second floor. The Princess was beautiful and as charming as ever, but she has a melancholy expression, as well she may (because of Greece and her own position between the two contending countries).

After lunch the Prince once more described the psychological difficulties involved. He pointed to the Bulgarians, who openly demanded the boundaries of San Stefano and shouted "Down with Yugoslavia!" and to Italy, which one could only hate and despise. Mussolini was the lout who had stood the whole world on its head. One could not trust him or the Italians in any way. I understood very well that he believed we were not innocent in the matter of the Bulgarian demonstrations, but had used them as a means to exert pressure. Several times the Prince emphasized the difficult position of Yugoslavia and his being married to a Greek princess, et cetera.

We then talked of the war situation and the prospects for peace. The Prince thought the English were taking submarine warfare very seriously. On the other hand, according to all reports, morale and determination in England were at a high level; they would not give in. Nevertheless, many people hoped that somehow an end could be put to this horrible war which was destroying everything. Only very recently a friend of his, the Duke of ——— had written him in this vein. How about our readiness to make peace?

I answered that Hitler probably still desired an understanding with England. But how was this possible? The Prince emphasized several times that it was a matter of confidence; there was widespread doubt that Hitler would keep his promises. To my question whether England would make peace with Hitler, he made no direct answer; but he obviously thought not. He made cautious inquiries about the internal situation in Germany, Hitler's authority, the authority of the Party, the chances for a change of regime, et cetera; also about the question of the monarchy.

In this connection, the idea was broached that perhaps a German conflict with Russia might constitute a bridge toward an understanding with the west. He apparently feared secret co-operation between the Russians and the Turks. Antipathy and mistrust for Italy came out again and again in his remarks.

In regard to our people he made a few observations: Hitler was to him a rather sinister puzzle; he didn't think much of Ribbentrop, but considered him the most powerful man in Germany.

*March 21, 1941:* Yesterday evening there was a meeting of the Council of Ministers. Three Ministers have resigned, among them the principal exponent of the English line, Konstantino-vitch.

Those who resigned apparently achieved a success, in that the rump government now lacks all support in Serbia proper— new evidence that adherence to the Three-Power Pact was achieved only under pressure and against all inner convictions. Zvetkovitch appears to be trying very hard to replace the three Ministers as speedily as possible in order to clear up the situation, as he finds his own position intolerable.

Extremely interesting report by the inspector of national defense. Very thorough and sober investigation of the general situation, full of respect for the Wehrmacht, but highly concerned about the final results of the war for the Germans on grounds that Goerdeler himself could have outlined.

The report recommended a pact of friendship or non-aggression with Germany, was in general for a clear and decent understanding but against capitulation—that is, adherence to the Three-Power Pact, which was impossible so long as Soviet Russia did not join it at the same time!

*March 22, 1941:* Berlin has now presented Belgrade with a sort of ultimatum: the pact must be signed by Tuesday or this "unique opportunity" will be missed. Heeren conveyed this threat today to Cinzar-Markovitch, Zvetkovitch, Kulenovitch (leader of the Slovenes in the Cabinet), and Prince Paul. Croats and Slovenes, of course, take it for granted that one must play along with this as security against Italy.

*March 23, 1941:* Today Heeren received instructions to tell the people here their decision must be made known by midnight because of the time that would be necessary to prepare the ceremony at the Belvedere. This represents the true

methods of our present leaders; they take no cognizance what-
soever of psychological effects, and leave the government here,
if it is still wavering, a tactically favorable pretext for refusing.
They have no choice but to agree, however. Results are unpredictable.

A visit from Dr. Ullmann and Bajkitch. The former is intelligent, with a broad view of things in general. He characterized this war as a conflict between a few *condottieri* over the
question of who shall set his stamp upon the world, not as a
conflict about the nature of the pattern itself. Organized
counterforces are to be found only in England. The tradition-
alists who fight for property, not of the capitalists but of a
leading class, and the working class in the old sense—those
wish a free order.

Bajkitch thought that since Bulgaria has yielded without
Russia making any move, the old Pan-Slav movement had
received a heavy blow; all opponents of a pro-German policy
were now gathered together under the aegis of the Anglo-
Saxons. But Ullmann believed that a German attack on Russia
would wholly destroy the fragile foundations of co-operation
with Germany now established here and in Bulgaria.

Weizsäcker telegraphed Heeren he should suggest to me
that in view of the situation I avoid visits in other capitals to
chiefs of state, prime ministers, and foreign ministers. I expected as much.

*March 25, 1941, Sofia:* I forgot to mention that the English
and Americans (now working together) have addressed a
sharply threatening note to Yugoslavia: if she joined the Pact
now she will be destroyed after the war.

Meanwhile the Yugoslavs have capitulated. It is interesting
that Konstantinovitch remains (as an observer?). Here in
Bulgaria a feeling of relief seems to prevail at the moment.
How the atmosphere will be when one realizes that Yugoslavia
has made demands is an open question.

Today the Yugoslavs signed. Actually they promised little
and received all kinds of guarantees. The Bulgarians follow
the affair with one damp and one dry eye.

*March 26, 1941:* Last evening I had supper in a cheap restaurant, the Battenberg, where citizens and German non-commissioned officers fraternize. The music consisted of German and Bulgarian airs, and on the wall, between pictures of a Bulgarian and a German soldier, there was a map showing Bulgaria's irredenta; it was illuminated during the playing of the Bulgarian anthem. The map showed Thrace and Macedonia as lost to Turkey and Greece; the demands against Yugoslavia were only "tactfully" indicated. Benzler, representative of the Foreign Office at the headquarters of General von List, was also there.

Afterward I went to the night club Etoile, managed by the Abwehr [German Military Intelligence Corps] and the SS Security Service. The chief of the Abwehr opened the dance. At the moment the officers of the SS bodyguard monopolize the scene; mostly disagreeable praetorian faces, but also among them honest non-commissioned officers as well as a few Bulgarians.

*March 27, 1941:* Yesterday afternoon I had an interesting conversation with Ivan T. Balabanoff, the apparently intelligent and energetic but enigmatic industrial leader. He left no doubt as to what high Bulgarian officials mean when they politely speak of being "reassured by the adherence of Yugoslavia"—anger over the guarantee of Yugoslavia's territorial integrity and distrust as to future developments. Balabanoff asserted that the Axis had lost 20 per cent of its followers here in the last twelve hours. Reserve officers who associate freely with Germans have received threatening letters. He seemed unconvinced by my comment that this flare-up would perhaps subside again.

Afterward I attended a large reception at Magistrati's for officers of the German Air Force. General von Richthofen stayed away because he was annoyed at the Italians for not having given him a decoration in Spain! I exchanged reminiscences of the very tense banquet of the Congress of Archaeologists on August 24, 1939, with the wife of the archaeologist and Prime Minister Filoff.

*March 27, 1941, Bucharest:* In the morning I received the

alarming news from Yugoslavia[1]—not entirely surprising, for I had felt from the beginning that all was not well there. Undisguised joy among the Bulgarians.

The affair is still obscure, but typical of the Balkans.

A plot with the English? Strange that Matschek and Kulovetch should stay. Is this voluntary? It is possible that Prince Paul advised the little King to take over this role in order to save the dynasty.

Just, our Military Attaché, has received reports from Berlin to the effect that Yugoslavia has swung around completely, and that a reaction in Turkey is feared. Minister Killinger has not been here for three weeks. This is peculiar in these times, with Neubacher an equally peculiar chargé d'affaires. Neubacher himself criticized Killinger's long absence, caused by a fight to maintain his authority against other Party offices in Bucharest (especially the Security Service; i.e., Gestapo). Situation typical of the Third Reich. Everybody against everybody else—a more and more inflated apparatus which functions only because of the industry of the German people, but which loses more and more of its real substance.

Mirbach reported that spirits in Rumania had shot upward. Better days might yet come! The Cabinet Ministers and others with whom I spoke regard all the borders with Hungary as provisional.

The chaos in Europe increases; the devil is at work. Neubacher said: "Adolf Genghis Khan—but Genghis Khan was an ingenious politician." He meant it as a compliment!

*March 29, 1941, Bucharest:* Called this morning on General Hansen, chief of the military mission. He, too, complained about the long absence of the newly appointed Killinger from which the Rumanians draw the conclusion that there is duplicity in German policy. I am convinced that there is such duplicity; the Party, of course, is still toying with the idea of seizing power through the Iron Guard since, as Neubacher told me, Horia Sima has been taken to safety in Germany.[2]

[1] The regime of Prince Paul was overthrown by a *coup d'état* March 27, 1941.

[2] Horia Sima, leader of the Iron Guard, had attempted a coup d'état on January 24, 1941.

Killinger had attempted to establish himself here as the sole political representative, especially against the SS, but so far without success.

I lunched with Senator Roth, leader of the German minority. He is desperate about the confusion the Party is causing throughout the German-speaking world. Schmidt, the twenty-eight-year-old "Führer," who was saddled on the German minority here by the SS (Lorenz, et al.), is without any real authority. At the head of the church, in the place of the highly deserving Glondys, they put a "Thuringian German Christian" who, however, immediately fell out with the Party because he opposed the idea that Christianity was centered upon "a soft, suffering hero."

One constructive value after another is being destroyed. The Legation is said to be a complete mess. Roth said we had to hope for victory with all our souls, and work for it, because otherwise everything German will be wiped out physically, but at the same time we could view the consequences of victory with only the gravest concern.

Roth was rather pessimistic about domestic affairs in Rumania. The government of generals is a temporary expedient maintained only with German assistance.

Göring told Antonescu the Führer had said to him he trusted only two people, Antonescu and Mussolini. Antonescu fed on this, while German functionaries worked underground with the Iron Guard. Antonescu had promised us to preserve the good elements in the Guard, while proceeding against ringleaders and common criminals. But the interpretation of the last two ideas was, of course, entirely arbitrary.

Toward evening I looked up former Minister Manoilescu. Neubacher views him with suspicion, believes that he conspires against Antonescu, and that I should be careful because Manoilescu was certainly watched. Actually Manoilescu was most cautious politically and spoke primarily about economic problems. However, now and then he made a few very interesting political remarks; for instance, one could now speak only of Serbia, no longer of Yugoslavia; or that he was first an engineer and then for many years an economist, but having once been Foreign Minister, and having been in the unfor-

tunate position of having to sign the Vienna Award, he had
only one thought; namely, to see to it that one day this was
rectified; the cutting up of Transylvania was madness.

*March 31, 1941:* Meanwhile the Germans have been evacuated from Croatia. All traffic on the Danube, and all freight
traffic in general, with and through Yugoslavia from Germany
and its vassals, is now at a standstill; this is also a serious interference in the conduct of the war.

*Budapest, April 2, 1941:* On the *first* Mirbach saw me off at
the airport. I flew here in calm weather, three and a half hours,
over beautiful Saxon villages, then the wooded and snow-
capped Carpathians, and finally over the Hungarian plains,
which had suffered severe damage from floods.

I was met here by Erdmannsdorf, whose diplomatic duties
seem to agree with him. Amazing meeting with the Heerens.
I had expected I might see her, since I knew that she had been
evacuated with the others. But he, too, had been called to
Berlin "to report." This is the famous method used in the case
of Welczeck, Eisenlohr, Dirksen. I am curious whether Ribbentrop will receive him at all.

As Heeren explains it, this was a typical Serbian putsch by
young officers, especially fliers, who want war. The outrages
against the Germans and against him were much exaggerated
by Berlin. There were but a few incidents and only on the first
day (against the German travel agency, against the engineer,
Mose, and, as far as he was concerned, simply some "boos"
during his drive from the cathedral).

Erdmannsdorf said that as early as Thursday [March 27,
1941], that is, on the day following the night of the putsch,
Hitler had summoned Sztojaj, had raved against Yugoslavia,
and had offered Hungary the most enticing pieces of Yugoslav
territory. As is his unhappy custom in such cases, he acted
entirely on impulse and in the manner of a small man. He
even dangled Fiume before the Hungarians, a dainty bite
which belongs to our Axis friends. He would have a talk with
the Italians!

Horthy has so far been able to arrange to have as few German troops as possible in evidence—in Budapest none at all. This will all change now.

In the afternoon I visited old Kanya. Sad to say he was pretty much of a wreck since his serious motor accident last September. He said he would like to write a book about mistakes in English policy during the last three years.

*April 3, 1941:* Today German troops are to march through. Last evening there were a lot of generals at the Hotel Duna Palota, although, as one old Hungarian Hussar major disdainfully remarked, more "engineers" than genuine soldiers.

The president of the German-Hungarian Chamber of Commerce was of the opinion that the monarchy was done for in Hungary. The country was now confronted with a roundabout effort to found a Horthy dynasty. Both his sons, however, amounted to nothing, despite the unfortunate protection given by Papa—least of all the Minister in Rio, whom old Horthy wished to shove on to Washington because of the higher salary. The Archduke Albrecht would be a more likely candidate for Regent. In the restaurant Albrecht was greeted several times with great respect, and an attempt was made to photograph him with us. I had an extended conversation with him, in which he expressed the view that a revolution must come in Hungary, but that it could be reasonably successful only if it were brought about jointly by the Imrédy group—which was a brain trust without popular following, and the Arrow-Cross group, which was "mass" without "brains."

Erdmannsdorff just called me to say that the Prime Minister, Count Teleki, had died suddenly during the night.

Evening. It seems to have been suicide. In the face of German mobilization against Yugoslavia he doubtless felt that the decision he feared so much, but had always evaded, had now become unavoidable for Hungary. He saw a tremendous danger in the mobilization and the consequent disruption of the national economy (already damaged by the floods), as well as in entering the war against England. It seems his nerves couldn't stand it. I hear that he went to confession the evening before. It is as if a devilish hand were at work in Europe.

This morning I visited Fabinyi, the former Minister of

Finance, a director general of the Credit Bank. He seems to be a very reasonable, experienced man. He wants a quiet, organic development in Hungary. He has no use for the ideas of the Archduke. Imrédy was an intelligent, first-rate man, but a bad politician. Of the Arrow-Cross crowd, with few exceptions, nothing good could be expected. It would be a great error, he rightly thought, if the Nazis should attempt to thrust upon Hungary an alien regime, led by their apish followers here. He, like Varga, has a veritable horror of the mobilization and of entrance into the war.

*April 4, 1941:* It is now admitted that Teleki committed suicide. I dined alone at the Erdmannsdorffs' instead of going to hear *Fidelio.* I had been looking forward to this, but, like all theaters, the opera was closed.

The Yugoslav Government (with Matschek in the Cabinet!) asks that the Italians, of all people, should attempt mediation. The situation, therefore, is not yet clarified. Berlin seems to consider the break as final, possibly even desirable. This would explain the trumped-up charges of atrocities, much after the pattern of Poland. It is not yet clear to me what line the Croats will take.

Face to face with this situation Hungary is depressed. Bárdossy as Prime Minister is apparently a temporary solution, for reasons of foreign policy.

I drove with Erdmannsdorff to the Gellért baths and up Mt. Gellért in the misty spring weather. We went walking. Merry people at the baths; outside all fresh and green, the chestnut trees with bursting buds; the castle shrouded in a fairy-tale mist like a palace of the Holy Grail, and, beneath, the majestic Danube. Now this country, too, wants (or does it?) to throw itself into the war. Long faces among the hotel staff. Twelve employees were called up this morning. And poor Teleki, with his sensitive nerves, sleeps the eternal sleep.

*April 5, 1941:* Train to the frontier. I drank a vermouth at Frau von Lukacz's. Her remarks confirmed the existence of an inner crisis in the government and the military which Teleki's death had revealed. A little while ago a war against Rumania would have been popular. But now the prospect of entering a war, and especially over Yugoslavia, with whom they had just concluded a pact of friendship at the behest of Germany, arouses general terror and the mobilization occasions greatest economic concern.

*April 7, 1941:* Vienna. I came here early on the fifth. Continual hum of airplanes; columns headed toward the southeast by way of Hungary. Herr Stephan, Director General of the Schenker Company, happened to be on the same train; this explains why Kronholz of Belgrade, now a refugee in Vienna, met the train. He was enraged at the lack of psychology in dealing with Yugoslavia; the break certainly could have been avoided. In any event, he said, after the revolution in Belgrade, Berlin was apparently set on having the war. The lies about atrocities against Germans were patterned very much after Poland. Kronholz confirmed the fact that these reports were untrue. Hitler, who had gone personally to the Belvedere,[1] was now acting out of wounded vanity.

Now the break is complete. They didn't even bother to present an ultimatum and thereby gain for Germany a favorable point of departure. After all, the Yugoslavs had merely changed their government. The proclamations which Hitler has issued are really in the very worst style and based on the most shopworn excuses his political muse has so far produced. This feeling is quite widespread.

Gauleiter Jury, whom I visited today, plainly said that the business displeased him and that it looked as if something had gone wrong. Naturally, General Gautier spoke even more sharply.

I went to see Baldur von Schirach. He had at first asked me to come at five o'clock, but afterward invited me to lunch. I finally went for coffee at three-fifteen and was picked up by an adjutant with a car. The conversation was interesting in so far as he expressed very moderate views and judged the entire Yugoslav business in a very critical light. Force alone would get us nowhere. He told how Matschek had in vain attempted

[1] Yugoslavia signed the Three-Power Pact at the Belvedere Palace in Vienna on March 25, 1941.

to get a guarantee from Berlin, and only after that had made up his mind to enter the Cabinet. He, Schirach, had sent a Viennese Croat to Berlin, but he had got only as far as to see Heinburg and had come back without having accomplished anything.

Schirach considered our entire situation very critical, particularly as regards America. The one chance was a decisive success in submarine and aerial warfare this summer. He described the extraordinarily great difficulties in matters of personnel and matériel which increased along with the extension of the combat areas. There is too great a strain all along the line.

The engineer R—— thought, however, we would achieve the war goals the Führer had set for this year; namely, the entire Balkan peninsula, Russia up to the Caucasus, the Near East, and North Africa!

Meanwhile, shortly before our invasion of Yugoslavia, our Russian friends concluded a friendship and non-aggression pact with that country [April 6, 1941]. A real warning.

Latest note: I met Neuhausen at the Hotel Imperial dressed as a major in the Air Force. He told me boastfully that he had been ordered to take over the direction of the entire economy of Yugoslavia, including the defense industry, and that he was personally responsible only to the Reich Marshal.

*April 10, 1941, Berlin:* Speedy and great successes in the Balkans. The Army is an incredibly brilliant instrument, with all the stronger characteristics of the German people, and filled with absolute self-confidence. It is tragic! With this magnificent instrument the destruction of Europe is being accomplished to perfection. In North Africa, too, immediate successes as soon as the German Army strikes. At the same time the Italian Empire in East Africa is nearing its end.

English airmen kept us in the cellar for three hours last night and punished Unter den Linden, the Opera, and the State Library, just as we once did the Guild Hall and Parliament. Madness strides on.

Popitz said the stargazers considered Hitler's horoscope for the month of April very unfavorable. Popitz doesn't put stock in this kind of thing but thinks it will have a psychological effect on the astrologically minded Hitler.

Weizsäcker confirms the belief that from the hour of the coup d'état in Belgrade, Hitler was set on battle, and, full of resentment, demands destruction and plans the wildest and most impossible solutions of the south Slav problem: Croatia under Hungarian domination, but Dalmatia to Italy!

Matsuoka was very restrained during his visit to Berlin [March 26, 1941]. He paid a long and much-publicized visit to Frau Solf, to whom he spoke of Eden as "my personal friend."

*May 4, 1941, Ebenhausen:* The defeats in Africa and Greece have doubtless damaged England's situation, because they endanger the entire status of England in the Near East. The repercussions in Turkey, Iraq, Egypt, and India are unmistakable. The isolationists in the United States are said to have gained ground, although, on the other hand, Roosevelt and all those who have put their money on him are redoubling their efforts.

In Berlin, among the Party, the military, and in part also among the people, the barometer has gone up perceptibly. The anxiety of people in the know, however, has not diminished. One cannot see a decisive success developing in the war situation, especially since the submarine warfare, on which such high hopes were based, is meeting increasingly effective defenses. A quick decision is necessary because food and other difficulties will increase very materially, especially if the attack on Russia is launched, for which increasingly intensive preparations are being made. To be sure an attempt is now being made, under pressure, from those who think this undertaking madness, to bring the bolshevists to heel by threatening to behead the whole lot of them if they do not do what Hitler wants.

But here is what is demanded of them: German exploitation of the Ukraine, access to oil for our war effort, and an attack on England. (This is approximately the program.) It would seem obvious that only people who are quaking with fear for their positions and their lives would yield to these demands and thus surrender Russia. Whether or not things look like this in Moscow I cannot judge.

A strange scene took place in Moscow upon the departure of Matsuoka. Stalin, to everybody's surprise, appeared on the station platform and laughingly said to Schulenburg: "You go on to Berlin and tell them, 'We want to remain friends!'" Then he clapped General Krebs, German Assistant Military Attaché, heavily on the shoulder with the words: "Well, well, a German general!" (A story told by Schulenburg.)

Contrary to an express agreement with Berlin, Matsuoka concluded a neutrality pact with Russia [April 13, 1941], although he had always excused himself with the Germans by saying he had to consult the Emperor and the Cabinet. In his farewell telegram to the Russians he exuded cordiality and emphasized that his stay in Moscow was the longest he had made. Naturally the Russians told him what we had concealed from him, that a German attack on Russia was imminent.

The situation is complicated by the continuous explanations of the Italians (in spite of their "victories") that they cannot carry on the war beyond this autumn. This is blackmail, of course, but also based on fact. Consequently Hitler meets all their wishes.

On *April 8* I conferred with Oster at Beck's. It makes one's hair stand on end to learn about and receive proof of orders signed by Halder and distributed to the troops as to measures to be taken in Russia, and about the systematic transformation of military law concerning the conquered population into uncontrolled despotism—indeed a caricature of all law. This kind of thing turns the German into a "Boche"; it develops a type of being which had existed only in enemy propaganda. Brauchitsch has sacrificed the honor of the German Army in submitting to these orders of Hitler.

*May 5, 1941, Ebenhausen:* The Balkan victory endangers the English position in the eastern Mediterranean, but it also means for us a new and severe strain on all our energies and entails more disadvantages than advantages. The first consequence is that the Bor copper mine has been put out of commission for half a year. In addition the Danube has been closed temporarily and we hear of rotten conditions in Belgrade.

Undersecretary Neumann, with whom I had lunch recently, was rather subdued. Conversations with Popitz and Goerdeler —the latter always unshaken in his sanguine prophecies—led to the conclusion that with the barometer at its present height it would be difficult to do anything to open the eyes of the generals; but perhaps very soon.

I saw Papen on *April 28.* He has aged somewhat, and seems more resigned. He thought the Turks were much more favorably inclined toward Germany than they were at first, but that they would resist any trespass on their territory. Papen says, "This kind of policy, furthermore, would have to be made without me!" Who knows?

On April 20 Weizsäcker's luncheon at the Adlon for the Governor of Rome, Giangiacomo Borghese, with Sophia, who had come for the visit of the Rome opera company. The opera was a tremendous success for the Italians, and I myself particularly enjoyed *The Masked Ball.* Unfortunately it was given in the ugly Deutsches Opernhaus—with Goebbels presiding in a wholly disinterested way—because the beautiful State Opera House has been destroyed by bombs.

After the opera I supped with Olga Riegele and Undersecretary Hueber [brother-in-law of Göring], who has again begun to think in very brutal military terms. We were guests of the American, Stallforth (at Horcher's restaurant), who had wanted to talk with me months ago. He had just arrived by Clipper. He is a man of sober and clear judgment. Recent events had given Roosevelt's opponents a great boost, but for the present this changed nothing. Stallforth's purpose is to press for peace with the leading people here, but up to now he has not been able to see Hermann Göring or anyone else. Very significant! I saw him once more at a musical evening and he said again with great earnestness: "Germany must bring this to an end by fall!"

In the company of Rantzau of the Foreign Office I recently became acquainted with a peculiar case, that of the beautiful and attractive young Englishwoman, Barbara Greene, who is formally engaged to Strachwitz of the Foreign Office, now stationed in Barcelona. She edits for the Foreign Office *The Camp*, a magazine, addressed to English prisoners. She said the readers maintained a lively contact with her. The prisoners of the Air Force receive the best treatment. There was a football game the other day between the German and English officers in which the latter won.

A shocking conversation a few days ago with Glaise-Horstenau, who has been appointed German Commanding General for Croatia at Agram. He had recorded two talks with Hitler revealing a mental attitude that makes shivers run up one's spine. Under the heading: "Reconstruction of Europe along new principles of real order and justice," a veritable chaos is being let loose upon the southeast. The basic principle is that in order to keep the Italians in line they are to get everything they want, no matter how absurd. There is no harm done if, later, they and the Slavs get into one another's hair. Second principle: the Serbs must be thoroughly squashed. The one sensible thing is that he doesn't want to push the borders of Germany as far as the Mediterranean.

The Croats have been ordered to come to an agreement with their mortal enemies, the Italians, who had sheltered and kept their present Führer, Pavelitch, for years. Agreement will be hard to achieve, however, since the Italians want almost the entire coast line—or at least the most valuable parts, and in addition want to exercise a kind of suzerainty over the Croats! Eventually there might have to be a German arbitration award, probably no more successful than that between Hungary and Rumania.

Montenegro is also slated to rise again. Italian Albania is to be expanded considerably, and Bulgaria is to have approximately the borders of San Stefano. Greece is to become an Italian dependency. And to think that for twenty-five years we have cursed the injustices of the Paris peace treaties!

The Hungarians are also to receive much, but they were intelligent enough to reject the proffered protectorate over Croatia.

The new German frontier, as well as that of Italy (Laibach), will push deeply into Slovenian territory. Resettlements are planned on a grand scale. In Berlin I met young

Prince Auersperg who lobbies for the incorporation of Gott-schee[1] into Germany, preferably through resettlement.

Glaise-Horstenau repeated a lot of Hitler's characteristic remarks. For example, with respect to the Jewish question in Croatia: the new masters there wanted to take measures only against recently immigrated Jews, but he had told them they must proceed radically, for it was the old established Jews who had the money!

*May 17, 1941, Ebenhausen:* There is such a mass of events and impressions that it is difficult to give the current picture in a few words. The war situation: in Germany's favor (1) the remarkably quick successes in Yugoslavia and Greece, thanks to the Army, which endanger the position of England in the eastern Mediterranean; (2) the fighting in Iraq [May 3, 1941], although apparently begun prematurely, constitutes a threat to the English position in the Levant, particularly because (3) the agreement with France (Darlan) is making progress, envisaging Syria as a base of operations for Hitler. Apparently France is in such a tight place that the people there know of no other way out than to play this game. (4) the fact that Rommel is holding his own on the Egyptian frontier, although with difficulty. (5) successes of the German Air Force against merchant shipping.

I do not know whether to add to the list of German successes the horrible destruction in England, which is claiming great cultural treasures as its victims, or whether I should not rather add them to the chapter on the suicide of Europe, along with the much less extensive but still heavy destruction in Germany.

Factors unfavorable to Germany are: (1) the steadily increasing strain on German resources; (2) the lag in submarine activities, contrary to Hitler's expectations, as a result of ever-more-effective counter-weapons; (3) the increasingly pointed antipathy of the United States, which seems bent on entering the war; (4) the rapid progress of moral degeneracy among the leaders—examples later; (5) in this connection there is the case of Hess.

[1] Old German settlement in Yugoslavia.

*May 18, 1941:* The effect of this last event, the flight of Hess to England, May 10, was indescribable, but immeasurably increased by the stupidity of the official communiqué. This was traceable to Hitler's personal explosions of wrath. The first one, especially, which implied that for months, even for years, he had presented to the people a half or even entirely insane "deputy" as heir apparent of the Führer. Winston Churchill briefly summarized the impressions abroad: "It is the worm in the apple."

Contrary to the high-flown purpose of Hess, the effect will be to prolong the war. At home, from a long-range point of view, it is a blow against the authority of the regime, but for the moment is a point for the radicals and for Ribbentrop. The latter, a few weeks ago, had had a violent quarrel with Hess about personnel matters (conflict between the SA Luther and SS Stahlecker to dominate the Foreign Office). Hess had received an incredibly rude letter from Ribbentrop to which he had replied—as one active Reich Minister to another—that Ribbentrop's letter revealed such a state of mind, the result of nervous exhaustion, that he preferred to resume the correspondence only when Ribbentrop had recovered his senses.

The background of Hess's flight is not yet clear. The official explanations are, to say the least, not complete. His sporting and technical performance alone showed that Hess cannot be called crazy. It is possible that he had reason to fear a move against him personally. I know that for a long time he has been doubtful about the methods of his lord and master. Although he behaved unspeakably when I left office I consider him as fundamentally not vicious, but as foolish and weak, possessed of idealistic and of course fanatical ideas. No doubt he frequently attempted to revive contacts with England, in most cases with the approval of Hitler.

According to information from his housekeeper, Albrecht Haushofer was taken away by two men at two o'clock in the night following Hess's flight, and had explained that he was going to the airport to take a trip! There is some uneasiness, inasmuch as other arrests have been made, among them, we hear, that of Gauleiter Wagner of Munich.

On *May 10,* in the afternoon, I went to see Popitz in Berlin. Meanwhile, day before yesterday, Ilse came back at last. I am thankful to have her again at a time when I need her so much. She had made preparations for Albrecht Haushofer's trip in a long talk with Carl Burckhardt in Zürich, and had told him that Haushofer was coming with two faces. [Ostensibly for Hess, but actually for the resistance movement.] Afterward she had a detailed conversation with Haushofer himself in Arosa after his visit to Geneva.

From Ilse's and Haushofer's statements it is apparent that Burckhardt, on the basis of the discussions with Professor Borenius in London, which he had told me about, and of further conversations with English diplomats, retains his belief that England still wants peace on a rational basis, but (1) not with our present rulers, and (2) perhaps not for much longer.

The air raids on Westminster Abbey, Parliament, and other places (which were triumphantly revealed to us on the same page of the newspaper in which the English were branded as "despicable cowards" for their attacks on German residential areas), naturally arouse an ever-increasing hatred.

Burckhardt told Ilse in Zürich that an agent of Himmler's had come to him to find out whether England would perhaps make peace with Himmler instead of Hitler—a new proof of the fragility of the Nazi structure. As an illustration of the clumsy propaganda methods used by our people, Burckhardt reported that when he offered to exert his influence in America toward a saner and more objective view of the situation, he had received the unbelievable answer that he would be well repaid.

The flight of Hess has now shattered every possibility of advancing our cause through Haushofer. After some weeks he was to go once more to Burckhardt, who meanwhile was to have got in contact with the British again. Then we were to have used the accumulated evidence to good purpose. This is now out, as Haushofer has been arrested.

The process of drawing new frontiers in the southeast is coming to an end. Their contours and the protectorates promised the Italians begger description. It has been confirmed that Hitler met all their wishes and thereby consciously entertained the thought in the back of his mind that murder and fighting between Italians and Slavs would follow, and that the Germans would very likely find it necessary to take action against the Italians, with whom he is furious!

The Russian question is still unsettled. There are whispers everywhere that Stalin will make a kind of peaceful capitulation. Weizsäcker doesn't put any faith in this and is convinced that Hitler is determined to carry out his campaign against Russia.

Typical remark of a neutral: when things go well with the English one can talk with them; when things go badly, they are unapproachable. With the Germans it is the other way around.

At the request of Professor Berber (he naturally has the title of "Minister") and despite great scruples, I have undertaken to write the next article on the political situation of Europe for his semi-official periodical. Dieckhoff has undertaken to do the one on America, and a man in the Foreign Office (Trott) that on East Asia—all three anonymously.

I stated all my conditions and emphasized that I could not write as a semi-official propagandist. Berber, who gives the impression of being very clever but somewhat mysterious, agreed to my conditions. The question, however, is whether it is practically possible. I should like to know whether Ribbentrop knows that Berber has requested me to do this. However that may be, it offers a chance to say a few things, and it is a good cloak.

I have some professional troubles. The MWT wants to extend my work with them for two years. But the whole program of the MWT becomes more and more problematical because of the encroachments of "managed economy" and because of the expansion of the German and Italian spheres in southeastern Europe.

I had dinner recently with the Bruckmanns. The latest of Hitler's inscriptions in Frau Bruckmann's guest book (this time for her birthday) was: "In the year of the achievement of German victory!"

A few days ago Frauendorfer called to tell me his woes. He is desperate about what he has to witness in Poland. He reported also that the secret Polish organization of resistance against German oppression was making rapid headway.

Two examples from his stories:

Himmler had one hundred and eighty Polish farm workers unceremoniously hanged because they had had intercourse with German women. Frauendorfer went personally to Himmler to protest against this action and to explain the impossibility of getting farm workers under such conditions. Answer: "I have studied each case thoroughly; I have had photographs sent me, and have ascertained that from the racial point of view hanging was justified in every instance!"

Governor General Frank, who is in hot water up to his neck, wrote to Martin Bormann that in his last conversation the Führer had ordered Polish farm workers to be treated like all other foreign workers, that is, humanely; for instance, they should be allowed to open savings accounts. Bormann replied that he had been present at all discussions, and knew that the Führer had not given any such order. On the contrary, he took the view that the Poles were not Europeans but Asiatics, and could be handled only with the knout.

*May 29, 1941, Ebenhausen:* The situation is highlighted by: (1) the successful German attack on Crete [May 20, 1941], which was insufficiently resisted by the English; (2) by the victory of the *Bismarck* over the *Hood*—more than canceled by the destruction of the *Bismarck* [May 24–27, 1941], which, to my mind, was rather foolishly ordered to St. Nazaire after the encounter off Greenland; (3) by the further deterioration of relations with America. People in general are in a bad state of mind. The economic strain becomes ever more evident.

The Hess incident, though systematically hushed up, did indeed affect the authority of the regime. Popular jokes are on the good-natured side. The thousand-year Reich has been shortened to one hundred years. Why? One zero less! Or in England Hess publishes a paper called *Der Türmer* [the Runaway].[1] Or a new title for Hess: Reich Refugee Leader [Reichsemigrantenführer].

Albrecht Haushofer is still imprisoned. Also Dr. Schmitt. The former allegedly because he encouraged the astrological interests of Hess—which is quite new to me.

[1]The name, of course, is a take-off on Streicher's "Der Stürmer."

Day before yesterday, Wednesday, there was a gathering at
the Sauerbruchs'. Sauerbruch, after some drinks, got into a
very lively argument with Pinder and Fischer, who both represented official viewpoints. Sauerbruch told how, at his first
lecture after the *Bismarck* went down, he had made a few remarks in honor of the dead, and had concluded with the words:
"Long live Germany and the Führer!" In the afternoon, apparently after denunciation by a student, the Gestapo called
him: it was absolutely required that in cases like this one should
say "Long live the Führer!" After that one could also mention
Germany. Comment superfluous.

On *May 22, 1940,* I delivered a short lecture at the Breslau
Fair on the economic problems in southeastern Europe. I not
only talked, but also managed to say a few things.

Gauleiter Hanke, formerly with Goebbels, with whom I had
had a serious altercation in Rome in 1933, expressly chose my
lecture among the meetings he honored with his presence. He
was extraordinarily cordial and in the evening made most
chivalrous remarks to the effect that this stupid incident now
lay far behind us. Since then I've heard very unfavorable comments about Hanke. He is said to be absolutely dishonest, and
maneuvers such as this were only camouflage. But to what purpose? Do these people actually sense that the timbers are beginning to creak? Comment is superfluous.

Next to Hanke sat a counselor of the Russian Embassy. With
a very naïve expression on his face he said to his other neighbor, Berve (Director General of the Schaffgotsch concern,
who made a very good impression): "I think I saw Field
Marshal von Rundstedt on the street. Is the Supreme Command located here?"

As a matter of fact he is in Breslau. I saw Rundstedt in the
hotel but didn't speak to him. I spoke, however, to his adjutant, Salviati, a cavalry officer recalled to active service. He
said the General Field Marshal saw clearly almost everything
that was wrong, but that was as far as it went.

*June 15, 1941, Ebenhausen:* The situation: (1) a decision
on the Russian problem draws nearer. According to the opinion
of all "knowing men" (in so far as there are any such), the

attack will most probably begin about June 22. With astonishing unanimity, however, come rumors—in the opinion of the same "knowing men" spread purposely—why?—that an understanding with Russia is imminent, Stalin is coming here, we are already peacefully in the Ukraine. (2) failure of the Iraq movement and the invasion of Syria by the English and the Gaullists [June 8, 1941]. This is England's and De Gaulle's reply to the prematurely conceived blow in Iraq and to Darlan's astonishing concession to Hitler, which, incidentally, was rewarded only meagerly by Germany.

The tug of war for the soul of Turkey, with promises from the German and English sides, seems to have reached its climax. The fear of the Turks that we shall hem them in completely must be very much to the fore. A German attack on Russia would bring this feeling to a new climax; the only question is whether the fear of the Turks will move them to come to terms with Germany.

The Russians seem to realize what is up, and are beginning to withdraw their poorly placed cordons of troops and to concentrate them in the rear. The prospects of a swift victory against Russia are still naïvely considered by the soldiers as bright. There are, however, also skeptical views; for example, Colonel Oster.

Nostitz came to me, very excited. He says we should do everything, even at the last minute, to reverse the decision to attack Russia. We could not avert an end to the war like that of 1918. Couldn't I attempt to influence Mussolini? For various reasons I cannot do that. I told Nostitz that I was not clear as to whether Mussolini was actually 100 per cent against the undertaking. (1) could it not be that a diversion of the overwhelming superior German weight from the Mediterranean (after the acute danger for Italy was removed) would be welcomed by him? (2) Is he, perhaps, skeptical about the outcome of the German campaign against Russia, and more concerned with preventing an overwhelming German victory than with the fear of a "defeat of the Axis?"

*June 16, 1941:* A series of conferences with Popitz, Goerdeler, Beck, and Oster, to consider whether certain orders which the army commanders have received (but which they have not as yet issued) might suffice to open the eyes of the military leaders to the nature of the regime for which they are fighting. These orders concern brutal and uncontrolled measures the troops are to take against the bolshevists when Russia is invaded.

We came to the conclusion that nothing was to be hoped for now. Brauchitsch and Halder have already agreed to Hitler's tactics. Thus the Army must assume the onus of the murders and burnings which up to now have been confined to the SS. They have assumed the responsibility, and delude themselves and others by reasoning that does not alter the essence of the problem—the necessity for maintaining discipline, et cetera. Hopeless sergeant majors!

The view was discussed that the corps commanders might refuse to carry out the orders and thereby bring about a showdown (fall of government). I doubt it. Moreover, this is a wild expedient which promises more dangers than hopes. At the moment the Chinese proverb is valid: *"Meju Fatse."* (There is no short cut.) Hopeless! Perhaps another moment will come during the Russian campaign, after it has become obvious that peace has not been brought nearer but is still farther away.

On June 9, 1941, there was a reception at Schacht's after his church wedding to his second wife, née Volger. There were many people present from "his majesty's most loyal opposition."

Afterward dinner at Sauerbruch's house, with Goerdeler and Gisevius. We considered political possibilities. Gisevius went later to Helldorf, who sent his car for him. During the conversation it became apparent that Goerdeler is often handicapped by quite outmoded conceptions. He does not grasp that the world really (although "unfortunately") is changing in a manner that can be regulated but not stemmed.

I delivered my Breslau lecture (on economic problems in southeastern Europe), with slight variations, at the request of the University Institute for Foreign Studies, before about two hundred foreigners, students and others, who are here to attend a course. Many Dutchmen, Belgians, Scandinavians, Swiss, and people from the southeast. I asked one Hungarian what all these people were thinking and what had drawn them to Berlin. To the latter question he answered: curiosity! Some of them were surprised that the Brandenburg Gate is still standing. In answer to my first question he explained that, with the exception of a few Mussert and Degrelle people, all Dutchmen, Belgians, Swiss, and Scandinavians were filled with hatred toward present-day Germany and hope for an English victory.

The death of the Kaiser [June 4, 1941] went almost unnoticed by the German people, although, personally, he had won more and more respect. The official formula was to treat the event with a "cool respect for outward decorum," but otherwise to preserve a deadly silence. Oster accompanied Canaris to the funeral, and was deeply moved.

*July 13, 1941, Ebenhausen:* This wartime paper is so bad that one cannot write on it with ink. A month has gone by since I last jotted down my impressions. The fearful contingency of an unprovoked attack on Russia has since materialized [June 22]. Even the bolshevists have been bowled over by our people. They had expected that at least some pretext would be found. The suddenness of the attack surprised them so much that their air force suffered very heavy losses on the ground, which swiftly resulted in a considerable German superiority. Nevertheless, the struggle is much harder than had been expected.

The Russians are fighting with tough and stolid bravery. As usual, heavy losses among German officers, particularly in the ranks of the youngest and best—among others Gebsattel's only son. At Agathe Tiedemann's in Vienna I also saw the picture of her eighteen-year-old nephew who was killed the very first day. I cannot forget his clean-cut (in the best sense of the word) German expression. A frightful, senseless, and unfathomable war!

The Berlin representative of the organization of White Russian *émigrés* called on me. He was in complete despair because he and his friends had staked everything on the Germans. He has come to the conclusion that the war is not being fought against bolshevism but against the Russian people. The most convincing evidence of this is the fact that Rosenberg, the mortal enemy of the Russians, has been placed at the head of the civilian administration.

Nostitz told me, and I agreed with him, that if Hitler goes on like this and it becomes clear that his aim is to put Russia first under Nazi Gauleiters (rejecting the co-operation of patriotic Russians), and then to split it up, Stalin may yet succeed in forming a patriotic Russian front against the German enemy.

It is grotesque that Stalin has just called off the anti-religious campaign, but nonetheless realistic. Certain sympathies, which we had at last gained in the world as the result of the German attack against bolshevism, are already evaporating. While Stalin orders prayers for victory, the Party in Germany (Bormann) steadily increases its attack on the churches.

Bishop Heckel, once a rather willing collaborator in all attempts to bridge the gap that divided Nazism and the Protestant Church, visited me recently and showed a perfectly clear understanding of the Party's purpose to destroy the churches. He brought along especially vivid evidence in the shape of notes on a meeting of Party functionaries in Madrid, at which the Gauleiter of the Foreign Organization of the Party had sharply proclaimed the incompatibility of Party and Church. He had demanded that Party functionaries and teachers leave the Church and that baptism should be replaced by a "name-giving" ceremony; that religious services at funerals, et cetera, should be dispensed with because the Christian religion, which took its orders from an "Asiatic" (Christ), was unsuitable for a German.

Bohle's reaction was typical when he was told about this. The matter had not been reported correctly; this kind of thing was at variance with his own views. These are the usual Party tactics, of course. Reconnaissance units and assault troops are sent ahead, and when the reaction is too strong, the Party carries out a pseudo retreat.

Since Stalin's "conversion," Nazi Germany has become the only protagonist in the world of the anti-religious movement.

The dissection of the Foreign Office progresses, but not in the direction of an objective reform. Favors are distributed to the Party mercenaries, the SS, and the SA. The latter have now been given the posts of Pressburg, Agram, Bucharest,

Sofia, and recently Budapest also, which has made the Hungarians furious because they have the impression that they are being put under a satrap, like the Balkan countries.

Hans-Dieter is in the front lines in Russia; our last news was dated July 3. He described the people and the country in the drabbest colors.

A few days before the beginning of the Russian campaign Popitz and I, in the home of that splendid Jessen, once more earnestly besought Beck, as the most distinguished representative of the officer class, to write a letter to Brauchitsch and ask him to protest against the orders to murder Russian captives. Beck finally agreed. He was encouraged in this decision by the news we brought him the following Wednesday at Paul Fechter's, that one commander of an army group—Bock, significantly enough, at the urging of a young officer of his staff —had actually refused to issue the order. Some army commanders, for instance Knobelsdorff, also appear to have refused to issue it.

Two recent conversations with the American Stallforth are worth putting down. Fired by the thought that the fight against bolshevism would give the isolationists in America an extraordinary boost, he redoubled his efforts to find a common meeting ground for Berlin and Washington. In speaking of my good relations with Phillips [American Ambassador in Rome], Stallforth had the idea of inducing Ribbentrop to send me to Phillips. His connecting link with Ribbentrop, Wuster, the Consul General in Rome, took up this proposal enthusiastically, and supposedly received Ribbentrop's consent at once. I told Stallforth the chances were 99 to 1 that Hitler would refuse. But I must admit that Ribbentrop's attitude—if the report is correct—is most interesting. Since then I have heard nothing further.

Popitz recently had a conversation with Crown Prince Wilhelm. He had come on the pretext of discussing his estates. Popitz had a good impression of him, his clear vision, his intelligence, and, what is more important, his earnestness; also his judgment about certain individuals. As to the main point, he expressly declared that he was ready to step into the breach and assume all sacrifices and dangers—about the extent of which he had no illusions.

Santa Hercolani, to the delight of everyone, is here to take her little son to the orthopedic hospital for treatment. She is depressed about political matters, particularly by the barbaric colossus which is gradually subduing all of Europe. In Italy people generally considered the war a strictly Party affair, in which the individual did not participate emotionally. There was deep dissatisfaction over the failure of the government machine, the corruption, and the insignificant performance of the Italian Army. Mussolini had lost much of his authority, particularly after his amateurish activities as a field commander in Albania, which cost so many lives. The Crown Prince had become old and gray as a result of his troubles and worries.

On *June 27* I delivered a lecture in Bremen, before the Academy of Administrative Law, on the Mediterranean in world history. The chief of the port administration showed me about the harbor and pointed out the extensive damage it had suffered. Losses were estimated at 16 per cent of the warehouses, sheds, et cetera. On the other hand, the giant combination of the Weserwerft and Deschimag concerns were untouched, as well as all the cranes. One is inclined to draw certain conclusions about Liverpool and other British ports, even if our people inflicted greater damage there. Actually traffic in the port of Bremen has not been halted even for one day. Nessenius now writes that there have been four daylight raids and four night raids in one week. One single air mine had destroyed twenty large structures, damaged forty severely, and 100 slightly.

From *June 5–7* in Vienna, principally to talk to old Riedl about fundamental problems of German economy in the southeast. A wise man of great charm. Conversed with Knoll, the intelligent, energetic Rector of the Academy of World Commerce. He is the representative of the MWT in Vienna. An old Austrian Nazi, but now very skeptical.

A few stories told in Vienna:

Hacha is lunching with Neurath, who hands him the menu. Hacha: "Where do I sign?"

Secretary of State Frank, the wild Sudeten German, finds an inscription daubed in red on the Charles Bridge in Prague:

*"Smrt Nemcum"* (Death to the Germans). He makes a complaint to Neurath, who calls in Hacha. Hacha: "Oh, these countrymen of mine! How often have I told them! Everything is to appear in two languages, and German always first!"

Hess was asked whether he didn't want to come back. Answer: "But I am not really crazy!"

Now I am walking a mental tightrope as I write my essay on Europe for Berber.

*August 2, 1941, Ebenhausen:* The situation: heavy Russian resistance, heavy losses, heavy English air raids in the west. Very meager results in the submarine and air war against the British merchant fleet. Consequently, low barometer readings, a general feeling of endlessness and doom.

I have had many conversations with Popitz, Goerdeler, and others about the question whether it is already too late for a change of regime, and whether or not a decent government would still receive an acceptable peace, now that our opponents can envisage the possibility of a complete crushing of Germany.

X visited me, at Popitz's request, on June 29. I explained to him that every public demand for a change of regime emanating from the enemy would have the opposite effect from that desired. The change of government was a German affair. All we wanted was an assurance from the other side that they would not exploit such a change of government and would be ready to make a reasonable peace. We did not need this assurance for ourselves; the absolute necessity of a change of regime was clear enough to us. But we needed it for the generals. X, however, thought all this was a lot of fuss. Nothing will come of this step.

Albrecht Haushofer is free. He was questioned, so to speak, as a witness, because it was assumed that Albrecht's report to Hess about his trip had something to do with the flight.

Popitz now wants Planck to go about from one general to another as a kind of circuit preacher, after the way has been prepared for him by Thomas.

Oster told me about the remarkable courage of Glaise-Horstenau, who called "Marshal" Kwaternik to account in the sharpest manner for the incredible cruelties practiced by the

Croats against the 1,800,000 Serbs, and who had even submitted a report on the subject. He told Kwaternik that in late
years he had lived through a great many things of this kind,
but nothing that could compare with the misdeeds of the
Croats.

Now that Japan has marched into Indo-China [July 23,
1941], East Asia will be drawn in also. This is bound to stiffen
America's attitude. Neither Japan nor the United States really
wishes to participate directly in the war so long as the prospects
of victory are still doubtful. But they are being driven nearer
and nearer to war.

August Westen (a big German industrialist in Slovenia, that
is old Austria), from Cilli, called on me and reported horrifying things, even of those Slovenian districts that had fallen to
Germany. Since Hitler used the slogan that this land must
become German, the Party gladiators have proceeded against
the old, established Slovenian population, in the most brutal
way, above all, against the intelligentsia and the bourgeoisie.
Respected and esteemed people, one of Westen's neighbors, for
instance, a Slovenian architect who was on the best possible
terms with the local German inhabitants, was taken out of his
bed at night and, with his wife and children and one small
suitcase, sent off on the train for Serbia. Others fared likewise.

Good news so far, thank God, about Dieter's personal welfare. The reports about the campaign sound bad enough.
Barbaric fighting and murder.

I have two lecture trips behind me. The first was to Brussels
at the end of June. I had a very good impression of Falkenhausen, who sees very clearly indeed, as does his Chief of Staff.
Physically Falkenhausen is a phenomenon. He is able to drink
enormous amounts in the evening without ever showing the
slightest aftereffects, and he is at his office shortly after eight
o'clock in the morning. Eleven years in China have stamped
out in him any tendencies toward drill-ground mentality and
dull mechanical obedience he might have had, and pumped
some adventurous blood into his veins. It is a pity he is not at a
more central spot. I shall remain in contact with him.

In my lectures I said all kinds of things; to my delight they
were understood.

During the last days of July I delivered lectures in Bochum and Dortmund before the Academy of Administrative Law of the industrial district. Astonishing how little effect the few air raids of the English have had on this German nerve center. Consequently there was no great depression here. There were many "Heil Hitlers!" In this respect typically provincial and also typical of industrial leaders, who are always politically inept and recognize only one real yardstick: profits.

Everybody in the know is reeling under the effect of Hitler's new orders which will triple the strain on our resources (particularly in view of the questionable nature of the "successes" in Russia). The manufacture of equipment for the Air Force is to be quadrupled (Guth thought they had until June 1, 1942, to achieve this; such are the dates on which one now figures). Tremendous increase in submarine and tank production. Setting up of a colonial army of two million men for an attack through Turkey on Baku, Mosul, and Suez.

Notable civic courage was displayed recently by the well-known Berlin physician, Dr. Munk, who gave an address at the Beuths' luncheon table. He spoke about Schiller as a regimental surgeon: "If a surgeon's assistant today permitted himself half the remarks young Schiller made under the "tyrant" Duke Karl Eugen there is no doubt at all what would happen to him. Perhaps, though, the Gestapo of the Duke was not so efficient as that of today."

*August 5, 1941:* Most malicious joke of the day: "What are the new materials made of?" "Out of the filaments of the Führer's imagination, the threadbare patience of the German people, and old Party shoddy."

*August 18, 1941, Ebenhausen:* Progress in southern Russia.[1] The air war on commerce has produced only meager successes. English aviation and the supposedly destroyed Russian Air Force attack Berlin. Geyr reported that the troublesome activities of low-flying Russian planes caused many casualties. Dieter reports to the same effect. Air bombs recently hit the building which housed the staff of the tank corps.

[1] On August 17, 1941, German troops reached the Dnieper.

The whole war in the east is terrible—a return to savagery. A young officer now in Munich received an order to shoot three hundred and fifty civilians, allegedly partisans, among them women and children, who had been herded together in a big barn. He hesitated at first, but was then warned that the penalty for disobedience was death. He begged for ten minutes' time to think it over, and finally carried out the order with machine-gun fire. He was so shaken by this episode that, although only slightly wounded, he was determined not to go back to the front.

Denunciations are on the increase. The destruction of all concepts of decency is illustrated in the following: Frau Jessen, from Ebenhausen, overheard a conversation between two officers who remarked that even after the greatest successes in Russia there still remained the problem of hunger and the winter. She repeated this to a lady in Ebenhausen, who reported her at once. Thereupon, an old resident here, who is blessed with a daughter fanatically attached to the Party, came to the house and explained to Frau Jessen that he must question her about her remarks. If she had made them, he would institute proceedings against her. Surprisingly enough, however, Weyrich, the local Party chief, had more sense than this foolish old . . ., and gave the matter no attention.

The chief political event is the publication of the joint declaration of Churchill and Roosevelt [Atlantic Charter, August 14, 1941], whose eight points remind me of Wilson's fourteen, but only superficially, for in substance they are generally mild and, above all, elastic. It is characteristic of our press that the matter is handled in cowardly fashion. The points whose effects Hitler apparently fears cannot be mentioned, but they are nevertheless attacked and crudely picked to pieces. The reader can find out only with great effort what they really are and then only inaccurately and incompletely.

*Ebenhausen, August 30, 1941:* Yesterday I returned from Jagd Klachau and Budapest. Before I left Ebenhausen the last time Guttenberg called me on August 15, at the request of Popitz, to say that I should remain in Ebenhausen to receive an important visitor on the eighteenth and nineteenth. On Sunday afternoon, the seventeenth, I received a visit from Langbehn, the attorney, whom I knew by name as a friend of Popitz's and as an associate of Albrecht Haushofer. He reported that Carl Burckhardt, who was spending some time in Germany on Red Cross matters, would soon be going to England on a like mission, and that it might be profitable, therefore, to have a talk with him.

This was the more necessary, first, because of paragraph 8 in the Churchill-Roosevelt declaration, which certainly would be interpreted by our generals as proof that England and America are not fighting only against Hitler but also want to smash Germany and render her defenseless. We were agreed that this interpretation was by no means the only one possible, but that it was certainly a very plausible one, as indeed the process of identifying Germany with Hitler was making progress throughout the world.

Evidence of this trend is to be seen in an English radio broadcast to the effect that Papen had said indiscreetly that before long the regime would be overthrown by a military dictatorship under Falkenhausen. The strange secret station "Gustav Siegfried" has also recently taken up this line. But, the broadcast continued, it made no difference whether Hitler and his outfit or the militarists were at the helm. If Papen said anything like this, he deserves to be hanged.

On *Monday, the eighteenth,* Langbehn came by car with Carl Burckhardt and took Ilse and me to his country place. There we were received by his pleasant wife, innumerable children, Shetland ponies, and mountain goats—a picture of utter peace. Both in the car and afterward we had long discussions along familiar lines:

(1) Every demand for a change of regime that emanates from the other side constitutes a tactical error, because we look upon this problem as a strictly internal question.

(2) On the other hand, identifying the Germans with Hitler—as can be read into Point 8 of the Churchill-Roosevelt declaration—destroys every reasonable chance for peace.

(3) German patriots make very moderate demands, but there are certain claims from which they could not desist.

It was moving to see how deeply shocked Carl Burckhardt

was over the progressive destruction of the best elements here (for example, the heavy losses among the officers in the east and especially among the nobility) and of the best qualities in Germany. He said that before the war Gauleiter Forster had told him a war would be excellent because many reactionaries would be killed. Similar remarks are said to have been made by Himmler, rather flattering to the reactionaries, though betraying a filthy cast of mind.

We liked it so much at the Langbehns' that we arrived in Munich almost too late to catch my train for Berlin, especially as the lighting gave out. Carl literally dragged my heavy trunk from the house to the car.

In Berlin I saw Popitz, Oster, and Dohnanyi, and also visited General Olbricht. They were unanimously convinced that it would soon be too late. When our chances for victory are obviously gone or only very slim, there will be nothing more to be done. Popitz hopes that Planck can soon go on his journey, after Thomas (accompanied by Rabenau?) has prepared the way.

The situation is serious enough even now. There is at hand a rather pessimistic report from the Naval High Command about the Battle of the Atlantic. There is anxiety over English-American expeditions to West Africa, from which point they could hammer away at the already demoralized Italians. The position of the Italians in North Africa, on the Egyptian front, is already so weak that they would long since have retreated beyond Tobruk but for Rommel's opposition.

The situation in France, particularly in the unoccupied part, is highly fluid; the policies of the leading people are obscure. Attempts on the lives of Laval and Déat [August 27, 1941]. Our friend Darlan, before the Indo-China affair with Japan, also cheerfully offered the Americans (to no avail) the occupation of Saigon, and Weygand is negotiating with the United States about a visit of the American fleet to Casablanca.

Meanwhile, all hell has broken loose in Croatia, Montenegro, and, to a somewhat lesser degree, in Serbia. Serbs in Croatia fire at the Croatians, apparently with Italian weapons, and the Italians have occupied the whole coast.

The occupation of Iran by the Soviet-British brothers-in-arms is also an embarrassing affair. Even the Führer's staff, whose reports are otherwise rosy, has now issued a rather subdued review of the situation: In Russia it is hoped that we can still take St. Petersburg and make progress in the south. But will we get to the oil fields? Perhaps up to the first fields (Maikop).

Hitler is pressing hard for swift advances, but the Army High Command has certain misgivings and, before advancing, wants to deliver a decisive blow to the Russians near Moscow. In any event, it is generally believed that there will be a Russian front through the winter. Hitler is flirting with the idea of an advance through Turkey. In short, anything can happen.

A significant conference of Keitel, Milch, and Thomas about the war-production program, which makes limitless demands. It would be immeasurably easier to meet these demands if, after a separate peace with France, that country could be fully integrated. But Hitler felt himself bound to Mussolini, as Milch emphasized, for he had promised to support his claims, which were unconditionally rejected by France. Milch had ventured the comment that nobody in Italy really stood back of Mussolini any more, but that Hitler thought Mussolini's fall would have unforeseeable consequences for Germany.

The Bishop of Münster, Count Galen, preached three very fearless sermons in July and August against the persecution of the Church and the murder of the feeble-minded. He castigated the general lawlessness and the methods of the Gestapo in language of unprecedented frankness. Himmler boiled over, and demanded immediate and drastic steps (presumably death by shooting).

Meanwhile, poor Kerrl was so frightened by the Bormann (Hitler) campaign that he begged Hitler to stop attacks against the churches during the war. Hitler sent for Bormann and, quite in line with tried-and-tested procedures, held it to be tactically correct to retreat a few steps for the present, much in the manner of the proverbial procession of Echternach; that is, the Gauleiters were ordered to desist.

Himmler, on the contrary, declared that in his opinion this was not an ecclesiastical problem, but a question of the security of the State (meaning "Party"). Therefore he had to go ahead.

He then had the impudence to call for the support of the
Army. So far Galen has been confined to Münster. Why does
Rome let Galen fight all alone? And what are our lordly princes
of the Church doing?

Hanna Nathusius was here and described the methods used
in Neinstedt against the feeble-minded people who had been
working so diligently at that place. They were marched through
the town to the station, and a few of them asked her why they
were not at least given the needle right there in Neinstedt. The
poor souls, therefore, knew exactly what they were in for. The
populace was so wrought up that a special Party speaker was
sent to Neinstedt. He tried to quiet them with the shameless
argument that they, the citizens, would now get more for themselves because fewer supplies would be used for the feeble-
minded.

Pastor Bremer, formerly of Florence, came to me greatly
worried because all clergymen were to be assigned to other
work on the grounds that they were not in a profession indispensable to the war effort. I am curious to see whether or not
the backward step of Echternach will be applied to this ruling
too. It is a measure that would be almost fatal to the Church.

The parents of a Baron Böselager, who fell in the war, announced his death with the words: "He died in the firm conviction that Christianity would triumph over unbelief."

On August 27, 1941, on my return trip from Budapest, I
saw in Vienna, poor, lonely Eichhorn, who had just lost his
only son in Russia. He was the grandson of the field marshal
who was murdered in the Ukraine twenty-three years ago. A
comrade of my regiment announced the death of two sons, the
last of the Counts of Kirchbach. Six generations of the family
have given nine Kirchbachs for the country!

My trip was undertaken for the purpose of cementing relationships with the newly founded Hungarian section of the
MWT. Incidentally, Archduke Albrecht arranged things so
that during the invasion of Yugoslavia he personally and
singlehanded could "reconquer" the huge old hunting grounds
of Belje which had once belonged to his father and which the
Karadjordjivitch dynasty had later owned and had consequently not parceled out. He immediately posted all the neces-

sary notices to announce that this was his property. Whether he will be able to hang onto it is a matter of conjecture. He is an intelligent, worldly wise, and ambitious man, who undoubtedly wants to be at the helm, and is somewhat opportunistic. For instance, he pretends to be more favorable to National Socialism than he would be if he followed his own inner convictions. He is skeptical about the outcome of the war. He banks on the Duke of Windsor who, he believes, is holding himself in readiness.

The most interesting political event of the trip was a long talk I had with Imrédy, who reminds me of Brüning. Physically he is weak, but he seems to have more capacity to act than Brüning. He wants to go along with Germany and desires a social and agrarian reform in Hungary, one that would come from the "right" and not from the "left." The aristocrats and the conservative gentry cannot grasp this, or not sufficiently, and on their part maintain that Imrédy falls between two stools: the Conservatives and the Arrow-Cross boys.

*August 22, 1941:* Hentig is now to go to Kischinev to the Army Corps of Schobert as representative of the Foreign Office. It is characteristic of our rattle-brained political leaders that on June 28 Ribbentrop had told him he need not be uneasy, for in two weeks one would shake hands with the Japanese in Novorossiisk (he meant Novosibirsk)! We were agreed that it is now high time for a change in regime.

*Ebenhausen, September 20, 1941:* The last weeks have brought a very low barometer reading, not only among the people but also, according to news from headquarters, in high places. There is strong Russian resistance; meager success in the Battle of the Atlantic; Iran is occupied by the English and the Russians; considerable English success in the Mediterranean in attacking the supply lines to North Africa; open rebellion in Serbia;[1] grotesque conditions in Croatia; hunger and a sinister state of mind in Greece; high tension in occupied France—also in Norway. Japan is in suspicious negotiations with the United States, the latter looming more and more as an actual military opponent.

[1] The German Army report announced on September 25, 1941, the use of Stukas against "irregular troops" in Serbia.

A very poor impression was made by Mussolini's visit to headquarters [August 25–29, 1941]; consequent great concern about Italy. The "weather frogs" have begun to climb again in the last few days as a result of important victories in Russia.

Interesting conversations of the last few days: Stallforth visited me in Ebenhausen after his return from Hungary. He made a good impression and I was astonished later to learn in Berlin that Weizsäcker as well as Schacht was doubtful about him. Schacht apparently had in mind certain transactions pretty far in the past. Stallforth himself had referred to this and indicated that he had had differences with Schacht.

I had an interesting visit in Berlin from a Herr Danfeld of the SD [Security Service of the SS]. This particular SS man, still very young, showed himself remarkably well informed in foreign political matters, sober in judgment, and astonishingly free in his comments. He remained an hour and a half, and broached certain subjects which I thought it more discreet not to discuss.

From all this it was apparent that in Himmler's outfit they are seriously worried and looking for a way out. I questioned Albert about Danfeld, especially whether he was an *agent provocateur,* which Albert flatly denied. He considered him decent and intelligent, but naturally made the reservation, inevitable today, that all these people have a code of honor and morals about which we cannot be absolutely certain.

Stallforth reported that Ribbentrop, after having at first agreed to the Phillips plan, had declared two weeks later that it was now too late. Stallforth regretted this turn of events all the more since W. von der Schulenburg (the translator of Mussolini's drama, *Caesar,* which depicts Caesar as a peacemaker) had talked with Mussolini, in agreement with Stallforth, and had found him very favorably disposed toward such an attempt. Mussolini was absolutely for peace, he said. We then discussed the possibility of meeting a responsible American of considerable reputation on neutral soil (Stallforth thought a general would be best).

Stallforth interpreted Roosevelt's policy thus: his chief aim was to bring about the downfall of Hitler; if this succeeded, peace would be possible.

In the course of the conversation I asked about the probable reaction in America to a restoration of the monarchy. He replied there would be no objection; Prince Louis Ferdinand would be downright popular. Stallforth pointed to Ribbentrop as the principal mischief-maker. Halifax, who, contrary to the assertions of German propaganda, enjoys a brilliant position in America, has indicated that Ribbentrop bears the chief responsibility for the war. History will one day confirm this.

Repeated conferences at Popitz's with Beck, Jessen, *et al.*, about the necessity of opening the eyes of the generals, and above all of impressing them with the need for speedy action.

Enough information about the Mussolini visit has filtered through to show clearly how vulnerable our situation is, and how every chance for a reasonable peace goes to the devil as soon as the other side sees victory ahead. For the most part Mussolini and Hitler talked alone and privately. Absurdly enough, the Foreign Office and the High Command got their information from reading Alfieri's cipher telegrams after he had talked with the Duce about the conference. The Duce, of course, did not tell his Ambassador everything. Nearly all reports agree that Mussolini painted Italy's picture in dark colors, and for the first time discussed his own status. For instance, he said he could not withdraw his demands on France lest he suffer a dangerous loss of prestige.

My last conversation with Popitz took place on *September 16,* in the presence of General Thomas. Thomas was only moderately satisfied with his trip to the front. Leeb was almost fossilized; the Chiefs of Staff of Bock and Rundstedt were good. (He has not yet been able to approach the latter, Sodenstern, and the former, according to Waldau, is unimportant.) The sole favorable factor is that Halder now sees things clearly. Planck is to leave soon on his trip.

We were rather concerned about Goerdeler, who is much too optimistic and too "reactionary." He has visited me often during these days and always refreshed me by his liveliness and enterprising spirit; but I was disturbed by his facile prophecies of an early breakdown of the regime. He also worries me with his somewhat childishly contrived plans.

On *September 3* Ilse and I had tea with Schacht and his

young wife, who is expecting a baby. Apparently Schacht sees things very clearly, but his judgment is always affected by his boundless personal ambition and his unreliable character. I believe if Hitler knew how to handle him properly Schacht would even now put himself at his disposal, unless he has given up the ship for lost. Regarding methods to be used in our enterprise, he flirts with three ideas: first, to begin by removing one stone from the edifice, namely Ribbentrop; second, he still thinks he might be sent to America, for which mission Stallforth considers him fit; third, he plans a trip to Italy in order to feel out Mussolini's sentiments about the peace question indirectly through Volpi.

Gisevius, who is now closely aligned with Schacht, successfully dissuaded him from making this trip, as he afterward told me. But he did urge him to write a cool letter ("Esteemed Mr. Hitler") in which he would say that although at their last meeting he, Schacht, had rejected a mission to improve relations with America, because at the time he had thought it futile, he now thought the matter should be reconsidered. These seem to me maneuvers unlikely to result in anything worth while.

Dohnanyi gave me a very good and detailed account of Mussolini's visit and the situation in Italy. Officers had told Canaris outright that Mussolini must and would be overthrown by the military in the course of the winter. Italian officers talked to Waldau in a similar vein.

Professor Ferri, of Milan, who was in Berlin on business and whom I met several times, once with Ilse and another time with Cosmelli, showed an astonishing frankness about the bad situation in Italy. The Party had come to the end of its rope and Mussolini personally had lost face to an extraordinary extent. The Italians looked upon the war as something which did not concern them, and which must be ended quickly one way or another.

Perhaps the current successes in Russia[1] will favorably influence the feeling toward the German cause in Italy and throughout the world. Should the Germans succeed in taking St. Petersburg, the Donetz basin, Maikop, and perhaps even Moscow, Russia could be written off as a really dangerous enemy.

[1]Kiev fell to the Germans September 19, 1941.

The base of supplies would be broader and the prospects of victory for the opponents would fade. That would be the moment to create a basis for peace. Actually, however, these successes, although they diminish the adversaries' chances of success, do not in any way assure the basis for a German victory. Therefore, under no circumstances should this chance be permitted to escape us as all others have done so far.

*September 1941:* It is astonishing that in wide circles, specifically in the Army, Hitler's prestige (not the Party's) is still great, and has even increased as a result of the Russian campaign, especially among officers. I dined with Waldau [General in the Air Force] and got from him the usual propaganda line that the military preparations of the Russians had been so fabulous that there could be no doubt of their intention to attack Germany at the right moment. "Once more the Führer was right and all others wrong."

I am not at all convinced of this. I believe the Russians were first of all afraid and would not have attacked us except in the event of an obvious breakdown. This is also the opinion of Schulenburg, Ambassador in Moscow.

In this connection it is very interesting that Hitler told Papen that after reaching the above-mentioned line in Russia we could perhaps come to terms with Stalin, who was, after all, a great man and had accomplished incredible things. Papen told me this himself.

Waldau told me about Mussolini's visit to Göring [August 25–29, 1941] and a small dinner for five, with Mussolini, Hitler, Göring, Cavallero, and Waldau. An unbelievable coolness had prevailed. Mussolini had hardly made a pretense of talking with Göring.

At a meeting of the Society for Southeastern Europe Ilse and I met the good Glaise-Horstenau. He was extremely pessimistic. The Third Reich, which was designed permanently to unite the Germans, had measurably deepened the breach between north and south. An unprecedented hatred toward Prussia was rampant in Bavaria and Austria. For this reason a Hohenzollern monarchy was impossible.

I visited the Bulgarian Minister, Draganoff, an intelligent, cool-headed man. It is quite obvious that he no longer sees any prospect of a German victory. He is also worried about Turkey. This concern is not shared by Papen. According to him the Turks want only to remain neutral. The Anglo-Russian alliance was just about the worst thing that could possibly have happened to them. Considerable German successes in South Russia would impress them strongly, and at any rate stiffen their resistance to British pressure.

I spoke to Papen before and after his call on Hitler. He again impressed me as weak. On the other hand, he apparently still has a lot of ambition. At the proper time he would like to take German foreign policy in hand and make peace for Hitler. In any event he talks constantly about the absolute need which he had urged upon Hitler, Ribbentrop, *et al.,* for presenting a "constructive peace plan" to all Europeans after the temporary end of the Russian campaign—a plan that would inspire their confidence and meet their hopes; and on this basis to strive for peace. Papen maintains Hitler did not object to this idea.

Papen told me of a blistering telegram Ribbentrop had sent him because of continual reports about the peace feelers he was sending out. Papen had answered sharply with an offer of resignation, but received a sugary-sweet rejoinder. I asked him about the statement that the secret radio had made concerning his alleged gossip about Falkenhausen. He declared that he had never heard anything about it, and, above all, had never uttered a single word that could be so interpreted.

*Ebenhausen, October 4, 1941:* Yesterday, in Berlin, Stallforth's secretary called me to say she had received information by telephone from him in New York that the "proposition" had been well received in America, and would I be ready to meet some "authorized person" in Lisbon? I answered that I was on my way to Bucharest, which is true, and Italy, where my daughter is. I could give an answer only after my return.

I have certain misgivings: (1) By whom is this person "authorized?" (2) Lisbon seems to me an unsuitable place because it is watched from all sides like a stock market, nor can I get there without creating suspicion. (3) What kind of "authorization" will I require to prove my right to speak for a group? (4) The various doubts concerning Stallforth are too important for me to enter rashly into this sort of thing.

I had dinner last night with Gisevius at the Sauerbruchs' (the *"Friend of all Men of Good Will"*), and traveled here with him. I broached this question without mentioning Stallforth's name, but hinting at the doubts which Schacht and the Foreign Office entertained about him. His reaction was favorable, but he was against Lisbon as a meeting place. He preferred Switzerland, or my alternative suggestion Spain (via Kurt Schmitt for the Munich Reinsurance Company).

Conversations with Dohnanyi and others, and especially a report from General Thomas, who has come back from the front, confirm the continuance of repulsive cruelties, particularly against the Jews, who were shamelessly shot down in batches. An SS staff physician, Dr. Panig, or something like that, had reported that he tried out dumdum bullets on the Jews and had had such-and-such results. He was ready to continue his researches and to prepare a report which could be used for propaganda against this weapon!

Dohnanyi told of a release of the High Command of the Wehrmacht [OKW] concerning the treatment of prisoners which had not yet been issued by the High Command of the Army [OKH]. It contained horrifying instructions which Keitel had commented on approvingly.

In church matters things are moving along at a lively pace. Whereas Galen and the Bishop of Trier have preached bravely in opposition, there is no leadership on the Evangelical side; consequently there is insufficient resistance. In the Warthegau the churches have now been reduced to the status of private organizations, which is a violation of the law; only adults can be members. It is revealing also that, as someone has assured me, Hitler personally gave orders that civilian populations be forbidden to participate in the field services for soldiers.

I had a visit from one of the most deserving leaders from South Tyrol, Franceschini, who was desperate over the state to which the German population there has been reduced, and over the general political chaos.

Day before yesterday I had a long talk with Popitz and General Thomas at Popitz's home about the further course of action. Both were alert, judicious, and discreet, although Thomas is not entirely immune to propaganda. In any event they both see things as they are; they are not reactionary but wish to move forward. A great problem, insoluble up to now, is where we can find names that carry weight with the workers. In this respect everything is smashed to pieces. It is becoming ever clearer what great destroyers the Nazis are in matters political and ethical.

The generals seem to be recognizing this gradually. A few days ago Fabian von Schlabrendorff, a reserve lieutenant and a lawyer by profession, turned up. He had been sent by General von Kluge in order to find out whether opposition was crystallizing at home, and to assure opposition groups that "one" was ready to act. He came to me through Guttenberg to get some information on foreign affairs. A very sensible man, but his comments revealed with what naïveté the generals approach this problem. Among other things he asked whether there was any guarantee that England would make peace soon after a change of regime was effected. I told him there were no such guarantees and that there could be none. Were it otherwise any shoemaker's apprentice could overthrow the regime. But I could guarantee him something else:

(1) That unless England and America were completely knocked out Hitler could get no peace.

(2) That a respectable Germany, on the other hand, would always have a very considerable chance to get peace, and an acceptable peace at that. However, a change in regime was our own affair—a question which we alone could decide, not our opponents.

He seemed to think that we would have to make peace immediately after the change. I had to explain to him that although peace was, of course, our goal, we would have to proclaim our preparedness to continue the war, at the same time emphasizing our readiness to conclude an acceptable peace. What else had to be done was another question. We agreed that immediately after the end of the pending offensive in Russia his general should send a suitable high-ranking man here for further discussion.

The whole incident is gratifying because, for the first time, some kind of initiative comes from that source. But I had to make clear to Schlabrendorff there was no way to avoid the nasty reality that there would be a period in which the disillusioned people might declare that Hitler had been robbed of the victory within his grasp and the new rulers couldn't get peace either. It is the old dilemma. If we wait until the impossibility of victory becomes clear to the whole world we shall have lost the chance for a passable peace. But we must not wait. Whatever the outcome, our inheritance will be a bad one.

*Ebenhausen, October 17, 1941:* Back from my fortnight's trip to Bucharest, Budapest, and Brazzà.

The situation can be summed up as follows: great and surprisingly quick successes in Russia, especially at Moscow. Resultant political crisis in Japan; the military party is obviously anxious to strike. If Japan enters the war it will be counted (by the generals too) as a new triumph for Hitler's policies. Actually the situation remains wide open. The immediate results would probably be: (1) increased difficulties for Russia and England (also China?); (2) greater strain on Japan's resources; (3) entrance of America into the war, and, therefore, (4) a broadening of the area of conflict and destruction; (5) additional reason for England to play (in view of the shortages of materials in Japan) for time.

In Rumania, the founding of the Rumanian group of the MWT. The political difficulties arising out of the conflicts between government circles, old parties, and Iron Guard, were surmounted by the initiative of the Rumanian founders of the MWT in a way that surprised us. We were presented on the very first evening with a *fait accompli*. The domestic political situation there is hard to understand, but in any event very uncertain. Every German success fortifies the authority of Marshal Antonescu, who, irreproachable personally, has placed his bet 100 per cent on Germany. Furthermore, he is the only man who has any authority at all.

Wilmowsky, Dietrich, and I called on Killinger, the German Ambassador, and were horrified at this brutal, uneducated, superficial sergeant major. He remarked that it would be best simply to set fire to Bucharest; it was nothing but a pig-sty. He was wholly indifferent and uninformed about the problems that interested us. He said, for instance, that after the war the economic problems of southeastern Europe would be only a question of markets.

*Ebenhausen, November 1, 1941:* After returning from my trip to the southeast I found the following situation in Berlin: (1) After the initial certainty of victory which followed upon the gains before Moscow, there was deep disappointment over the revival of Russian resistance in the center, favored by bad weather. The only consolation is the progress in the south, toward the oil fields. (2) There is growing concern about the strain on the whole machinery, as well as the difficulties of procurement. (3) There is increasing recognition of the un-bearable conditions developing in all occupied countries. (4) There is revulsion on the part of all decent people toward the shameless measures taken against the Jews and prisoners in the east, and against harmless and often distinguished Jews in Berlin and other large cities. (5) There is a slowly increasing disposition on the part of the military leaders to go along no longer with this infamous and filthy business.

I met Popitz, Jessen, and Goerdeler, and discussed the whole situation with which we should be faced in the event of Hitler's fall. Goerdeler was obviously keeping something up his sleeve, so one got the impression that under certain circumstances he might attempt a separate course of action. It is planned that I shall approach Witzleben once more through Falkenhausen. Goerdeler, who, I believe, keeps nothing from me, came to me the following day to tell me about some steps he had taken be-fore the war, with the approval of the generals, in England, America, and France.

He had approached numerous leading statesmen, among them Churchill, Sumner Welles, Daladier, Vansittart, in order to acquaint them with the situation in Germany and to sound out their attitude. In my opinion the conclusions he draws from these talks are, as always, exaggerated and too heavily colored by his own wishes. He regards Churchill as favorably disposed toward us and forgets that everything that has happened in the meantime has worked to sharpen antagonisms and destroy sympathies.

Falkenhausen and General Thomas have visited Brauchitsch and report that he comprehends what beastliness is rampant. He is also gradually awakening to the fact that a share of the responsibility is his. If Hitler should be eliminated, he has decided to take action. This at least indicates some progress. Falkenhausen, who opposes the hangman's method (even if he was not able to prevent one of his subordinate commanders at Lille from having hostages shot!), only escaped being kicked out by a hairbreadth, but seems to have been saved by Brauchitsch.

Every day it becomes clearer how far our spiritual and moral standards have degenerated. At the Rheinhaben table the shooting of the hostages was mentioned,[1] and very reasonable people, such as Admiral Groos, regarded the measures as proper. General Thomas reported a similar instance: a big industrialist had declared, on the occasion of the Poensgen celebration, that the murder of prisoners was quite right, for in this way one could get rid of a useless race. Thomas answered him: "I hope something of the sort will not happen to you someday."

Gritzbach, an intimate friend of Göring, called on Popitz. He was shocked by the execution of Jews. Terrible scenes took place in their houses during the night. The populace in part was so disgusted that the Nazis found it necessary to distribute handbills saying the Jews were to blame for everything, and anybody who sympathized with them was a traitor to his people.

Popitz told Gritzbach that it was his duty to lay these things before his master [Göring]. Gritzbach answered that he would be glad to do so, since Göring certainly had the same sentiments, but that Göring would not take action because the order had come from Hitler himself. Hitler had been asked that Jews who were war veterans should not be compelled to wear the Star of David or be subject to expulsion, at least those who

[1] October 19-20, 1941. As a revenge for the murder of the German commander of Nantes fifty hostages were shot.

had won the Iron Cross. "No," was the answer. "These swine got their decorations fraudulently in any case."

The Jews were forced to sign a statement that they had evacuated their homes voluntarily (at two o'clock in the morning and under the surveillance of the police!), that they had participated in communist activities, and were transferring their property to the state.

Just as Bishop Galen has exercised not only a powerful and direct moral influence throughout Germany but also a certain indirect influence, it has been demonstrated that an energetic protest often does have an effect. Thus the Evangelical Pastors' Association protested against an order of the Bavarian district association of the Red Cross ordering all clerics thrown out of the association "because of the interconfessional nature of the Red Cross." The Pastors' Association used the sharpest language in its protest, and suggested that it would perhaps be better to exclude all pastors from the German nation, among them countless numbers who fell in the war, who were wounded, or who received the Knight's Cross, et cetera. Result: the order was revoked. Also they persuaded Göring to agree that the Air Force, which until now has had no religious services, is to have chaplains.

It is said (accurately?) that the best fighter pilots, Mölders and Galand, made energetic protests to Hitler or Göring against the persecution of the churches and had offered to return their decorations. Unfortunately, according to what Father Noppel (former rector of the *Collegium Germanicum* in Rome) told me, the German episcopate is not at all united. The majority, under the leadership of the old pacifist cardinal, Bishop Bertram of Breslau, was opposed to an open struggle and against "political" rather than religious methods. The proponents of drastic action, Galen and Preysing, were therefore in the minority. People such as Bertram will get nowhere at all with people such as Hitler and Himmler. Bishop Gröber of Freiburg, once dubbed "Brown Konrad," is now completely disillusioned by the regime according to Noppel.

Hans Berndt Haeften gave me a gruesome example of the Nazi way of "governing." Benzler, the German Counselor in Belgrade, had desperately inquired what to do with the 8,000

Jews herded together in that city, and made suggestions as to how he thought the problem might be handled. In the Foreign Office (that is, Luther) there was indignation over such softness. Luther got in touch with Heydrich, who immediately sent a "specialist" down to Belgrade to clean out these poor people.

*November 30, 1941, Ebenhausen:* I have had no time to write for quite a long while. On the *twelfth* I celebrated my sixtieth birthday in gratitude to the Giver of all good gifts, especially for the greatest gift of all, Ilse. The good round figure of sixty doesn't trouble me, but many other cares are growing. Every discerning person must see clearly that black clouds are piling up around us, in matters material, moral, and even military. The masses generally still drift along with the stream. They grumble, but are fundamentally without will or judgment. This is also true of the mass of the officer corps.

Typical of this was a recent afternoon I spent at the home of Harald von Königswald with his father-in-law, Falkenhausen [the Dante scholar], Reinhold Schneider (a poet—a pleasant, intelligent, deeply earnest, but sick man), Kameke, and Udo Alvensleben! Great discussion about the proper attitude to take. Udo, who had come from the front, was astonished at the growling at home and depressed by the degree to which the officers had been turned into "yes" men—men who neither noticed anything nor wished to notice anything. It is true, of course, that the average soldier and officer simply does his duty. But the highest commanding officers certainly bear a higher political responsibility, particularly during that revolutionary and lawless period since 1918.

We (Ilse was in Berlin for four weeks, thank God!) met Udo later at the Hammersteins'. The master of the house, in his unshakable pessimism and complete rejection of the regime, constituted a superb contradiction to his guest.

I had numerous talks about the situation in general with Thomas, Lejeune-Jung, Popitz, and an intensely interesting evening with Oster, Dohnanyi, Guttenberg, and "Bamme."[1] The picture is somewhat as follows: the food situation is getting more and more serious, especially as the prospects for the

[1] Probably General von Rabenau.

next harvest are very bad. The potato and turnip crops are now badly damaged; the raw-material problem is difficult, and the gasoline- and fuel-oil shortage is perilous. The German and Italian fleets are largely immobilized. If Maikop is not taken soon the threat will grow into acute danger.

The morals of the people have deteriorated through the battle against Christianity as well as through the spreading corruption and various other sinister phenomena. Udet committed suicide [November 17, 1941] after a serious quarrel with Göring, the reasons for which are not completely clear. As a result, accidents like those of Mölders [crashed on November 22, 1941], Wilberg, and Briesen, which were probably normal, lead to a general whispering campaign. The effects of the dishonesty of the propaganda and of the whole system are becoming stronger and stronger.

On the military front: in the west there are very slight successes in the Battle of the Atlantic and in the air war. In the east there is further astonishing Russian resistance, particularly in the south, where Timoshenko has made successful counterattacks, and where the weather has caused difficulties (insufficient protection against the intense cold as a result of premature optimism), and tremendous wear and tear on equipment. At the center of the front, near Moscow, somewhat greater progress has been made in the last few days. In Libya there has been a heavy, dangerous offensive, dangerous also because of the moral repercussions among the Italians.

Foreign affairs: a tremendous to-do in Berlin, but essentially meaningless; a mass signing of the Anti-Comintern Pact [November 25, 1941].

*Ebenhausen, November 30, 1941:* A great point of weakness is the political and economic situation in the occupied territories. Hatred and distress are spreading day by day. For the moment things are going best in Denmark, but young Topsoe reports even from there that the atmosphere is really bad. There is complete economic and financial collapse in Rumania.

On the occasion of a dinner given by Funk for Bulgarian business leaders I had a long talk with Schwerin-Krosigk and

Neumann. Schwerin-Krosigk still tried to find good in every-thing. He admitted the folly of the methods but praised the administration in Germany as a makeweight, and claimed that in various fields he had observed excellent achievements. A closer examination revealed that these accomplishments were attained in those places where old officials were still in high posts and where they still guided and directed the younger officials. This is the explanation in a nutshell. The good element in the old administration and in the old Germany was so strong and so deeply rooted that it continues to be effective even today; but it cannot stand the wear and tear much longer. It is exactly the same with the Army.

About three weeks ago I had an interesting talk with Schacht, who visited me for no particular reason. He apparently wanted to have a heart-to-heart talk. He does not feel easy at present about the famous letter he recently addressed to Hitler. He said he had written as follows: In the spring he had replied in the negative to Hitler's question as to whether something could still be done to keep America out of the war. Now a new situation had arisen as a result of certain developments. Of course he could not promise that an effort to this end would now be successful, but it was not altogether impossible if an attempt were made to initiate discussions with the Americans (through him, naturally), first on economic problems, and then lead them on into discussions about peace.

This whole complicated series of deductions is not convincing. He was of the opinion, in any event, that all attempts to establish contacts with someone on the outside would have to be made under the official protection of Hitler. This seems rather like squaring the circle.

Interesting communications from Popitz and Langbehn from headquarters, where the latter has been busy trying to get people out of Himmler's concentration camps. This is often possible through payment of large sums! He described the amazing measures that were taken for Hitler's security, and on the other hand the fluid state of mind existing within the SS. Two souls dwelled in each breast in strange combination; one a barbaric Party soul, the other a misunderstood, aristocratic soul. Langbehn repeated the wild remarks he had heard from individual SS leaders, full of criticism of the Party and of Hitler, and concern over the outcome of the war.

There was a great quarrel between Hitler and Keitel, during which Hitler hurled mad reproaches at Keitel. Keitel, deeply discouraged, babbled about suicide, and took himself off to Brauchitsch. The break, however, has been healed. The incident is not significant. It is, at most, symptomatic.

I am told that I am soon to give a lecture before Witzleben! (Purpose: to work on him.)

I heard two stories which show what effect the wearing of the Star of David has on people. Mme. Chvalkovsky met a worker in North Berlin who had sewed on a large yellow star with the inscription: "My name is Willy." And she rejoiced that this evil regulation was turned into ridicule.

A herculean worker said to a poor and aged Jewess in the train: "Here, you little shooting star, take my seat!" and when someone grumbled he said threateningly: "With my backside I can do what I like."

On the other hand, here is evidence of growing fanaticism: A deaf little old Jewess entered a store. A young SS officer barked at her: "Do you know what time it is?" She didn't understand. Again he put the same question, ruder, but with the same result. Whereupon he took her roughly by the shoulders and pushed her out with the words: "It is five minutes to five. You can't buy anything until after five o'clock. Out with you!"

*Ebenhausen, December 21, 1941:* Christmas and the year's end draw near. Since I made the last notations the situation has changed considerably. The prospects, domestic and international, for an end to this criminal insanity become dimmer and dimmer. Those in military power have been told a hundred times that they will be forced to a decision only when their position is shaken or when they are in the situation in which Ludendorff found himself in 1918, when he called desperately for peace.

Perhaps they will move only when both of these situations are upon them. Now the time is almost ripe. The food situation has deteriorated rapidly (potatoes especially are scarce), there is increasing scarcity of raw materials (especially oil), a dangerous loss of industrial workers to the Army, conspicuous failures in Russia (and in North Africa), and a simultaneous bogging down of the submarine war.

For several weeks now Brauchitsch and Halder have felt that their position was weakened. They are justifiably indignant that they have been made scapegoats for the reverses in Russia, although it was Hitler alone who, against their advice, insisted on the double operation—in the south toward the oil and in the center toward Moscow. Now they begin to see the light.

On *December 2* at a reception at Sztojaj's (Hungarian Minister), the 150 per cent Nazi, Frau von Brauchitsch, rushed up to me quite without reason and overwhelmed me with friendliness, complaining about the difficulties besetting her husband. Shortly afterward she talked in a similar vein to her nephew [Haeften] and said she would be delighted to arrange a tea in order to bring me and Brauchitsch together.

A little later Brauchitsch himself confessed to his nephew that it was necessary to take action and that he wanted to confer with me. Halder expressed similar sentiments to Thomas. Still later, however, Halder withdrew his statement in conversation with someone else. My informant maintains that he had said we must wait now for the spring and a final triumph over Russia.

The Japanese successes, of course, have raised the spirits of many people. It is not a bad thing for peace negotiations, if the English and Americans are a little hard pressed. Nevertheless, entirely aside from the fact that a Japanese success is deplorable from a higher European viewpoint, the Japanese attack is bound to prolong the war.

Because of the swift Japanese successes the other side must now play for time more than ever before. Furthermore, the first Japanese victories are still problematic in their significance, because they were achieved largely by the element of surprise and by the use of closer bases of operation. This surprise is the result of the unscrupulousness of the Japanese military party, which forced the outbreak of war and attacked Hawaii while Nomura and Kurusu negotiated with Hull. This was an act of unprecedented shamelessness, even after the experiences of these last years. Japan will eventually be defeated because of her physical weakness. This picture might change, of course, if the Japanese strike decisive blows in the first stages of the war and seize complete mastery of the Far Eastern sea lanes. Meanwhile Hitler is systematically attempting to eliminate the generals as a factor of power. He addressed some sharp words to them in the Reichstag [December 11, 1941] when he screamed against the domestic foes of the regime. Rundstedt is replaced, typically enough, by Reichenau, and Bock has been kicked out. Brauchitsch and Halder are perhaps already on their way out. When Kleist had to retreat near Rostov he received a nasty and senseless telegram from Hitler "that further cowardly retreats are forbidden." Only after the "Supreme War Lord" had flown to Mariupol was he convinced that the retreat was necessary.

Particularly stupid is the untruthfulness of the army communiqués. They are bound to destroy all confidence. Dieter soon noticed how false the official interpretation of the "situation" was. We are now greatly worried about him. The tank troops are among those hardest hit.

On the whole it seems that discipline and organization still hold, but the condition of the troops, particularly as a result of the loss of matériel, is in many respects serious. A consequence of the setback is that France and the Balkans have been drastically stripped of military units. This is especially dangerous in the Balkans, where Bulgarians and Italians replace the Germans and are assigned "pleasant duties." But, most important of all, instead of discharges there is now more drafting, which endangers agriculture and industry.

The irresponsibility with which our political leaders went into this war and continue to expand its scope is doubtless without parallel in history.

Very characteristic of Ribbentrop's theatrical recklessness was his order that the South American diplomats who called to declare war or to "break off relations" should be received in the waiting room, standing, by a young counselor, who tore up the documents before their eyes and then had the diplomats shown out by the doorman. Childish!

Personal note: The law faculty of the University of Göttingen offered me the chair of public law (primarily international law). There is much to be said against it, but it also has much that is attractive, in view of the way things are moving now. Professor Smend, deputy dean, my old friend of the days of the political round table, came to Berlin and lectured me for two afternoons in a most moving way on the challenge of this position. I answered that I would think it over. In spite of the attractiveness of the work and the convenient cloak it would offer me I finally refused.

What has engrossed and disquieted me most during the past weeks were the numerous conferences on questions concerning a change of the regime. One major difficulty is Goerdeler. He is too sanguine, always sees things as he wishes to see them, and in many ways is a true reactionary, though otherwise he has splendid qualities. Nevertheless, we finally agreed on the chief issues. Also, despite all doubts about his position, we agreed that the Crown Prince must come to the fore. Beck assented, although through past connections he knows the Crown Prince well.

The principal difficulty with Beck is that he is very theoretical. As Popitz says, a man of tactics but little will power, whereas Goerdeler has much will power but no tact(ics). Popitz himself often manifests a slightly professorial manner, the somewhat abstract views of an administrator. Nevertheless all three are capital men.

I was always afraid that we had too little contact with younger circles. This fear has now been realized, but only to reveal new and formidable difficulties. First of all, I had a long talk with Trott during which he passionately contended for the avoidance, within as well as without the country, of any semblance of "reaction," "gentlemen's club," "militarism." Therefore, although he, too, was a monarchist, we should under no circumstances have a monarchy now, for a monarchy would win the support of the people and would not win confidence abroad. "Converted" Social Democrats, that is, Christian Social Democrats, one of whom (a former Reichstag representative) he named, would never go along with us on the monarchy and would wait for the next group.

To these negative points he added the one positive thought that Niemöller should be made Chancellor of the Reich. He was, on the one hand, the strongest internationally recognized exponent of anti-Hitlerism, and, on the other hand, the most popular reformer here and the one most likely to appeal to the Anglo-Saxon world.

Afterward I met the alert, cultured Peter Yorck—a genuine offspring of his highly intellectual and sometimes too theoretically inclined family. He expressed similar sentiments. Finally, at his own request, I went to see Yorck again. There I met Moltke, Trott, and Guttenberg. All four, under the leadership of Trott, set to work on me furiously.

On the day of my departure, at Popitz's, Fritzi Schulenburg hammered away at the same theme. Of the five young men he was easily the most sober-minded, the most politically conscious, but, on the other hand, the most prejudiced against the Crown Prince, because his father had absolutely enjoined him to oppose any such possibility because of the stand taken by the Crown Prince in the crisis of 1918. So far as Prince Louis Ferdinand is concerned, he apparently considers himself the man of the hour, though he lacks many qualities he cannot get along without. He seems to have done so by insisting that they are part of his inheritance.

Goerdeler takes an almost completely unfavorable attitude toward the ideas of these young men, who, on their part, disapprove of him. He maintains that he himself has good relations with the Social Democrats. In the matter of the Crown Prince he is less positive in his opinion.

Beck firmly supports Goerdeler in this as he does in most questions. Popitz, more than anyone, favors the Crown Prince as an immediate solution. All three emphasize that we should not permit ourselves to be unduly influenced by passing moods of the people; but Goerdeler, of course, overestimates the degree to which people in general resent the present system and long for a liberating action.

I am trying to find a kind of connecting link with the younger men by arguing somewhat as follows: The premise "no reaction, but attempt to get popular support," was correct. Therefore, it is most earnestly to be desired that we get, as head of the government, a man whose name will be considered both as a deliverance and a program. This is important, too, in the interest of foreign policy, even if only to a limited degree. The latter qualification is necessary because the national character of this change, rising out of the peculiar will and needs of our people, can be maintained only if we do not look over our shoulder at other countries. Also because the Christian-pacifist circles among the Anglo-Saxon peoples, on whom Trott counts most heavily, are entirely useless as a dependable political factor.

In general I am against Trott's theoretical and illusionary outlook. Unfortunately such a personality as we hope for is not there. I am convinced that the man Trott proposed [Niemöller] has some unsuitable characteristics. He is somewhat unbending, non-political, and not a good strategist. Aside from all this, I think that, after the first effect had worn off, he would not be a successful symbol. On the contrary, he might even create opposition.

In this state of affairs there is nothing left to do but to act without such a popular personality—for act we must, and that very soon. It is clear that the situation having advanced so far, the role of a new government will be utterly thankless, one taken on in the middle of a mess—yes, a kind of liquidator's role.

We must keep in mind that we may be used only to clean up and will then be replaced by others, or that we may fail altogether. The task is to manage this as well as is humanly possible. Moreover, we shall have to fashion a government that is as free as possible of the odor of reaction, militarism, et cetera. Action, however, is now the main thing!

So far as the Hohenzollern family is concerned, the situation is serious enough. Nevertheless, in spite of all doubts, this is one way which still offers the greatest hope of co-ordinated action. The decision will have to be made according to the situation of the moment; and the one who swings into action first will have the most to say.

Trott asked me whether I would back out if Brauchitsch accepted the Niemöller solution. I countered by asking whether he, Trott, wanted to influence Brauchitsch in this sense.

All of these talks will naturally be pointless for the present if the news I reported above proves true.

*December 22, 1941:* It is true.[1] Brauchitsch and Halder have been overtaken by a political Nemesis about which they have been warned often enough. Hitler will—perhaps successfully at first—attempt to distort this into a military Nemesis, that is to make them the scapegoats for a defeat for which he himself is to blame.

The reports from the Moscow front sound very bad; also those from North Africa.[2] It is possible that the first political consequences will be seen in Italy.

*December 22, 1941:* The more one ponders the removal of Brauchitsch the stronger grows the impression that a crisis of the first magnitude is near at hand. The work of many months [influencing Brauchitsch] has come to nothing, but perhaps there is more to it than that.

The campaign of lies is in full swing. The Party spreads the word around far and wide—convincingly to the ignorant—that "the generals wanted to storm ahead senselessly but the good Führer exercised his genius to call a halt, averted bloodshed, and made it possible for many to have a furlough."

The precise opposite is true. Hitler pressed for the advance against the adverse opinion of the military leaders, and forced the offensive in the south and in the center. Brauchitsch realized that he couldn't go after the oil before he had finished with Moscow. But these Field Marshals have only themselves to blame for such treatment.

I am considering making one or more speeches at a psychological moment to serve as a signal.

*December 29, 1941:* According to the latest news Halder has not been fired, but he has told a fellow officer that he did not know whether he would last much longer.

An extraordinarily pessimistic letter from General Geyr

[1]December 19, 1941, Brauchitsch dismissed. Hitler took over the supreme command in his stead.

[2]December 17, 1941, Kalinin was taken by the Russians. December 25, 1941, Bengasi retaken by the British.

dated December 19. He had only a small and completely exhausted detachment under his command. The situation was extremely serious, more so than in Africa. Not only the Guderian Army Group but the whole Army was at stake. The Russians sprouted new defenses like Hydra's heads. His report, along with Dieter's, demonstrates the unprecedented irresponsibility of the Hitlerian "strategy" from October on and the complete lack of preparation for a winter campaign.

# 1942

*On the train, St. Margrethen to Munich, January 24, 1942:*
A trip to Brussels, Paris, Geneva, Zürich, Arosa. The purpose
of the journey was a lecture before the staff of Witzleben's
Army Group in Paris. I had thorough discussions with Falkenhausen and Witzleben.

The situation just previous to my departure was marked by
repercussions of the crisis in the High Command posts and by
the continuous successes of the Russians on the one hand and
the Japanese on the other. With respect to the first point the
situation has become even more serious than at the time of my
last notes, because of the dismissal of Guderian and Hoepner.
The former left with a manly farewell order of the day: "The
Führer has dismissed me from my post." The latter was kicked
out in the meanest and most dishonorable way, the official
notice speaking of the "former" colonel general.

Reichenau's death occurred [January 17, 1942] during my
trip. Hitler exploited it from the Party point of view by issuing
a rather clever order of the day. On the occasion of Brauchitsch's dismissal, in his nervous excitement, he had completely
messed things up. At the same time he entered upon a peculiar
and well-staged retreat by sending Rundstedt a letter through
Schmundt, entrusting him with the duty of representing him
at Reichenau's funeral. In addition, he reinstated Bock (there
were photographs of the two together published in all papers),
and put him at the head of the Southern Army Group.

Before my trip I had numerous discussions with Popitz, Goerdeler, Beck, Jessen, Planck, as well as with Oster and Dohnanyi, about the general situation, the tactics to be adopted, and particularly about the line to be followed in my talks with Falkenhausen and Witzleben. Astonishing optimism, especially on the part of Beck and Goerdeler with respect to the possibilities of both generals. Goerdeler composed a document to be used, and we went over it. Jessen and I insisted on a change to the effect that there shall be no "reaction" and no useless efforts at trying to undo the past. The whole thing did not entirely please me, but I took it along and afterward gave it to Witzleben.

Planck reported about the systematic strengthening of the SS, which is now to get an air force! It seems that being in a tight spot "Göring has moved over toward the SS." On the occasion of his birthday [January 12, 1942], when the usual fantastic tributes were brought to him, Göring—according to Planck's report—brought Sepp Dietrich to the fore and introduced him as the "pillar of the eastern front." At the same time he hurled verbal barbs at the stale old generals.

The generals have only themselves to blame that things like this happen. Goerdeler reported a session preceding Brauchitsch's dismissal in which Hitler, Göring, Goebbels, Himmler, and Ley participated—a charming little circle. Göring, still in the dark about conditions, had suggested that Brauchitsch be called in, too, but his proposal was brusquely waved aside. Goebbels had then asked for Keitel, but was told by Hitler that a man with the brain of a movie doorman would be of no help.

On the last evening (*January 15*) I met Glaise-Horstenau at a reception given by the German-Hungarian Society. He told grotesque things about developments in the southeast, and reported further that at his table Meissner had just made loud and bitter complaints about Ribbentrop—he was a frivolous fellow, his foreign policies were fatal, he was physically and mentally worn out, and he would not live to see the end of the war.

I arrived in Brussels on the afternoon of the *sixteenth*. The train was very late. Dinner with one hundred and two officers;

I was the only civilian. I had ample opportunity, here and later, to talk with Falkenhausen. My impression of him was, if anything, even more favorable than last time.

He is intelligent, clear headed, sober (that is in judgment; otherwise he is a bit of a gay blade). As a result, his position is endangered. I was in complete agreement with him. This week he wanted to go to Paris. He has just delivered an address to his officers in which he made clear to them the seriousness of the situation, and he underlined the unqualified necessity of obeying his commands. His military resources, incidentally, have been reduced to a minimum. He praised the King of the Belgians and thought that his second marriage had done no harm to his reputation in the country, except among some sections of court society, especially among those who would have preferred that he marry their daughter!

After a long wait at the station in the evening I finally left for Paris at 3 A.M. I was met by Schwerin, Witzleben's personal aide-de-camp, and very comfortably quartered in Witzleben's apartment at the Ritz.

First, I had a long discussion with Schwerin, who made an excellent impression on me and with whom I was in complete agreement. He belongs to the group of Peter Yorck, Hellmuth Moltke, *et al.*, but is firmer, clearer, more realistic. I invited Major Crome, of Stülpnagel's staff, to lunch at the Hotel Scribe. Jessen had made the arrangements for my trip through him.

I spent the evening in St. Germain, at first with Hilpert in the hotel that served as staff headquarters, and then with Witzleben in his villa. I had met him only once before, at a banquet Hitler gave for Mussolini in 1937. He didn't feel very well this evening and looked older than his age. He was somewhat dull, especially at the stiff and boring gathering following my lecture. Nevertheless, I had a good feeling about him —a man of clear purpose and good perception.

After dinner I gave my lecture on Living Space and Imperialism. I had the feeling that the majority did not really understand it. Schwerin told me later, to my gratification, that he had heard I was one of those diplomats who say nothing and who arrange a lecture in Paris in order to go shopping (shopping for what, and how?).

I spent the morning with Stülpnagel, who impressed himself much more than he impressed me. He is, of course, in a most disagreeable situation. His staff had implored him, as he told me himself, not to shoot the hostages, but to resign, which he unquestionably should have done. He offered the usual excuse that by not resigning he could "prevent worse things happening." At least he should have said that he was acting on express "orders of the Führer." Now he is more hated in France than almost anyone else.

Speidel, to whom I wanted to go next, was called away, so I went back again on Monday afternoon with Crome. They were puzzled by the German policies in France and not much edified by Stülpnagel's attitude. But "public enemy No. 1," they said, was Abetz and his outfit. Since Abetz was not there I visited his deputy, Schleyer, just as I did a year ago, at noon on Monday. He is now a "Minister." I had to rub my eyes to realize that a whole year has gone by. He still held the same opinions he had held a year ago; namely, the double-headed policy toward France.

Abetz was now in Berlin and would, he hoped, bring back a clear-cut policy which would really offer France something and thereby bind her more strongly to us. What he did not say was only that the Party and Abetz himself do not want to desert the French Quislings, that is, Marcel Déat, Luchaire, et al., who in the eyes of all decent Frenchmen were bribed swine. Consequently, in their relations with Pétain they remain bogged down in duplicity.

Sunday noon at Tirpitz's with Marthe Ruspoli-Chambrun. Marthe was in a Gestapo prison for three months after being denounced by a compatriot. But she came through it all right. She is as pretty as ever, clever, refined, adroit in speech, and charming. Marthe said the people had thought very highly of the German military, and that it would not have been difficult at all to come to terms with France; but all this had been spoiled. Now all classes of people were possessed by a consuming hatred and a longing for our defeat.

It is significant of present relationships that this Frenchwoman asked me whether she should show me Mölders's letter. She also knew about the Galen sermons. She told the following good story: After she was taken to the Gestapo prison the sergeant major asked her whether she wanted anything. This clever little person answered: "Yes, I have heard that the Führer has made such fine speeches. I should like to read them!" The man promised to get them for her, but returned sadly with the following announcement: "You see, they don't give us any toilet paper here, and this newspaper has already been assigned to the toilets."

On Monday evening there was a stag dinner at Wolf Tirpitz's: Fatou, Darlan's representative in Paris; Bruneton, an industrialist delegated to handle social questions; Fay, the historian and director general of the National Library; Fort, representative of the United Steel Works; and Major Beumelburg, of Stülpnagel's staff. Most interesting politically were Fatou, a tall, blond man, very crafty, and the spritely and cultivated Fay, whom I visited with Schwerin the next morning at the *Bibliothèque Nationale*. He showed me very beautiful Carolingian Gospels, et cetera, from the time "when we were still one."

The political conclusion I could draw from the conversation was that a real understanding with France was still possible (almost no one was for England), but not by the means used thus far. No patriotic Frenchman—and there would be no purpose in dealing with any other—would even consider entering upon a discussion unless two conditions were met: (1) evacuation of central France (especially Paris); (2) the return of most of the prisoners of war.

The Pucheu circle was pointed out to me as the most promising group of "patriotic Frenchmen" one could work with. The English and the Americans do not yet want to give up Pétain. Pétain himself seems to add up to something more than his contemporary, Hindenburg, who at the end was only window dressing. Pétain is apparently at heart a clear opportunist, that is, he will wait to see which way the rabbit runs and let no opportunity slip through his hands, whereas Darlan obviously puts his money on Germany. But perhaps they show each other their cards under the table.

Monday morning I went to see Witzleben again. He seemed much more lively. Schwerin was there, too, as he was the first time. We were agreed on every point. Like most other officers, he was not really informed about the situation in the east. He now wants to send an officer there in order to get information. Falkenhausen and Witzleben think that Beck's and Goerdeler's idea of "isolated action" is utopian.[1] On Monday I discussed my impressions with Schwerin.

I left Paris for Geneva on the evening of *January 19, 1941.* In the sleeping car to Culoz, where I had to wait two hours, a nice porter—the really good type of Frenchman, pleasant, heir to an old culture—told me despairingly about the food and fuel situation: 150 grams of fat and butter! Minute quantities of meat, and bread scarce.

Nostitz picked me up in Geneva. I had long and rather worried talks with him and Kessel. In the evening I dined with Martin and Alice Bodmer at the Restaurant Meroyaume.

As I wandered along the Rue de l'Evêché in the old part of the city, while the chimes in the cathedral tower rang out merrily and untroubled, Kathleen Schwarzenberg leaned out from her window above. I felt the wicked world suddenly recede and turn into fairyland.

The most important event for me in Geneva, however, was a two-and-a-half-hour conversation on the first afternoon with Carl Burckhardt, who had just returned from England. He was, to make a long story short, not so hopeless about an acceptable peace as I had feared. I had been apprehensive lest the idea that Germany and Nazism were one was already a *fait accompli.* This, apparently, is not yet the case.

However, he sees no chance at all for peace with the present system (at best a dictated peace). Among people of the upper classes hatred against us was almost pathological. Neither could we disregard the circle which looks upon a conservative Germany (in a higher sense) as being just as impossible as Nazi Germany. But at the moment the idea in government circles, not only in the group around Halifax and Hoare, but also

[1]The arrest of Hitler was to take place only after the commanders in the west had assumed complete individual authority. At that time, however, there were not enough seasoned troops in France.

among those nearer to Churchill and in court circles, is that an arrangement with a decent Germany must be made.

He said he had been asked again and again about the generals. Ribbentrop was considered absolutely unspeakable—the most hated man of all, although the word "hate" doesn't quite describe the feeling they have for him. The name of Hess was never mentioned in conversation. There was great skepticism about the possibility of a change in Germany. In answer to a query about peace conditions, Burckhardt, so he reported, made only vague indications that the boundaries of 1914 might well be demanded. The moderation of this seemed to have excited a certain surprise.

*February 3, 1942, Berlin:* I finally arrived in Berlin after the customary wartime travel experiences, what with trains being late, train schedules changing, et cetera. I had lunch at the Adlon with Werner Schulenburg (from Rome). He gave me the usual picture of Italy, bitter complaints about my successor's [Mackensen's] intellectual inadequacy and his sergeant-major mentality. Schulenburg had a long and interesting talk with the Pope, who thoroughly regretted my retirement. Without a doubt Pacelli still loves Germany and wishes that it could be maintained as a strong moral power. Naturally not in its present form.

I reported on my trip to Popitz, Jessen, Beck, and Planck.

*Berlin, February 14, 1942:* The military situation in Russia seems to be somewhat stabilized, but there is still a great amount of wear and tear on resources and energies. Dieter writes from Brest-Litovsk. It took him thirty hours to make the last one hundred and fifty kilometers. Fifty per cent of the German locomotives are in service on the eastern front!

Karl Otto Hassell fell on November 6, 1941; Lorenz Jürg Hassell fell on January 16, 1942. An endless sacrifice for the destruction of European standards.

In the Far East there are further great Japanese successes and Anglo-Saxon failures.

The *Gneisenau, Scharnhorst,* and *Prinz Eugen* have run the blockade from Brest to a German harbor [February 13,

1942]. A brilliant achievement in the name of a criminal political system.

Berthold called on me yesterday. He is one of those who joined the Party out of honest idealism. After his experiences in his eastern sphere of duty he gives the impression of a broken man. What he reported from Russia, not only about the mass murders of Jews, which demoralize both the perpetrators and the onlookers, and immeasurably befoul our honor as a nation, but also about the brutal treatment of the Russians, and, of late, interestingly enough, of the Ukrainians as well, exceed anything yet known.

Even Koch, who was hitherto considered halfway decent, participates to the fullest extent. He wants to make southern Russia into a "Land of Goths" settled by Germans. It is said that to the north will be the "Land of the Vandals." One is tempted to look on this as a bad joke.

Frank, who in some respects—for instance, in ecclesiastical matters—is still moderate, is a weak character and under heavy attack by the SS. One of his most intimate colleagues, Lasch, "governor" first of Radom and then of Lemberg, was arrested because of gigantic robberies of jewels, works of art, et cetera.

Berthold was in South Tyrol, too, and described the hopeless conditions there. Because of alleged skeptical remarks the German Gestapo denounced him to the Italians, who deported him.

The arbitrary "degradation" of Hoepner, without any court-martial, has been substantiated after a scrupulous examination of the situation. He had ordered a retreat. General Count Sponeck was sentenced to death by a court-martial sitting under Göring on Hitler's orders. He had said in his defense that he would do exactly the same thing again in a similar situation—a soldierly utterance which, however, in view of the mentality of Hitler, who had ordered the court-martial in a sputtering rage, made it difficult to pardon him.[1]

A strange situation exists on the eastern front because Russian paratroops and cavalry and ski troops, who have broken

[1]Sponeck was let off with imprisonment. After July 20, 1944, an execution commando of the SS appeared at the Germersheim prison and shot Sponeck without a new trial.

through the lines, are working with partisans behind the German front. In one case it was established that these partisans had held target practice on a drill ground behind the German front.

Oster and Dohnanyi visited me, somewhat disconcerted by the news that the Gestapo was watching them closely. It was also interested in Popitz and myself. Everybody is rather intimidated. Still more unpleasant is the fact that Witzleben is not only ill but has given his men some orders, not at all helpful to us.

I spoke with Goerdeler and Jessen. It seems that at the moment nothing can be done about Hitler.

*Berlin, March 3, 1942:* The situation is marked by: (1) ever-greater successes of the Japanese; (2) a shift toward the left in London; (3) a waste of German resources in Russia; (4) further deterioration of economic and food conditions in Germany. Goerdeler predicts complete failure by spring 1943 —probably somewhat exaggerated; (5) the stiffening of German-French relations (remark of Hitler: "The French seem to want to blackmail me. When I have finished in Russia I shall use an entirely different tone with them!"). Hitler's proclamation at the anniversary of the founding of the Party reached a new low in language and mentality.

One is forever confronted with riddles. After all that has happened the generals, with Halder at their head, have again got cold feet in the presence of Hitler. A report from Etzdorf, February 27, 1942, states that in the opinion of the military the Führer has again been right as against the generals in deciding to hold our forward positions in Russia. Halder has told Etzdorf that he could talk quite freely and informally with the Führer for hours on end, even with his hands in his trouser pockets!

Dieter wrote me from Russia, February 15, 1942: "The changes in personnel have reached tremendous proportions, including promotions, which have strongly affected the stability of the officer corps. In the higher posts, from division commander on up, there reigns a wild confusion, and each incumbent of such a post takes it with the idea that he will be leaving it tomorrow morning. Allegedly things are in such good shape that everyone can take in his stride the constant insecurity of the situation which results from this endless confusion.

"Nevertheless, this is at the moment to be looked upon as the lesser evil. More dangerous is the complete loss of confidence between the higher commanding officers and the highest leaders. Every opportunity is being used to weaken the independence of the higher commanding officers. The military commanders can really give no orders at all without inquiring "higher up" about every stinking little detail, particularly anything involving the slightest retreat. These gentlemen are thus kept on a short leash.

"There is endless discussion about the least measures which might be taken to turn to 'advantage' the 'extra' time and to 'raise the spirits' of the troops. Commands are made and revoked three or four times. The stubborn clinging to every dirty bit of Russian soil has been unnecessarily costly in blood, and through these methods of warfare numerous chances for achieving real success have had to be sacrificed. It is clear that under such conditions an offensive is likely to be even less successful than otherwise.

"The situation is not entirely bad here, but elsewhere it must be an incredible mess. In my opinion a general stabilization of the front is not yet in sight, and can hardly be expected until the beginning of the spring thaw. Then we shall at least get some rest. The old troops of the summer offensive are the pillars of the front and head and shoulders above the soft troops of the French occupation. But they are naturally worn out, and not in shape for further action without a period of rest at home. But this can hardly be thought of because of technical railroad difficulties. . . ."

I recently spent an evening with Beck, who, touchingly enough, had me to supper. His daughter, who had just lost her husband in Russia, acted as hostess. The death of his son-in-law (Neubacher) was a great loss.

I read him Dieter's letter of February 15. He thought Dieter sized up the situation very accurately. Beck did not believe that Witzleben had gone soft, but that perhaps Halder had.

*March 22, 1942:* People are feeling the effects of the severe period at the end of the winter, which has endangered the crops and also the effects of reduced rations. The economic strain is steadily growing as regards both human and material resources. This does not prevent a rise of the barometer in Party circles, among many of the military and among the intellectual Philistines; also in Italy, as Ilse reports.

The latter can be accounted for by the apparent failures of the English[1] and the Americans, and by the victories of the Japanese. There is also a feeling of relief that the Russians, when all is said and done, have not accomplished much. So extravagant plans are being made again: "Complete destruction of the British Empire, hand in hand with the Japanese."

What is actually happening is that the destruction of all standards is progressing at the double-quick, and at the same time the supremacy of the white man is breaking down; finally, the stealthy bolshevization of the world. It is said that Hitler himself is not entirely enthusiastic over the gigantic successes of the Japanese, and has said he would gladly send the English twenty divisions to help throw back the yellow men.

I spent an interesting evening recently with Langbehn. He still suspects all sorts of things are being planned around Himmler. A person in that corner is in a better position to act than one in Beck's entourage, where things are going to pieces, especially since the last disappointment with Witzleben. The incident has been rather satisfactorily patched up, but, for all that, some remnants of suspicion still linger on: Popitz against Oster, the younger group against Popitz, *et al.* I am trying to smooth things out. For instance, today I shall go with Oster to see Beck, who is at the center, and who must hold all the strings.

Recently I had a visit from my friend Schwerin. I am always in perfect agreement with him, but that in itself does not mean much.

The excellent Jessen has lost his eldest son in the east. Blows are falling right and left in a terrible fashion. The wear and tear on troops and matériel in the east is colossal. It is an open question whether an offensive on a large scale is possible, and

[1]March 28, 1942, Bengasi again in the hands of the Axis powers.

what reserves the Russians are in a position to build up behind the present front.

The other evening at Sauerbruch's interesting stories from the front were told by General Stapf, who has been fired from his post as commanding general because he showed a will of his own. About thirty-five divisional commanders have been relieved of their posts!

As presiding officer of the court-martial in the Sponeck case, Göring had very clearly stated that the Führer wanted his generals to obey and nothing else. How childishly naïve and thoughtless the average German officer is, even the intelligent ones! This was demonstrated to me during a conversation with Colonel von Holtzendorff at a dinner of the Second Guards Regiment. Incidentally, he spoke in an appreciative way about the Italians in Libya. He said Goebbels was "so friendly" as to come now and then to the tank troops at Wunsdorf and give them enlightenment! Recently he had "very correctly" said that now, for once, we had a really successful ally, but we were already babbling about the "yellow peril." Very cleverly keyed to the simple military mind.

*March 1942:* I view the situation of the tyrannized smaller nations with particular bitterness because, on the one hand, I have always been convinced of the need for closer economic and cultural co-ordination, and, on the other hand, I have always emphasized the necessity of looking upon the smaller nations as free, self-determining, sovereign factors. Even as a young man I put this concept in writing, and now I see with what impossible methods the Nazis treat the matter. This became clear to me when, a few days ago, on the invitation of Seldte (of all people!) I went to a lecture by Professor von Genechten, a Mussert man, and Attorney General of Holland. He said many true things, but with impossible premises and conclusions.

The following story aptly illustrates the tragic situation of humanity during this process of self-destruction. In 1995 the last superplanes of the Axis and the Anglo-Americans are fighting it out to the finish. The orangutan in the primeval forest says: "Heavens, now I have to start all over again."

Another anecdote illustrates the stupidity of the Party. "At

a crossroads three cars, each with the right of way, collide—
Hitler, the SS, and the fire department. Who is to blame?"
Answer: "The Jews."

At the request of Professor Wagemann I am taking over as
permanent delegate of the German Institute for Economic Research to similar institutes already founded or yet to be founded
in the southeast, perhaps also in Denmark. I am doing it because my work for MWT has been very indifferently supported
and because I can be useful to the MWT as a connecting link.
Above all, my presence in Berlin and my real activity would
thus be more effectively camouflaged.

*March 24, 1942:* I had an evening conference day before
yesterday with Olbricht and Oster at Beck's. We agreed that
Beck must hold all the strings. Goerdeler's son has indulged in
the superfluous luxury of sketching out his political thoughts
and giving them to a number of people. An SS man returned
them to him with a friendly warning. His own captain had denounced him! Thanks to the energetic support of his regimental commander and his own defense, the court-martial let
him off with a very mild sentence.

Grotesque intermezzo: the same colonel told a member of
the court-martial that he would get a kick in the rear if he
didn't stand firmly and defend Goerdeler's son. The whole
story is evidence of the divided spirit in the muddled Wehrmacht, which has no real leader.

Hitler has locked up several railroad executives in the east.
They are scapegoats for a situation in which the railroads have
been unable to meet the exorbitant demands made upon them.
They have been neglected for years in favor of the great super-
highways and "prestige" buildings. When Dorpmüller remonstrated, Hitler proudly answered that if he could have a general
and a wearer of the Knight's Cross condemned to death and
inflict punishment on other generals, he could certainly lock
up a few railroad directors.

*March 28, 1942, Ebenhausen:* During the last days in Berlin
I had detailed discussions with Jessen, Beck, and Goerdeler.
Prospects not very good. Beck was formally adopted as the

head of our group. It looks as if Witzleben might lose his post.

Yesterday I had a lengthy discussion with Papen, who had called me after his arrival from Ankara. He is remarkably uninformed about domestic developments, even those in the army leadership. Apparently his aim is Turkish mediation in the hope of arranging a peace. In his opinion the main concern of Turkish politics, now as before, is to keep out of the war. He believes he can bring about Turkey's entrance into the war on the side of Germany, provided that after a "successful offensive" in Russia, Turkey offered mediation and was rebuffed by the Allies.

I do not believe this train of events will proceed so smoothly and according to plan. Why should England be so stupid as to make a flat refusal of mediation, particularly after possible further disasters? England and America have one thing in their favor—time.

At the top here there is apparently some concern about a landing operation. On the other hand, there is enough optimism about the development of the North African campaign to warrant hopes of conquering Egypt! Great successes are also expected from the summer campaign in Russia. Whether they will be decisive is very doubtful.

Yesterday afternoon I had a visit from Oster and Dohnanyi. Archduke Albrecht was here earlier, extremely displeased by the appointment of Horthy's son. He believes that the next step will be his designation as Horthy's successor. He declares that Horthy, Jr., is little inclined to be friendly to Germany, and that the appointment of Kallay to replace Bárdossy [March 10, 1942] will work out in the same way.

Furthermore, the steadily increasing differences between Rumania and Hungary, recently aggravated by an offensive speech by Mihai Antonescu, constitute a knotty problem for German policy, because Germany wants both countries to supply troops for use against Russia, and can grant neither one what it demands at the expense of the other. The anti-German elements in both countries thereby continually receive fresh stimulus.

Last Sunday [*March 22, 1942*] Bossy, the Rumanian Minister, gave a large musical tea which Ilse and I attended. Frick was the guest of honor. It is absurd that when people like Prince August Wilhelm appear at such functions they always take the spotlight—a glitter of sham gold which cannot hide the real situation at all.

The new Croatian Minister, Budak, told me of the joys of Croatian independence. In reality a large part of the country is already in the hands of the rebels again.

Since I contemplate a trip to southeastern Europe I called on Draganoff. He said that if the Bulgarians went to war it would benefit neither themselves nor the Germans. Moreover, the Bulgarians are always turning their eyes in the direction of Turkey. Conversely, according to Papen, the Turks are afraid of the Bulgarians and would be more willing to go along with Germany if they could thus get full security against the Bulgarians.

*March 29, 1942, Ebenhausen:* I arrived here early this morning with Ilse. I forgot to record that Ilse had read some copies of letters from Hess to his family. He appears as a fairly decent fellow, is satisfied with his treatment in an English country house, and is comfortable. All letters close with a "Heil Hitler!" Politically naïve, inasmuch as he believes that his action will someday bear fruit.

Recently I read two documents which illustrate very well how matters stand with us. An order of Keitel's to the Armed Forces reveals a downright servile attitude toward the Party and concludes on the note that the Armed Forces must be brought into closest identity with the Party. The second was an epistle written by Hess's successor (and evil spirit), Martin Bormann, to a Gauleiter. It reveals an absolutely diabolical hatred of Christianity as such, which the Party program is pledged to defend, and not directed solely against the churches. Moreover, his line of argument shows a lack of education and an idiotic falsification of history that would be hard to beat.

From the notes of a trip to Vienna, Budapest, Sofia, and Bucharest:

*Sofia, April 13, 1942:* I talked with King Boris. The King received me with great amiability. He said that when he learned of my arrival he wanted to see me at once because he had heard a great deal about me, especially that in Yugoslavia I had exercised such a good influence on Prince Paul. The conversation did not follow any special pattern, but touched on Yugoslav and Italian politics, World War I, the political developments leading up to the present war, the war situation as of today, postwar tasks, Bulgarian politics, and in conclusion my present activity and the work of the MWT.

As regards Yugoslavia the King discussed with some spirit the political blunders made after the death of King Alexander. Prince Paul, whose human qualities he praised highly, had not been politically equal to the situation. King Alexander, who had originally hated him but who had later come to a better relationship, had handled the situation in Yugoslavia very differently. He, King Boris, had once told King Alexander: *"Tu sais, toi et moi nous sommes beaucoup plus balcaniques que Paul."*

I replied that as regards King Alexander this was certainly quite correct. King Boris said that Prince Paul had made a mistake in permitting himself to be estranged from Stoyadinovitch. To be sure, Stoyadinovitch had finally gone off on the wrong track, inasmuch as he had lost his perspective and wanted to play the role of a "Führer" or "Duce." He, King Boris, had always used his influence to induce Yugoslavia— after changing the impossible methods of government in Macedonia—to join Bulgaria in building a peaceful bloc on the Balkan peninsula.

In discussing Italian policies, he was discreet but quite critical, although he spoke of Mussolini personally with great appreciation. He obviously views Italian policy in Croatia and elsewhere with deep concern. He asked pointed questions about Mussolini's personality and governmental methods, as well as about the significance and character of other personalities. The King's questions revealed a special interest in Ciano. On the whole King Boris seemed to have very little respect for Italian politicians, except Mussolini.

In the course of this discussion we spoke repeatedly of World War I. King Boris told me about his own experiences as his father's representative at Headquarters. He emphasized several times that relationships in this war and the prospects, too, were entirely different from those days. He seemed convinced of ultimate victory. British policy before the war, he said, was irresponsible, especially in the treaties of guarantee. When I expressed my regret over the destruction in Europe and the setbacks to the white race, he replied that this was England's fault. We should not close our eyes to the fact that we are in the midst of a great revolution which cannot be understood in terms of the past. He had clearly recognized this, he said, and from the beginning had looked forward. Unfortunately such was not the case everywhere, and if changes were now being brought about forcibly and rashly this was due only to the shortsightedness of many politicians.

As far as Bulgarian policies are concerned the King declared that he had, to his great satisfaction, found that the Führer had complete understanding for his present attitude. It was important, especially as regards Turkey, that Bulgaria should stand intact and ready with a well-equipped army.

About domestic problems and the ministerial crisis just ended King Boris spoke only briefly. For economic reasons the change in the Cabinet had been long overdue. He had only waited for Easter to be over, and for a quiet moment, to make the decision without interference by parliament or pressure from any side.

The essential elements in the Bulgarian political situation are apparent from my notes on the conversation with King Boris. The German course is rather widely recognized as the correct one. However, matters are complicated by the conflict with Russia for which there is strong sympathy here because of an inextricable mixture of communist and Slav sentiments.

The economic situation is very difficult, particularly for the urban middle and lower classes. There are breadless days. Corruption is growing, as in all countries affected by the war. As an example, I wanted to buy some socks, which are to be had only with ration points. Countess Lerchenfeld and I asked for some in a little shop, received without a moment's hesitation a statement that we could have them, and the owner brought them out by the boxful. At this moment a policeman entered the shop and stood beside us. Countess Lerchenfeld indicated to the merchant that we would wait, but he quite calmly completed the transaction without asking for points. The next day she inquired about this special case and found out that the proprietor had hired the policeman so that no one else should spy on him.

The King is very intelligent and adroit, and the authority in the country. He plays the keyboard of his people with a sure hand. The Church plays a considerable role, in close conjunction with the State. This is probably the healthiest of all Balkan peoples. The peasant character is clearly evident even among the educated groups. I have a good impression of the military. Many of the leading personalities have a military-peasant character (for instance, the new Minister of Agriculture, Petroff). On the other hand there is a tendency toward conspiracy, party intrigues, et cetera. There is always a great deal boiling away under the surface. The structure of the state is still young, not firmly built, and certainly very sensitive to setbacks.

*Budapest, April 14, 1942:* It was very cloudy, windy, and foggy on our flight from Sofia via Belgrade to Budapest. As a result of the tremendous floods Belgrade is unrecognizable. In Semlin I happened to meet Dörnberg on his way from Budapest. He had just landed because of a breakdown. We arrived in Budapest right on the dot.

After a visit to what seemed to me the very peaceful offices of the Hungarian-branch of the MWT, I walked along through the beautiful streets, zigzagging up to the castle, where at six o'clock Prime Minister von Kallay received me at the suggestion of Sztojaj. He was in a Cabinet meeting but remained with me for half an hour.

An amiable, intelligent elderly gentleman. When he heard that I had come from Sofia and had talked to the King he was extremely interested and asked for information about Bulgaria's attitude after the King's visit to the Führer's headquarters. He also wanted to know about the remarkable Cabinet crisis. He assumed that the latter had something to do with the visit to Hitler. I doubted that, and described the long-standing differences in the realms of economic policy, related the not entirely trustworthy version the King had given me, and explained that the sudden decision to take up the matter of the change in ministers was now traceable, according to reliable information, to communistic machinations. In this connection we discussed the personality of the King, whose father Kallay knew well. He was especially interested in the fact that for the present the Bulgarians would not participate in the war. Kallay then described the situation of Hungary and dwelt particularly on the tremendous burden that the mobilization and the conduct of the war had placed on the country—in one year something like a half-billion pengö.

*Bucharest, April 16, 1942:* At nine o'clock the little two-motor Douglas plane, *Hohentwiel,* rose over Budapest, and at eleven-twenty we were here. Over the Carpathians, almost three thousand meters high, there were several gusts of wind and air pockets, otherwise it was very quiet and beautiful. I was met here by the Legation (Mirbach) and the local branch of the MWT.

In the afternoon I had a long conference on institute matters and then went to see Neubacher, Minister in charge of economic affairs at the Legation. He was once mayor of Vienna and told interesting stories about local affairs. The system here rested solely upon the Marshal. Nobody else counted. Mihai Antonescu was significant only as a shadow of the Marshal, who was with him all day long.

The Iron Guard movement was not supported by us because the Führer held the Marshal in high esteem. But it certainly was not dead. It was well organized and very active, especially among the youth. Nor did they have any other choice, for if they were not National Socialists they would have to be communists. Unfortunately, the whole situation reminded him strongly of the life and activities of the illegal Nazi Party in Austria. But of course the movement had been robbed of its leaders. They were called "the potatoes" because their heads are underground.

In discussing the personality of Manoilescu with Gigurtu, during an interesting trip into the oil sections of Sinaia and Predeal, we fell into a lengthy political conversation. He thought it was a very cheap way out to blame the Vienna arbitration award on Manoilescu. A new government could not and would not have acted otherwise.

An engineer of the Konkordia Company had just made a remark to him, Gigurtu, about the harm done to Rumanian honor. He said he had answered that honor was a beautiful word but that the essential thing was to serve one's country, and that such service could only be rendered in this way.

Unfortunately Manoilescu had certainly made one mistake, and that was to permit the return of the King and Lupescu. The King had wanted to arrange a reconciliation with the Queen, which would have been a blessing, for Carol was a very clever ruler. The Queen certainly was most charming, but she seemed to be unlucky. She had failed to respond to the effort for reconciliation. Now she was shabbily treated by the Antonescus.

Gigurtu said the Marshal was a decent man, but he did not understand that the Rumanian people were intrinsically and deeply royalist and that one must therefore place the monarchy first. Instead he and his wife wanted to play king and queen. The most dubious influence was that of Mrs. Goga, an unscrupulous, clever person, who, although a Transylvanian Rumanian, was an agent of the Central Powers even in World War I, and who was still to this day a German agent. Besides, she was grafting shamelessly. Both Antonescus, as a matter of fact, hated Neubacher. They got along better with Killinger. While we were talking in front of Gigurtu's house at Predeal two cars passed and their passengers waved at us. In one was the Marshal with Mrs. Goga, in the other Mihai Antonescu with his wife.

It is practically impossible for a private person to get meat; this shows how incapable the state is in economic organization. However, Gigurtu stopped about a half or three quarters of an hour out of Bucharest and quite openly bought meat in great quantities for the next week from a butcher in a small town. For money one can get anything in Rumania, but the masses of the people are poor and can buy nothing.

The political conflict is going on underground. The government has few supporters and is considered a vassal of the Germans. The old parties still have many adherents. There is great fear of Russia, and therefore Germany's friendship is desirable, but there is hatred for Hungary, and the longing for Transylvania overshadows everything.

On *April 18, 1942,* I had an audience with Queen Helen. The Queen, who looked very beautiful and charming, received me as an old friend, inquired about everybody, and spoke with great sympathy of Prince and Princess Paul of Yugoslavia, who were in Kenya. Only after ten months did the Grand Duchess Helen (in Athens) receive news from them. In great surprise she told me that King George was inspecting troops in Palestine. When I asked about the Crown Prince of Greece she said that he, whose views were so different from those of George, had been asked by many people, including herself, to stay on in Athens, but he had gone away with his brother out of family loyalty. The Grand Duchess Helen had said to him: "You are so very clannish!"

The Queen acknowledges that she recognized the absolute political necessity of a pro-German policy for Rumania, but complained bitterly about Antonescu's regime. She said that she and her son were actually enslaved, isolated, and kept from all activity. They would not let the King go to the front, and she had been allowed to visit the military hospitals only after much opposition—for Madame Antonescu wanted to have a monopoly on this kind of thing. Antonescu had taken part of the palace that belonged to the royal family without so much as informing them. The King couldn't even have professors come there to continue his studies. But nevertheless George Bratianu came in the guise of a professor. The worst of it was that Antonescu was a decent, clean man, but endowed with a one-track mind and as stupid as an ox. He was ordered around by the other Antonescu, who was plainly a scoundrel, exactly like Ciano. The strength of his position could be explained only by his relationship to the wife of the Marshal.

Another dangerous and influential person was Mrs. Goga, who had great charm through which she got everything, and who shamelessly enriched herself. She was worse than Madame Lupescu. The Queen apologized for telling me so much gossip, but conditions really were abominable.

*Ebenhausen, April 27, 1942:* Yesterday an unexpected session of the Reichstag with a speech by the Führer. A mixture of brutal megalomania and weakness, demagogery, and ignorance about the fundamental nature of the state.

At the end of April I sent word to Frau von Weizsäcker that I would drop in for coffee at three-thirty, in order to meet her husband, too. On *April 29,* contrary to custom, I was conducted directly to him in his study. He carefully closed the windows and doors, and announced with some emphasis that he had a very serious matter to discuss with me. He brusquely waved aside my joking rejoinder. For the time being he had to ask me to spare him the embarrassment of my presence. When I started to remonstrate he interrupted me harshly. The conversation was in two parts, and the second he was obliged to ask me to keep secret from everybody, including my wife. He was determined, in case of trouble, to deny everything.

Every time I asked for enlightenment he cut me short. If I were not willing to listen to him he would simply have to stop short of part two. This matter had cost him sleepless nights. Part two meant great danger to him and to his family.

I declared that all this was a riddle to me and that his behavior was incredible, but that he should go ahead and speak. He then proceeded to heap reproaches on me as he paced excitedly up and down. I had been unbelievably indiscreet, quite unheard of; as a matter of fact, "with all due deference," so had my wife. This was all known in certain places (the Gestapo), and they claimed even to have documents. He must demand, most emphatically, that I correct this behavior. When I attempted to interrupt he became annoyed and said again and again: "Get this straight! If you do not want to understand me then I must break off." I explained I must at least defend myself, but he disagreed abruptly. He paid no attention to my objection that he seemed to associate himself with these unsubstantiated accusations.

Then came the second part. I had no idea, he said, how people were after me (the Gestapo). Every step I took was observed. I should certainly burn everything I had in the way of notes which covered conversations in which one or another had said this or that. Apparently he meant himself. He opposed my efforts to get at the facts behind all this; this concerned my future behavior, not the past. Finally he said: "Now, *auf Wiedersehen*, but please not too soon!" And then he continued: "You wanted to call on my wife; please come on over."

During the whole talk I controlled myself only with the utmost difficulty. I did it in view of the danger that apparently exists for my family. I suppose that when the question of my visa came up the Gestapo warned him against me, and now he felt it his duty (or was it his duty?) to keep me at a distance.

Deeply depressed by this experience I went to Frau von Weizsäcker. At first I assumed that she knew nothing about all this. In the course of the conversation I remarked quite casually that the main motive that ruled the behavior of mankind today was fear. Her answer struck me as being somewhat embarrassed. Afterward she followed me into the corridor and said pleasantly that I should not be too upset. Finally she remarked that after all there were automatic telephones, too! Then I knew she was informed about everything and wanted to bridge the gap between me and her husband. But I was not very anxious to put a foot upon any such bridge.

*May 1, 1942:* Trott called on me. His chief, Weizsäcker, had sent for two of his subordinates to warn them about me. I was being watched because I had criticized the regime, said Hitler must be removed, and such things. I met Trott again a little later and he told me his chief had subsequently given an order that in no event was I to be told of this. Trott also said that Papen, upon his departure from headquarters, had heard how Hitler had inveighed against the diplomats and had pointed to me and my wife as particularly impossible types.

*May 8, 1942:* Nostitz paid me a visit. He told me that earlier he, too, had been warned against me several times. On *May 13* I met Trott. He had meanwhile seen Gisevius, who had asked him to tell me not to take this seriously. At the bottom of it all there probably lay the fact that the Weizsäcker group had taken at face value certain so-called English peace feelers that were really of no consequence and was now worried lest the view that England would not make peace with Hitler should disrupt their efforts. Gisevius himself later told me the same thing. As a matter of fact Nostitz gave me to understand that the time when England would absolutely refuse to make peace with Hitler was past.

On the *evening of May 17* at the Bismarcks'. The nephew, Haeften, told how he had chanced to overhear a telephone conversation of his chief, Luther, in which the latter had inquired about the state of my visa. The other party had answered that Schellenberg was in general opposed to my taking a trip because they could watch me less effectively if I were away.

*Ebenhausen, August 1, 1942:* For several months I have not been able to write in my diary because certain information I received toward the end of April made it imperative to exercise more caution. The whole occurrence confirms some symptoms of the present situation.

(1) The absolute "will to power" of the present rulers, in contrast with the Weimar regime.

(2) The Cheka methods used by them.

(3) Their inferiority complex as against the "upper class."

(4) Their instinctive aversion to every person with real character.

(5) The fact that all opposition and all criticism, even those arising out of the most patriotic motives, are looked upon as punishable crimes.

(6) The consequent trembling fear on the part of everybody.

According to confirmed rumor Hitler has a particular dislike for Ilse and me. In view of the character of the man I consider this a compliment. On the other hand, the memory of my conversation with Weizsäcker torments me, because—even after taking into account the validity of all possible tactical considerations—there still remains his way of going about it, which, to put it mildly, is incomprehensible to me. It seems that there is indeed a general increase in distrust. But my recent experience seems to show that I am the object of particular attention.

I do not know whether or not I have recorded the fact that I received a German visa for my trip to Bulgaria, Rumania, and Hungary in April only after great difficulties and at the very last minute. Now I have been refused a visa for a trip to Hungary (for the Institute of Economic Research). Some subordinate in Luther's division signed a letter in which the Foreign Office asked me to abandon the trip.

Popitz told Langbehn, without any prompting on my part, that the trip must be taken later, because the cancellation had created an embarrassing situation abroad. The one danger of advancing such an argument is that the answer will be: all right, but this will be the last time.

If all efforts are in vain, then my activity for Wagemann is finished. The work for the MWT cannot be carried on in this way indefinitely, and thus my excuse for staying in Berlin would disappear. Probably this is what these fellows really want to achieve. Without any qualms at all they have carried out a successful process of "intimidation" and "isolation" among those people who see the trend of things clearly and are thinking over ways and means of keeping the wagon from slipping into the abyss, whether the war ends in victory or defeat. The success of this policy is of no great practical significance in that the possessors of military power thus far have adopted a servile attitude and nothing has therefore come of these deliberations to date.

The leaders of the SS are much more alive to their goal, and also know the dangers and the impossibility of certain methods. Because of Heydrich's death [June 4, 1942], the development of this "black" movement has once more been suspended, but the embers burn on. It is naturally a sinister sign of the hollowness of the system.

Bruckmann suggests that I write a biography of Hardenberg—a fruitful thought in case of a severe limitation of my present work in Berlin, since I would then have an opportunity to go to Neuhardenberg.

The political situation has now developed in such a way that all those who really love Germany and know what this is all about are going through an acute inner conflict, unique in history, at least with us. The military situation today is not bad in itself. Russia has already suffered extraordinary losses of important territories.[1] Of course the Russians are holding in the center and at the pivotal point between center and south, and have also avoided a battle of extermination in the south. In Africa the English have stopped Rommel's offensive short,[2] but if they in turn do not successfully take the offensive, the Axis will probably push on farther.

On the other hand, heavy English air raids of considerable material and moral effectiveness. Still worse ones are to be expected. But a real "second front" is still lacking. Submarine war is successful but not decisive. The Japanese have become rather quiet. It may be that they are preparing great blows. Economic resources are strained on both sides.

At home we have very critical shortages of food, industrial products, and man power. The many foreign workers constitute a danger. No end to all this is in sight. The other side cannot now make peace with Hitler, but must play for time.

Italy goes along in a resigned way, somewhat relieved by improved conditions in Africa and in the Mediterranean, but full of horror at the duration of the war. Petrucci, the Italian Consul General in Munich, thinks that Mussolini has been thoroughly worn out by the extraordinary demands that have been made on his strength and his exaggerated sex life. He simply has no new ideas. Relations between Ciano and Ribbentrop were bad. Ribbentrop continually wanted to instruct and direct Ciano, and Ciano said each time: "I have just said that." The Italian military are furiously angry because the Germans show no respect for their achievements.

In the occupied territories relations are very strained, thanks to the evil methods of the Party, especially in Czechoslovakia after Heydrich's terrible blood bath. The two razed villages, whose men were herded together and shot, women deported, and children subjected to forced training, serve the propaganda of the Allies. The same thing has now happened to a village in Norway.

[1]The Donetz basin in German hands, July 30, 1942.
[2]Rommel reached El Alamein August 27, 1942.

In France, too, there are numerous tensions, and a repetition of Draconian measures. In Poland horrible things continue to take place which give one nightmares and make one blush for shame.

Frank disapproves of these things, but is powerless because his own record is not clean. He is therefore completely in the hands of the SS. The SS leader who has been put at his side, or, more accurately, has been placed above him, treats him as if he were non-existent. For instance, he doesn't even bother to answer his invitations.

Hitler's famous speech against the law [April 26, 1942], together with the shooting of Governor Lasch, which, although justified, was done without trial, more or less made Frank beside himself. He asked and received authority from Hitler personally to make a speech in support of the legal system, which was welcomed with wild applause by the people of Munich, and especially by the students [July 21, 1942]. Hitler did this quite in conformity with his cunning recipe of double-dealing, in order to throw dust in the eyes of the people. It works, too.

The great campaign which Himmler had initiated against Göring and his outfit, because of the particularly lively corruption in this circle, has momentarily been brought to a stop as Hitler doesn't want a scandal now. Here lie the facts behind the grotesque comedy of Göring conferring the flier's wings on Himmler.

With the military it is the same old story. Bock has again been given his walking papers. The generals have merited no other treatment.

There is a strong increase in the brutal treatment of the Jews. The "mixtures" [half and quarter Jews] are also coming in for worse treatment. Old Weinberg, at eighty-one, is now in a concentration camp. More and more people are being deported. In Poland, as already stated here, they are simply murdered.

The case of Kaufmann is especially bad. This good and irreproachable man was a former Minister and officer in World War I. Hindenburg had accepted his resignation with high commendation. The Gauleiter of Munich put him to work in a factory, forbade him to ride on a tram or to visit restaurants. Finally, one of the higher officials insulted him coarsely and struck the defenseless man in the face with his fist.

The fight against the churches also follows its appointed course. In a particularly crass instance Bishop Heckel recently begged me for help. Müller, the Evangelical Bishop's Vicar in Hermannstadt, Rumania, was publicly accused of being a "traitor to his people" and otherwise insulted by the local group leader, Andreas Schmidt, a young ruffian. When an attempt at amicable settlement failed, Müller felt it necessary to take action against Andreas Schmidt. Killinger told him that he sympathized with him fully, but that he should avoid bringing suit before a Rumanian tribunal. Müller declared that this was agreeable to him if Killinger would take care of the matter. Killinger explained that he was not in a position to do that because Andreas Schmidt was not under his jurisdiction, but that he would furnish the money and visa for Müller to fly to Berlin, and would write to Luther in detail. The latter would then set the matter right in co-operation with the Office for Germans Abroad. The Consul General in Hermannstadt would accompany him.

Müller appeared at the airport. The first snag was that the Consul General excused himself from taking the trip. In Berlin, Pastor Müller was put up at the Adlon Hotel, went to see Heckel, and reported to Luther. Thereupon the Gestapo came to Heckel and said they knew Müller had been with him. Where was he staying? The Gestapo then appeared at the Adlon and took Müller's passport away. A few days later it was returned to him with the visa canceled! There was no sign of life from Luther.

On *June 5* Ilse and I spent two and a half days at Warnitz. I had a most enjoyable visit with Henry Stackelberg, Professor of Economics at Bonn, an intelligent man, lively, clearheaded, and cosmopolitan.

During Ilse's stay we lunched with Diels (alert, hard to see through, bursting with ambition, probably unscrupulous). By chance Klee, who had just come back from South America, was also there. What he has gone through in Germany has bowled him over. Budak, the Croat Minister, quite intelligent, a rabid Croat nationalist, made no bones about having participated indirectly in the assassination of King Alexander. He was of the opinion that the Croats were undeniably grateful to the Italians for all assistance rendered during their exile, but they would in no case accept them as masters or turn Croatian territory over to them.

*June 10, 1942:* I had dinner with Ilse at the Swedish Minister's in honor of Sven Hedin, who told Ilse a highly interesting story about how Charles XII had appeared at midnight before his friend Heidenstam, while he was writing about the battle of Poltava. Heidenstam heard a clinking sound and in came Charles XII, sat himself down in an easy chair opposite him, laid his hands encased in long white gauntlets on the arms of the chair, and said: "You are mistaken; I prayed at the battle of Poltava." I found that Hedin had aged and was likable only within limits. The purpose of his trip was a childish hope that he could do something to stop the atrocities in Norway.

I had a conversation with Tschammer. In the present ruling clique he is a square peg in a round hole, but admittedly no genius. I dropped in on the good Brauchitschs. Little good to report about their passive cousin, the field marshal. Ley had promised him a car. Now, after his dismissal, Brauchitsch is shamelessly laying claim to it—so far in vain!

Professor Hohn, Himmler's scientific adviser, asked me on the suggestion of Jessen to come to see him on June 29 about a possible honorary professorship for me. Jessen believes that this type of activity would provide a good cloak and put me in a position to say a great deal. I gave Hohn an outline of my ideas and writings, but it is not clear whether he will take the matter up seriously.

On *July 11* with Ilse in Ebenhausen. She stayed on there. The morning after our arrival we visited Frau Else Bruckmann, where our visit was interrupted by poor Frau von Kaufmann, who begged me for more help. Else Bruckmann told all kinds of stories of Hitler's early years. For instance, Goebbels had been recommended to Hitler but at first the latter was not willing to receive him. Later he was persuaded to do so. Afterward there was a great quarrel and Hitler wanted to throw

Goebbels out, whereupon Goebbels threw himself at Hitler's feet, whimpering in the most undignified way.

Her report of Hitler's last visit was more vital. This spring he had written in her guest book: "After the most difficult winter of my life, and at the beginning of a great new year." This was considerably toned down from the 1941 inscription, which read, "In the year of the achievement of victory." The signature was miserably written.

On that same day, after a long conversation on aeronautics, Hess had satirically written underneath: "The period of adventures is not yet over."

Most shattering, however, is the fact that Hitler is said to be "very pleased and optimistic" over the war in the east. He would build a great East Wall at an appropriate place and then be free to act in other directions. The land that had been conquered with so much blood could not be given away again, but had to be kept in German hands. He had gone on to say that among our allies the Finns were especially brave, but naturally the Japanese were even braver, because they fought an ideological war. So, of course, did the bolshevists. But bravest of all were the Germans, and of these the SS, because they did not have "Christian inhibitions" like others. In the future he would see to it that these inhibitions were stripped from all Germans!

A good joke is being told. A man in the streetcar mumbles: "Nothing to eat, nothing to smoke, nothing to drink—Heil Hitler!" As he keeps repeating it over and over the conductor perks up his ears and tells him that if he does not keep quiet he will be arrested. But the man goes on repeating his phrase. The conductor halts the car and calls a policeman. "What did you say?" asked the policeman. "Nothing." The policeman then asks the other passengers, one after another. The first answers: "I was asleep." The second: "I was reading the paper." The third: "I was talking with someone." The fourth: "I am worn out and don't pay attention to anything." The policeman leaves and the streetcar goes on. The man continues: "Nothing to eat, nothing to drink, nothing to smoke, but solidarity among the people [Volksgemeinschaft] is first-class!"

*August 4, 1942:* Yesterday, with Uexküll, I visited Kurt Schmitt with the intention of interesting him in Kaufmann's case. Unfortunately it was in vain. He had intervened on behalf of other non-Aryan cases with Police President von Eberstein, who had declared that he would not again raise a finger because, first of all, there was nothing he could do, and second, they were already accusing him of being too slow in the noble work of clearing out all the Jews from the "capital of the movement," as Hitler had ordered. Schmitt himself told of dreadful cases that had caused him many a sleepless night. For instance, the widow of the commander of his company, who had fallen in World War I had been deported! It was to be assumed that all these people have been murdered, for nothing more is heard of them. Two respectable old ladies whom he knows, and who were also to be deported, had tearfully begged him for poison. What a frightful exhibition of bestiality!

*Ebenhausen, August 28, 1942:* When I returned to Berlin ten days ago I found a veritable wave of optimism which emanated especially from the military, government officials, and small minds. The victories in Russia,[1] the submarine successes, et cetera, would bring peace. An entirely different interpretation of events on the *evening of the nineteenth* at the Sauerbruchs' with Popitz, Planck, Olbricht, and Beck. They believed the victories would serve only to prolong the war because the other side would the more inevitably be forced to play for time, that is, to wait for increasing technical superiority, especially in the air. They estimated the number of airplanes produced per month to be: Germany, about 1,500; England, 1,300; Russia, 1,000; America, 4,000.

Important recent events: A new Minister of Justice, three deaths among leading airmen, Brazil's declaration of war, ambiguous attitude of Serrano Suñer.

The decree by which Frank is deposed (that is limited for the present to his already undermined post of Governor General) puts in the shade all previous proclamations. The decree charges the man, who until now has been president of the

[1]August 10, 1942, Maikop and Krasnodar in German hands.

revolutionary tribunal and who is to act in the capacity of "guardian of the law," with the express authority to depart from all existing law [August 24, 1942]. The jurist Thierack, who is not ashamed to carry out this self-castration of justice, has been described to me by a former colleague, who knows him extremely well, as a mixture of stupidity and trickery.

Three deaths from airplane crashes within the space of a few days are of particular significance. The Duke of Kent's death saddens me because of the lovely Marina. Horthy II [August 20, 1942], whose disappearance from the scene renders the "Horthy dynasty" scheme impracticable as a solution of the domestic muddle in Hungary. The third case is that of the admirable Gablenz. It is typical of our present situation that the death of such a man, who had achievements to his credit and was of a critical and independent disposition, should immediately give rise to rumors that he was murdered.

Brazil's declaration of war [August 22, 1942], at the very moment of Germany's great successes, is morally impressive. At the same time, though stoutly denied by our press, it will have considerable significance in the battle against the submarines in the western Atlantic, and in any American plans pointing toward Africa.

Portugal immediately and loudly proclaimed its fraternal sympathy for Brazil and underscored it heavily, while delicately hinting to us that it all meant nothing. Serrano Suñer reveals himself more and more as an unreliable recruit for Hitler. He deals in "Latin solidarity." In Spain things are boiling. In Turkey, too, the sharply neutral attitude is again gaining ground. The increasingly serious air raids on German cities are very real. The Americans are more active now in the Far East than they were in the beginning. The Japanese are having more and more trouble with them.

*Berlin, September 4, 1942:* There is increasing pessimism about the possibility of bringing the war to an end. Very heavy fighting in Russia, dangerous exhaustion of troops, and ever greater strain on our man power. In Africa we are making efforts, so far unsuccessful, to regain the offensive. Rommel is temporarily out. He had suggested Guderian as his successor and this called forth a burst of fury from Hitler. The grotesque game of tin soldiers which Hitler plays with the generals has been enriched by a new case. Stumme, commanding general of a tank corps, was sentenced to five years' imprisonment because a staff officer from one of his divisions, carrying plans for the deployment of his troops, fell into the hands of the Russians. He was immediately pardoned, with Göring promising him a new command, and is now being sent to Africa as a substitute for Rommel. An unmilitary, un-Prussian farce. It parallels the catastrophic developments in the field of justice. Thierack, the new Minister of Justice, delivered a wild speech: "Rather punish nine innocent people than let one guilty man escape." Someone comments wittily: "It is really risky to be innocent."

Goerdeler visited me in Berlin. He is going to the Russian central front on an economic mission with very convincing material but little prospect of success.

He told me about a vile, bombastic speech Göring made to the Gauleiters: "We don't propose to go hungry. The people in the occupied countries can feed on Cossack saddles."

We discussed the foreign situation. It is not yet quite clear what the great change in the Japanese Foreign Office means, especially the resignation of Togo. He was formerly considered rather a man of peace. Is it a victory of the military party? Oshima is supposed to have been in Moscow and to have urged a separate peace; otherwise Japan would attack Vladivostok. The idea is obvious. But the so-called "mild German conditions" specified in that connection sound fantastic and are unacceptable for Russia. They provide that the Ukraine and Caucasus are to be under German sovereignty! Germany is to help in getting Russia an outlet to the Persian Gulf.

Spain suffered a political crisis which ended with the dismissal of Serrano Suñer.

Day before yesterday I went to see Jessen. He was somewhat more optimistic about the possibility of a change of regime, but it wasn't convincing to me. It seems that Himmler is worried and is again toying with the idea that perhaps he could get a peace. Stuckart is mentioned as a candidate to succeed Heydrich. He is a moderate man. Schellenberg is also mentioned.

*Berlin, October 4, 1942:* An unbelievably empty, somewhat halting speech by Hitler [September 30, 1942] on a low moral level, aesthetically more vulgar than ever. He adopted the tone of a street urchin against the enemy. Factually interesting is that the tenor of his remarks is subdued, his demands obviously much reduced.

At the center of the system there is increasing agitation and on our boundaries the fermentation is growing stronger. Big quarrel with Denmark because, believe it or not, the "King of Denmark did not reply courteously enough to a congratulatory telegram Hitler had sent him on his birthday." Poor Scavenius was really given a dressing down by Ribbentrop through Renthe-Fink, the German Minister in Copenhagen. Both Ministers were recalled, and there were threats and pitiful kow-towing on the part of the Danes, who are afraid they will be sent a Gauleiter and who even want to send the Crown Prince here on a mission of apology.

Yesterday, *October 3, 1942,* lunched with Bossy, the Rumanian Minister. Very pleasant people at the lunch. Immediately after the meal Bossy sat down with me and poured out his troubles. It was impossible that things should go on this way. A senseless war was being waged for the sake of prestige and the regime. Did I not see an opportunity for peace somewhere? Unfortunately I had to answer that I did not.

Afterward we were driven home by the Italian Counselor, De la Porta, and his wife. When we stopped at our apartment, and after the ladies had got out of the car, De la Porta let loose much like Bossy, but even more vehemently. In obvious and grave concern he made no bones about his pessimistic observations. A terrible catastrophe could be averted only if Germany took the initiative. Neither side could completely defeat the other, and nothing but endless, senseless devastation lay before us if we did not somehow arrive at a peace. The best thing would be for the Germans to make a gesture, confirmed by acts with respect to the occupied territories and their future. He thought the recent speech by the Führer offered a "ray of hope" in that he no longer spoke of a new order for Europe under German domination and such impossible things. To my question as to whether Myron Taylor had sounded out Italian sentiment while in Rome he of course gave an absolutely negative answer. On the contrary, he had told the Pope that now things had to be fought through unrelentingly to the bitter end.

*October 10, 1942:* Hitler's last speech has generally been interpreted abroad as evidence of weakness and clearly a retreat. In spite of its bombastic tone the same is true of Göring's speech in the Sports Palace [October 4, 1942]. This speech, however, in contrast to Hitler's, was an indisputable success here at home. Of course low and demagogic means were employed, but it did raise the war spirit and also enhanced Göring's own almost unassailable position. His black opponents, the SS, have been chased back into their rat holes, but of course they have become even more rabid and scheme for revenge. Since the SS view the outcome of the war very realistically, that is skeptically, they are driven to the necessity for finding a way out.

On *November 1, 1942,* I spent the evening with Beck at Etta Waldersee's; her husband was present for a time. Beck was thoroughly pessimistic about military matters. Generals are continually being sent home in half-dozen lots. In his very calm, practical, thoughtful way, Beck sadly observed that the decomposition of the Army goes on apace.

Last week end Nostitz visited me in Ebenhausen and advised me, with forceful and certainly well-intentioned arguments, to be very cautious. But the whole group around Weizsäcker gives more and more evidence of being weak and easily influenced. Nothing that smacks of action can be expected from that source.

*Berlin, November 2, 1942:* The political standards of our master are sinking even lower, if that is possible. The propaganda machine is so worn out and the situation so precarious that they resort to the cheapest devices. For instance, Goebbels's last speech, in my opinion an ineffective one [October 18, 1942]: "Once people fought only for ideals; for example, for Socialism or National Socialism (!), for faith in a simple or in a more varied form. Now we fight for our daily bread." "Complaint is the laxative of the soul."

The situation in the east is stalemated. Nevertheless, Hitler merrily told the Gauleiters that in the summer of 1943 "he would take Moscow and the Caucasus, would defeat the Russians, and dictate the peace."

Our submarine war is quite successful but not decisive. In North Africa there is very heavy fighting;[1] a sweeping English victory there—not yet decisive, but it might be of far-reaching importance.

Rieth reports a veritable babel of politics from Tangier, where he is now Consul General. Americans and Englishmen, Frenchmen and Spaniards, Italians and Germans, are all feverishly active. The Americans are particularly energetic. Propaganda is humming and everybody expects that Africa will become the focal point of the war. There is latent antipathy between France and Spain because the latter wants to have part of French Morocco and will probably go into action if the Americans advance into North Africa, not to fight them but only to secure this territory for themselves.

Patitsas, the Greek Undersecretary, called on me on October 30 and said he had just come back from Rome. On every hand he heard that the Italians were extremely sorry they had ever got into a war with Greece. In the future "friendship" must be the password between the two nations which are so closely related culturally. Patitsas gave me to understand that the treatment accorded him in Rome had differed very greatly from the proceedings in Berlin. It was incomprehensible to him how quickly the Germans had managed to destroy the love and admiration the Greeks had felt for Germany at the beginning of the occupation.

Patitsas found that people in Italy thought very badly of the war of Mussolini and Germany. The overwhelming majority of the population appeared to be thoroughly weary of the war and feared nothing more than German supremacy. Apparently they are beginning to take notice of this feeling here, too, and the press has recently been ordered to toss daily bouquets to Italy. As usual, this order was carried out very crudely.

[1]October 25, 1942, the English Army attacks at El Alamein.

On *October 26, 1942,* I dipped into history and saw the very superior film on Bismarck. I again confirmed my conviction that films must falsify history first, because they condense facts too heavily; second, because of the need for dramatic effect. For instance in this film Holstein, brilliantly portrayed by Krauss, plays much too large a role. The effect of the film is hard to estimate; that riddle, the "masses," is incalculable. Many believe it works against the monarchist idea.

On *October 19* I lectured in Stuttgart. We were cordially received by Strölin, the chief burgomaster, who sees things quite clearly; a rather nice chap. The Deputy Commanding General, Oswald (who said at dinner that he believed in the "intuition" of the Führer) was able, to my great relief, to facilitate Ilse's trip on the following morning. I returned to Berlin that evening.

Stuttgart is a really delightful city, old yet new, in which the works of nature and man have developed together. Before going to Stuttgart I went with Ilse to the meeting of the Dante Society in Weimar. Weimar has suffered markedly from its popularity with the Party. Also it is getting more and more difficult to organize things like the Dante meeting. Food, lodging, and assembly halls are all problems. Nevertheless, it was a pleasant oasis in this barren period. We breathed freely again.

Some of the lectures were interesting. German professors often cannot differentiate between writing and speaking. Falkenhausen was fresh and effective in his treatment of *Dante and the Stars.* Gertrud Bäumer presented a very remarkable discussion of her new Dante novel. She defends the historical novel on the ground that only thus can an era and its people be portrayed plastically. This may be, if the author is really a master and if he has very conscientiously studied the sources.

I enjoyed most of all the talk of a young German-Russian engineer, Holbach, now an officer, who was present for the first time and explained in an animated, fresh, and brief manner what it was that drew him to the Dante Society. It was the fact that modern natural science had dissolved the whole proud nineteenth-century enlightenment, with its allegedly final conclusions, into uncertainty and relativity, and forced us to seek solid ground somewhere else.

A number of interesting evenings in Berlin. I spent an afternoon devoted to religion at Frau ——'s; excellent religious discussions among members of three faiths as to the significance of "the image" in religion. The most effective, because the most primitively religious, was an orthodox priest. The whole affair was refreshing; it was proof that an effective Christianity is still alive. The one holy church, however, is still far away.

I attended the meeting of agrarians where Professor von Dietze spoke. I was most impressed by the one woman present, Marion Dönhoff, who manages three estates. I put her on her train for East Prussia, after drinking a glass of wine with her at Töpfer's. There is comfort in such moments in the agreement about things that matter; but we cannot help seeing the awful shape of things to come which we are unable to prevent.

*Ebenhausen, November 13, 1942:* The barometer sinks lower and lower in Berlin. It is becoming ever clearer how right it was to tell the generals that a change in regime must be accomplished while Germany is still undefeated and intact. By now it has become highly questionable whether the other side is at all inclined to give an acceptable peace even to a different Germany. I see only one chance: to abandon Japan. On the one hand, Japan's entrance into the war had the effect of making the United States conduct this war as her own and to throw in all her resources. On the other hand, the Anglo-Saxon may well be influenced by the prospect that Japan might soon be defeated if an understanding were reached with us.

If the regime were changed today we should have to be prepared for unhappy consequences in lands to the southeast and perhaps even for desertion by Italy. In disagreement with Popitz and others, I am of the opinion that we must do everything possible in advance to avoid the latter contingency. However that may be, all of these evil prospects must not be allowed to keep us from overthrowing a regime which is ruining us at home and which means far worse ruin at the end of the war.

*Ebenhausen, November 26, 1942:* The barometer is still going down. Stalingrad begins to play the same role as Verdun. The prospect of a new winter campaign appears more and more probable—with an enemy hard pressed and fighting under tremendous difficulties, but still unbroken.

In addition there is increasing severity in the air raids. Munich is being attacked, too. All our possessions in the attic barely escaped destruction, great fires burned in the whole area, and the neighboring house was a heap of rubble.

We have had heavy losses in Russia. Dieter writes in a most serious vein as of November 16. The trend in his letters from August 9 to November 16 is frightening.

Dangerous disturbances might begin any time now in neighboring countries. The Finnish Minister in Washington, Procopé, has made some very unorthodox statements. It is significant that he called attention to the fact that in Finland there is no persecution of the Jews.

Japan has announced it needs a large supply of iron, otherwise it cannot attempt any great undertakings. The picture one gets of the feeling in Greece should be mentioned here, too. Schmitt, my political barometer, with whom I dined yesterday at Uexküll's, made remarks which, coming from one who has always been so obedient and optimistic, proved how low public opinion has now sunk. He said that pictures of Hitler were thrown into the street with curses after the air raid on Munich. Ilse, who picked me up today, said that there was also a great deal of cursing of "the enemy." Vicco Bülow told about the "commendable" (!) disposition of those cities in the west, such as Cologne, which were most heavily hit, to hold out to the end.

A decline is nevertheless inevitable, and nothing can be expected from the so-called feelings of the people as such—fury against Hitler, for instance. We are a most curious mixture of heroes and slaves. The latter applies particularly to the generals, who have succeeded in an almost fabulous manner in getting their authority reduced to zero, especially as against Hitler. After the reverses in the east he again fumed like a maniac, for when things go wrong it is not "the most brilliant military leader of all time" who commands, but "the generals."

Sauerbruch, who visited Hitler recently, found him old and broken. In conversation he had muttered strange, disjointed phrases like: "I must go to India," or "For one German who is killed ten of the enemy must die." Sauerbruch thought he was now unquestionably out of his mind.

Hitler has thrown out Bock, List, and Ruoff as Army Group Commanders. Also a number of commanding generals, among them the intelligent Gustav Anton Wietersheim, who had advocated a timely withdrawal from Stalingrad; and finally he even got rid of Halder. Zeitzler, Chief of Staff with Rundstedt, is to take Halder's place.[1] According to all reports he is an unpleasant man. The "Supreme Head of the State" is now personally commanding the Southern Army Group. He treated Keitel most savagely, that man who through his servility has assumed the heaviest guilt. When Olbricht recently asked Keitel how things were, Keitel answered: "I don't know; he tells me nothing; he only spits at me!" Hitler put him out after a wild explosion, but a few days later actually reinstated him.

Popitz had visited Küchler [Northern Army Group]; Goerdeler has also called on him and, more important, on Kluge [Central Army Group]. They found complete understanding, especially about the necessity of keeping in contact. But is there still time? Who knows whether they will not be kicked out too?

Popitz confirmed terrible reports from the East, particularly the brutal massacre of many thousands of Jews. A Swiss attorney, who had saved a few Dutch Jews through bribery, said sarcastically to an acquaintance: "You Germans are such great organizers; why, in the face of your transportation difficulties, do you first ship so many thousands to the east instead of simply murdering them at home?" This man returns to Switzerland with truly edifying impressions. He will not keep them to himself!

The Pétain-Laval government is compromising itself more and more deeply in the Jewish question. Tension in France is mounting daily.

My visa has again been refused. It is not unlikely that Ribbentrop, who is getting more nervous every day, is behind it. This time they probably didn't even check with the SD [Security Service of the SS]. H. B. Haeften has emphatically warned against any activity at the moment. A St. Bartholo-

[1]December 10, 1942, Zeitzler succeeded Halder as Chief of the General Staff.

mew's night was quite conceivable at a time of such critical developments.

On *November 15* I gave a well-attended lecture on Cavour before the German-Italian Society in Leipzig. During lunch at the Rathskeller I was much amused to hear a general of the Air Force, who sat next to me, jubilantly remark on my "allusions" to the present.

Similarly, the Berlin editor of the *Frankfurter Zeitung* told me he had written an article about my essay on southeastern Europe primarily so that he could quote a few sentences of mine, for the newspaper itself dared not say such things.

*Ebenhausen, November 13, 1942:* Gloomy predictions of recent times with respect to the war situation have been outdistanced by military events. Severe defeats in North Africa; the larger part of the Italian forces fighting there has been destroyed—principally as a result of a gasoline shortage. A dangerous situation has been precipitated by American landings in North Africa [November 8, 1942]. Complete stalemate in the east.

Unfortunately, there is little hope that any power will bestir itself to keep us from rolling on into disaster. At the "top" there is increasing nervousness. A very poor speech by Hitler in Munich [September 8, 1942]. New arrests, both right and left. Our subaltern generals should be thrashed. Part of the time they think like corporals; the rest of the time they think only of themselves.

Ilse and I were much impressed yesterday by General G——, whose desire for comfort and security prevents all action on his part. He is really interested only in whether they will give him another post.

General Quade, official spokesman for the Air Force command, spoke officially in loud, strong, and rosy terms, and then whispered to me: "What is going to happen now?"

I liked General Kaupisch when I saw him again. At the Rheinbaben table he said, in great concern: "We are now probably at the turning point." This is a very widespread feeling.

Hitler and others are pinning their hopes on the new secret weapon. I am convinced that even if "terrifically effective," it will serve only to increase destruction and prolong the war. It is becoming more and more clear what a mistake Hitler made in holding the long, crooked front at the beginning of last winter, and how foolish was the order which demanded a decisive victory be won at Stalingrad as well as in the Caucasus.

I paid a visit to Fromm three days ago to talk with him about not being able to ride any more. When I apologized for coming to him on such a trivial errand in these serious times he blustered away in such a manner that I got angry and very vigorously insisted that the situation was terribly critical. Thereupon he abandoned his blustering tone and blamed everything on the politicians. Then this German officer said: "Yes, but our Führer has more strategical ability in his little finger than all the generals together!"

*Ebenhausen, December 20, 1942:* A bad month lies behind us. The double break-through by the Russians at Stalingrad with the encirclement of one and a half armies has been kept secret [November 23–25, 1942]; there are further retreats in Libya; the Allied position has consolidated in North Africa. These are compensated only by considerable German submarine successes and small repulses of the enemy at Tunis. These things do not equalize the situation. In addition, there is the increasing exhaustion of man power.

There was an impressive report a few days ago by Waldau, a high Air Force officer, about the imminent mobilization of schoolboys fifteen and sixteen years of age for anti-aircraft duty at home. They were not to come from the boys' high schools, for they are already out of school at that age. This would have a dreadful effect on the next generation of the intelligentsia in intellectual as well as moral respects. At the same time it is an obvious sign of weakness, for these flak batteries will, in the future, be composed of one third soldiers, one third children, and one third prisoners of war.

Throughout the whole world there is increasing activity against us: in the occupied territories, in Italy, in neutral countries, especially in Turkey, Portugal, Spain, and Chile. Atrocities in Poland are exploited very dramatically in the House of Commons. There is increasing nervousness here at home arising out of anxiety over the outcome of the war and fear of domestic disturbances.

At the last inspection of newly appointed officers Hitler was absent. Göring took advantage of the occasion to make a bitter and incredible attack on the generals—i.e., the superiors of those present. Although not long ago Göring had asserted that Hitler was doing everything himself and was "commanding" the individual battalions "from his bunker," he now asserts that the generals are responsible for the failure of the campaign last winter and this.

Frighteningly impressive report by Waldersee, who has just returned to us from the captivity of Stalingrad. He told how insane were the commands from the top, how high generals behaved like subalterns in their abject obedience, and about the conditions of troops and matériel after their heavy losses.

There are some important changes in my professional existence. Clodius of the Foreign Office and Undersecretary Neumann told Wilmowsky that I was a heavy burden for the already badly compromised MWT, because Ribbentrop was vigorously attacking my activities, especially as the Gestapo was watching me and making my trips impossible. Wilmowsky was most unhappy, but understandably enough accepted the resignation which I offered on the spot. We agreed that I should leave the executive committee but should remain on the board of trustees. This I am to do on April 1, since at that time, as chance would have it, there is a broader opportunity to do some work for Wagemann in the Institute for Economic Research. To be sure everything will be more difficult there.

My leaving the MWT certainly serves some purpose, as I have recently been warned several times about the Gestapo. For that reason I would perhaps do well to keep out of sight, so that I can at least continue to work in some way. Wilmowsky brought me the news that someone had deliberately looked him up in order to warn me through him. Frauendorfer told me, too, that the former Gauleiter Josef Wagner sent me greetings and a warning. Frauendorfer, SS man and wearer of the gold Party badge, was most impressive in his boundless despair about all he had lived through in Poland. It was so terrible that he could not endure it. Now he wants to go to the front as a simple soldier. Continual, indescribable mass murder of Jews. SS people rode around in the ghetto after the curfew hour for Jews and used automatic pistols on anybody who was still out, for example, children who still lingered playing in the streets.

The radical leftists are beginning to get more active. I had a very satisfactory exchange of ideas with the younger group— Peter Yorck, Haeften, Schulenburg, and Trott at Dohna's.

Bottai, who was in Berlin to attend the dedication of the Studia Humanitatis [December 7, 1942], made an interesting observation to Almuth at a luncheon party given by Grillo, the Italian Consul in Munich. The whole war was a mistake, for communism was today more firmly marshaled behind National Socialism and fascism than it was behind bolshevism, which was now acting in a democratic way. The Italians who turn up here (Colbertaldo *et al.*) are shocked at our conditions of slavery and barbarism. I was especially struck when, at the dedication of the Studia Humanitatis, the Italian Professor Grassi quoted from the farewell message of Giordano Bruno to Germany at Wittenberg. One becomes almost melancholy at hearing these beautiful and prophetic words.

An interesting, very arresting performance of the second part of *Faust*. Never before had the earthly "fiasco" of Faust seemed so clear to me. Ethically and aesthetically he needed grace from above in order to be saved. At the moment when his end was obviously in sight he said:

> *"Dass sich das grosse Werk vollende,*
> *Ein Geist genügt für tausend Hände*
> [To bring the great work to an end
> One spirit suffices for a thousand hands]."

Under the disintegrating influence of our times spiritual confusion is growing here even among the best people. For instance, that excellent fellow Brandenburg, severely wounded as a flier in World War I and now Ministerial Director, called me at luncheon a "hyphenated Christian" because I had written about the tasks and achievements of the German Evangelical pastors in the periodical *Pfarrspiegel!* One must refrain, he said, from senseless activities (see the sonnet of

Reinhold Schneider); instead, one should content oneself with prayer. Jesus Christ and nothing else.

I have read an interesting English novel by Eric Knight, *This Above All*. It presents a not-very-happy picture of England, despite a really constructive purpose.

Italy becomes more and more of a puzzle. Mussolini tries to pull his people together by making a speech, which in tone ("Churchill, whose mouth reeks of alcohol and tobacco!") follows well-known patterns, but which contains one sentence that gives pause. Ciano shortly thereafter repeated it: The war was now attaining such gigantic proportions that the entire world was at stake, et cetera, and even territorial questions lost their significance! There are indications that the Italians are attempting to sound out the other side in Lisbon. It is not clear whether this is being done with or without the knowledge of the Duce.

Langbehn has had some talks with an official Englishman in Zürich [December 12, 1942] and an American official [Hopper] in Stockholm, with the approval of the SD. Under the already familiar conditions (change of regime) there were possibilities for an acceptable peace, above all with England, which looks upon America and Japan with great concern and fears bolshevism. But there was also some possibility of coming to terms with America. She does not want chaos in Europe and does want a free hand to deal with Japan.

*December 31, 1942, Ebenhausen:* The last day of a year in which the German position became steadily worse. Has any man in history ever before so lightly taken on so terrific a responsibility? Has ever a nation submitted with greater apathy?

I have just read the news of Nevile Henderson's death. The official German press lies shamefully on this occasion. This man, who worked to preserve the peace up to the very last minute in August 1939, they now call a "saboteur" of peace. Ribbentrop's bad conscience comes out clearly on the crucial point, the reading of the sixteen points. They have the cheek to write that he did not "pass on" the memorandum. One witness less and one gentleman less!

Darlan's death [December 24, 1942] still somewhat mysterious. It seems to have relieved the tension between the English and the Americans.

A visit from Nostitz who has returned from Switzerland. We discussed the improbability of a timely change of regime, and the necessity of providing the diplomatic missions with immediate instructions and to have them take certain measures which would make clear the distance between us and the present regime. I emphasized the necessity of not delivering ourselves into the hands of foreigners. Our swinishness must be judged before our own tribunals. Therefore there should be immediate court proceedings against the criminals who now rule over us.

I had a long talk about Weizsäcker on the basis of conversations the latter apparently had with Kessel, who told Nostitz about them. Nostitz defends Weizsäcker. I simply said not everyone could behave that way; that called for a particular sort of character. He has properly been blamed for the famous speech he made to our diplomats returning from America in May 1942.

A great communist conspiracy has been uncovered in the Ministry for Air and other government offices. Apparently it is composed of fanatics filled with hatred for the system. They seem to have planned the creation of an interim organization which could function in case the bolshevists won.

# 1943

*Berlin, January 22, 1943:* If the generals had it in mind to withhold their intervention until it was absolutely clear that the corporal is leading us into disaster, they have had their dream fulfilled. The worst about it is, however, that our definite prophecy has also been fulfilled; i.e., that it would then be too late and any new regime could be nothing more than a liquidation commission. I suppose we cannot say for sure that the war is lost, but it is certain that it cannot be won and that the prospects for persuading the other side to make an acceptable peace are very small indeed. Consequently the generals are much more aware that something must be done, but at the same time the domestic and foreign fronts have become much weaker.

According to the reports of people who, like Jessen and Gisevius, have pipe lines to the Army both on the battle front and at home, there is now a real possibility for peace. The evil of the situation is revealed in the fact that at this same time there come reports from the "enemy's side" which give rise to ever-increasing doubts as to whether they are now holding out for complete destruction of Germany. I have probably noted down before that after my visit to Walchensee, at the end of the year, our efforts to make contact with England through Langbehn in Switzerland, and with America in Sweden, were yielding tolerable results. Gisevius, on his part, reported somewhat less favorably from Switzerland. The word "occupation," i.e., the occupation of Germany as a condition for negotiations, has often been advanced in this connection. The optimists among us think, however, that even in that event the familiar arguments (America, Russia, Japan) could still be exploited politically.

In our inner circle there are strong differences of opinion, fostered by Beck's all-too-lenient leadership. There are serious doubts in different quarters about Goerdeler, at least as a political leader. Also about Popitz, who is reproached for his earlier questionable attitude under Göring as well as for serious mistakes in financial policy, and for his all-too-long co-operation with the regime. Falkenhausen is rejected by many as having participated in the regime of terror. I, personally, hold myself as aloof as possible from disputes about personalities and try to stiffen Beck's backbone. Furthermore, I maintain that the number of usable people is too small and the good qualities of those mentioned too great for such squabbling. Gisevius works hard for Schacht.

The newest version, and one toward which Beck seems to lean, is that before a real cabinet is formed and alongside a later cabinet there should be a small directorate: Beck, Schacht, Goerdeler, myself, and a general. I have nothing against this. Leadership by Goerdeler I also consider hazardous.

Long conference with Beck on *January 16, 1943,* during the air raid, which did some damage to his house. On the way home I passed five large fires. On the next day Ilse and I wanted to go to see the Jessens. There was a new air-raid alarm. Ilse got stuck in the subway at the Potsdamerplatz and I was put out on the street at Schmargendorf and ran as fast as Nurmi through the Heidelbergerplatz, Rüdesheimerplatz, Breitenbachplatz to Popitz's and his comfortable air-raid shelter, complete with a bowl of punch. From his attic, also somewhat damaged, we saw a gruesome spectacle.

I could breathe again at a meeting of the Wednesday Club where Spranger delivered an excellent lecture on the spirit of our a<sub></sub> ... <sub></sub>d Christianity.

Sc⸍ arze (Elsa Arnim's husband) told me on *January 10, 1943,* that they wanted to elect me President of the Academy. But I consider it quite impossible that Hitler would agree.

Sauerbruch, who belongs to the Senate of the Academy, will do something about it from above. It would be quite a good platform. I spoke about the matter with Kurt Schmitt, too. It is very characteristic of the situation how depressed, indeed how desperate, Schmitt was. At times these people cannot be loyal enough to the regime or optimistic enough. Schmitt told revolting stories about Göring's fiftieth birthday. Gifts amounting to about one million gold marks, among them a Sèvres service of 2,400 pieces, given by three industrialists. Cost: 500,000 reichsmarks. A French hunting lodge, stolen in France and destined to be placed on one of Göring's hunting estates, three medieval statues, valued at 16,000, 17,000, and 18,000 reichsmarks. Gritzbach [adjutant to Göring] had telephoned Schmitt and mentioned the statues in case he was at a loss as to what to give! Schmitt gave them, too, obedient fellow that he is. .

Recently I had an interesting visit from Oster. He read me a document which set forth Himmler's views about war and peace in the east. From this it must be concluded that this man is either a knave or a fool—or both.

I had numerous conferences with Popitz, Goerdeler, Beck, and Guttenberg, who is leaving us, withdrawing from the line of fire and going to Agram.

Quite interesting, but not very gratifying, was an important discussion between the youngsters and the older members of our group at Peter Yorck's. The youngsters, who in contrast to the older men are presenting a united front toward the outside, were led by the witty Hellmuth Moltke, with his Anglo-Saxon and pacifist inclinations. I was again favorably impressed by Gerstenmeier, with whom Popitz and I had a talk before the meeting. Beck presided. He was rather weak and reserved. There was a sharp contrast, particularly in the realm of social policy, between the younger group and Goerdeler, which the latter unsuccessfully tried to conceal. Goerdeler is really something of a reactionary. The unity of the younger group, incidentally, does not really include Fritzi Schulenburg, who is more of a realistic political thinker. I am glad the youngsters have enough confidence to talk over their doubts with me.

*Ebenhausen, February 14, 1943:* The last few weeks have brought the most serious crisis we have experienced thus far in the war, actually the first real crisis, unfortunately not only a crisis of the leadership and of the present regime but a crisis for Germany.

It is symbolized in the name "Stalingrad." For the first time Hitler was not able to get out from under the responsibility; for the first time the critical rumors are aimed straight at him. There has been exposed for all eyes to see the lack of military ability of "the most brilliant strategist of all time," that is, our megalomaniac corporal. This was concealed up to now by a few intuitive master strokes, the lucky results of risks that were in themselves unjustified, and the shortcomings of our enemies. It is clear to all that precious blood has been shed foolishly or even criminally for purposes of prestige alone. Since strictly military affairs are involved this time, the eyes of the generals were opened, too. The behavior of the unfortunate General Paulus, to whom the Russians can now present the field marshal's baton,[1] is being sharply criticized. This, if ever, was the time for him to show some of Yorck's spirit. If he could not do that, he should not have come out of this disaster alive.[2]

Gustav Anton Wietersheim (commanding general of a corps), who in conflict with Paulus "was kicked out," now appears as a really great figure, but that doesn't do us any good now. The one general who defended his views most valiantly, and consequently fell into disgrace and received no decorations or recognition, was Strecker. He and his excellent Chief of Staff, Groscurth, turned out to be the ones who fought the longest.

Even Herr Zeitzler, Hitler's chosen Chief of the General Staff, now sees what is going on and has summoned up enough courage to resist idiotic orders. For two days he did not appear at the staff meetings and in this way put across his own ideas. Kluge and Manstein, too, after the harm was done, managed

[1] Colonel General Paulus was promoted to field marshal by Hitler on January 31, 1943.

[2] Paulus, according to a plan of the resistance movement, and in agreement with Kluge and Manstein, was at the proper time to have broken out of Stalingrad and headed westward. At the same time Kluge and Manstein were to have taken over independent command of the Army, which was to have been the signal for the *coup d'état* in Berlin.

to get more freedom of movement. And Herr Fromm, this weather vane, now trumpets brave opinions. But in spite of all efforts, what is still lacking is a spark plug.

There are more and more reports to show Hitler's dangerous mental condition. The present government is celebrating its tenth anniversary by fighting for its own existence at the expense of the German people. It is significant that Hitler did not dare to speak on January 30! Who would have believed this a short time ago—or that Göring would disappear into a bunker during his speech because of an air-raid warning.

*Ebenhausen, February 14, 1943:* The dangers for Germany lie at that one spot where the enemy will penetrate, somewhere along lines stretching from Spain to Turkey on the one side and up to Norway on the other. A sign of the times is to be seen in the dismissal of all halfway independent people from the Italian Cabinet [February 6, 1943]. Ciano goes as Ambassador to the Vatican, where he will have every opportunity to make contacts with the other side. All those who are of real stature and character are dismissed: Bottai, who as far as I know stood well with Ciano, a humanist; Pavolini, a friend of Ciano, a cultured writer; Grandi, former Ambassador to London; Thaon de Revel, who has an English mother. Therefore a concentration of all government functions in Mussolini, a sign that the war will continue. In addition Mussolini is still sick. Dr. Sauerbruch has gone to see him.

In Berlin I had countless conferences with ———. Aside from the lack of spark plugs there are strong differences over questions of personality, particularly with respect to Goerdeler and Popitz. I work for both, though not with the idea that the former shall be number one. As a contrast to the present regime, the most highly "personal" of all, we must first of all create an impersonal directorate led by the military. Goerdeler continues to misjudge the state of "ripeness" and consequently the possibilities. This does not, however, affect the necessity for action. But we must be clear about the realities and shape our methods accordingly.

*Ebenhausen, March 6, 1943:* Sad to say the serious crisis mentioned at the beginning of my last notes did not precipitate the cleansing storm, the bitterly necessary, intensely longed for change of regime. That alone could still afford us at least the chance of a tolerable peace, an inner healing, and the recovery of Europe. Vain are all efforts to pour iron into the blood stream of the people, who are supporting a half-insane, half-criminal policy with all their might.

The military events alone, the irresponsible leadership of this megalomaniac and irresponsible corporal, should have induced them to act if the inner rot were not enough. At the moment the acute crisis has dissolved into a more subtle lingering one. A remark by that opportunist, Fromm, to Olbricht is illustrative of this: In view of the improved situation on the southern part of the eastern front the change was now no longer necessary. Olbricht, however, will do nothing without Fromm, and the leaders in the east continue to vacillate.

General Field Marshal —— accepts a check for more than 250,000 marks for his sixtieth birthday. That he did not formally reject it might still be excused, but it is incomprehensible that he cashed it instead of storing it away in a strong box before the eyes of trusted witnesses, as forever "untouchable."

Our spirits were low at all our meetings. Goerdeler, in his desperation, again toys with the idea of taking some kind of partial action on the theory that the whole building would collapse like a house of cards. That is not the way. Certainly the situation is "ripe," but not so ripe that one can run such a risk. Even today Hitler's prestige is still great enough—if he can keep on his feet—to enable him to take counteraction that would mean at least chaos or civil war.

Gisevius, who has frequent meetings with Christian circles in foreign countries, told me that I am held in good repute by the Pope. At the same time he warned me against entering into too close relations with Heckel and Gerstenmeier, who were regarded by the confessional churches and the real Christians of foreign countries as compromisers. Thus there are always internal squabbles. I argued strongly against this exaggerated destructive kind of weeding-out process and defended Gerstenmeier especially.

A mad proclamation by Hitler which he did not dare read

himself. He arranged that the infamous Esser should bring it out. Seventy-five per cent of it was Jew-baiting, the rest was an announcement of the sharpest kind of demands on the occupied areas—tactically as stupid as possible. Wagemann, returning from the Hague, reported on the growing tension there. The shooting of hostages brought retaliation in the form of ten murders of Mussert people for every hostage killed.

Minister Thomsen, upon his appointment, reported at headquarters and at Karinhall. He went with illusions and came back completely converted. He found Hitler outwardly maintaining an irresponsible confidence in victory, busily drawing up building plans for embassies, et cetera—an undignified drama.

Göring kept him a whole day, was very friendly, drove him about in the forest, and presented a grotesque figure. He appeared early in a Bavarian leather jacket with full white shirt sleeves. He changed his costume often during the day, and appeared at the dinner table in a blue or violet kimono with fur-trimmed bedroom slippers. Even in the morning he wore at his side a golden dagger which was also changed frequently. In his tiepin he wore a variety of precious stones, and around his fat body a wide girdle, set with many stones—not to mention the splendor and number of his rings.

The big speech by Goebbels reached a new pinnacle of filthy demagoguery directed against the upper class. Here is an example of the effect on imbeciles. The wife of Minister Thomsen steps out of the subway. A man in uniform, heavy with braid—she thinks it was a police officer—storms up to her, snatches an ordinary, much-worn kid glove off her hand, and bellows: "Haven't you heard that Goebbels has forbidden the wearing of kid gloves?" A peroxide blonde passing by chimed in: "Quite right!" Incidentally, Goebbels had not said anything against kid gloves; he said that in such times as these one couldn't handle things with kid gloves. But the stirring up of animosities and hatreds is getting worse, and what makes it still worse is that it originates in "high places."

In spite of this neither the military nor the civilian lambs, who choose their own butchers, disappear from the scene. There would be little to say against this if they were the only ones to be butchered. But the real victim is Germany as a whole.

Löser, the Director General of Krupp, an intelligent man who sees things clearly, recently said that the leading people, with the servile Krupp-Bohlen and the cold-blooded, egotistical Zangen at their head, stood behind Hitler because they thought this was the way to make large profits and keep their workers in line. Clear realization of national needs was found much more frequently among the workers. Of course it was very difficult to determine the real mood of the workers, because everybody was spying on everybody else.

A week ago [*February 27, 1943*] I went to Cologne with Ilse. My lecture reminded me of the one I gave in January 1937, when I was on active service, in the large auditorium of the university. To my astonishment I was again received with great honor. In spite of four daylight alarms on the same day there were 1,500 people at the lecture!

In the evening we dined at Winkelnkemper's. Toward the end of the meal came an air-raid alarm. Since they told us that all trains left promptly in spite of everything we went on foot and in total darkness to the station, hanging onto a faithful hotel porter. At first we sought shelter under the viaduct and then climbed into a train filled with soldiers.

We were headed for Niederlahnstein because we wanted to visit Henry Stackelberg (Professor of Economics in Bonn) at Röhndorf. There was no information available; every minute we hoped the train would leave, but actually we stood on the train platform without any kind of protection during a very bad air raid, the worst since May 30, 1942. The attack was most severe just around the station and the Rhine bridge. The Stackelbergs, who had come from the lecture, were on the same train and all but embraced us when we arrived.

We spent a restful day of recuperation at the Stackelbergs'. His brother, Herbert Stackelberg, who is chief of administration in Norway, came late. He told about Terboven, an energetic, brutal, and dangerous fellow who kept an eye on his goal. Almost anything could be expected of him if the regime fell. Falkenhorst was the usual general without political will or courage. A few of his subordinates were better. His deputy in Oslo, whom they called "the Austrian," had been sent away as useless.

The mood of Cologne is a mixture of great courage, dull indifference, and a deep bitterness. Separatism seems still to be weak.

A particularly repulsive new spectacle is the sight of sixteen-year-old children on anti-aircraft duty. Now the first boys have fallen! This business of taking away the best among a whole class of potential soldiers is a waste of capital and at the same time a new blow at the upper class, for these children are the higher-grade pupils.

I got to the night train after all kinds of tiresome detours through a city sown with time bombs. Happily there was no alarm when we left, but later we had plenty throughout the whole industrial area. The stations made a ghostly impression.

Just as we had scheduled the lecture in Cologne to coincide with the tremendous air raid there, we arrived back in Berlin just in time for the first really severe attack on March 1. First to the theater with the Waldersees to see a charming performance of *The Parasites,* the closing words of which were superbly spoken by Walter Frank: "Justice exists only on the stage." Frantic applause. Afterward we had a very pleasant, leisurely meal at Borchardt's.

But then hell broke loose! Very soon the neighboring building began to burn, soldiers were called out of the shelter for rescue work, sparks rained down on the courtyard, and ashes began to drift in everywhere. A few telephone operators in the shelter began to behave badly and in spite of everything sang indecent songs, et cetera. Finally, when the firing died down somewhat, Waldersee and I seized our wives and walked through the center of the city, where fires were blazing in many places—Hedwig's Church, the arcade, about thirty roof fires in the Friedrichstrasse, et cetera.

An effort to reach the subway failed, so we went on foot through the Tiergarten, where we walked, at my suggestion, on the wooded side, since it was easier going. We did not know that there were time bombs on the other side, one of which exploded the next day. Another lay for days at the entrance to the

Bendlerstrasse. There were gruesome scenes also at the western end of town. All windows at the Waldersees' were broken. In our house an incendiary bomb had landed in the next apartment. Many people are entirely or partly burned out. Almost all buildings and collections in the Botanical Garden are destroyed. For us personally the most staggering thing was that poor Raimute Hassell lost everything, all souvenirs, books, and papers. She and little Fritz just missed losing their lives. With her procurement certificate she gets very meager replacements and some things she can't get at all.

I am withdrawing from the executive board of the MWT. There was no real work there for me anyway, not being allowed to travel. In the Institute for Economic Research I am not very happy either. However, that is a secondary matter, since I need a job as a cover. Sometimes I get fed up with Berlin (that is these futile attempts to overthrow the system) and long to settle for good at Ebenhausen and do only literary work. But that would certainly be wrong and cowardly.

An interesting and grotesque situation has come to light in the Foreign Office—the dismissal and arrest of the so-called Undersecretary of State Luther of the Personnel Division, a most powerful man and very intimate with Ribbentrop. This uncouth, presumptuous, false, and probably corrupt fellow had criticized Ribbentrop, orally and in writing. What is most probable is that the SS really isn't interested in him but set a trap for him in the hope of getting something on Ribbentrop. Now the whole unbelievable Luther outfit is being put under a magnifying glass. We really have beautiful conditions in the Third Reich, which presumes to be so superior to all other systems!

Foreign affairs at the moment are particularly critical in Finland, inasmuch as the attitude of the authorities there is more and more vacillating. The new Foreign Minister, Ramsay, with whom as well as with Ryti I had dinner at Erklö's one evening in September 1939, is a "Sir" and of English descent. Only the intransigence of the bolshevists, or rather the differences among the Allies, still binds the Finns to the Axis.

In Spain things do not look very good for us either; nor in Portugal. The Germans fear a landing, and Hitler is planning in such an event to occupy the northern ports for the protection of our submarines. Tovar, the Portuguese Minister, told me recently that he considered a landing of the English in Spain or Portugal out of the question, and justified it with the the pretty argument: "They simply don't need to. They have certainly enough landing places where they would be enthusiastically received!"

Morell, our Air Attaché in Ankara, who seems an intelligent man, expressed himself about Turkey somewhat as follows at a tea at Air General von Bülow's: (1) The Turks would like to stay neutral. (2) They have an enormous fear of Russia, who is out for their hide. (3) They will fight if we invade. (4) They would not fight if England undertook to do something in Turkey. The latter eventuality seems to be quite likely if the English are figuring on a consolidation of our eastern front and on a spring offensive. Rumania is of decisive importance in the war because of her oil. The English know this, too. Perhaps they will first take the Dodecanese as an air base.

The developments in Italy are, perhaps, at the moment the most interesting. Mussolini was so sick that Queen Elena called Sauerbruch on the pretext of visiting a sick or wounded general. Afterward Sauerbruch was not even allowed to see him, because he was better, and there was fear of the effect of such a visit on world opinion. Sauerbruch told us about Italy. Three weeks ago today Mussolini, quite restored, received the correspondent Heymann for a forty-minute interview before the latter's trip to Germany. He told him that Italy would go through thick and thin with Germany.

At the same time he admitted that he had dismissed the Ministers [February 6, 1943] because of their "clique building." When asked whether he saw any danger for Italy he answered: "No, not so long as we are in Tunis." But in the long run the Italians were pessimistic about this. The world news service of the Stefani Agency (French edition) carried an official pronouncement on the change of Ministers in Italy, in which it was said that Mussolini was again taking foreign affairs into his own hands, for politics must now again assume equal importance with the conduct of the war. The peoples of Europe, who had all alike shed their blood without counting the cost, had to be given the hope that they had not fought in vain, or something like this. All peoples, in other words! And: the war could not be brought to an end with weapons alone. Even clearer is the Stefani commentary on the official, very adroitly phrased communiqué about Ribbentrop's visit to Mussolini.

Strange to say this commentary was published in the German press (unlike the pronouncement, which was suppressed), but only in the *Völkischer Beobachter*, of all papers. The text said that Mussolini was again firmly following the line he had always pursued, which had led him from the Four-Power Pact (with England and France!), by way of Munich (the relinquishment of Czechoslovakia), to the peace efforts of August 1939 (compromise over Poland!). At the end was this sentence: In this task he had the complete co-operation of the great and far-seeing German Führer. In other words, the goal is peace and the Axis nations must go after it. If Hitler will not go along it will be done without him.

But will anyone still make peace with Mussolini? Perhaps. With Hitler, however, certainly not, unless it be Stalin, and the latter only if Germany completely renounces all claims to Russian territory and influence. This Hitler can hardly accept. For the time being he is openly working the anti-bolshevist line for all it is worth, implying that the west must, in all reason, come to an agreement with him. In his mouth the plea is a waste of breath, the more so since he himself is taking giant strides in the direction of bolshevism. Or does he want to bluff Stalin? Mussolini has the advantage over Hitler of being able to resign if the worst comes to the worst and if it is to the interest of his country.

*Ebenhausen, March 28, 1943:* I transfer to the Institute for Economic Research. On the whole it is not very gratifying. One bright spot is that I can ride for the time being at the old Behrmann summer stables at Hundekehle (Grunewald), which the Brandenburg detachment[1] has reserved through the good offices of Captain Hohl.

---

[1] The Brandenburg Division had been formed as a unit that could be counted on for the *coup d'état*.

Is evil winning out everywhere? Kurt Hammerstein [the general] is mortally ill. I went to see him—a miserable picture. In spite of his weakness—I was only with him ten minutes—he passionately implored: "Above all, don't make a 'Kapp Putsch.'[1] Tell that to Goerdeler, too."

This admonition is justified, for without a real organization the temptation to make desperate isolated attempts gets stronger. For instance, there was recently a violent conflict between Jessen and Oster. Oster had accused Jessen of mistaking wishful thinking for reality. Goerdeler is desperate about the futility of all our efforts. He claims that Goebbels, Frick (with Stuckart as mentor), and Bormann had jointly come to the conclusion that Hitler is insane and must be put on the shelf.

Luther, Undersecretary of State in the Foreign Office, has finally landed in a concentration camp. It is grotesque that he thus wins belated sympathy because he apparently recognized and openly stated that Ribbentrop is mentally unbalanced. When he saw at headquarters how things stood with him he telephoned his principal colleague, Büthner (who managed to save himself): "It is all over for us; order two wreaths at Grieneisen's [Berlin undertaking establishment]!"

The generals are enough to drive one mad. My old colleague Etzdorf, who is with them as representative of the Foreign Office at headquarters, despairingly told me that now, after conditions had improved somewhat, everything was swimming in butter again. "The Führer was right again." Hopeless!

It is tragicomic that Zeitzler, of all people, should show the most courage, that is, of course, in purely military matters, otherwise he is obedient. Etzdorf further said that at the beginning of the Russian campaign the rattle-brained Führer had deliberately rejected Stalin's offer to abide by the Hague Convention. He had likewise forbidden a response to the Russian gesture of allowing post cards sent to prisoners. A conscienceless *condottiere,* and colorless at that.

I had met Etzdorf at a lunch to which the good-natured but completely naïve Hansi Plessen [counselor of embassy in Rome] had invited me on March 20, 1943. His older brother was also

[1]A revolt of disgruntled right-wing elements against the nascent Weimar Republic in 1920.

there and told very interesting stories about Giraud, whom he had escorted to Kleist after he was taken prisoner. This was a meeting between two really soldierly gentlemen.

The latest watchword at headquarters, which Etzdorf reported and which seems to have originated with Manstein, is: "We will simply defend Fortress Europe." Trott said he had had lunch with Axmann (leader of the Hitler Youth), who had just returned from a visit with Hitler, and was completely saturated with Hitler's optimism. ("This time I will liquidate the Russians.")

I had a similar impression a week ago at the mess of the War Academy. General Schmund delivered a lecture that was completely "in line" and said to me across the table: "I was at the front and was again overjoyed to find there a steadfast faith, a feeling of superiority, and a deep contempt for our allies!" For a general this last remark was extremely silly and got my dander up, whereupon he noticed that he had gone too far.

The well-known horseman, Colonel Bürkner (commandant of the riding and driving school), was charming with his radiant blue eyes. He is said to be most indiscreet in the mess of the riding school he commands. Someone remonstrated with him at table once, whereupon he is said to have boldly declared: "I can depend on my orderlies"—a remark which these men received with stormy enthusiasm.

A story the good Heinz Albers-Schönberg told me recently at Frohnau belongs in this same category. It seems that one never says "Heil Hitler!" in the flak batteries, but as a joke someone did so recently to a non-commissioned officer. He replied: "Don't ever let me hear that stinking greeting!"

I have seen a great deal recently of the officer corps. Once I gave a lecture to the officers of the anti-aircraft division, and afterward had lunch with the staff. A fairly poor impression. On a pretty low level. The division commander told me that while on duty during air raids in his command tower at the zoo he was continually disturbed in his work by annoying telephone calls from Gauleiter Goebbels, from Göring, and even from Hitler. When there were only a few planes reported shot down Göring would immediately begin to talk of "the blackest day in my life."

On *March 11, 1943,* the Wednesday Society [meeting] at
the house of Professor Stroux in Lichterfelde, was most impressive, for both the neighboring houses to the right and left
were completely burned out. The good man then spoke about
the concept of harmony in antiquity—a theme on which one
at first had difficulty concentrating, particularly since he read
his essay almost without looking up. The subsequent discussion,
however, was most interesting and instructive for me as an
amateur.

On *March 25, 1943,* I had dinner at Plettenberg's in the
Netherlands Palace with Ulrich Schwerin and Fritzi Schulenberg. Schulenberg told me that "they" had informed him my
telephone was to be tapped from the next day on. I was surprised only that this step should really be taken now. He said
I should be very cautious. The purpose of the Gestapo was to
identify the friends of suspected persons. But I should not by
any means suddenly give up telephoning my friends altogether!
The reason advanced for this measure (that is not the real one
in the eyes of his informer) was that I had visited Boris in
Bulgaria, and further that I had contacted the French Minister
in Budapest, who was known as a De Gaullist.

Previous to the evening at Plettenberg's, a theological afternoon at ——. Very remarkable people were there: Guardini,
whom I liked better than his writings; August Winnig (former
Social Democrat), outspokenly Christian; Gertrud Bäumer;
and clergymen of the three faiths. Theme: "Evangelism," that
is, "how can the gospel be brought to people today?"

I tried to show how educated youth might be reached.
Gertrud Bäumer thought that entirely new approaches should
be made, without the clergy, in order to avoid the opposition
of youth, et cetera. To my astonishment, Schacht's daughter,
Frau von Scherpenberg, was also there. She is a former Social
Democrat and had me introduce her to Winnig as an "old
party comrade." She said her father was not much molested
any more and lived in retirement in the country.

Three weeks ago I delivered my Mediterranean lecture in
Munich to the German-Italian Society.

Munich is still much agitated by the discovery of a conspiracy among the students (the Scholl brother and sister

[February 16–18, 1943]). The Party is trying to make them out as communists. I have read the simple, splendid, deeply ethical national appeal which brought them to their death. Himmler apparently did not want any martyrs and ordered a stay of execution, but it came several hours too late. It is important for the future that such an appeal should have seen the light of day. It seems that Professor Huber, also arrested in the meanwhile, was the author. The brave Scholls died on the gallows, courageous and upright martyrs [February 22, 1943]. Report by an eyewitness.

*March 29, 1943:* Mussolini was to have paid a visit to Hitler last week, but canceled it. Remembering numerous discussions with him, I was interested to hear that he had urged Hitler to arrange a peace in the east even after war had broken out. Hitler had refused because he had to hang on to the Ukraine: "otherwise there would be no water for his pipes." Hitler still seems to cling to the illusion that he can get a peace with England.

Yesterday an outright offer was made to England to join with Germany in guaranteeing the freedom and security of the "west" in the form of an article (by Kircher) in the *Frankfurter Zeitung*.

Meanwhile, Mr. Wallace, Vice-President of the United States, made his address on the three ideologies. The "Christian-democratic" view had to prevail over the "Prussian-militaristic" view (in spite of its unquestionable qualities which were used to advance a wrong purpose). The third ideology, the "Marxist," would have to be rejected. Except for the usual identification of Hitlerism and Prussianism (which I reject), the speech shows the deep-seated differences between the eastern and western allies, and indicates what opportunities there would be for a different German regime. In this connection Gerstenmeier had a highly interesting conversation in Sweden with clergymen and —— about the secret Germany, part of it in the presence of the British Chargé d'Affaires. The same question always comes from abroad: "Is there a secret Germany? Why does it put up with all that goes on?"

On the occasion of Wallace's speech, the *Neue Züricher*

*Zeiting* for the first time takes sides unmistakably with Germany's enemies. A speech by the Turkish Prime Minister is clearly pro-Anglo-Saxon.

A grotesque byplay: Old Prince Chigi, Italian and fascist, visits the American Archbishop Spellman in Vatican City in order to confer on him the Cross of the Order of Malta (certainly not without Mussolini's permission!). The *Osservatore Romano* treats bolshevism as a thing that must be completely rejected, but emphasizes that it is an indigenous European growth which by chance has matured in one country (Russia). Consequently there was no reason for the Pope to take sides against this nation.

In Russia we are now attempting an about-face, that is, to pose as pro-Russian (but anti-bolshevist). It is too late. Someone eagerly told me that they want to make a "Wang Ching-Wei" [puppet] out of General Vlassov. They just stagger unsteadily 'round and 'round.

*Ebenhausen, April 20, 1943:* Today all Germany is ordered to put out flags [for Hitler's birthday]—"Love of the free man." Never before has this been done with so little enthusiasm.

The longer the war lasts the less I think of the generals. They have undoubted technical ability and physical courage, but little moral courage, absolutely no broad world vision, no inner spiritual independence or that strength of resistance which rests on a genuine cultural basis. For this reason Hitler was able to make them subservient and bind them hand and foot. The majority, moreover, are out to make careers in the lowest sense. Gifts and the field marshal's batons are more important to them than the great historical issues and moral values at stake. All those on whom we set our hopes are failing, the more miserably so since they agree with all they have been told and permit themselves to indulge in the most anti-Nazi talk, but are unable to summon up enough courage to act.

At the moment, for a change, some hopes are put on Guderian. The prospects, however, are infinitesimal, although action is more imperative than ever if we are not to experience a complete catastrophe at home and abroad.

In view of the imminent end in Tunis the Italian question comes to the fore for the time being. A complete understanding was not reached between Hitler and Mussolini, who finally showed up [April 7–10, 1943]. I do not know whether it is true that Mussolini declared the situation in the Mediterranean could not be saved unless Gibraltar was taken. Neither do I know whether the rumor is correct that Hitler raved and ranted and wanted to arrest him! In any case things look menacing.

Notwithstanding, General Balck (recipient of the Oak-Leaf Cluster on the Knight's Cross) was able to get up recently at the Rheinbaben table and preach (obviously in clichés). He had just come from the eastern front where he had a talk of an hour and a half with the Führer. He was unshakably convinced of the greatness and brilliant generalship of the "Führer," who alone had saved the military situation, the Army, and Germany this winter (he shouted these words!). He, Balck, believed that we were now nearer to victory than one or two years ago. The Russians were as good as defeated in the field, our troops overwhelmingly superior. The Stalingrad venture should have led to a complete success had reasonable foresight been used. One could not judge such things afterward, but only in the light of the situation prevailing at the beginning. (Mad nonsense! If this were true there would never be such a thing as an inexcusable failure, for a military leader seldom acts from sheer insanity.)

Our misfortune had been that the Russians had attacked north and south of Stalingrad and at both points had encountered Rumanian armies which, of course, like all armies of our allies, they rolled over. Still, this situation could have been brought into balance, he said. The relief army, immediately drawn up under Manstein, would have been successful, indeed it was only thirty kilometers from Stalingrad. But these Russians—apparently not participating sufficiently in our "Kaiser maneuvers"—had rather incredibly attacked and beaten the Italians north of Stalingrad. Afterward the Hungarians had not only taken to their heels, but for the most part had gone over to the enemy. They had by far the worst army, their glib tongues and good looks notwithstanding. (So goes the story. But where in all this was the foresight and wisdom of our "brilliant Führer?") The relief army, therefore, had to be diverted in order to fill in the gigantic gap in the lines. All those present sat through this with their mouths open.

Amazing things are reported by Hans Holtzendorff from his personal observations. Hitler had arrived in Dnepropetrovsk by plane, had been lifted out of it, and had staggered forward, supported by two men. Same thing going back. During the discussion with the assembled higher officers, who were demanding that the forward position be abandoned, he had become so enraged by the doubts of one of the participants that he tore the epaulets off his shoulders.

An ever-increasing nervousness has marked these weeks. Yet it is often difficult to distinguish between reality and fear, and of course also between fact and rumor.

Fritzi Schulenburg, a deputy governor, old SS leader, and active soldier, was arrested at three o'clock one morning because on the occasion of the arrest of a fellow officer who had made rebellious speeches someone said that Schulenburg had been looking about in Potsdam for "reliable" officers. Schulenburg was released after a few hours, having defended himself very skillfully, but the matter still smolders. It is amusing that Keitel should have dressed down the weak-kneed Fromm, of all people, for having received such a fellow as Schulenburg.

I myself have been warned four times that my telephone is tapped, that I am probably watched in other ways, too. Hohl had heard that a purge like that of June 30 threatened the opposition.[1] The whole group around Oster, for some time the butt of attacks by the SD, is very excited.

On the pretext of violations of the foreign-exchange control laws, Dohnanyi, his wife and brother-in-law have been arrested. The Advocate General's office has found only a minor violation, however. The investigation is being conducted by Roeder, an officer in the Advocate General's office of the Air Force, who seems to be ambitious, and who has already been

[1]Hohl had previously visited me (Berlin, 28 Fasanenstrasse) to implore me to persuade my husband, who was in the greatest danger, to leave, if possible to go into a sanatorium. I refused, because my husband realized his danger but would not, in the interest of his own safety, give up his efforts to overthrow the regime and to save Germany from plunging into disaster. He always said to me: "I cannot sit here with wide-open eyes, remain inactive, and look on while the wagon rolls down into the abyss." Note by Ilse von Hassell.

active in the case against Sch.-B. It is to be feared that the whole project will break down. Dohnanyi, on top of everything else, seems to have made a blunder at the time of his arrest. He surreptitiously indicated to Oster that a compromising document was in the strong box. It promptly fell on the floor and was picked up by an official of the Advocate General's office! A first-class mess.

I recently called on Beck (*April 1*), who is ill, after having undergone a major operation by Sauerbruch. He was still quite weak. His handsome head reminded me of Frederick the Great.

Sauerbruch, whom I saw twice on behalf of Beck, claimed that he knew I was on the list of the most dangerous people and hence in serious jeopardy. Rantzau (Foreign Office) told me that it was known in the Foreign Office, too, that I was being watched. I shall therefore do nothing right now about a travel permit, especially since, even though the SD might give me permission, Ribbentrop would probably sabotage it.

Ribbentrop recently even refused to let an article of mine appear. Schmidt, chief of the press section, informed me of this with the remark that officials of the Foreign Office, including those who are on the inactive list, must have the consent of the Minister for Foreign Affairs if they want to publish their writings. This after five years of writing without permission, and just after I had changed my status from the "inactive" to the "retired" list.

*Ebenhausen, April 20, 1943:* Sad to say the excitement is also affecting my private contacts. Many people are afraid.

I have seen little of Goerdeler and Popitz recently. For some time now the usually enterprising Jessen has been very depressed. He wanted to see nobody. His wife, however, managed to get him to creep out of his shell and have Ilse and me come over for a very cordial, if not exactly encouraging, evening. There is little to be done at the moment. Capital people.

Ribbentrop has now become completely rabid. He hates the entire old Foreign Office (in which I, too, found much to criticize, but for other reasons than Ribbentrop). Diels, whom I saw recently on a trip to Magdeburg (for the founding of a branch of the Institute for Economic Research), told me about the mad things he had experienced with our so-called diplomats in Bucharest and Sofia. He also told me that Ribbentrop had said to Hitler that the only thing that mattered in the Foreign Office was a National Socialist mentality, and that he wanted forty SS men, forty SA men, and forty Hitler Youth leaders, so that he could replace the older members of the Ministry.

All the latest changes in the Foreign Office [April 17, 1943], therefore, can be looked upon as a blow against the old officialdom. Dieckhoff, to be sure, goes to Spain. Like the late Moltke, he is one of the few in the good graces of Ribbentrop. He is also temperamentally submissive. Woermann and Gaus are even less satisfactory in this respect. The former goes to Nanking, the latter seems to have been eliminated. Weizsäcker should really have gone long ago, because occasionally he had attempted to show some resistance, at least in small ways. His successor is insignificant, entirely inexperienced, and an out-and-out creature of Ribbentrop. He owes his career, aside from the qualities mentioned, to his very beautiful, ambitious, intelligent, and astonishingly civilized wife. Incidentally, the Party doesn't especially like Steengracht, who has been a member only since 1931.

Weizsäcker has a post at the Vatican which could be very important, but which it certainly is not under this regime. He merely lends himself to the Nazis as the usual false front.

*May 15, 1943:* Hentig is very caustic about Weizsäcker (much too little resistance). It is remarkable how often a deeper probing of Swabians reveals a lack of firmness of character and a peasant shrewdness concealed by their good nature. Compare Kiderlen, Neurath, and Weizsäcker.

The united front of clear-sighted men is crumbling; it is partly their own fault. The whole Canaris outfit has shown weakness and in general has not quite lived up to expectations. If the "good" people are not so wise as serpents and guileless as doves nothing will be accomplished.

This is all the worse because things are storming ahead so rapidly that some "action" becomes ever more imperative. On the one hand the political situation would not be entirely hopeless for us if the system were completely overthrown; on the other hand defeat from without and catastrophe from within draw nearer and nearer.

As far as defeat from without is concerned, Tunisia followed upon Stalingrad [May 8, 1943]. The frantic propaganda that seeks to disguise the severe defeat in Tunisia as a success can certainly no longer fool anybody. Mussolini is taking measures toward military concentration. Counselor Weber (International Institute of Agriculture) told me that after a temporary preference for very young people such as Vidussoni, he was again taking on older and tried men. Scorza, the new Undersecretary, had coined the interesting slogan: "The Duce, the thousand-year dynasty, and the Catholic Church." This illustrates the radical difference from us.

Mussolini and Hitler have not reached a full understanding [April 7–10, 1943]. Mussolini had demanded a decisive shift to the defensive in Russia and the building up of strong reserves for the west and south. The visits of Horthy [April 16–17, 1943] and Antonescu [April 12–14, 1943] were also unsatisfactory. Horthy was asked to replace Kallay, and Marshal Antonescu to replace Mihai Antonescu with people more loyal to the Axis, so far without success. Quite the opposite. Kallay defended himself energetically against Imrédy's attacks by adjourning parliament. Mihai, the lovely boy, was "sick" for a few days, but has now recovered. The tactless and brutal treatment accorded to Horthy is typical of our rulers. When summoned alone to Hitler, Horthy was confronted by a council of three.

The attitude of Finland appears to be most dangerous at the moment. Turkey also presents an extremely bad picture, although Papen still manifests optimism. In Holland there is bitter tension and silent fighting. Shocking reports come from the good Frauendorfer in Poland. While Frank publicly declares he wanted to give Poland a dignified and free existence, and while the gang tries in vain to befuddle world opinion about the Katyn murders, the SS in Poland carries on most shamefully. Countless Jews have been gassed in specially built chambers, at least 100,000. But the Polish intelligentsia, too, is being decimated, just as before. Frauendorfer and Berthold, no longer able to work in the Government General, have enlisted as ordinary soldiers. Frank found this very understandable, and only admonished them to go to the Army and not to the SS. But the SS took Frauendorfer to task, officially and in writing, because, though an SS man, he had reported to the Army. He was threatened with stern measures.

Meanwhile the unhappy remnants of the Jews prepared to defend themselves, and there is heavy fighting which will certainly lead to their complete extermination by the SS. It is Hitler's achievement that the German has become the most loathed animal in the whole world.

We are saddened by Hammerstein's death. He was a very wise man politically, and clear-sighted in military matters. Decent through and through. The one thing that hampered him, as he himself used to say laughingly, was a need for personal comfort. He could, however, have rendered great service when the critical moment came. Beck has improved since his serious operation, but is still not very well.

*Ebenhausen, June 9, 1943:* This state is deteriorating more and more into an immoral and bankrupt enterprise under the leadership of an irresponsible gambler who can scarcely be called mentally normal and who is surrounded by riffraff. And thus we roll on toward disaster.

None of the "field marshals" is acting as if he knew any higher concept of duty. Yet even the obvious interests of the professional soldier in his career, and purely strategic considerations, ought to prompt them to act. New evidence of this is the way the African campaign has led to catastrophe. Incidentally, this far-from-glorious end was a complete surprise to the Führer's headquarters. At the very end Hitler tried shamelessly but vainly to pull his darling Rommel out of the mess, for which Rommel was largely responsible, and then let efficient, straight-shooting Arnim shoulder the burden of blame.

Zeitzler's right-hand man, Warlimont (Deputy Chief of Staff of the High Command of the Wehrmacht) returned from Tunisia to the Führer's headquarters just before the surrender. I have been told on responsible authority that he wanted to be taken to the Führer to report that it was possible to hold out until fall. Answer: "Yes, the Führer would be much interested in this, but the announcement has just been made that Tunis and Bizerte have fallen!"

Recently I caught myself unconsciously avoiding a subway car in which I saw a general.

Many deliberations—that is not really "many," since caution dictates that there be few meetings. The impossibility of action has a crippling effect. Nevertheless, at every opportunity I have conversations with Beck, now slowly recovering, with Popitz, and with Guttenberg, who came over from Agram. Things are taking a dreadful turn.

The Dohnanyi affair smolders on and acts as a strong brake on our plans. It is said that Dohnanyi's chief, Canaris, has taken the offensive, since it has become obvious that the foreign-exchange matter is not really serious and, in any event, just a pretext. A few days ago I had an enlightening evening with the lawyer Wirmer, with Dohnanyi's brother-in-law, Klaus Bonhoeffer, and with the trade-union leader, Leuschner. They are thinking along clearly national and religious lines. They say that important elements of the former Social Democratic Party share these views. At the same time there is deep defeatism, no hope for a favorable outcome of the war, and hope of doing away with the regime only after a military catastrophe. One hears more and more often "Let us hope the English will be in Berlin before the Russians."

After Tunisia, general concern is focused on the possible defection of Italy. It is a question, however, whether such desertion will be sufficiently rewarded, and whether the fear of becoming a battleground will not have a deterring effect.

On my departure from Berlin I was told that the Allies were exercising rather abrupt pressure on the Italians, offering them the prewar *status quo*, with Tripoli, but without Abyssinia and without their Balkan possessions.

Detalmo told me about clandestine newspapers in Italy, for instance *La Ricostruzione* and *Europa Federalista,* and another which Detalmo himself helps to distribute, *L'Italia Libera.* These papers are passed from hand to hand. An Italian anti-fascist professor told me that Croce and Sforza were mentioned as the coming men.

In their pessimism people are clinging to the idea of a "new weapon," which, according to whispering propaganda, is to be used soon. It is supposed to be a rocket gun which can reduce whole sections of a city to ashes from a great distance and at one blow—a terrible vision! The submarine war is not going well. English air raids, on the other hand, are having devastating effects, especially those on the large dams at Dortmund, Wuppertal (Barmen [May 18, 1943]), et cetera. I traveled to Partenkirchen with some people from Dortmund, Essen, and Gelsenkirchen and was shocked at their reports. The Dortmunders were still in complete confusion, bitter and hopeless. If on top of the heavy damage to war industries these raids increase in violence and scope, disaster is near at hand.

It is open to question whether the English and Americans really want to run the risks of a landing. But they will probably do it on account of Russia (in a double sense), and in order to have their hands free against the Japanese. There are psychological reasons, too! The only question is where.

*May 24–25, 1943:* Recently I paid a visit to nice Frau von Bethmann at Hohenfinow with Stensen-Leth, the Danish Counselor of Legation, and old Kühlmann. In spite of everything there is a wide chasm separating me from people like Kühlmann. He is a capitalistic parlor democrat, completely materialistic and with no real convictions. I had a long talk with Stensen-Leth. He talked very openly about our incomprehensible political mistakes and the hopelessness of the war. He thought that Best (new Minister to Copenhagen, a Nazi) showed a certain understanding of the situation in Denmark. He was resolutely liquidating the wholly impossible Danish Nazis and was avoiding the errors Renthe-Fink had made from trembling fear of the Party.

Li told me that the opposition groups in Italy, even those with conservative and clerical leanings, were against the dynasty because it had identified itself too strongly with fascism. Indeed, this was also the feeling of the many revolutionary officers, who were headed by Cadorna's son. If this is true the result will be chaos.

The question arises next whether our people have grasped

the seriousness of the situation and the criminal levity of our political course. Langbehn maintains that even some of the highest leaders of the SS understand this and the necessity of getting rid of Hitler.

Desperate over the threatened catastrophe and the inactivity of the military, certain "well-meaning" people are discussing more frequently the possibility of using the SS to overthrow the regime if all other means should fail. They argue that this might not only put this organization into our hands but would also prevent domestic disorders. They say that afterward the SS will, of course, be dissolved, too. The question first, is only whether Himmler and company would dare play such a game and co-operate in the friendly manner desired; second, what effect this procedure would have abroad, for every foreigner justly regards the SS as the very incarnation of the devil.

*Ebenhausen, July 4, 1943:* A few days ago (the end of June) I returned from a very successful trip to Brussels. Surprisingly enough, through the influence of the Army, I received not only a visa for the lecture at Falkenhausen's headquarters, but an extension of my diplomatic passport, to which I am no longer entitled.

[From a letter to Frau von Hassell] ". . . At eleven-two o'clock I drove with Falkenhausen and his principal aide, Dumoulin (Foreign Office, Hammerstein's brother-in-law, now a lieutenant colonel) to the château of Seneffe, thirty-five kilometers from Brussels, after having picked up the celebrated Elisabeth Ruspoli on the way. You will remember that we met her at the Leyens' at Unterdiessen in 1938. Her husband was one of the two Ruspoli brothers who, despite their rather advanced age, died very courageously as parachutists. A square in Rome is now named after them. We drove by way of Waterloo and the strange monument there.

"Seneffe is a real fairy-tale château with flower borders, a veritable sea of roses, and a huge park with magnificent trees. We stayed in one of the pavilions; in the château proper only a few rooms are used for receptions. The military commander at Paris, Heinrich Stülpnagel, appeared for tea with his aide, an old friend of my childhood, Hans Hartog, really a forester but now a lieutenant colonel.

"In the morning I had a long walk with Falkenhausen. Stülpnagel joined us for part of it. I cannot write my thoughts, but you undoubtedly can imagine every single one of them. . . ."

It was very useful for me to meet with Falkenhausen and Heinrich Stülpnagel. Thanks to the skill of the former things in Brussels are going moderately well on the whole, although the recruiting of slaves on the one hand and the course of the war on the other have made the situation worse. Unpleasant friction has grown between Falkenhausen and his subordinates. Karl Otto Kameke had urged my being invited to give the lecture, which I myself had initiated for other reasons, chiefly because he hoped that I might be able to influence Falkenhausen.

Kameke's chief, Reeder, told me at length and in some excitement what the trouble was. The principal complaint was that Falkenhausen was too soft with the Belgians—and unpredictably so at that—allegedly under the influence of his friend Elisabeth Ruspoli. It is charged, further, that she was responsible for the lack of real confidence between Falkenhausen and his officials.

My impression is that both sides are to blame. Perhaps Falkenhausen does not run his office in a businesslike way. On the other hand, the bureaucracy understands neither his personality nor his objectives. This old China hand is in his way something of a bohemian, off duty perhaps rather frivolous, and his working habits are not those of a Prussian civil servant of the old school. For years he has felt our situation was very serious. For that reason he aims at holding onto as many reserve positions as possible, to be ready for a change in regime. In any case, the estrangement between him and his officials is regrettable and harmful. Particularly damaging are the openings he offers to Party spies, who have long been after his scalp.

I discussed all this with his colleague Stülpnagel, who makes an excellent impression, intelligent, clear-sighted, a fine type of Prussian officer. We were in complete agreement on this problem, as on others. Every dependable man and post is vitally important, particularly one like Stülpnagel, the more so because our chances of bringing about a change are so slight. For even if no decisive blow at the regime can be delivered from Paris and Brussels for lack of strength, these positions are nonetheless important, and the highly intelligent, far-sighted Falkenhausen is indispensable.

I therefore undertook during a long walk the disagreeable task of making clear to Falkenhausen how extremely nervous the Party had become. I said the Gestapo was collecting material against all persons like himself, and that we should on no account play into their hands. By way of illustration I told him how various people were watched and that I myself was under observation. I added that my confidential source had informed me that he, Falkenhausen, was being carefully watched and that they had already collected quite a lot of evidence, especially concerning his too-intimate relations with the Belgians. He seemed impressed, and took my remarks with good grace.

I felt the same thing was true of Elisabeth Ruspoli, and dropped a hint to her in the course of the evening's conversation, assuming that she had the greatest personal interest in holding her friend.

Illustrative of the somewhat narrow way in which officials there judge Falkenhausen is their great indignation over a letter written by the King to Hitler behind their backs about the conscription of workers. It afterward appeared that Falkenhausen not only knew all about the letter but had even had it drafted by a German officer.

Incidentally, I came home with the impression that salvation could not come from this quarter.

*July 4, 1943:* Thank God Beck is improving at last! The poor sick man was watched even in the hospital. Oster went to Sauerbruch to let him know about that.

*Ebenhausen, July 18, 1943:* I was welcomed here with the news that the local police (at Hohenschäftlarn) had received orders from the Gestapo to watch me as a potential revolutionary. This is confirmation of Goerdeler's statement during his recent visit that nervousness and, consequently, the observance of "all dangerous people" were increasing.

Guttenberg has been called back from Agram and thoroughly questioned about the Dohnanyi affair. They were chiefly interested in his relations to a certain imaginary individual whom no sensible person knows. The questioning seems to have gone off quite well. The chief of the investigation felt around a great deal. The Dohnanyi affair is a public scandal. Months spent in an endless investigation undertaken without legal warrant against a high military official.

It is characteristic that when Sauerbruch took Beck to Frau Sauerbruch's house in the country near Dresden to recuperate he was immediately questioned about it by the police.

Goerdeler and I are in despair to see everything drifting to ruin without a hand being raised to stop it by those who have the power.

In the east things are going badly.[1] Russian resistance is extremely strong and supported by very superior new matériel. Our communiqués are ambiguous and full of whitewash. Meanwhile the bomb has exploded in Sicily.[2] As a result of air and sea supremacy the operation was successful. The fall of the naval base at Augusta without serious resistance seems very peculiar. According to various reports the Italians can't hold out any longer.

With the increasing damage from air raids we must indeed admit that our position begins to look extremely dangerous. The increasing partisan warfare on the Balkan peninsula is also an element of danger. Countess Lerchenfeld, from Sofia, with whom I had dinner told me of serious happenings in Bulgaria which make it appear that the situation there is very uncertain.

All reports agree that in their desperation those in "high places" are flirting more and more with the idea of a separate peace with Russia. For Hitler it is the only way out. Mussolini and Japan have been urging this for a long time. Ribbentrop is grasping for this rope, and Hitler, who was at first deter-

[1]The German offensive at Bielgorod of July 6, 1943, came to a standstill on July 15 because of a counterattack by the Russians.

[2]July 10, 1943, Anglo-American landing in Sicily.

mined to hang on to the Ukraine, et cetera (thus making a Russian solution impossible from the start), is now supposed to have softened and ready to be contented with the borders of 1914. But such a show of weakness will rather stiffen Stalin against any agreement, the more so since he, like everyone else, cannot trust Hitler to abide by a treaty.

Yesterday (*July 17*) I had breakfast with Schacht at the hotel. Unfortunately he telephoned to announce his arrival! He has practically no hope left. He gave an interesting account of his final resignation, on which occasion Göring distinguished himself by writing a letter in an extremely devious and bad style. In Berlin I saw Popitz and Gerstenmeier a few times. I also saw Trott and Langbehn.

A highly courageous action was undertaken by Wurm, as the "eldest bishop" of the Evangelical Church. This may prove of real significance. He is making a protest to Hitler and to all Ministers against the methods of the regime, the lack of justice, persecution of the churches, and atrocities in the occupied areas.

It will, of course, have no effect, and may even bring personal harm to Wurm, but it might be of great historical importance that at least the Evangelical Church openly and clearly disapproved of the whole filthy business—a move for which our friends, the field marshals, unfortunately seem to lack courage.

Something of my personal life: a fine performance, on *July 19, 1943,* of Calderon's *Leben ein Traum*—a very good translation by Komarel—at the Schauspielhaus. I went with Wolf-Ulli and the two Brauchitschs. Wolf-Ulli is very close to me in every respect.

*July 20, 1943:* The other day when I was asked by Faupel to give a lecture before the German-Spanish Society the Foreign Office suddenly insisted on censoring my lectures in advance. Why now, after a dozen public lectures?

Hitler, contrary to the views of Goebbels and others, ordered that the *Frankfurter Zeitung* cease publication as of September 20, 1943, after it had annoyed him for ten years. Thoroughly logical. The paper was only a fig leaf, a false label. Objectively, of course, this action is most regrettable.

Feverish preparations are being made in Berlin by all government offices for emergency quarters in the event of destruction by air raids. Complete destruction of the most essential sections of Berlin, including the transportation facilities, cannot be met by emergency offices and the like.

A typical story: Churchill, in the course of a grand tour, comes to St. Helena. "Well, everything seems to be ready. He can paint it himself!"

*Ebenhausen, July 20, 1943:* I talked with Dieter about Hitler's foreign policy before and after the outbreak of war. I developed the following theme: The real basis of the whole catastrophic sequence is ignorance of the world, coupled with an entire lack of restraint. The political instrument was the military alliance with Italy and Japan and the consequent division of the world into two camps—moreover, in a manner which created a balance of power unfavorable to Germany.

The decisive turning point toward war was the occupation of Prague. All preceding actions, including the Anschluss and the incorporation of the Sudetenland, the world had accepted. The significance of "Munich" was that the world swallowed these events, but with a firm determination not to tolerate further German seizures without a fight.

There is absolutely no foundation for Hitler's assertion that England, after Munich, had decided to attack Germany as soon as it was strong enough. The English resolution, after they had learned their lesson and had become distrustful of Hitler's assurances, was rather to improve their military position so as to be able to resist further aggressive action. It is also highly probable that had German policies been handled skillfully England would not have prevented a settlement of the Corridor question.

If it is true that Hitler later reproached Ribbentrop for having given him poor advice in proposing that he take Prague first and the Corridor later, then he was justified in the reproof. Henderson himself told me in the spring of 1939 that Prague had been the greatest disaster because it had destroyed all faith in a moderate policy and in Hitler's word. If instead Hitler had taken up the question of the Corridor after a time things would probably have gone well. The seizure of Prague was all the more foolish since further developments were bound to make Czechoslovakia absolutely dependent upon Germany.

I see the errors of English policy first, in the treaties of guarantee which were bound to make Germany nervous without actually protecting the states in the east; second, that England —following a poor precedent—failed to announce with utmost earnestness at Munich that it would take military action in case the agreement was violated. All of this, of course, does not excuse Hitler's policies.

Henderson was also right when he once said that it was impossible for Hitler and Ribbentrop to maintain simultaneously two different assertions: (1) England had wanted to defeat Germany for a long time and was arming to that purpose. (2) England was decadent and weak and would not fight, therefore one could ride roughshod over England's objections. The second assertion is the one that represents Ribbentrop's actual conviction. This complete misinterpretation of the situation moved him always to fan the flames and in the decisive days of 1939 to help recklessly in bringing on the war. The historic responsibility, however, will fall on Hitler.

The Hungarian Ministers who were in Germany a short time before the outbreak of war were especially uneasy because they felt that the very Cabinet officer whose special responsibility it was to weigh the facts of foreign affairs and to warn against a provocative policy worked instead most actively for a policy that inevitably led to war.

Thus these men started the war against Poland with criminal recklessness, risking the intervention of the Western Powers, completely misjudging the power relationships and, above all, without any idea at all of the significance of sea power. They thought they had created the necessary security by making a treaty with Russia, although they themselves took this step with the mental reservation which became apparent in 1941.

There is absolutely no foundation for the assertion that Russia wanted to attack, or would have attacked later. We have here the most pernicious example of the preventive war which Bismarck condemned. If Germany "stumbled" into the two-front war in 1914, Hitler wantonly brought it on in 1941. Russia had only one feeling about an intact Germany—fear. Russia would never have attacked Germany, or at least never have attacked successfully, so long as Germany possessed an unbroken army. It suffices to imagine what would have happened if Germany, after the fall of France, had remained in possession of a fully intact, powerful instrument of war, instead of wearing it out in battle against an underestimated Russia. The fight against Russia which Hitler started was just as reckless an undertaking as the war in general. After it had started there was at least one chance—the only "morally" good chance, from the propaganda point of view—to wage it exclusively against bolshevism and to make our watchword the liberation of the Russian people, with whom Germany had no quarrel.

The opposite happened. Hitler united Russia behind Stalin against Germany. Incidentally, one might also point out the folly of aligning ourselves simultaneously against Poland as well as against Russia—a violation of the A B C of any German policy in the east.

A further ruinous decision was that of declaring war on the United States. Annoying as it was to see this power supporting the other side, it was stupid of Hitler to seize the initiative and turn the United States from a supporter of the other side into our major foe, who would use the full force of her strength against Germany. It may be that Hitler thought he owed this action to Japan. If so, it was the only instance of treaty loyalty in Hitler's career and a truly strange and disastrous one at that.

Finally there was the mistaken policy of extending the area of fighting as far as possible by the invasion of hitherto neutral territories. This procedure became the more unfortunate when the policies applied in the majority of these countries turned them into reservoirs of hatred and revenge.

In general the foreign policy of the Third Reich is characterized by a dangerous mixture of foreign and domestic considerations. The method symbolized by the names of Quisling and Mussert became especially pernicious.

*July 24, 1943, Ebenhausen:* Germany is gradually being strangled. Reports from Sicily are very bad. Those from the east are not good. In addition, fake army communiqués, poorly co-ordinated with those of the Italians.

The meeting of Hitler and Mussolini in Italy (Hitler's device of quoting Mussolini's past utterances was useless) apparently went off without achieving harmony [July 19, 1943].

Almuth came back quite crushed from a meeting with Marchetti, the Italian Consul General, and Consul Grillo. Redoubled pessimism. He was deeply impressed by the air bombardment of Rome [July 19, 1943], which (and this was the reason for the bombing of San Lorenzo) destroyed the main railroad facilities of Rome and severely interrupted traffic. I do not believe that Italy can survive a crippling of Rome, the transport center. Italian geography makes this clear. On his trip to San Lorenzo the Pope was so stormily besieged by the people shouting *Pace!* [peace] that his car was damaged and he had to change to another.

Things are developing exactly as I predicted they would in my reports of 1936–37. Italy's great misfortune is her victory over England in the Ethiopian crisis of 1935–36. The false estimate of England to which it gave rise led Italy to depart from the historic line of her foreign policy: "Never against Great Britain!"

Petrucci, the former Italian Consul General in Munich, seems to have quoted some of my anti-Nazi statements in the Foreign Ministry in Rome, and cited my name. Happily he was rebuked for this indiscretion, so I hear, and I hope the matter will have no further consequences.

*Ebenhausen, August 15, 1942:* For two and a half weeks I haven't written anything, but things are developing so rapidly that an accurate delineation would be a work of art. Four outstanding events mark the period we have just traversed at such a gallop: the fall of Mussolini [July 25, 1943], the air bombardment of Hamburg [July 25, 1943], the conquest of almost all of Sicily, and developments in the east, particularly southwest of Bielgorod.

Here at home there seems to be great confusion "at the top."

This was noticeable in the reaction to the Italian developments, in the confusion following the attack on Hamburg, in the case of Goebbels, and finally in Hitler's leadership in the east, which is becoming more and more disastrous. Anyone who sees these developments with any clarity at all begins to burn with a white fury over our high military leaders. They have gone beyond all expectations in their servility. My last conferences on this subject with Popitz, some of them in the presence of Langbehn, Leuschner, and Trott, made it evident that at least to one of these generals it now appears urgent to avoid complete descent into the abyss. This man, Stülpnagel, had sent Grumme to Popitz because he didn't altogether trust Goerdeler's effusions.

Reports [from Langbehn in Switzerland] state that the Anglo-Americans have absolute confidence in victory, are determined to see it through to the end, and in particular to destroy Berlin. The American source of this information is good, although there is undoubtedly more room for doubt than Langbehn admits. It is still absolutely necessary to strengthen the only argument that might still count at the last minute—namely, that complete chaos in Germany would serve the interest of neither England nor America, especially in relation to Russia.

Air bombardments such as that on Hamburg can only produce chaos. Therefore, the one solution is a new and decent government in Germany. It is of the utmost importance to make the other side see how matters stand, but we can do that only if there is at least a good likelihood that something will be done.

Stalin dissociates himself more and more from the Americans, whose tremendous successes he fears. His Free Germany Committee has no meaning in itself, but is important as a symptom. If Hitler comes to terms with Stalin, the resultant disaster cannot be imagined. It would be different with a decent, self-respecting Germany. This Germany would have to exploit all opportunities. There is only this one expedient left—to make either Russia or the Anglo-Americans understand their interest in a sound Germany.

Actually, a healthy European heart is to the interest of the east as well as the west. In this game [*Mühlespiel:* being on good terms with both sides] I prefer the Western orientation, but if need be I would also consider an agreement with Russia. Trott agrees with me entirely; the others are doubtful for theoretical and moral reasons, which I understand. But they are gradually coming around. Popitz, who is always very anti-Italian, hopes, even though he doesn't say so plainly, that the King and Badoglio will fail so that we can be entirely free in our movements. I think that a mistake. A success for the King and Badoglio would be of greatest importance, but is most improbable in view of developments. They will fall between two stools and will not be able to give the people what they expect from the change, immediate peace. The fact that the enemy does not seem to be treating Badoglio any better than Mussolini will not have an encouraging effect on our generals.

But those generals should say to themselves how completely different the situation would be if, at the same time, or shortly thereafter, there was a parallel development here. They will wait, however—if indeed they ever do anything—until this chance, too, has gone. All these people fail to understand that Hitler's idea is to drag Germany with him into ruin if he does not succeed.

Many people congratulate me because Mussolini's fall proved the correctness of my estimate of the situation. This is a hopeless over-simplification.

Events in Rome did not surprise me in that I had always calculated that Mussolini, unlike Hitler, could one day resign. But I did not foresee that he would be torpedoed by his associates. I had thought that fascism was an empty shell, but I had not imagined that it would disappear so quickly and so ingloriously.

A highly significant episode: The day after the events in Rome we were dining at Marchetti's with Grillo. The latter told us that Farinacci had fled Italy by plane with a safe-conduct from Mackensen, and had arrived in Munich. When the commandant of the airport had appealed to him for help, Marchetti had answered that he knew no Mr. Farinacci! And in alluding to Mackensen's letter he had said: "I take orders only from my sovereign!"

At the decisive moment the King again showed a considerable capacity for action, but unfortunately it changes nothing in this desperate situation. I still wonder what Grandi and company had in mind. Did they think they themselves could take the helm? Or did they really want only to save the country? Mussolini's passive attitude was such that I assume he must be in a bad physical state. Detalmo was mistaken; he had thought the King and Badoglio did not have a chance, and yet it was they who acted.

The effect of all this on our higher ups was apparently most surprising. First reaction: the German representatives in Rome should arrest the ringleaders! Incidentally, no instructions for publicity! Second reaction: it is a "fundamental error" to think that fascism is dead, as Jodl is supposed to have said to Hitler. Hitler would revive it again. Hence the insane scheme to rescue Mussolini by paratroopers and reinstate him. The third reaction, as Planck seriously told it, is that Hitler toys with the idea of making the little King "Emperor of central Europe," with himself as Chancellor.

Guariglia [the new Italian Foreign Minister] has always impressed me as serious and intelligent. But how can anyone conduct foreign affairs in such a situation? A dreadful heritage. Perhaps it would be even worse with us. At the meeting in Tarvis (Guariglia, Ambrosio, Ribbentrop, and Keitel) no unanimity seems to have been achieved. How could there be! No communiqué.

*August 2, 1943:* Guttenberg visited me. Wolf-Ulli was there, too. They had grilled Guttenberg very thoroughly on the Dohnanyi case and complained about him to Canaris, as well as about Gisevius and one other person. For the time being he goes back to Agram.

The danger of air raids is throwing all Berlin into confusion. At the Institute there were two long deliberations about finding ways and means to escape the raids; rather fruitless. Wagemann came back from his trip to Hanover completely shaken. The good man sat at his desk in shirt sleeves (the heat is intense) with a bottle of vermouth at hand. He was near, or really, in tears. He had seen terrifying scenes and said that it simply could not go on this way. In Hamburg from seventy to eighty thousand people were without shelter.

*August 4, 1943:* I have had very useful discussions with Popitz and Trott about the relations between the two generations and the necessity for building a bridge between them as far as basic political questions are concerned. In this exchange of opinions a rather unnecessary difficulty is introduced by the concept of "socialism"—another cuckoo's egg that Nazism laid in the German nest. The term "socially conscious" has come into disrepute. But words are not of final importance.

*August 19, 1943, Ebenhausen:* It is very amusing to see how sudden interest in me personally is shown by all those who think that a turn of events might be at hand—just as dear old Rümelin always used to send cigarettes from Sofia whenever he read in the papers that I might become Undersecretary at the Foreign Office, or something like that, if there were a change in government. It is a pity that one can hardly hope for such a turn of events, and that the noble task of a German Badoglio would be only one of hopeless liquidation. Nevertheless, everything possible must be done to bring about this change in order to save at least the basic elements of the Bismarckian Reich. Old Nitti has backed Badoglio in America—very interesting as a symptom.

Yesterday I had a visit from Frauendorfer. He was very alert, very sensible, and equally desperate. He had a poor impression of the strength of the so-called Atlantic Wall.

Apparently it was possible to save almost everything from Sicily. New proof of the military slowness of the Anglo-Americans. Our performances have been and still are conspicuous in view of the rotten leadership at the very top and the enormous material superiority of the other side.

Frauendorfer repeated an utterance of Hitler's (made years ago) : One should not speak of "many enemies, much honor," but "many enemies, much stupidity." A severe but just judgment by Hitler on himself. He has not only made enemies of 80 per cent of the nations of the world, but has simultaneously mobilized against himself all the great forces of the intellectual world: capitalism, bolshevism, liberalism, church, and Jewry. In the midst of this desperate situation I am trying to put my mind out to grass. Lately I have been fascinated by Jaeger's *Paideia*, which yields surprising insights into antiquity and the future. In addition, Weizsäcker (Karl Friedrich) and Heisenberg on the *Cosmic Picture of the New Physics*. In this field great changes lie ahead of us.

*Ebenhausen, November 13, 1943:* I have made no notes for a long time, I think since the end of September. Yesterday was my sixty-second birthday and I was reminded of the seventieth birthday of my father, November 11, 1918, which he celebrated so unhappily after having looked forward to it with childlike joy. Today we do not seem so far gone as we were then; in fact, however, things are much worse, because it is the second time within one generation.

The situation grows worse by leaps and bounds, at home as well as at the front. The military situation is marked by unexpectedly great Russian successes and the rising sea of hatred which we owe to our insane policies. The domestic situation is deteriorating in two ways: first, there is a growing inner tension. The higher-ups, through Goebbels's megaphone, are deliberately inciting hatred against the upper class as a skillful and effective means of diverting the hatred that would ordinarily be directed against the Party. There are economic and food troubles, a deterioration of morals, and at the same time a dull and apathetic attitude toward all big questions. Second, there is a deterioration in the sense that the prospects of bringing this war to a halfway bearable conclusion for Germany through a change of regime become ever more slight.

To be sure the Moscow conference [Hull, Eden, Molotov, on October 29, 1943] in no way diminished the conflicts among the Allies. The treatment of Austria in the communiqué is significant. She was dragged in by the heels, apparently as the sole material question on which there was unity. But these conflicts remain barren for us because Hitler cannot make use of them. He represents the one factor which enables our enemies to get together in spite of all differences.

I met Goerdeler at the station. He maintained that Churchill had made an authentic statement by way of Sweden to the effect that he could make no binding arrangements before the government was overthrown in Germany. But if the revolt should succeed and should prove itself possessed of sufficient authority, he believed that a practicable way would be found.

A particularly unfavorable element is the course of events in Italy. The rash conduct of Badoglio, the shortsighted policy of the English toward the change of government in Italy, the meager military achievements of the Anglo-American armies. On the other hand there are Hitler's brutality and the vengeful and stupid methods he uses in Italy, which surpass in baseness anything done thus far. The whole country is being plundered and thousands of Italian officers and soldiers, who only did their duty faithfully, are being shot on orders of the maniacal Hitler. All these things now conspire to make of the Italian overthrow, which might have had a liberating influence on us, a source of new evils. In this category belongs the weakening of the Italian monarchy. It is always the same picture. The other side does not present a constructive and progressive program, but Hitler-Germany shows itself to the world as so absolute an evil that there is no way for us to benefit from the mistakes of our adversaries.

The case of Langbehn is particularly disastrous to our plans for bringing about a change in Germany. Langbehn, who still enjoys the hospitality of his "friend" Himmler [in the concentration camp], is being severely questioned, especially as to why he brought Popitz to Himmler. An attempt is thus being made to establish some connection between what they thought they had learned about Langbehn's business in Switzerland and the Popitz-Himmler talk. They are trying to interpret this talk as if Popitz and Langbehn had been attempting to entice Himmler to follow this line. This is why questions are continually being asked about men who might be back of Popitz, especially generals. This is a bad situation, first of all for Langbehn, because Himmler, for his own protection, won't let him out as long as the Party suspects him.[1] It will also be bad for Popitz, who may

---

[1] Langbehn was in Switzerland with a *"double"* face; he went with Himmler's permission, but actually to represent the resistance movement.

yet be cross-examined, and finally for everybody who is working on the scheme.

On the other hand, perhaps Himmler's fear of being exposed will to some extent protect Langbehn, Popitz, and others. Popitz was rather depressed by the whole business, particularly because Himmler had reacted sourly to Popitz's attempt to inquire about Langbehn's fate. Our work is rendered more difficult, too, by the growing tendency of important groups to reject Popitz.

At least, Goerdeler says, the "younger circle" as well as the representatives of labor were absolutely against Popitz. Yet at times I had the impression that the younger group (and also a part of the older group) were much more strongly opposed to Goerdeler. The latter has prevailed, however, through his tireless activities.

Incidentally, after a series of warnings Goerdeler had decided to retire for a time into a hospital, in order to get out of the line of fire. But that didn't last long. Recently his stenographer has been arrested. Whether or not this was in connection with him is not clear, because she had also worked for others. Nevertheless it is another warning.

They have now indicted Dohnanyi. According to what I was told by Oster, who had seen the indictment, there were certain minor irregularities (foreign exchange matters), but Goltz, his defense attorney, was rather optimistic. Nothing political has thus far been revealed, despite the zealous efforts of the fiendish prosecutor. Oster is now indicted, too, because of UK appointments that he made. It is all part of an attack against Admiral Canaris's organization, which rubs the Party the wrong way.

Goerdeler reported that the preparations have now made some real progress. There was determination to act in Berlin and at the front. He mentioned the names. I repeatedly asked whether the action included the kernel of the matter [the immediate removal of Hitler], but received no definite answer. Goerdeler still toys with the mistaken idea that we should go ahead even without this essential action. I am against this.

Furthermore, he brought up the question of personnel. Some circles were now in favor of Schulenburg as Minister for

Foreign Affairs, because he had warned against war with Russia. At the bottom of this lies the thought that through him we could either make peace with Stalin or exercise pressure on the Western Powers through the fear of such a separate peace.

The labor people, he admitted, seemed to prefer me because the other solution smacked too much of reaction. He, Goerdeler, knew Schulenburg only superficially, but found him a stolid and not very impressive person. He suggested that I come to an agreement with him as to the form of our cooperation; he was ready to work with us. At any rate his readiness was demonstrated by the fact that he was willing to let himself be smuggled across the Russian lines in order to talk with Stalin about a negotiated peace with a new regime in Germany.

I declared myself opposed to handling this as a question of "candidates"; within the confines of our most intimate group it was simply a matter of confidence. I was on very good terms with Schulenburg and was happy and willing to have a very thorough discussion with him, however, not in the spirit of a "distribution of jobs," but in order to work out a basis for cooperation. Personnel questions, such as who is to be Minister, Undersecretary, or Ambassador in some capital—as the central figure of our peace negotiations—were matters for later consideration.

I later defended this point of view even more sharply in talks with Popitz, who seemed to be little pleased that Goerdeler had brought on such a discussion of candidates. As to the major issue, he took the position that he would undertake only a project which he could reasonably expect to be successful.

With him and Goerdeler I was also in agreement about the terribly difficult and fundamental decision as to whether it was not already too late, and whether it would not be better to let the catastrophe run its course. We believe that in spite of everything it is imperative, for moral reasons and for the future of Germany, that an attempt be made before the end if there is any opportunity or prospect at all. Above all, it is essential that through this effort immediate trials be started against the Party criminals.

Unfortunately, I found Beck less well than the last time I

saw him. He is suffering from an unpleasant bladder trouble which seems to have been pretty hard on him.

On *October 9, 1943,* I lunched with Schulenburg. He still looks at things, and at individuals, too, from the Foreign Office point of view. But, aside from this, we understood each other very well. A clear and level head, with sound instincts. He is not so young as he was. Naturally we did not discuss any matters of positions or posts. Incidentally, he thought that Steengracht saw the situation correctly.

On *October 1, 1943,* I visited Rogeri, who seemed to have aged. He is very unhappy. He had talked with Mussolini in Munich for an hour, found him physically in bad shape, mentally alert, and quite moderate ("no revenge"). Rogeri also visited Marchetti in Garmisch (the Italian Consul General in Munich, who had been interned. Incredible!). Marchetti can go out for walks, et cetera. He is determined not to work for Mussolini.

An awful speech by Hitler, on the lowest level. He is embarrassed because he does not know how to explain his failures.

*Paris, Bordeaux, Dax, Reichenberg, October 1943.* On *Friday morning, October 15, 1943,* I was picked up by car at Dax by a Lieutenant Kaufmann sent by Commander in Chief Blaskowitz. Kaufmann, a young philologist, modern languages, is planning to be a military interpreter.

At noon I went to lunch with the Commander in Chief at Castle Tonart (medieval, built by English kings as a moated fortress, large park and farms). News came of the occupation of the Azores, very symptomatic of the situation. I had lunch with the staff and others, including Gregor, the German Consul General at Toulouse, son of the opera director. Next to me the Chief of Staff, Colonel Feyerabend, and a Major von Renteln, the commander of the Cossack regiment now in garrison on the Atlantic coast together with the "Free Indians." The Cossacks are stationed here because they cannot be relied upon at the eastern front! An indication of the strain on reserves.

German soldiers are mostly very young chaps, or quite old. Renteln, with bushy hair and mustaches, in field uniform, a real soldier of fortune but also a gentleman. He was a Russian officer for nineteen years, a colonel at twenty-seven, at first with the Imperial Horse Guards, later with the White Russians (Yudenitsch), then a German enlisted man, and now at last a major again. He said, his men were good soldiers, but at the Russian front they had begun to go over to the Soviets. They wrote him from Russia through secret channels, expressing great attachment to him. According to their stories, they were getting along famously "over there."

After lunch I had quite an interesting political conversation with Blaskowitz and Gregor. The latter showed us a directive from Berlin. The conflicts among the Allies, which were actually very great, should be played down in any public speech. Livonius had told me that Blaskowitz was "refreshingly optimistic" in speeches to his officers!

I suggested to Blaskowitz that we also have a private conversation, whereupon he asked me to see him at half-past six and dine with him before the lecture. The conversation with Blaskowitz was not very successful. He sees things essentially from the soldier's point of view. He hopes for an increasing slump in American interest in the European war, and for "some" military event which will make it easier for us to hold out until a political opportunity shows up. For example, a severe defeat of the Anglo-Americans in Italy. He does not believe a landing will take place in France, but if it comes it will be very bad.

The Paris scene is not much changed since 1942. The French are more self-confident, but I noticed no open unfriendliness. I had tea with Mima [Princess G., a Russian émigrée]. She was somewhat older, but lively and unchanged. She is stubbornly optimistic about Germany, which, she said, was Europe's only hope against bolshevism. The Paris correspondent of the *Gazette de Lausanne,* who had had lunch with her, shared her hope. I tried to explain to her how things really were. She gets no money now from America and is again selling her valuables.

I spent the evening with Marthe Ruspoli—an amazing evening. She is actually the center of a group of German officers, all intellectuals of high caliber, and all opponents of the regime.

The Italian Ambassador Buti decamped—with his possessions—a few days before the armistice. He was obviously informed. The other Italians were interned.

Hartog just telephoned that Stülpnagel can't see me today because Sauckel is there. Is he being difficult, or lazy, or doesn't he want to see me? Hartog is quite fed up with Stülpnagel, who was soft and timid.

On *October 20, 1943,* back in Berlin. Here I had two musical delights: with Ilse to the Furtwängler concert—the Seventh Symphony—and with her, Wolf-Ulli, and Frau von Brauchitsch to *Fidelio.* For me this is one of the most divine creations of mankind. The second act—the prisoners in the courtyard of the castle—is most timely and moving.

*December 5, 1943, Ebenhausen:* Meanwhile the situation on the battlefields is little changed. In the east the heavy, pulverizing battles go on, but without a real Russian breakthrough. In Italy the Anglo-Americans hack away without imagination and with slight success. In the Pacific the game of cops and robbers continues without any important results. Above all, the crushing impression and the terrifying effects of four great air raids on Berlin.

I shall never forget my feelings on the day [*November 22, 1943*] after the first big raid when I walked from Hundekehle, where, still in ignorance of the proportions of the catastrophe, I had been riding as usual, to Halensee, from Charlottenburg to the Fasanenstrasse, from there through the Hardenbergstrasse, past the burned-out Memorial Church, through the Tauenzien—Kleist—and Nettelbackstrasse to Lützow Square, through Admiral von Schröderstrasse to the Tiergartenstrasse. In Emserstrasse I found the Waldersees engaged in salvage work in front of their completely destroyed house, where they had sat celebrating her (Etta Waldersee's) birthday with good wine and a goose, until just three minutes before a demolition bomb landed on their flower-decked apartment. "Our home died in beauty," she said bravely. If they had decided to go downstairs one moment later they would have lost their lives.

Most of the cellars withstood the blast, but the losses are considerable. In the badly damaged Charlottenburg Palace the world-famous Golden Gallery is destroyed. An airplane loaded with bombs had crashed through the strongest bunker. The young von Hülsen couple and about thirty employees of the royal house were killed. Dear Wilhelm Arnim, with his lofty, unworldly spirit, and his brave wife are no more. The old west side of Berlin, for Ilse and me the real abode of tradition and our youth, is gone. Almost all the houses in which at one time or another we had spent peaceful hours have been destroyed: the Uexkülls's; Ursula Krosigk's (as well as the bookstore she had so courageously built up); the house of Seebohm, the good old admiral, who is ill and in the hospital; that of Aschoff, our fine old family doctor; our dentist, Derig's; Dagmar Dohna's studio; Plettenberg's beautiful apartment in the Netherlands Palace, in which we had just spent that pleasant evening, and so forth.

In addition the old Habel Restaurant, the Kaiserhof, the Bristol, the Eden, many of the ministries, but not the new chancery, Rosenberg's Ministry for Eastern Affairs, or the Propaganda Ministry. The devil, who seems to be ruling the world, protected them. But the French and English embassies are gone. The English destroyed their embassy as we did ours in Belgrade. My old headquarters, the Central European Economic Association, is reduced to some burned-out walls. The Institute for Economic Research was spared, like an island, by the first raid, but during the second raid most of the building, including my room, was made uninhabitable by a demolition bomb that landed across the street.

The subsequent disorganization is typical of all government offices and institutes—everybody is busy with problems of restoration and emergency quarters; no real work is done. The achievements in the field of transportation are amazing. These facilities are being restored with unbelievable speed. After the fourth big raid Ilse and I left Berlin yesterday morning. The train left on the minute, and after a very normal trip, with dining car, et cetera, we arrived at our destination on the dot.

The political situation has not changed much. The most important recent events are: the meeting in Egypt between Roosevelt, Churchill, and Chiang Kai-shek [December 1, 1943], and in Persia between Roosevelt, Churchill, and Stalin

[December 6, 1943]. Their purpose is to bring stronger political pressure to bear on Germany. The nervous efforts of our people to draw a parallel to Wilson's fourteen points is interesting.

Popitz told me the air raids had not led to any kind of organized work on the part of the "nonexistent cabinet." Everyone jogs along in his own way! Leadership principle! Only in a nation like the German can things function as passably as they still do. A lot more will have to happen before we reach complete chaos!

I met Goerdeler and Schulenburg once more to discuss opportunities in foreign affairs. The latter swears that it is possible to come to terms with Stalin, to my mind with exaggerated optimism. Of course I, too, see in this game of playing with both sides the only opportunity for a new regime, but not in the sense of double-dealing. The manifestation of fairness toward England is vital. This must be supplemented by keeping open the possibility of an understanding with the East.

At these conferences I resisted with all my strength the discussion of candidates for jobs—apparently with some success, for when I happened to meet Goerdeler later in Potsdam on the tram (as I was about to go to see Schacht at the Palast Hotel), he, too, took the only possible point of view that all that mattered was that our "Band of Brothers" should hold together. He didn't express it this way, though, but used the language, unfortunately not unfamiliar to him, of one to whom position in life means very much. He said, "We are all agreed that you must be Minister for Foreign Affairs!" One could only draw the conclusion that he believed we were concerned here with the distribution of "honorable" offices.

Planck is always extremely pessimistic, but in the main he has been right. He maintains that if Rome falls, the Pope will be taken along "for his own protection." Our people are certainly capable of this. Thus instinctively everybody believes that we dropped the bombs on Vatican City the other day.

Gericke told me Hitler had said to General Toussaint (amid violent accusations against Mackensen who despite all his servility to the Party is under house arrest at Neurath's hunting lodge in the mountains) that the only person who judged the situation in Italy correctly was I, and that those who had fired me ought to be called to account! In that case he should begin with himself. How changeable these people are who lack any real background!

Gleichen told of Mussolini's unhappy position. Of all places, he apparently lives in the house of our old friend Count Serego-Alighieri at Gargagnano. Disappointed, inactive, bitter, he sits there, shorn of power, completely in our hands and in those of the Petacci sisters, who have turned up again. A melancholy end which I would not have expected.

Doertenbach who was at the embassy in Rome until September 9, 1943, shares Rintelen's view that Badoglio wanted to honor our alliance and was persuaded to desert us only because of our behavior. When he did break with us he was in such a desperate situation that he acted both stupidly and disloyally.

It is questionable whether the King was in the know at the time of Rahn's audience. Doertenbach thinks it possible that Mussolini's men, for instance Buffarini, may be playing a double game, that Buffarini is acting in agreement with Grandi and is waiting for the opportune moment to toss a monkey wrench into the works. It is indicative of Mussolini's weakness that, after Ciano betrayed him so shamelessly, he is already flirting with the typically Italian idea of taking him back again.

The level to which a certain section of German science has fallen was demonstrated to me by a lecture I heard in the Berlin branch of the German Academy. The lecture was on race policies by Professor von Verschuer, the man whom E. Fischer had dared to propose as his successor in the Wednesday Society. A superficial palaver, tailored to Party purposes, a veritable disgrace.

A kind of social life on a modest scale has developed in Potsdam as a "place of retreat" from Berlin. Blessing has just arrived from Rumania and said that fear of bolshevism would almost inevitably hold the Rumanians solidly in our camp. The same would doubtless be true of the Estonians and the Letts. But we have ruined all our chances with the Poles, and the attempt now made to win them over comes too late.

Our policy has produced veritable masterpieces of mistaken methods. This was demonstrated to me in a conversation with

J. Wallenberg. As a Swede, he does not desire our collapse, but he sees no way out. Goerdeler maintains that Churchill had asked Wallenberg to say that he would look with benevolent interest upon a new regime in Germany; in other words, under Goerdeler's leadership. Schacht doubts this, or rather he does not believe that this message was meant specifically for Goerdeler. I incline to the same view. Goerdeler, incidentally, again brought up the question whether it might not be possible to achieve a change without getting rid of Hitler first. Beck is not willing to go along with that. Neither am I.

On the following morning I had breakfast with Schacht at the Palast Hotel, and afterward a short walk in the direction of Sans Souci. He was exceedingly open and frank. It pleased me when he admitted he had at first fallen for Hitler. His outspoken, absolutely personal, burning ambition is disturbing. It leads him to misjudge his own position. He gave it to be understood that he would not take over a ministry or any other office under somebody else as Chancellor. At first it seemed to me that he wanted to hold himself in readiness for special tasks, but afterward I realized that he considered himself as the appropriate head of a government, and had me in mind as a kind of assistant for the technical aspects of foreign policy.

On the essentials, however, we were completely agreed. He, too, held it to be our duty, in spite of the bad situation, for moral as well as political reasons, not to let the wagon roll into the pit but to climb into the driver's seat first, although there will be little honor in it and little to be salvaged. Schacht shares my view that no success can be expected without the previous elimination of Hitler. Likewise, he is of my opinion that a loyal effort must be made to come to terms with the Anglo-Saxons and all double-dealing avoided. The threat of an agreement with Stalin remains in the background. Unfortunately the whole thing is probably a will-o'-the-wisp.

I forgot to jot down two items from the record of my successor in Rome. While Mussolini was suffering his crushing defeat in the Grand Council, Mackensen drafted a telegram in which he said that Mussolini had the situation firmly in hand. When someone suggested to him that evening that it should not be sent, he misjudged the situation so completely that he expressly ordered it dispatched. Still more insane was that when the new chief of government, Badoglio, first sent for him he pretended to be absent and sent Doertenbach, the young counselor of embassy in his stead to this important conference.

*Ebenhausen, December 27, 1943:* General G believes that a landing will be made in the west. He hopes to get command of an armored division, is completely absorbed by this idea, and consequently very much centered in himself. A political ostrich, in that he is trying to draw nearer to the SS, because he will have mostly SS men in his army and consequently wishes to mobilize the black influence in his favor! He seems to be a good soldier, but otherwise undoubtedly of small caliber.

Unfortunately I had a similar impression of —— who has come on furlough from Belgium. He is childishly proud of his general's stripes and completely absorbed in his official duties and his local problems and achievements. It is remarkable how strongly the German virtue of "doing a thing for its own sake" can prove a hindrance to a truly political grasp of conditions.

Perhaps I was particularly sensitive about political matters for a number of reasons. First, the impressions made by the increasingly terrible effect of the air raids in Berlin were so overwhelming that one's every fiber trembled with anxiety to get rid of our regime and to save at least the essentials of a future for Germany before a catastrophe wipes out the last chances. Connected with this is the fact that shocking political chaos prevails among our adversaries. Acute conflicts among the Allies are only superficially veiled, if that. There are contradictory and tactically unwise political statements, such as Smuts's speech. There is an apparently irresistible advance of communism, particularly in North Africa, Corsica, and metropolitan France. There is deep annoyance among the small states and the French over the lack of consideration with which the Great Powers override their wishes. All these are factors which, in the event of a timely change of regime, might make it possible to conduct a not entirely hopeless foreign policy.

The people who disapprove of Badoglio's behavior now believe that there is nothing left to do but just to see things through. They do not realize the Italian situation is entirely different from that in Germany, and that Badoglio, shuttling back and forth between loyalty to the alliance and recognition of the impossibility of fighting on, operated with the least possible skill.

For us the situation is simply this: With Hitler the war will certainly be lost, because it will be fought to a catastrophic end by both sides. It does not lie in Hitler's nature to yield, nor can he hope to bring about a decision favorable to us. Neither are the Anglo-Americans prepared to deal with Hitler. I think the possibility of arranging a separate peace with Russia, which perhaps once existed, is also gone. The one definite point on which the other side is united is that Hitler must first of all be laid low. Only after this goal has been reached can (and will) their differences come to the surface.

Politically it is up to us to make clear to the other side their interest in a healthy Germany. With a leader like Hitler, however, after all that has happened, this would be impossible—if only because nobody believes him. A complete break with Hitler's policies is the decisive step. What takes place later is of secondary importance. In any event a new government should have as broad and deep a foundation as possible.

A further point which made me especially irritable about —— is the case of Falkenhausen. This intelligent and farsighted man, in defiance of all warnings, has made things far too easy for the Party and the Gestapo. He has been a thorn in their flesh for a long time. The petty men who had always turned up their noses at him have been proved right. He has been so stupid about his relationship with Elisabeth Ruspoli and has offered his political enemies so many points to attack, that he is now really about to fall, at a moment when he is needed more than even before. The whole affair is a discouraging business. What is there to hope for if the finest horses fall into the ditch?

But more important than all this was the fact that during the week before Christmas, according to reliable sources, the first concrete prospect for attaining our goal materialized. How often we were told this! I never put much faith in such talk.

But the statements of reliable people sounded so convinced and so convincing that I really began to take it seriously. A few days before my trip came a reverse: "Postponed until January." Reason: "Because Hitler had vanished." During the decisive days Goerdeler was with me often, and after the action was called off he was furious, understandably enough. He said the generals would never make a decision, but would wait for complete catastrophe. After waiting two days in vain with Wuffi, on *December 23, 1943,* I had a long and gratifying talk with Schwerin, whom I again found most agreeable and who is very active.

I was satisfied with a number of conversations I had with Kessel. He had accompanied Frau von Weizsäcker to Berlin. She came to look after her house, which was badly damaged. I did not get into any serious discussion with her. Kessel, however, maintained that Weizsäcker was pressing for action with utmost vigor. This is easy to do from the Vatican! Before that he certainly did not get very involved.

I spoke with Trott, shortly before my departure, in the same way as with Schwerin. He judges the situation much as I do. On his official trips he has had the opportunity, as have few others, to look at things from the outside and even to make contact with Englishmen. His English acquaintances were greatly concerned about Russia and deeply interested in developments here. They were, however, suspicious lest a change should turn out to be only a cloak, hiding a continuation of militaristic Nazi methods under another label.

On *December 17, 1943,* our apartment at 28 Fasanenstrasse also got it. With two neighboring houses it was in a rather isolated spot in that area. Incendiary and phosphorous bombs made a bad mess of it, and would have destroyed it entirely if the fire engines had not come quickly. The first bomb came through the roof just over my desk. Emmy [the maid], according to her story, put this fire out, but then the flames from the next house set fire to ours again. I spent one evening and the night at the Sauerbruchs'. Waldersee was there, too. Sauerbruch, amusing and curious as always, told interesting tales from earlier times, particularly about the Munich putsch and Hitler's scarcely heroic performance. He also reported that an

SS leader (Turner) had told him about a conference of high SS leaders in which one of them had said that when the time came to re-establish contact with England they still had me, and that the Führer's opinion of me had changed considerably. Another example of our ups and downs: The nincompoop Ziegler, who once basked in the warmest sun of grace, has been chased out into the cold because he made defeatist remarks; it is alleged that he has even been arrested. As he protested in a "cavalier" fashion that Pietzsch entertained the "same views," Pietzsch, too, fell into disgrace.

Popitz is deeply depressed. First, naturally, because of developments in general, then because he rightly assumes that, when a change of regime takes place, he will not be in the front row, at least not in the position he wants (Minister of Education), although he has worked so long and with all his strength in this enterprise. I think he is exactly suited for this post, and am wholly in favor of using his considerable gifts in this way. Beck doesn't like him. Goerdeler, too, is against him. The latter maintains that he had no personal antipathy to him, but that the Social Democrats would not tolerate him because he had too long sympathized with Göring and had co-operated too long with the Nazis. To my mind this is not sufficient grounds, particularly as we are short of men. I can't yet see clearly how far this judgment is correct, or whether Goerdeler is hiding behind the Social Democrats.

Actually, Popitz's professorial manner has alienated many people. Goerdeler thinks Popitz would be suitable for the embassy to the Vatican. Not bad, for Beck would reject Weizsäcker for this post, and, indeed, for any post, especially because of Weizsäcker's speech to the diplomats who were returning from America in May 1942. His final words then were: "We do nothing without the Führer; his will is our will."

Popitz is concerned because of Goerdeler's "parliamentary" methods. He always acted like the leader of a coalition. This is true. For me, too, Goerdeler is too much a man of the old methods, but things have now progressed so far here that all such considerations are no longer of decisive importance. Anyway, the first cabinet will probably be used up quickly.

At Goerdeler's suggestion I had a detailed discussion with

Kiep. I had thought of him as a possible undersecretary, or something like that, because of his good knowledge of the Anglo-Saxons. But he considers himself more suitable as chief of the press section, that is as a *porte parole* in Anglo-Saxon affairs.

# 1944

*Ebenhausen, January 2, 1944:* The new year begins with
the darkest of prospects. Anxiety and horror still hold sway. It
is with this feeling that I go back to Berlin. Should I keep on
working there? Is there any sense in it at all?

A very interesting book on Stalin by the American, Eugene
Lyons. It was written before the German-Russian war and is
neither "orthodox" in the Allied sense nor exaggeratedly anti-
Hitler; therefore, relatively objective. The picture one gets of
Stalin is, to be sure, much less agreeable than the one Schulenburg draws, but very cogent and convincing. The author is
apparently prejudiced in favor of Trotsky.

*Ebenhausen, February 7, 1944:* Situation: a very serious
deterioration of the situation in the east. Heavy air raids,
which will certainly destroy about half of Berlin. The landing
of the Anglo-Americans at Nettuno, though with very modest
results for the time being. Increased pressure on the neutrals,
to which Argentina has already yielded. Bolivia's attempt to
get out from under the net the United States has thrown over
Spanish America has been of no avail. On the other hand, the
differences among the Allies continue and even increase.

Indicative of the situation is the stink bomb *Pravda* has
thrown at the Anglo-Americans in the form of the news report
that Ribbentrop had negotiated with Hoare in Spain. The
result in Germany was a heightened suspicion on the part of

the rulers, who assume that it was not Ribbentrop who was making contact with the English, but other groups. Schwerin says that they suspect some younger group in the Foreign Office. About the same time Kiep was arrested. He was the victim of a stool pigeon of the Security Service of the SS. Furthermore, Hellmuth Moltke has been questioned, and since he apparently refused to make a statement, he was held. Whether he is still confined I don't know. I always have some doubts about him because of his unrealistic political mentality.

Elisabeth Thadden has been imprisoned because of church affairs and was denounced by the same stool pigeon as Kiep and his wife. Frau Solf, widow of the Ambassador, Scherpenberg, Schacht's son-in-law, and Fanny Kurowsky [were denounced] in the same way and at the same time. The stool pigeon is a Dr. Reckse of the Charité Hospital. Bernstorff is still imprisoned, too. He has been accused of being connected with Langbehn's trips, apparently on no grounds at all. The latter will certainly be held indefinitely, because Himmler is afraid for his own skin. "Puppi" Sarre also is still "in." It is rumored that Popitz is somewhat in danger of being involved in this same matter. Schwerin confirms this, and also Stauffenberg, whom I met in November at the Jessens', with whom I was impressed. He said we should be extremely cautious in making statements and in meeting people, especially in meeting Popitz, who was being closely watched. Stauffenberg thought that there was nothing special against me at the moment.

Our conversation was interrupted by an air-raid alarm which sent us to the cellar. Contrary to our arrangement, Jessen had invited Popitz. I wanted to be alone with Stauffenberg, who was brought over after the alarm. Popitz is nervous and irritable, a result of the understandable bitterness he feels for Goerdeler, who really treats him badly. But he takes these things too personally—an attitude which hurts no one as much as himself. His doubts about Goerdeler's methods are justified. Stauffenberg handled the conversation very skillfully but did not succeed in dispelling Popitz's misgivings, which he shares, at least in part. The trouble is the fact that Beck has no real conception of politics and has put himself entirely in Goerdeler's hands.

The whole business, of course, is so much waste motion; nothing will happen anyway!

I was in Hamburg for three days. That city is still filled with an astonishing if ill-founded confidence. The North German provincial city (a category in which I really never counted Hamburg) is still the main pillar of our system. The remarkable effectiveness of the propaganda was to be felt even among the really select patrons of the National Club, where I had lunch. Near me sat that good and pleasant man, Admiral General Albrecht, who said to me: "When will this streak of bad luck come to an end?" And, as I shrugged my shoulders, he added fervently: "It must now, it really must!"

*February 23, 1944:* There was a heavy air raid during the last days of my stay in Berlin. A terrible sight in the morning, especially in Halensee. So far there have been from fifteen to seventeen severe attacks. Result: 50 per cent of Berlin is destroyed or heavily damaged. Why shouldn't they go ahead with the other 50 per cent? Nothing will be changed by the exhortations of the Bishop of Chichester and the former Archbishop of Canterbury, Dr. Lang, who warn against excessive raids.

The military situation is something of a stalemate, thanks to the slowing up of the Anglo-Americans in Italy. To be sure Beck and others believe that they do not want to do more than tie down some of our forces. I don't think so. Thanks to the excellent work of the middle level of German command, as well as of the troops in the east, our people forced their way through the encirclement at Tscherkassy. It would make a dog howl to see how much officers, soldiers, and people achieve and endure, under the most miserable leadership at the top level, both political and military. The opportunities we missed in the east alone are enough to send those responsible to the gallows.

The spiritual confusion and the moral deterioration caused by Hitler were vividly illustrated recently by two things: Seydlitz, Daniels, Schimatis, whom I knew at the Army High Command (he made a very fine impression), have sent over the Russian radio a very tempting appeal to surrender to the soldiers encircled at Tscherkassy. German military history contains not even an approximate parallel. One would doubt the authenticity of the broadcast but Daniels addressed a personal appeal to a former captain of his old battalion in Rastenburg, now commander of a division. This kind of thing can't be made up. ("The world is out of joint, oh, cursed spite, that ever I was born to set it right.")

Another sign is the state of our law and the nervous investigations of the SD. Ewald Heinrich Kleist listened in on a trial before the People's Court in Potsdam against the publisher Boness, who was condemned to death. An SD man told Ewald Heinrich in cold cynicism before the trial that the sentence had, of course, been decided upon long ago. This was the impression at the trial, too: a comedy brutally played out, ending in legal murder, testimony given under duress, a brutalized defendant, a shamelessly limited defense—and German judges take part in such proceedings! The presiding judge, a particularly bad individual called Crohne, betrayed himself when he said to poor Boness: "Would you maintain that you have been mistreated? I inquired of the SD and have established the fact that you have neither been mishandled nor examined under duress!"

A whole group of people has been arrested on the denunciation of a stool pigeon, looking for connections in Switzerland, probably in conjunction with the Langbehn case. Frau Solf and daughter, Elisabeth Thadden, Zarden, the former Undersecretary in the Ministry of Finance, who meanwhile seems to have committed suicide, Kiep and his wife, and Hellmuth Moltke.

The success of Soviet propaganda among German prisoners of war was a hard blow for Hitler. Apart from Seydlitz, et cetera, Soviet recruiting among the troops was partially successful, so that German non-commissioned officers were parachuted in the Crimea as agitators. They were caught and shot. Now a counter-indoctrination is to be undertaken against this successful "re-education," as Colonel von Völkersam pungently called it. The colonel heads this project in the Air Force and naïvely described it recently at the Rheinbaben table. A grand program of political indoctrination will be carried out in the entire Wehrmacht, from the commanding general down to the last grenadier.

Before Rintelen is allowed to take over an army corps he has to go through this course. The intelligence level of most officers will guarantee a certain amount of success, but they will never forge a real weapon this way.

The foreign situation has deteriorated dangerously, especially in Finland. Heavy pressure on Spain, which may one day lead to a domestic blowup. In Turkey, on the other hand, the pressure of the English had led to a temporary stiffening. In Bulgaria, conditions are growing even more unstable. Wolf writes from France that all intercourse with foreigners has been strictly forbidden. Firle, who heads the Merchant Marine Department in Paris, confirms the fact that only the "dregs" among Frenchmen still support the German side.

The other evening I went to Gottfried Bismarck's to see his brother Otto. He confirmed the reports of Rintelen and Doertenbach on Italy in all essentials. The report of the High Command of the Armed Forces on the course of events in Italy is a tissue of lies. Otto Bismarck judges Ciano more favorably than I do.

Two examples of our lack of good taste: They photographed Ciano in his cell through a hole in the wall. And Mussolini, apparently entirely powerless, was prevailed upon to have himself photographed at chess—which he does not play at all!—in the act of "checkmating the King!"

Popitz I found disgusted and nervous—which is understandable. He has been told that proceedings against him and Goerdeler are in the air. Goerdeler has received sharp warnings and seems to be unable to make a move. Stauffenberg told Popitz the generals no longer wanted to receive Goerdeler. Everything is going to the devil!

*Ebenhausen, March 13, 1944:* I am down with a swollen knee which can be flexed only with considerable pain, this time the right leg. It was my right foot that I injured in a fall from my horse nine months ago. I am furious. I have been so agile until now. Is my age beginning to tell? In any case a warning which one must attempt to turn to advantage. It is a bitter pill.

In March 1944 three big daylight raids on Berlin—the first ones very disconcerting. The inner city was not touched, but the surrounding districts were heavily damaged. The Americans often drop their bombs in a senseless way, for instance over Schlachtensee or Nicolasee, or on the harmless country town of Templin.

*Wednesday, March 8, 1944:* Planck is completely pessimistic, almost resigned. Unfortunately he is also pessimistic about Brussels, where he is not going any more. Keitel, stupid and narrow-minded—possibly influenced by the Elisabeth Ruspoli case—forbids all intercourse with foreigners. Thus the last bridges for the future are cut off.

In Brussels, Keitel yielded completely to Party pressure and agreed to the appointment of a high police and SS leader who is not under Falkenhausen.

The situation on the southern part of the eastern front is very bad. The chief political danger at the moment is Finland. These people want to end all this. Of course the Russians make it very difficult for them. For the time being frigid relations exist between Turkey and England, between the United States and Argentina, which is being supported by Chile, Bolivia, and Paraguay. One can still say in general that as far as foreign developments are concerned all is not lost if . . . !

I had lunch with Otto Christian Fischer at the Club. He is really very sensible about Hitler, but has nevertheless built up the thesis that the only thing left now is to let things take their course in a war of exhaustion. At some point the enemy, too, would reach the bottom of the barrel! And this at a time when our material disadvantage is becoming more and more pronounced, with the air raids, especially on the aircraft industry, getting more severe every day! In the west we can hardly get any planes into the air.

Goerdeler, naturally, spoke very differently when, after a long interval, he came to see me in Potsdam. He speaks of the "last phase" which we are now entering upon. He keeps himself very much in the background, after warnings from all sides.

Jessen does not yet give up hope for the younger generals (Stauffenberg).

A disturbing visit from Berthold. These people, who were once idealistic National Socialists, now realize the imminence of the catastrophe and have only one idea: How can we save ourselves personally, and our Bavaria, from this chaos and from the responsibility for what has happened? Prussia can bear that burden! They hope naïvely that Bavaria will receive somewhat better treatment from the enemy. They want to join up with Austria, perhaps under a monarchy. This kind of thing was being discussed publicly at local meetings in the west. He was disappointed that I, as a "Hanoverian," did not at once agree. Of course he labeled it all as the first cell of a Germany that would later grow together again.

I forcibly described the dangers and illusions of this kind of policy. One point I did concede. If complete bolshevistic chaos ruled in the north, then the cell idea might become practical; in that event, I would prefer to see Bavaria and Austria together to seeing Austria by itself, because they would be better able to survive.

Two significant Berlin jokes: "I would rather believe in victory than run around minus my head!" A completely bombed-out person says: "After the destruction of all equipment and furnishing essential to the war effort, I have retired from my dwelling, 'according to plan.' "

*Ebenhausen, April 8, 1944:* I have been laid up three weeks with this inflammation in my knee, and have had enough leisure to recuperate from my strenuous stay in bomb-battered Berlin, to reflect, to read, and to write a little book about Pyrrhus, which was fun. Our sons, who were our great joy at Easter, discussed the book intelligently and made some good suggestions.

The situation in general is getting worse and worse. Events move in the usual spiral, that is it looks again and again as if a halt could be made on the precipitous path, especially as a result of the strategic mistakes of the Anglo-Americans and the growing political differences among the Allies. Also the Russian advances are so much of a threat to our eastern Allies that they have to go along for better or for worse. In this connection the arrogant intransigence of the Russians—in the case of

Finland—stands Germany in good stead, and in the case of Hungary, the ruthless and determined activities of the Nazis. The energetic intervention in Hungary at first had the desired result, but in the long run it will prove a dangerous point of weakness; for fear of bolshevism now keeps the Hungarians on our side, but only in the role of galley slaves.

In this connection there is interest in the Russian declaration that they have no demands to make on the Rumanians, an obvious attempt to shatter that already fragile front. Of course by their attitude on the Finnish question they have made success more difficult. The very lame Ribbentrop interview reveals how unpleasant the Russian declaration is to Hitler. Of course he does not dare to publish the exact wording. Thus no temporary stalemate or transient improvement in the situation can save us from slipping further along the downward path. This is especially true because of the almost unbearable wear and tear on the Russian front and, in the event of an invasion, on the other fronts as well, and because of our increasing inferiority in matériel as a result of air attacks on our aircraft industries.

A few days ago Schacht visited me on my sick bed. It was very pleasant out on the upper veranda in sunny weather. He said that his son-in-law was still "in," supposedly only as a "witness," and was treated well (in Fürstenberg-Ravensbrück). He also was at the famous Thadden "tea" and was denounced. Schacht no longer sees any hope for a timely change of regime, but he maintains, as I do, that if it should come—but only then—there would still be all kinds of political possibilities. Apparently he still thinks he is the man of the hour.

One point with which he dealt in great detail was an immediate separate peace with France (perhaps with Daladier). Alsace-Lorraine was to be a kind of autonomous buffer state under German sovereignty, but so managed economically that between Alsace-Lorraine and France there would be just as little of a customs barrier as between Alsace-Lorraine and Germany. This arrangement would bring a most welcome prosperity to that district and the apple of discord would disappear. I believe, however, that no French government would today accept German sovereignty over Alsace-Lorraine.

*Ebenhausen, April 4, 1944:* . . . Even now a change in regime would mean an improved political outlook. The immediate trial, before a regular German court, of the criminals who now rule over us would exonerate us morally and would cleanse the German escutcheon. This would be a great political gain.

The abdication of Victor Emmanuel "after the taking of Rome," and the appointment of Umberto as Regent, is represented in our press as punishment for the "traitors" and as evidence of the political muddle and the inevitable advance of bolshevism. In my judgment this is entirely wrong. It seems to me that they have cleared away—if only for the immediate future—the elements of conflict, and have temporarily silenced the controversy over the monarchy, thus creating a kind of united front to which the communists must also adhere, whether they like it or not, as Moscow has recognized Badoglio in order to out-maneuver the Anglo-Americans.

*Ebenhausen, May 27, 1944:* The situation is marked by the increasingly nervous expectation of "invasion" on the part of both friend and foe. Will it really come? It is still considered questionable, but I believe in it. When? Where? With a sidelong glance at Russia, Anglo-Saxon public opinion is demanding action. In England "in order to finally end this burdensome war." On the other hand, Hitler and his henchmen see in the failure of an invasion the only real chance left to them.

Destruction and scarcities of raw materials increase, and the food situation may become critical at the latest early in the summer. The possibilities of a separate peace with Russia have also diminished, and Russian war aims are becoming tougher. They now officially demand, over the protests of the English, that the entire German Wehrmacht shall be carried off into slavery. It may be that this demand is meant as a tactical expedient, or to provide the Russian people, after they reach the German border, with a more attractive (?) war aim.

But the presentation of this demand gives food for thought, as does the curtain of silence that has fallen over the "promises" to the so-called Free Germany Committee in Moscow.

Across the Channel, to be sure, they still represent Russia—probably also for tactical reasons—as perfectly ready to come to terms with a German military dictatorship, whereas only the democracies are the protectors of freedom. It is also asserted with increasing precision that a far-reaching secret understanding has been reached between Japan and Russia.

On the whole there are no prospects for peace. At the same time differences are increasing in the Allied camp. Stalin's declaration concerning his readiness to negotiate with the Vatican has faced the officials of the Catholic Church with a considerable dilemma. The pressure on neutrals grows heavier. We have become more modest and are even content with the attitude of Turkey, although she has completely cut off the export of chromium, which in the long run is indispensable to us.

In this connection the following incident is significant. The news agency, Interpress, had asked permission to publish in the German press that part of my article, "Greater Europe" (written two years ago!) dealing with Turkey. The article appeared in numerous German newspapers. One might have expected Ribbentrop to get excited about it, for it was published without prior consultation with the Foreign Office just after the beginning of the conflict with Turkey. Apparently, however, it suited the purposes of the Foreign Office very well to have an unofficial voice—but one which abroad is considered official—say something nice to the Turks. As a result, the *Pester Lloyd* called the article "a German voice concerning the suspension of chromium shipments," which was, of course, not even mentioned. *Habent sua fata articoli.* This saying also proved true in another sense of my article, "A New European Balance," in the periodical *Auswärtige Politik.*

The official Wehrmacht newspaper for officers, *Was Uns Bewegt,* has been renamed *Der Offizier des Führers,* a crazy title. The first issue is made up of disgusting and, in my opinion, ineffective Byzantine blather in praise of Hitler. The impression one gets of increasingly devastated Berlin, Unter den Linden, and the beautiful Gendarmen-Markt, is shattering.

Withal, the Berliners sit in the sunshine, in the midst of wreckage and debris, on the benches on Unter den Linden as if there were peace. The attacks are crippling life more and more, if only because of the general nervousness which increases every day. During the day I usually walk to our old air-raid shelter at 28 Fasanenstrasse.

An incident which took place recently at the Beuths' seemed significant to me. Someone expressed the opinion that we had indeed been forced to attack Russia, otherwise the Soviets would have attacked us. I burst out with: "I am absolutely convinced of the contrary!" Whereupon there was a very obvious, embarrassed, and frightened silence. At last someone said: "But it would be terrible if you were right!"

The new offensive of the Anglo-Americans in Italy [May 11, 1944] is more serious and is making headway. Nevertheless, I could understand the entire strategy only if they were soon to attack in other places as well. In this way they can achieve certain results, but nothing decisive. I am waiting for the moment when Hitler declares that in order to save the Eternal City, the Pope, and the art monuments, he had magnanimously ordered the evacuation of Rome,[1] under no pressure from the enemy.

Serious situation in Bulgaria and Rumania; it would not take much to bring about a collapse in both countries. It is hard to understand how they were again able to parry the blow aimed at Jassy. Otherwise, in the opinion of General Xylander, who has just come from Rumania, things would have ended right there.

A certain consolidation seems to have taken place in Hungary, of which the entrance of Imrédy into the Cabinet is perhaps proof. They maintain their hold over the people by making the customary appeals to mob instincts (Jewish question, anti-upper class policy. This class, to be sure, leaves much to be desired.) Horthy is engaging in passive resistance, but seems to be overreaching himself more and more. Westrick related at Beuth's that Kallay had told him the greatest diplo-

[1] June 5, 1944, the Allies entered Rome.

mat in Europe was Antonescu. He was considered the best-loved friend of Hitler, and still had his agents everywhere on the other side.

According to various reports, the SS, even during the days just preceding the change of government in Budapest, had brutally prepared the way. For instance, they had treated the old Royal Italian diplomats outrageously, making the members of the so-called Badoglio Legation run around for hours in the courtyard.

At the Adlon recently I met Guttenberg and Koschak, the crafty new Croatian Ambassador. The former gave a rather sad account of conditions in Croatia. Banos Subasitch, my old acquaintance from Agram, a friend of Prince Paul, seems to have taken over the government in exile with Peter. That would be very interesting—a Croat!

We spent one evening at the Jessens'. It did us good to be with them. Unfortunately he had had a serious automobile accident and had broken about everything one could imagine. Sauerbruch is now patching him up. Jessen is one of the few who in the innermost recesses of his heart still seems to hope that a revolt will take place (Stauffenberg).

I had a visit from Schniewind. News about Langbehn varies. His wife is more optimistic, his comrades lately more pessimistic. Schniewind spoke of Goerdeler very critically. Originally he, Schniewind, had promised him to co-operate as Minister of Economic Affairs, but about a week ago he had withdrawn this promise. He doesn't think that Goerdeler is the proper man. When Goerdeler asked him why he had told him that he lacked the power of decision. This I cannot understand, for this is just what Goerdeler has. It looks to me as if Schniewind considered the members of a future government as liquidators who will afterward be damned for having signed intolerable terms. I said that even then one ought not to hesitate.

*Ebenhausen, June 12, 1944:* The world lies under the cloud of the "invasion" [Normandy, June 6, 1944]. It is almost ridiculous how both sides, after the long, nervous tension, welcomed it with a sigh of relief. Nothing can be said as yet about the outcome. It is strange, first of all, that the day of Dunkirk was chosen. Could it be that our adversaries were really influenced by such toying with dates? Secondly, that the other side did not take advantage of the opportunity it had to make propaganda capital out of the taking of Rome. Instead, this great impression was immediately blotted out by the greater event of the invasion which followed it directly.

At the same time there has been a noticeable letdown in air raids on Germany, which may prove that enemy air power, too, is not unlimited. During the ten days of my stay in Berlin there was no alarm; only a warning during the meeting of the Wednesday Club on May 31, the day of my arrival, at Sauerbruch's house, where Beck spoke very well and in a very polished manner about Foch. His estimate of the man appeared to me too favorable.

Beck was really his old self again, but this "old self" has indeed, in the course of time, proved to be more of a pure "Clausewitz," without a spark of "Blücher" or "Yorck." Jessen attended this meeting again, after his serious motor accident, but was on a stretcher and was taken home in the evening. He reported that Hitler as well as Himmler had attempted, independently of each other, to feel out Stettinius. Answer given to both: "Not with you!"

The last announcement by the German Officers' Committee in Moscow, on the occasion of the invasion, is very interesting. The sense of it is: "We Germans have nothing to gain in an Anglo-American advance into the heart of Europe. Therefore defend yourselves effectively and come to terms with the east!" The latter part was not said in so many words, of course.

According to English reports two Stockholm correspondents of well-known German newspapers renounced their German citizenship under romantic and improbable circumstances —giving back their passports through the window of the Legation. The English radio broadcasts a conversation that supposedly took place between one of them—Count Anton Knyphausen, brother of Benckeser, brother-in-law of the imprisoned Kuenzer—and the English Minister. He is reported to have said the German nation was composed of 17 per cent of Nazis and interested hangers-on, 80 per cent of those who always run along with any crowd, and 3 per cent of sensible people. The English, he said, should not believe that the air terror would bring them victory. The war could be brought to an end only by means of a successful invasion (this was said before the invasion) or by bringing to the helm the 3 per cent with whom an acceptable peace could be made.

A further evidence of the spiritual confusion which Hitler has bequeathed to the poor German people is the "Vermehren" case in Turkey. Vermehren, a member of the German Military Intelligence Corps, seems to have worked for the Secret Service, and he and his wife escaped in an English airplane. Now all the rest of his family have been locked up as hostages. Flügge is said to have been interested in this group.

Popitz said that his neighbor, Haverbeck (a businessman), through whom he had first met Langbehn, had been locked up for six weeks as a witness against the latter. Today this is standard procedure! During this period he was interrogated three times by a criminal lawyer called Lange.[1] Principal object, the affair Popitz-Himmler. Lange had remarked that Popitz ought to be cross-examined, too, but that was too difficult. Haverbeck was then honorably released, and Lange, who lives in the neighborhood, has since frequently come to have tea and to exchange eggs and other produce with him!

One of the most shameless cases of Party justice and of impudent perversion of the law through regular judges is the proceedings against Rohr because of his participation in the burial of a Russian prisoner. Eight months' imprisonment. The Supreme Court at least had the courage to suspend the sentence and to refer the case to a district court outside Pomerania.

*June 8, 1944:* At noon Goebbels invited a select group of high officials, industrialists, et cetera, into his "throne room" for a lecture on propaganda—in all two hundred persons. I was invited either through my association with the Central European Economic Association or the Institute for Economic Research—a very effective label and cloak for me. Goebbels presented himself beautifully as one of the upper "bourgeoisie."

[1]After the attempt on July 20, 1944, Lange was an examining attorney against Popitz and Hassell.

He wore an elegant gray suit without insignia, used unemotional language, and confidentially addressed himself to "men in the know." He gave the appearance of being very frank in revealing his methods. He made a decided impression on most of his audience as a "very intelligent man."

Only a few noticed that here spoke a man who had reached the end of his rope. There were numerous contradictions and slips; more especially, he completely ignored the fact that propaganda in foreign countries is fundamentally different from propaganda at home. He drew an unqualified parallel between "the propaganda for National Socialism, which finally, in spite of all hindrances and setbacks, led to war and victory, and the propaganda for war and victory." There was one dangerous sentence, designed for his own glorification, that the victory of National Socialism was the result of propaganda!

As to foreign propaganda, he absolutely rejected the importance of the psychological factor. To be sure one could take advice, he said, on this or that point, from someone who knows foreign countries, but on the whole human beings were human beings. He obviously had never entertained the thought that no propaganda will do any good abroad if the policies pursued wreck everything.

For domestic propaganda he had two axioms: (1) continuous repetition, even when one personally feels that one couldn't listen to it any more; (2) to speak in such a way that the intellectuals would still be interested and yet so that the "woodcutter" (who was his prototype of the common man) would understand.

Axiom for foreign propaganda: the battle against bolshevism and against the Jews. In respect to both of these points Goebbels slipped sadly. As regards the first, he remarked (rather to the astonishment of many) that a really successful advance of the Western Powers into the heart of Europe would naturally remove the danger of bolshevization and hence (he didn't say this, but he implied it) the effectiveness of this propaganda device! As regards the Jews, he explained, after having emphasized that the war would end with the complete defeat of one or the other side (which issue would be virtually decided this summer), that one day the "Great Powers" would certainly sit down together again at the same table and "shake hands," and ask one another: "Now, how did all this come about?" And with one voice they would be forced to answer: "The Jew was to blame!" The last word in wisdom!

*Ebenhausen, June 13, 1944:* Last night we wanted to start on our trip and have dinner with the Schniewinds in Solln before leaving. But it could not be done. There were heavy American daylight raids on Munich and the suburbs, especially on the Bavarian Motor Works and the railroads. No trains to Berlin from the main station. Other runs were also interrupted. Whether we can leave today is doubtful, for during the night there were heavy raids by the English on similar objectives.

During the day we could see hundreds of silver birds flying undisturbed in the gleaming sunshine. The Ebenhausen district was not hit. But we got it all the more strongly during the night—worse than ever before. This harmless village was in the thick of it. Many bombs fell. A big fire at Schäftlarn, near the monastery. A powerful hit whistled close over our heads and "blew" Wolf Henning and me literally from the east terrace into the house. The bomb landed a hundred yards from the house and a hundred and fifty yards from our stable loft near the inn.

*Ebenhausen, July 10, 1944:* Disaster is looming ever more closely on the horizon. So far all signs pointed to a rather long siege, but now there is more and more reason to believe that the end is not far off. There is evidence of dissolution among the troops. The army leadership and the Russians themselves were apparently surprised at their successes between Dünaburg and Kowel. In East Prussia German soldiers are on the run; three commanding generals have sacrificed themselves. The retreat is proceeding at a rate that was never reached in 1918.

The terrible effect of our hopeless inferiority in the air weighs in the scales against us. The increasing shortage of raw materials, especially of motor fuel. "V-1" apparently has considerable effect but is hardly decisive. If "V's" with higher numbers have greater effect their use will merely be a measure of desperation which will make this awful war even more terrible, and will destroy every reasonable prospect of peace. At most they can only postpone our catastrophe somewhat, and that means to make it worse. The invasion, too, is gradually gaining.

In Italy there is a steady retreat, and we no longer hear about the submarine war. I was told that Ribbentrop had sent Professor Berber to Geneva under "Red Cross" camouflage to try to get some limitation of war in the air! And then V-1s! What psychology!

This is no time for jokes, but two stories of "Count Bobby" [popular figure of fun] illustrate how things are. (1) He is drafted, and says to the staff surgeon: "I would like to serve at the Führer's headquarters!"

"Are you crazy?"

"Is that one of the requirements?"

(2) He is looking at a globe and it is being explained to him that the large "green" area is Russia; the red area, the British Empire; the pale lilac, the United States; and the yellow, China—all giant areas.

"And that little blue spot?" he asks.

"That is Germany!"

"Hm. Does the Führer know how small it is?"

Chvalkovsky developed his ideas on the German-Czech and Czech-Russian question very clearly. He would be entirely right if we only had a rational leadership. I should like to make use of his train of thought in an article which the new periodical of the government general at Cracow has asked me to write. Incidentally, what a magnificent idea to start such a publication there now! In many ways people there are still absurdly uninformed; we notice that from conversations on the train. Chvalkovsky told me that Beneš's rival, Osuski, had said that Hacha and Chvalkovsky had pursued a very correct policy, for they had saved the Czech nation.

One day I had lunch alone with Sagoroff, the Bulgarian Minister. He is a pleasant and intelligent man with many illusions who still believes in a happy ending. In his Legation two rooms are still habitable, one of them really a vestibule in which we lunched and afterward sat. His description of conditions in Sofia might give rise to misgivings in spite of all his optimism. In general, almost any day now things may begin to crack in one of our "vassal" countries, be it in Finland, Bulgaria, France, Hungary, or elsewhere. The Hungarians, of course, are fighting for their lives, but it is significant enough that when the Allies entered Rome, Apor, the Hungarian Minister to the Vatican, refused to serve Budapest any longer. In Italy tragic conditions prevail. The neo-fascists are a rabble, and in the south there "rules" a combination of aged men, little unknown people, and active communists.

The other day we saw Degrelle in the Potsdam Palast Hotel without recognizing him. What opportunities our clumsy oafs and criminals have ruined in all these countries! I was particularly shocked by the reports of Grundherr from Denmark, whom we met in Friedrichsruh. Best, he said, is a very sensible man but he cannot prevail against the half-demoniac, half-stupid directives from "above," and General Hanneken is a rough, imbecilic ruffian. Best himself lives in the Dagmar House. Other floors lodge the SS and the lower floors are used as a German jail. A clever combination!

Every act of sabotage against munition factories, et cetera, is countered by the Schalberg people, who are largely recruited from the rabble, with senseless attacks on movies, theaters, and restaurants. The murder of German soldiers or of Danes friendly to the Germans is not met by punishment or the shooting of a hostage. Instead a simple policy of revenge murder is carried out, that is some innocent Danes are killed. Hitler wanted a ratio of 5 to 1; Best reduced it to 2 to 1. The hatred created everywhere is boundless.

A meeting of the Wednesday Society was held at Popitz's. He spoke about the "State." Somewhat heavy going, atmosphere depressed. Beck has lost all hope of an attempt. With Wolf-Ulli I went once more to Popitz. I visited Jessen just before that; he is still confined to the house because of his motor accident. He seems still to have some hope.

At Popitz's we talked about the frightful Kiep case. He and Fräulein von Thadden were condemned to death on charges of defeatism—perhaps they are already dead. They were denounced by that swine of a stool pigeon, Dr. Reckse. Between my visits to Jessen and Popitz I met Sauerbruch on the street. He had just visited Thierack, the bloody Minister of "Justice," to ask a pardon for Kiep. He is always ready to help and very courageous. Thierack acted as if he knew little or nothing at all about the case, but hinted at "connections with the enemy," and warned Sauerbruch against interceding for people who were condemned to death. This was very much frowned upon by those "above!" Moreover, the matter of a pardon was his affair; the Führer didn't bother about such things.

I have already mentioned our visit to Friedrichsruh. On invitation of the Bismarcks we were there from Saturday evening, *July 1,* to *Monday morning, the third.* Wonderful sunny weather. It is marvelous what these two have made of Friedrichsruh—he in the park and she in the house. But everything seemed small beside the memory of the great man himself, in the house, at the crypt, in the little museum. It was almost unbearable. I was close to tears most of the time at the thought of the work destroyed.

Germany, situated in the middle of Europe, is the heart of Europe. Europe cannot live without a sound, strong heart. During recent years I have studied Bismarck, and his stature as a statesman grows constantly in my estimation. It is regrettable what a false picture of him we ourselves have given the world—that of the power-politician with cuirassier boots—in our childish joy over the fact that at last someone had made Germany a name to reckon with again. In his own way he knew how to win confidence in the world; exactly the reverse of what is done today. In truth, the highest diplomacy and great moderation were his real gifts. A picture, probably by Werner (?), portraying Bismarck as strong and forceful beside the collapsed figures of Thiers and Favre, is a good example of the foolish concept of Bismarck which we ourselves have spread abroad. This scene is quite accurately drawn, for instance the draping of Thier's cloak. I suggested to Bismarck that the picture should be removed. Many others deserve the same fate.

*Ebenhausen, July 11, 1944:* From the evening of *July 6* to noon of the *eighth* I was in Karlsbad. The trains were overcrowded. On the return trip we sat and waited for four hours at

Marktredwitz because, as a result of heavy raids on the main station of Leipzig, the trains from that city were hours late. A pretty, energetic little conductoress impressed us with her really moving account of the way she was overworked. She had the whole train to take care of alone, and, although only twenty-three years old, she had to cope with hordes of surly, irritated travelers.

We traveled through lovely German Bohemia. There one still finds an entirely different, quiet, friendly atmosphere, in contrast with the Reich proper, in spite of severe raids on Breux, where we saw the smoke-screen installations. Many "Heil Hitlers!"

We were very well received in Karlsbad. I had a pleasant conversation with an Austrian colonel, who thanked me for showing a refreshing objectivity to which one was no longer accustomed. Also I went to see Walter Bloem, who served as a major at the age of more than seventy; his son, also a writer and a major, is serving with him there. The commanding officer is Major General Herludt von Rohden, burning with ambition, nervous and feverishly active, a cadet with little fundamental training but working hard to get it. He asked me to help him in his literary tasks, and at his invitation I attended a staff meeting. How people strive and work and sacrifice in this Germany of ours! A decent nation with a tragic destiny.

Yesterday I had a visit from Nostitz. Gloomy report about feeling in Switzerland. Carl Burckhardt is deeply pessimistic about Europe's fate. Nostitz disapproves my working with Berber, because "it compromises me abroad." Before he had always warned me against being "imprudent" at home. In other words, lie abed and do nothing!

I tried to explain to him the purpose of my work, the practical aspects of it as well as the personal tactics involved. That anyone could identify me with the regime I will not believe as long as I live. He told me that Halem had been sentenced to death, and one of the Mumms, too. The other Mumm was sent to the penitentiary. Krauel refuses to return to Germany. These are events that one would never have believed possible.

Nostitz also told a beautiful story about the unpredictable and unstable Berber. He had asked Carl Burckhardt, a Swiss citizen, whether one could speak freely with the members of the consulate! Nostitz was deeply impressed by the "quiet dignity" of the German people; he completely overlooks the factors of fear and stolidity.

I asked Geyr what the generals in the west were thinking. Answer: "They are doing their duty," and he gave me to understand that the basic attitude was one of complete resignation. Only through a lucky coincidence Geyr had escaped the air raid which wiped out almost his entire staff. Rommel, who happened to be there, also had a narrow escape. Geyr said he now got on very well with Rommel, although he had not at first.

In Speidel (with whom I had once had a long talk in Paris) Rommel has an excellent, clear-headed Chief of Staff. In addition to Rundstedt, Sodernstern has also been suddenly dismissed. I was interested in Geyr's description of how impossible it was for the staffs to make their headquarters in villages because their presence was immediately betrayed. They have to take cover in the forests, bivouacking and living in tiny huts!

*Ebenhausen, July 13, 1944:* Immediately after Geyr's departure there were renewed air raids. Very uncomfortable in the cellar because some of the many waves of planes flew very low. One plane was shot down not far from us, and the crash had a sinister sound.

We were greatly concerned about Almuth, especially as the train from Ebenhausen only went as far as Grunwald. (Our departure today impossible, yesterday, too.) Thank God she came home safely, but exhausted and deeply shaken by her terrible bicycle ride through burning streets. In the neighborhood of the Bavaria Ring one couldn't get through because of fires, wreckage, and the tangled mass of electric wires. The heaviest daylight raid yet on Munich. A number of barracks, an orphanage, several kindergartens, et cetera, were hit, with heartbreaking losses. This looks like an answer to the "Robot" bombs. Hitler is supposed to have been in Munich day before yesterday. No mail, no papers, no telephone.

## Editor's Note

BY

HUGH GIBSON

The foregoing entry in Hassell's diary was made only a few days before the final attempt on Hitler's life, July 20, 1944. The events of that day have been told admirably by Allen Welsh Dulles in *Germany's Underground* (Macmillan, 1947), the best and most authoritative account that has been published.

The Gestapo was closing in on the conspirators and the attempt could no longer be deferred. Goerdeler was in hiding, a warrant having been issued for his arrest. Moltke was already in prison, and Oster under house arrest. There was no time to be lost.

Count Claus Schenk von Stauffenberg, one of the inner circle of the conspiracy in Berlin, had recently been appointed Chief of Staff to General Fromm, Commander of the Home Army with headquarters in Berlin. In this capacity he attended meetings at Hitler's Supreme Headquarters, and it was decided that in addition to organizing the uprising in Berlin he would have to carry out the assassination. With a bomb in his brief case, Stauffenberg arrived at Hitler's headquarters in East Prussia and was passed through by a series of guards. He found that the conference, instead of being held in the usual underground concrete shelter, was to take place in a flimsy surface structure.

Hitler presided over the meeting with Stauffenberg on his right. Having made his report on replacement troops, Stauffenberg set the mechanism of his bomb, placed it by Hitler's chair, and took his leave.

As luck would have it Hitler rose unexpectedly and went across the room to look at a map. He thus escaped death by a matter of seconds. If the meeting had taken place in an underground shelter, where there was no escape for the pressure all those present would have been killed. As it was, the windows and wooden walls of the building gave way. Although four died of wounds the rest escaped with their lives.

Stauffenberg waited until he heard the explosion, saw various people blown out of the room, Hitler among them, and took off for Berlin in his own plane to report the success of his attempt.

In the meantime General Beck, Field Marshal von Witzleben, Hoepner, Olbricht, and other military members of the conspiracy, gathered at the Ministry of War, ready to take over the government as soon as word was received that Stauffenberg had carried out his mission.

They waited with growing anxiety until at three-thirty, they received a telephone message from GHQ that there had been an explosion and there were a number of casualties. At the same time Stauffenberg telephoned through his adjutant to report his safe return—and the death of Hitler.

Then things began to happen, but not at all in the way that had been anticipated. The conspirators had sent sealed orders to all district and field commanders which were to be opened only when they received a telegram from Berlin giving the code word "Walküre." These orders, which aimed at outwitting the Gestapo, provided for the imposition of martial law, the occupation of all public buildings, and the suppression of political activity. Each general was to arrest the Nazi and SS officers in his district and the secret headquarters of the Gestapo was to be taken.

The Walküre message was released and the whole telephone and teletype service of the Ministry of War was set to work sending out word of Hitler's death and orders for supplementary measures against SS and Party leaders.

The conspirators had counted heavily on the blind obedience to superior orders so deeply ingrained in the German character, but they had failed to realize the extent of the demoralization that had been wrought by the Nazi regime. From the outset things began to go wrong. Olbricht informed General Fromm that Hitler was dead and urged him to alert the Replacement Army, so essential to the success of the uprising. Fromm was cautious and telephoned Hitler's headquarters. Keitel told him the Führer was only slightly injured. Fromm refused to act and was arrested, but unwisely not held incommunicado. Then other generals began to wobble. The troops which had been stationed near Berlin did not arrive so rapidly as they should. Even Beck took time out for an attempt to reach Supreme Headquarters and ascertain whether Hitler was really dead.

The afternoon wore away without the prompt and decisive action that had been planned. Some of the generals lost their nerve. The radio had not been seized. The officer ordered to occupy the Reich Chancery and arrest some SS officers, instead of obeying sought the advice of his subordinates, with the result that he was taken to Goebbels, who convinced him that the plot had failed by getting Hitler on his private wire. Then, instead of carrying out his first orders, he set out to intercept the troops moving in to occupy Berlin and sent them back to their stations in the country.

By evening the Nazis had re-established themselves in command and the conspiracy began to crack. Once they realized that superior orders were not obeyed instinctively the generals were lost. They practically gave up trying.

Fromm had been liberated by some nearby troops and proceeded to arrest those who had arrested him in the afternoon.

Beck asked to be allowed to keep his revolver and shot himself. Then Olbricht, Stauffenberg, Merz von Quirnheim, and Lieutenant Werner von Haeften were taken into the courtyard of the Ministry and shot. A number of others, among them Yorck von Wartenburg, Dr. Gerstenmaier, and Berthold von Stauffenberg, were awaiting execution when word came that all prisoners were to be kept for Himmler's use in gathering information about the conspiracy.

Then began a terror that ended only with the downfall of the Nazi regime.

# After
# July 20,
# 1944

BY

WOLF ULRICH VON HASSELL

On July 13, 1944, my father wrote the last words in his diary. Munich was cut off from all railway service at that time because of air raids, but my father was nevertheless determined to get to Berlin, for once more an "action" was in the air. He succeeded in traveling northward by roundabout ways, and on July 16 finally reached the quarters we shared in Potsdam.

After the failure of the attempt on Hitler's life on July 20, 1944, had become evident, it was clear to my father that the last hope for an overthrow of the regime had gone up in smoke, that nothing could now stay Germany's fate. My father did not want to elude his own fate either. Outwardly unperturbed, he carried on his daily routine.

On July 24, in the Grunewald, he happened to run into Gisevius, who was awaiting a chance to escape. He told me later about this remarkable meeting. Gisevius was filled with bitterness and deeply depressed by the failure of this last attempt at an overthrow of the regime. He complained that he and his particular friends had been excluded from the final phase of the preparations and planning for the future. But my father saw only the act itself, which at this late hour had revealed to the world the struggle of the other Germany. It depressed him that discord should so soon come to the fore.

Finance Minister Popitz had been arrested as early as the morning of July 21, 1944. My brother telephoned that day and the following day in great concern. On July 26, 1944, he succeeded in getting to Berlin to see our father once more. As in old times, we three dined together at the Adlon. Two days later, on July 28, my father was arrested at his office. Shortly before I had received a warning from Potsdam and was able to tell my father that his last hour had struck. He received the Gestapo seated at his desk.

Professor Peter Jens Jessen was the last of this group to be taken by the Gestapo. As a result of his motor accident he was still extremely weak and could not walk alone. I was with him frequently before his arrest. He longed only to be taken to his comrades. On the eve of July 20 Count Stauffenberg and the other principal figures had been at his house to talk over their plans once more. The Gestapo never knew of this, as indeed they never did grasp the whole story leading up to this attempt at an overthrow of the Hitler regime. The Gestapo could work with terror and criminal methods, but not with real insight and intelligence.

After my father's arrest I went to the Prince Albrech-strasse, the headquarters of the Gestapo (the so-called Reich Security Headquarters). Despite the dictates of common sense I wished to leave nothing undone to save my father. I accomplished nothing. I was thrown out and they threatened me with arrest. But, above all, they lied to me again and again with oily courtesy.

At least I was able to bring small comforts to my father up to the last day of his imprisonment, in the form of food, cigarettes, and reading matter. The Gestapo had spread a fine-mesh net of branch offices throughout ruined Berlin. The relatives and friends of the ever-increasing number of prisoners met in these and in the bombed anterooms of the Berlin prisons. We smiled at one another and tried to give advice and help.

My father was first taken to the concentration camp at Ravensbruck in Mecklenburg. There they had set up a special section for "prominent guests" of the Gestapo. The sculptress "Puppi" Sarre, who had been a prisoner since the autumn of 1943 in connection with the Langbehn case, told us later about the concentration camps. She had seen my father there, and wrote us afterward: "Even the guards were impressed by his serenity, his confident mien and manner. In one instance I observed how the SS guards, probably without knowing it themselves, treated him with respect and admiration."

In Ravensbruck it may still have been comparatively tolerable for my father. One letter from him describes how the prisoners were taken for a walk in the courtyard, and when the weather was good they were permitted to sit on the steps and eat their food in the open air.

On August 15, 1944, my father was brought over to Berlin in chains. For a few days he lay in a cell of the Moabit Prison at 3 Lehrterstrasse, a dirty old building, severely damaged by air raids. Then the Gestapo took him to the cellar prison at 8 Prince Albrechtstrasse, the special prison of the Reich Security Headquarters. Here they at once began the cross-examinations, which lasted day and night. The fighters of the German resistance movement met in the corridors and washrooms of the prison.

My father filled in the long days of waiting in the concentration camp at Ravensbruck, and the brief hours between examinations at the Prince Albrechtstrasse, writing his memoirs.[1] This activity occupied and diverted the tireless worker. The manuscript, in which my father recorded his life from childhood, filled one hundred and fifty single-spaced typewritten pages. The narration ends with the years 1926–30, when my father was Minister in Copenhagen. In each of the few letters which he could send us during his imprisonment he mentioned this work and the comfort he found in immersing himself in a better past. His reminiscences breathe contemplation and calm. "A prison cell," it says at the beginning, "is a good place to start one's memoirs. One has time, too much time, for meditation. The past life takes shape before the spiritual eye in stereoscopic plasticity. One sees one's life and oneself stripped of all sham."

Except for this, there is scarcely any mention of the present. But toward the end, and without any connection with the con-

[1] Shortly before the Russians marched into Berlin I was able to recover these memoirs from the weakening hands of the Gestapo, along with other papers belonging to my father, his ring, his watch, and his cigarette case, things which he had carried with him to the very end.

text, my father wrote these lines in verse on the edge of the manuscript:

*Du Kannst uns durch des Todes Türen*
*Traumend führen*
*und machest uns auf einmal frei.*

On September 7 and 8, 1944, the so-called People's Court, with Freisler presiding, opened proceedings against my father, Goerdeler, Leuschner, Wirmer, and Lejeune-Jung. Schlabrendorff says he saw my father once more in the course of these days in the corridor of the Reich Security Headquarters. With the self-possession of a cavalier of the old school, my father approached him and whispered as he passed by: "My death is certain. When you get out please give messages to my wife. My last thoughts will be of her."

As in most of these proceedings before National Socialist revolutionary tribunals behind closed doors, the decision against my father and his four companions in the trial of September 7–8 had been determined beforehand. As early as September 5 my father was informed by Lammers, chief of the Reich Chancery, that he had been deprived of his civil-service status:

"The Führer has, as I now officially inform you, ordered that you be deprived of your official status as a retired civil servant because of your participation in the events of July 20, 1944. All rights derived from your former office are hereby forfeited."

The text of his indictment was presented to my father in his cell only thirty-six hours before the trial.

Three fourths of its contents were completely new to him, he wrote. Only that version which suited National Socialist propaganda was to be heard before the court. The accused were given hardly any chance to defend themselves. In addition, they were hampered by fear for their families and by the desire not to involve any of their comrades who were still alive.

Nevertheless, these five men of the resistance movement gave Freisler some difficult hours. Out of the group of invited Party guests and government representatives whose presence was ordered to intimidate them, there soon leaked some reports of the trial, although any talk about it was strictly forbidden.

Many of those present were too deeply stirred to remain silent. At the end they no longer knew who was judge and who the prisoner. An eyewitness told me about the trial and about the exemplary behavior of my father. He concluded his account with the words: "He was truly a noble man, but too noble for this world."

The sentence was carried out on my father, Lejeune-Jung, and Wirmer at the prison in Berlin-Plötzensee two hours after it was read. Along with them that afternoon of September 8, 1944, there were put to death Colonel Hansen, Lieutenant Colonel Smendt, and Count Ulrich Schwerin-Schwanenfeld, who had been especially close to my father in the group of fighters against Hitler. On Leuschner the death sentence was not carried out until September 29. Goerdeler had to live on for five months in the cellars of the Prince Albrechtstrasse. He was executed with Popitz and Delp, the Jesuit priest, on February 2, 1945.

# Epilogue

BY

ILSE VON HASSELL

After the heavy air raids on Munich at the beginning of July 1944 I had to give up trying to accompany my husband to Berlin. Very worried, I let him make the attempt to get through alone. On July 21 I received his first letter from Berlin and at the same time the shattering news of the failure of the attempt. In his next letter my husband wrote: "Beck has fallen at the front. Great sorrow over the end of this noble man." I received three more letters with similar news, the only documents the Gestapo took with them from our house.

Before me lies a note written in 1942 by my far-sighted husband:

I shall send telegrams and telephone calls under the name "Hausmann." If a search of the house is imminent: "Siegfried arriving soon." If my arrest is imminent: "Leaving soon to join Siegfried." In either case, withdraw our bank balances in Berlin and Munich; for Berlin, signatures are attached. If there is still a chance to do so, remove or hide the package of documents in the library and my old brown leather case. (Perhaps in the woodshed behind the large logs, then push the top ones over them.)

We soon hid these documents in various places. The diary notes for 1936–41 were already safe in Switzerland. My husband wrote in school copybooks, but later he often used tiny leaves of calendars and small notebooks, so that he could quickly stick them under the rug if the Gestapo should come unexpectedly.

When, in May 1942, we were repeatedly informed of the special affection the Gestapo felt for my husband, he sent my son, Wolf-Ulli, to Ebenhausen to bury the diaries. That was easier said than done, but my son and I stood there with a Ridgeway's Pure China Tea box, which closed fairly well, tried as best we could to make it more secure with wire, and carefully buried it among some roots in the damp earth of the forest. After a very wet summer my husband and I dug them up again in the fall of 1942, and just in time, for some of the writing was already quite blurred. Even now we can often make out the words only with a magnifying glass. We later hid the notes behind some stone work in a grotto of the garden.

On July 28, 1944, at three o'clock, violent ringing roused us from our sleep. Two Gestapo officers stood at the door with our trembling local policeman. They asked for my husband. Filled with indignation that these scoundrels had triumphed, I angrily said that I found their conduct incredible. All our lives we had unselfishly served Germany! They were reasonably polite, declared they had orders to search the house, and went to my husband's desk. I said: "Please do not put things in too much disorder. My husband is very orderly and it would make him angry. Here are papers concerning bank matters; here are notes for lectures and articles; here are letters. Take what you need and put the other things back where they belong."

Curiously enough, they allowed themselves to be ordered about, looked hastily through everything, and studied in detail only the satirical poem, "Ten Little Grumblers," which they found on my husband's desk. I was on pins and needles because in the same room, five steps away, my husband's last diary notes were hidden in a photograph album. I tried to entice the Gestapo people to my mother's desk in the next room, and watched with relief as they burrowed around in the drawers filled to overflowing with old letters.

Again they asked for my husband. I knew that it had never been his intention to hide, so I gave them precise information: "Mornings, until half-past seven, he is in Potsdam, 35 Seestrasse, then he rides—of which, of course, you disapprove—

and at nine-thirty he is at his desk in the office at 6 Fasanenstrasse, second floor."

Thereupon the Gestapo people declared that they had to
arrest my daughter Almuth and myself. They took us to
Munich, first to the Gestapo, where we were asked all the same
questions over again. The Gestapo building was badly damaged by air raids, so we were taken in the Black Maria with
two charming murderers to the prison in Ettstrasse.

After my husband's arrest my son Wolf-Ulli went straight off
to the Gestapo in Albrechtstrasse on the morning of July 28.
He explained that he had been with his father the whole time,
was acquainted with his every thought; if they seized his father,
then they should arrest him, too. This impudence apparently
convinced the Gestapo that he knew nothing. In any event, he
remained free. When he came to Munich he said to the Gestapo
that since they could see that he was free they should also release his mother and sister. The Munich prisons were filled to
overflowing. This is the only rational explanation for his success in getting Almuth and myself installed in Ebenhausen,
under the condition that we be "restricted" to that community.

After the verdict was made public on September 11, we
were not imprisoned again. On the other hand, my younger
daughter, Fey, was arrested at her Italian estate Brazza, and
brought to Innsbruck two weeks later with her two little boys,
aged two and three. There the boys were literally torn from
her by two nurses of the NSV [National Social Welfare Corps],
and she herself was taken to the local jail where she was put
among criminals. Then, as a *Sippenhaftling* [member of the
family of a politically suspect person, held as a hostage], together with relatives of Stauffenberg, Goerdeler, Hofacker, and
other participants in the resistance movement, she was dragged
for eight months from one concentration camp to another and
suffered great hardships.

My younger son, Hans Dieter, was sent back from the front,
arrested in Ebenhausen during the night of October 29, and
incarcerated in the special prison of the Gestapo for members
of the Wehrmacht, at the fortresses of Germersheim and
Küstrin, which were later "evacuated" to Lake Constance.

Shortly before the end of the war Fey and Hans Dieter

escaped Himmler's last execution order by a hairbreadth. My daughter's little boys were completely lost. I found them at last in July 1945, after weeks of searching, in the former NSV home, Wiesenhof-Hall, near Innsbruck, under the name of the "Vorhof brothers."

Immediately after Goerdeler's arrest, in the middle of August 1944, I received the last letter from my husband from the concentration camp at Ravensbruck. There was a postscript: "I am being taken to Berlin." There, Wolf-Ulli was cynically told his father would need no more books; he would not have time for them. Almost every day Wolf-Ulli went to Albrechtstrasse—difficult, galling trips—without being able to see his beloved father again. I learned of the sentence from my son. He telephoned on the morning of September 11:

"Have you seen the paper? There is news in it."

"The worst?"

"Yes, the worst."

It had been my wish to share my husband's fate, but they never examined me. My only solace at being still alive is that he wanted it that way. I regard my husband's notes, which he often wrote in desperation and which he wanted one day to use himself, as a legacy and a mandate.

I am full of gratitude for the happy life I lived at the side of this knight without fear and without reproach, who inspired me every day anew, who never disappointed me, whom I could admire in all things, both great and small, even up to his death. The last words he wrote, with absolute composure, a few minutes before his execution, went through many Gestapo hands and finally reached me four months later. They do not belong to me alone. His greeting to "all friends" is destined for all those who, within and without our country, were united with us on the same principles.

May there be truth in what Daque says about the beliefs of ancient peoples, that the souls of the upright, the strong, and the noble, who sacrifice their lives, enter again into the life stream of the whole people and work toward the salvation and the good of all.

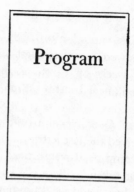

# Program

Written by U. von Hassell after consultation with Beck, Goerdeler, and Popitz, January–February 1940 [planned for use in the event of a change of regime after action to prevent the invasion of Belgium].

1. The German Government is determined to carry on with all its strength the war into which Europe has unfortunately been plunged until a peace is assured which guarantees the existence, the independence, the freedom, and the security of the German Reich and nation, and which restores in the main the old frontiers between the Reich and Poland.

2. The German Government, convinced that the entire German nation in arms stands back of this demand, will strive toward an early peace on this basis. For this reason its members have resisted the plans of the former German Government, which, by violating the neutrality of neighboring states, would have destroyed these prospects for peace.

3. The German Government leaves to the judgment of history the principles and achievements of National Socialism. It recognizes whatever sound and progressive ideas were included in it. Unfortunately, in clear contradiction to these ideas, the former German Government undertook to pursue for some time a policy calculated to kill the soul of the German people and to undermine its economic well-being.

4. An intolerable Party tyranny was erected through a system of self-seeking Party bosses and imposed upon the entire nation like an iron net.

Any free expression of opinion, even in non-political spheres, was branded as a crime; every free intellectual movement was shackled. Spying and slander, in unprecedented proportions, became the order of the day. The administration of justice, especially in criminal proceedings, was subordinated more and more to Party viewpoints. The conduct of the Gestapo violated the fundamental principles of morality and destroyed human personality. Severe violations of justice and law, attacks upon the person, life, and liberty of innocent people remained unpunished, indeed were encouraged from above. Just recently there were occurrences in connection with the war, tolerated by the highest officers in the state, which are without precedent in German history. In this same chapter belong the terrible outrages perpetrated, unpunished, by the Party against the Jews.

5. The organism of the state was in the course of being completely undermined and destroyed by the Party. The once incomparable German bureaucracy was stripped of its most important functions and reduced to lower and lower levels of operation. The Party bosses everywhere were given all actual power and this they abused.

6. In economic matters, the former government carried on in recent years an ever-more-unconscionable exploitation of the resources and energies of the nation, and a reckless squandering of money, especially for show buildings of all kinds, whereas for social purposes, particularly for housing programs, only inadequate funds were provided. The orderly administration of the finances of the state had ceased, whereas the tax burden had grown almost without limit.

7. In addition, since the beginning of the year 1938 a foreign policy was carried out that took on a more and more adventurous character. The people were made to believe that the disregard of all principles and agreements constituted "Realpolitik." Through lack of political wisdom on the part of all participants war finally came, threatening, after twenty years of painstaking reconstruction, the destruction of the highest European values to the advantage of bolshevism. The German Government does not abandon hope that the adversaries of Germany will recognize the necessity of making peace now on

the basis of the principles mentioned above; of giving the world an opportunity of attaining health and happiness based on the will of all nations in good faith to build a community of peoples with the least possible armaments, and through spiritual and economic exchanges. The contradictions inherent in the Paris treaties after the World War are the deepest cause of the misfortunes that now have overtaken the world. If Germany's adversaries fail to recognize this, the German Government will not hesitate to draw the conclusion that it must continue the war to the very end.

8. Until it is possible to re-establish a constitutional way of life, the supreme power in the German Reich is to rest in the hands of a regency; the regency shall consist of the regent and two associates. This regency shall appoint the Ministers of State.

9. In order to lead the German people from the way of life under the former system into new and healthier paths, the regency decrees:

(a) The National Socialist Party shall be dissolved in all its branches. The Minister of the Interior shall decide upon the necessary measures. He may appoint commissioners for that purpose. He shall advise the regency as to which organizations of the Party, as for instance the NSV [National Socialist Welfare Organization], the Winter Relief Work, et cetera, shall be taken over. He shall especially examine whether the SA [Storm troops], the NSKK [National Socialist Motor Corps], the NSFK [National Socialist Flying Corps], among others, can be reorganized into new formations. The SS shall be dissolved. In so far as it can be merged with one of the organizations already mentioned, measures will be taken to that effect. The Minister of War shall order the transfer of the individual members of the SS or the SA into the Wehrmacht. The Minister of the Interior shall carry out a provisional reorganization of the police and shall submit to the regency proposals for definite action.

(b) The Labor Service shall be retained but reorganized. Recommendations to that effect shall be made to the regency by the Minister of Labor.

(c) The Labor Front shall be rebuilt from its foundations. The Minister of Economic Affairs, in agreement with the Minister of Labor, shall decide upon the necessary provisional measures and submit recommendations to the regency.

(d) The organization of the national economy shall temporarily remain unchanged. It shall be organized in conjunction with the general reform of the state. The Minister of Economic Affairs shall take care of the necessary changes in personnel.

(e) The property and income of all Party organizations and of the Labor Front shall be transferred to the Reich. The Minister of Finance, in agreement with the competent Ministers, shall decide upon the necessary regulations and make recommendations to the regency about the use of these funds.

(f) In order to prepare for the reconstruction of the state, the regency shall set up a constitutional council under the chairmanship of the Minister of the Interior which shall draft recommendations. These recommendations must be based on the principle that a unified German state shall be organized along political and economic lines that take special cognizance of historic tradition. They shall ensure the co-operation of the people in the political life of the Reich and a control of the state based on local and corporate self-government.

(g) The Minister of Justice shall make the necessary provisional arrangements to restore the shattered dignity of the law; to assure an administration of justice through judges who are subject only to the law, and to carry out the necessary changes in personnel. He shall make preparations for the final reconstitution of the judiciary. All proceedings against individuals in violation of law and justice shall be quashed.

(h) The Armed Forces are at once to be put under oath to the regency. The regent is the Supreme Commander of all the Armed Forces and appoints the commanders of its separate subdivisions.

(i) The executive power in all the Länder except Prussia, in the Prussian provinces, and in the occupied territories, shall be exercised by military commanders appointed by the regent.

(k) The Reich-Statthalters are abolished. In Prussia the regent shall exercise the highest executive power.

(1) In all spheres of government the civil service shall be reorganized in such a way that career officials shall replace those appointed for Party reasons. The regency shall determine which officials shall be appointed by it, and which by the appropriate Minister.

(m) The regency shall appoint a council which shall scrutinize legislation passed since January 30, 1933, and shall recommend to the regency which laws, orders, and regulations are to be annulled. All regulations issued by the National Socialist Party or one of its organizations shall be considered invalid. Especially the legislation with regard to the Jews.

(n) This Council on Legislation shall appoint a commission which shall make recommendations as to how the relationship between state and church shall be regulated. The pre-eminence of the state shall be considered as the guiding principle.

(o) During the war the press shall be subject to the censorship of the executive authority. For the period after the war new regulations shall be issued on the basis of freedom of the press within the framework of the security of the state.

(p) Science and teaching are to be free.

(q) During the war literature shall be under the supervision of the executive authority. After the war the state and nation shall be protected by legislation against abuses in the field of literature.

10. The regency is aware that its task is infinitely difficult and that it is scarcely calculated to win popularity quickly. It is called upon to liquidate a system which has laid heavy burdens upon the German nation for a long time to come. It will endeavor to carry out this process without any feeling of revenge, and to liquidate the burdens in such a way that the smallest possible material sacrifices will be demanded. Nevertheless, these sacrifices will be heavy enough. The German nation—of this the regency is convinced—will courageously make these sacrifices, finding compensation in the fact that law and justice have thus been vindicated as well as decency, morality, and true freedom.

# Index

dam; arrested by the Gestapo after July 20, 1944; tried before a People's Court, acquitted, transferred to the Sachsenhausen concentration camp, 339

Blaskowitz, Johannes, Colonel General, 1883———. Commander in Chief of the German Army in Poland, 1939; resigned in protest against SS interference; later Commander of the First Army Corps in France at Bordeaux, 79, 80, 100, 109, 323, 324

Bloem, Walter, 1868———. A writer, 354

Bock, Fedor von, Field Marshal, 1880———. Died in the defense of the city of Hamburg, 80, 110, 202, 214, 229, 235, 261, 274

Bodelschwingh, Friedrich von, 1877———. Prominent German Protestant leader; Director of the famous Bethel Institution; first Protestant Reich Bishop; resigned 1933 in protest against Nazi policies, 44, 78, 150

Bodelschwingh, Friedrich von. Protestant Minister at Schlüsselburg; nephew of the Bishop, 43, 78

Bodmer, Martin, 1899———. Member of the International Committee of the Red Cross, Geneva, 240

Bohle, Ernst Wilhelm, 1903———. A Bradford (England) leader of the foreign branches of the National Socialist Party, 201

Bonhoeffer, Dietrich. Protestant minister; lecturer at the University of Berlin until 1939, when the Nazis forbade him to continue his lectures; arrested in April 1943; executed in April 1945, 304

Bonhoeffer, Klaus. Lawyer; legal adviser of the *Lufthansa* (German Air Lines); arrested in October 1944 and executed in April 1945, 304

Borenius, Tancred, 1885———. A Finnish citizen; temporarily Professor of the History of Art at the University of London, 170, 171, 194

Boris III, 1894–1943. King of Bulgaria 1918–43, 154, 161, 249, 250, 251, 252, 253, 295

Bormann, Martin, 1900———. One of the principal Nazi leaders during the last years of the Hitler regime; became Chief of the Party Chancery in May 1941 after the flight of Hess; condemned to death *in absentia* at Nuremberg; believed to have died in the fighting for Berlin, 1945, 164, 196, 210, 249, 293

Bosch, Robert August, 1861———. Head of the famous Robert Bosch Corporation at Stuttgart; philanthropist; financed the travels and anti-Nazi activities of Dr. Goerdeler, 56, 82, 92, 97

Frank, Dr. Hans, 1900——. President of the Academy of German Law; member of the Reich Cabinet; Governor General of Poland, 1939–43, 100, 103, 165, 196, 242, 261, 265, 302, 303

Frank-Fahle. Official of the I. G. Farben Corporation (foreign operations), 115, 121

Frauendorfer, Dr. Max, 1909——. Administrator in the Government. General of Poland, 165, 195, 196, 277, 302, 303, 318

Freisler, Dr. Roland, 1893–1944. Chairman of the Workers' and Soldiers' Council of Kassel in 1918; Undersecretary in the Prussian Ministry of Justice; President of the People's Court at Berlin; killed in an air raid while trying anti-Nazi conspirators in 1944, xiii, 362

Frick, Dr. Wilhelm, 1877——. Reich Minister of the Interior, 1933–45; Reich Protector of Bohemia and Moravia, 1943, 29, 293

Fritsch, Werner von, Baron, 1880–1939. Colonel General, Commander in Chief of the Army, 1935–38; ousted in a quarrel with Hitler; sought and found death in battle before Warsaw, 1939, 23, 24, 50, 75, 90, 143

Fromm, Friedrich, 1888–1945. General of Artillery, Chief of the Armaments Section of the War Ministry and Commander in Chief of the Home Army; executed March 1945, 137, 139, 276, 285, 286, 299, 358

Funk, Walter, 1890——. Undersecretary in the Ministry of Propaganda; Reich Minister of Economic Affairs and President of the Reichsbank, 31, 33, 60, 85, 105, 110, 145, 148, 225

Fürtwangler, Wilhelm, 1886——. Orchestral conductor, 29, 171

Gablenz, Karl August von der, Baron, 1893–1943. Director of the *Lufthansa* (German Air Lines); killed in an air accident in 1943, 266

Galen, Clemens August von, Count, 1876–1946. Bishop, later Cardinal, of Münster; outspoken opponent of Nazism; died of exhaustion and starvation on his return from Rome, 1946, 210, 211, 218, 223, 239

Gaus, Friedrich Wilhelm, 1881——. Chief of the Legal Division of the German Foreign Office, 301

Gerstenmeier, Eugen, D. D. Member of the External Affairs Office of the German Protestant Church; head of the *Evangel-*

Thomas, Georg. General of Infantry, Chief of the War Production and Armaments Division of the German Ministry of War; arrested in 1944; liberated at the end of the war, xi, 53, 127, 128, 132, 136, 173, 204, 209, 210, 214, 218, 219, 222, 224, 228

Timoschenko, Semjon, 1895——. Russian Marshal, 225

Tischbein, Friedrich, 1880——. Civil servant, 5, 40, 66

Todt, Fritz, 1891–1942. Professor; Inspector General of Road Construction, 124, 131, 162

Togo, Shiegenori, 1882——. Japanese Ambassador in Berlin, 1937–39 and in Moscow 1939–40; Foreign Minister, 1941–42, 267

Trautmann, Oskar, 1877——. German Ambassador to China, 1935–41, 20

Trott zu Solz, Adam von, 1909–1944. German Rhodes scholar at Oxford, 1931–33; on a mission for the German Underground in the United States, 1939–40; Counselor of Legation at the German Foreign Office; arrested and executed in 1944, 20, 230–232, 257, 278, 294, 310, 315, 316, 318, 332

Tschammer und Osten, Hans von, 1887——. Reich Sports Leader, 263

Udet, Ernst, Lieutenant General, 1896–1941. German air ace, 225

Umberto, Crown Prince (later King) of Italy, 1904——. Abdicated 1946, 55, 343

Vansittart, Sir Robert (now Lord), 1881——. Formerly Permanent Undersecretary of the British Foreign Office, 111, 221

Victor Emmanuel III, 1869——. King of Italy, 1900–44, 308, 316, 317, 328, 343

Vlassov, Andrej Andrejevitch. Russian Lieutenant General; captured by the German Army; formed a Free Russian Army to fight alongside Germany; extradited by the Allies to Soviet Russia and reported executed, 297

Wagemann, Ernst, 1884——. President of the Institute for Economic Research, 247, 259, 277, 287, 317

Wagner, Adolf, 1890——. Minister of State; Gauleiter of Munich and Upper Bavaria, 16, 26, 193

Wagner, Josef, 1899–1945. Gauleiter and Governor of Silesia until 1940; Reich Price Commissioner; executed in 1945, 27, 136, 277